HOLDING THE POLITICAL CENTER IN ILLINOIS

INTERPRETING THE CIVIL WAR
Texts and Contexts

EDITOR
Angela M. Zombek
University of North Carolina, Wilmington

Aaron Astor
Maryville College

Brian Craig Miller
Mission College

Joseph M. Beilein Jr.
Pennsylvania State University

Jennifer M. Murray
Oklahoma State University

Douglas R. Egerton
Le Moyne College

Jonathan W. White
Christopher Newport University

J. Matthew Gallman
University of Florida

Timothy Williams
University of Oregon

Hilary N. Green
University of Alabama

The **Interpreting the Civil War** series focuses on America's long Civil War era, from the rise of antebellum sectional tensions through Reconstruction.

These studies, which include both critical monographs and edited compilations, bring new social, political, economic, or cultural perspectives to our understanding of sectional tensions, the war years, Reconstruction, and memory. Studies reflect a broad, national perspective; the vantage point of local history; or the direct experiences of individuals through annotated primary source collections.

HOLDING THE POLITICAL CENTER IN ILLINOIS

Conservatism and Union
on the Brink of the Civil War

IAN T. IVERSON

The Kent State University Press *Kent, Ohio*

© 2024 by The Kent State University Press, Kent, Ohio 44242
All rights reserved

ISBN 978-1-60635-479-7
Published in the United States of America

A version of chapter 3 appeared in *Civil War History* 68, no. 4 (December 2022): 347–70.

No part of this book may be used or reproduced, in any manner whatsoever, without written permission from the Publisher, except in the case of short quotations in critical reviews or articles.

Cataloging information for this title is available at the Library of Congress.

28 27 26 25 24   5 4 3 2 1

For Drisana

CONTENTS

	Acknowledgments · ix
	Introduction · 1
ONE	Prologue · 9
TWO	A Hell of a Storm · 22
THREE	The Common Cause · 46
FOUR	No Man's Land · 77
FIVE	The Great Debates · 108
SIX	Race to the White House · 144
SEVEN	The Union in Peril · 175
	Epilogue · 203
	Notes · 207
	Bibliography · 249
	Index · 266

ACKNOWLEDGMENTS

Far more people than can be named here contributed to this book and to my development as a scholar. First and foremost is my graduate advisor, Elizabeth Varon. Her keen insights and thoughtful comments have added immeasurably to this project, and her mentorship has meant the world to me. Other faculty members at UVA also provided a helping hand on many occasions, especially Caroline Janney, Justene Hill Edwards, Stephen Cushman, Kirt von Daacke, Alan Taylor, Christa Dierkscheide, S. Max Edelson, Worthy Martin, and William Hitchcock.

Early mentors in the Northfield Public Schools and at Princeton University were instrumental in launching my career as a historian, especially Earl Weinmann, Mark Thornton, Wendy Warren, Joseph Fronczak, Sean Wilentz, and Matthew Karp. This book has also benefited from conversations with a range of scholars who generously volunteered their time to engage with my work. I offer special thanks to Michael Burlingame, Daniel Crofts, Michael Fitzgerald, William Freehling, Jack Furniss, Gary Gallagher, Michael Holt, and Frank Towers.

The staff at the Abraham Lincoln Presidential Library in Springfield were very helpful in assisting my search for relevant manuscripts and newspaper sources. I also thank the staff members at the libraries of the University of Chicago, the University of Michigan, the University of Illinois Urbana-Champaign, and the Library of Congress for their help in the archives. Thanks also to those fellowships that contributed financial support to this project, namely the King V. Hostick Scholarship, Platzman Memorial Fellowship, and the Humane Studies Fellowship.

It has been a privilege to work with Clara Totten, Angela Zombek, and the rest of the team at Kent State University Press. Their professionalism, generosity, and efficiency deserve special recognition.

I am also grateful for the kind support of colleagues at both the Civil War Governors of Kentucky Digital Documentary Edition and the John Dickinson Writings Project, especially Chuck Welsko, Brian Trump, Jane Calvert, and David Hoth.

My faith community in the Episcopal Church—in Charlottesville, Versailles, and the Twin Cities—has provided tremendous support. Special thanks to Lachlan Hassman for helping me to deepen my relationship with Christ.

I am grateful to the many friends who have provided so much laughter over the years, especially Will Marfleet, Jack Peters, Erik Mandsager, Cory Gett, Bennett Falck, Noah Cloak, Abe Cooper, Zartosht Ahlers, Gerry Angelatos, Josh Morrison, Brian Neumann, Peyton Hoyal, Taylor and Emily Boomer, Matt and Brianna Frakes, Kevin Lonabaugh, and Harrison Redepenning.

My late grandfather, Howard Roscoe, inspired my love of history at an early age. I ask for the intercession of all the saints that he may find eternal rest. Thanks, and blessings also to my surviving grandparents, David and Linda Iverson and Doreen Roscoe. My parents, Todd and Ellen Iverson, and my sister, Emma Iverson, have given me overwhelming love and support. I couldn't have done it without you guys.

Finally, I extend my gratitude to my lovely wife, Drisana Iverson. Her care, attention, and encouragement have made me a better scholar and a better man.

Illinois in 1860 (Mary Lee Eggart)

INTRODUCTION

Amid the tumult of the 1856 campaign season, the *Chicago Journal* offered its readers a working definition of conservatism:

> Conservatism is a commendable element in our national politics. It tends to adjust an equilibrium in times of distraction and factious contention. It is the make-weight in times of extreme outbursts of passion or popular excitement, placing the weight of reason in each scale of the balance, and thus producing a counterpoise. It has the respect for that which our fathers established, in their patriotic desire to enact a truly model Republic, and resolves in its dispassionate reverence for original principles, to sustain and preserve unimpaired the system of government which they instituted. This is conservatism in its true sense, as applied to the politics of this country, and in this sense, we have respect for the man who is governed by its spirit, and shapes his political conduct according to its dictates.[1]

Neither revolutionary nor reactionary, conservatism for Americans of the mid-nineteenth century represented the political center, a middle path that balanced the passion of the moment with the wisdom of the past. In a moment of tremendous social, political, and economic change, it served as a guiding star for many as they sought to balance their hopes for the future with a profound fear that forces beyond their control would destroy it.

Students of the Civil War era tend not to emphasize this conservative disposition when investigating the origins of the United States' greatest conflict. A consensus has emerged among historians that the institution of racialized chattel slavery, above all other forces, caused the outbreak of war between the United States and the self-styled Confederate States of America in 1861. As a result, many have, quite understandably, focused their attention on those voices at the margins that worked to bring the moral quandary of slavery to the forefront of national politics. This impulse has generated many fine works of scholarship detailing the efforts of abolitionists, both Black and white, to advance the cause of human freedom.[2] But other scholars have recently begun to uncover the significance of this conservative impulse, rightly recognizing that the late antebellum period "was an era in U.S. history in which self-described conservatives dominated American life."[3] By emphasizing the political preeminence of moderates, especially in the free states, these works challenge the idea that those at the ideological extremes shaped the content and tenor of political discourse. They have also restored the centrality of the Union in the political thought of Northerners, a concept whose "meaning has almost been completely effaced from popular understanding of the [Civil War]."[4]

For many white Northerners of the mid-nineteenth century, the Union represented the safeguard of political liberty, economic prosperity, and social tranquility. As recorded in the pages of an Illinois newspaper, they considered the Constitution "the most sublime institution of human wisdom" and credited the Union with "the fairest scenes of individual and national happiness." While the rest of the world remained subject to "the shackles of tyranny and oppression," the white men of the United States enjoyed an unprecedented combination of political liberty, constitutional stability, social mobility, and economic opportunity.[5] Fearful of backsliding into tyranny or leaping into anarchy, they jealously guarded against any threat that might corrupt or undermine the Union and pledged to defend "the fundamental principles of republican government."[6] While partisans contested the application of these principles, most would have recognized historian Michael F. Holt's description of republicanism as a government "whose basic function was to protect the liberty and equality of individuals from aristocratic privilege and concentrations of arbitrary or tyrannical power."[7] For the overwhelming majority of white Northerners who sought to preserve or, if they thought it lost, restore this vision of government, the label of *conservative* fit quite well.[8]

Yet, conservative Northerners of the mid-nineteenth century did not reflexively oppose change. As historian Andrew F. Lang has persuasively argued, "conservatism did not mean rigid, static aversion to modern progress" but instead "meant approaching the uncertainness of the present with reasoned caution, using the rule of law and the proven, limiting principles of constitutional democracy to make necessary, periodic, and often fundamental alterations to conserve a nation's exceptional attributes."[9] Indeed, as affirmed by another leading scholar, Adam I. P. Smith, the "advocates of a conservative course, or of conservative principles, also regarded themselves as the advocates of progress."[10] Such was the case in 1859 when the *Islander and Argus* of Rock Island, Illinois, hailed the Democratic Party as both "the progressive party of our Great Republic" and also "the conservative party of the Union." The editor elaborated that the party, known then as the "Democracy," could claim this dual identity because it promised a future "in which Liberty is tempered by Law; in which Order is maintained, but in which no man's Freedom is infringed upon; in which national power and individual rights harmoniously co-exist."[11] In other words, it moderated the conflicting impulses in national life, ensuring a prosperous future while maintaining the inheritance of the past.

It is important to note that the boundaries of what constituted a conservative position shifted over time as unexpected events forced moderates to reevaluate how best to preserve the Union, republican government, and economic opportunity for free white men. Many of the same politicians and voters who denounced the repeal of the Missouri Compromise in 1854 subsequently rejected its restoration in the form of the Crittenden Compromise in 1861. Some might frame this reversal as evidence of radicalization. Yet the conservative Republicans who took this path believed that in both instances they were preserving the American Revolution's legacy from forces determined to undermine it. The same mindset also helps to explain Douglas Democrats' shifting position over the winter and spring of 1860–61, during which longtime advocates of popular sovereignty reversed course and became champions of the Crittenden Compromise only to then metamorphize again, in the wake of Fort Sumter, into militant advocates of the war against secessionism. The underlying consistency in these policy reversals was a steadfast commitment to maintaining the Union at all hazards.

Holding the Political Center in Illinois tells a familiar story in a new way by returning conservatism to the forefront in this critical state. In doing so, it departs from some recent works on conservatism in antebellum America that have defined the term narrowly and have sought to trace the lineage of the modern conservative movement.[12] This book also challenges the view, advanced by historian James Oakes, that antebellum Republicans self-evidently "constituted the left wing of the American political spectrum."[13] Rather than impose a left–right dichotomy recognizable to Americans in the twenty-first century but alien to those of the mid-nineteenth, this book takes into consideration all claims to the contested label of *conservative*, such as that of the Republican *Chicago Journal*.[14]

Illinois's geographic, economic, and demographic diversity makes the Prairie State an especially interesting place to study self-identified conservatives. Divided by contemporaries into distinct northern, central, and southern regions, Illinois presents a microcosm of a heterogenous antebellum North. While Cyrus McCormick's mechanical reaper increased agricultural yields beyond anything imaginable a mere decade before, internal improvements like the Illinois & Michigan Canal and the Illinois Central Railroad connected entrepreneurial farmers to eager consumers in the expanding eastern cities of Philadelphia, New York, and Boston.[15] Rapidly integrating into the national economy, Chicago became the "gateway city to the Great West" as its population swelled from barely two hundred in 1830 to more than one hundred thousand in 1860.[16] As the new metropolis struggled to integrate a flood of Roman Catholics from Germany and Ireland, in the state's hinterland, newcomers from New England clashed with established "Suckers" who had migrated from Kentucky, Tennessee, or Virginia. At the center of an expanding nation, these diverse voices clashed over issues such as immigration, religion, education, temperance, and, of course, slavery's potential extension. In this period, the state's citizens marveled at their unbounded agricultural and industrial potential and grappled with the tensions corollary to cultural heterogeneity.[17]

Over the course of the 1850s, it became clear that Illinois would play a critical role in national politics. With most of the South thoroughly Democratic and the Upper North staunchly Republican, the three Border North states of Pennsylvania, Indiana, and Illinois, served as critical fronts in the battle for the presidency. While Democrat James Buchanan secured these critical fifty-one electoral votes in the 1856 election, his margins of victory in each state were hardly resounding. Illinois appeared especially vulnerable. Buchanan won only a plurality of 44 percent of the vote, with the opposition divided between the Republican John C. Frémont and the Know-Nothing candidate Millard Fillmore. If the Republicans could secure the support of Fillmore's voters in the Prairie State in 1860, they would add a critical swing state to their column and clear a path to the White House. Alternatively, if Stephen A. Douglas could maintain his party's traditional dominance in Illinois, Republican prospects at the national level markedly dimmed.[18]

By analyzing the evolution of a single state within a framework of national politics, this book responds to the call of historian Jack Furniss to place federalism at the center of nineteenth-century political history. In the 1850s, national operatives in Washington, DC, lacked the means to dominate the political system. Instead, as scholars such as William E. Gienapp and Michael F. Holt have recognized, "loose coalitions of state parties, each of which functioned to a large extent independently of the others," drove national politics. By recognizing that state organizations, not national parties, "formed the core of the political system," this book emphasizes how local conditions, preferences, and prejudices shaped American politics in profound ways. The Democratic and Republican Parties that developed in Illinois contrasted in important ways from corresponding organizations in states like Massachusetts, Pennsylvania, and even neighboring Indiana. The conservative race to the center that shaped politics in Illinois did not occur in the same way in every Northern state. Nevertheless, the way each party ran that race—tailoring its message to local conditions to build a viable coalition within an unstable political environment—illustrates a dynamic that shaped electoral politics throughout the Union.[19]

Holding the Political Center in Illinois charts the political trajectory of the state from the introduction of the Kansas-Nebraska Act through the firing on Fort Sumter. Some readers will recognize the places, characters, and events in this book from the many fine works that have charted the rise of Abraham Lincoln.[20] Lincoln plays a prominent role in the following pages, but he does not occupy center stage. Instead, he emerges as one of many political leaders who sought to contain the chaos inadvertently unleashed by the state's most prominent politician of the 1850s, Stephen A. Douglas. Building on historian Michael E. Wood's effort to reinterpret Douglas as a national political figure in his own right rather than "a speedbump on Lincoln's road to greatness," this book explores how and why the "Little Giant" remained a potent force in Illinois and national politics until his untimely death in June 1861.[21]

In doing so, this book does not seek to exculpate Douglas or diminish Lincoln. Instead, it aims to complicate our understanding of these men and their parties by examining their shared instinct to preserve a republic they believed was destined for greatness. It makes the case that in Illinois, Douglas's Democrats and Lincoln's Republicans, as well as the Know-Nothings and oldline Whigs, who tried to remain aloof from both camps, shared a common economic vision for Illinois and the western prairies beyond the Mississippi where their sons and daughters would eventually make their homes. They imagined a society in which free white men would carve out homes and communities while governing themselves under the auspices of the Constitution and the Union.[22] Except for a small number of administration (later Breckinridge) Democrats, Illinois voters rejected the idea that slavery was a positive good and deserved protection from the federal government throughout the national territory. Although white Illinoisans disagreed on the extent to which slavery threatened the West and whether the federal government should intervene to restrict its expansion, most concurred that the institution was undesirable.[23]

Nevertheless, the Prairie State's electorate remained deeply hostile to free and enslaved African Americans. While Illinois Republicans sometimes defended the abstract natural rights of Black Americans, members of all parties staunchly opposed Black civil and political rights and expressed support for the Fugitive Slave Law. Indeed, the marginalization of Black abolitionists and other radical voices emerged as a recurring theme throughout the period. For Illinois conservatives in all camps, an abstract distaste for slavery blended effortlessly with palpable racism.[24]

For all this common ground, Illinois's partisans clashed on a wide range of issues and battled ferociously to claim the political center and the mantle of *conservative*. Throughout this period, political coalitions in Illinois remained fluid. The disruption precipitated by the passage of the Kansas-Nebraska Act did not neatly reorganize voters. Instead, it initiated a process of realignment that continued through the beginning of the Civil War. The question of popular sovereignty remained the dominant force shaping allegiances, but other issues, such as immigration, temperance, and former party affiliation, also proved significant. Personal enmity between leading figures in the parties also played a part. Notably, even as Republican leaders in the East sought détente with Douglas and Republicans in Indiana formed a coalition with Douglas Democrats in opposition to that state's pro-Buchanan Democratic machine, the antipathy between top Illinois Republicans and the "Little Giant" prevented such an alliance in the Prairie State.[25]

Amid this intense competition, leaders on all sides orchestrated a drive to the ideological center, which led to a brief but significant convergence in the spring of 1861. While partisanship reemerged as a divisive force in Illinois and the rest of the North during the war years, it remains essential to understand why so many Democrats and other antiabolitionist Northerners enthusiastically enlisted to fight against their Southern slaveholding countrymen. The united reaction against secession that propelled Lincoln and Douglas to make common cause in the opening months of the Civil War arose out of an unconditional commitment to the Union that defined the politics of self-identified conservatives.

This book relies heavily on two source bases to determine voters' feelings, and both warrant further explanation. Modern public opinion polls did not exist in the antebellum United States. Thus, any attempt to establish the motives of the public or any group of voters requires some degree of inference. For all their eccentricities and flaws, partisan newspapers provide an excellent window into the thoughts and feelings of local communities. Although directed to some degree by party higherups, these papers spoke directly to local audiences. They served as the main channel of political information for ordinary voters. To be sure, their editorials sought to persuade, but they also hoped to reflect and magnify existing feelings within a community. In addition, these papers printed the proceedings of local party meetings, where voters expressed their views directly. By adopting resolutions and selecting delegates to party conventions at the state level and beyond, ordinary party members made their views known. Thus, while far from perfect, the partisan press provides scholars with more or less accurate readings of the community's political temperature. The correspondence of prominent political actors, candidates, newspaper editors, and local activists provides an additional glimpse into the minds of ordinary voters. Some of the letters received by figures such as US senator Lyman Trumbull came from ordinary farmers, merchants, and craftsmen. But even those letters written by county politicos to state leaders provide keen insights into the local climate. While newspaper editors sometimes overlooked the storm clouds on the horizon in their defiant editorials, these same men rarely held back bad news in private letters to public officials and party leaders.[26]

The prologue, chapter 1, offers the background necessary to understand the complicated political, economic, and ethnocultural forces that had begun to reshape Illinois in the early 1850s. Chapter 2 investigates the passage of the Kansas-Nebraska Act and the disintegration of old partisan alignments. While the anti-Nebraska forces that emerged from this moment agreed that Douglas had violated a sacred national compact, old allegiances as well as new ethnic and religious tensions prevented them from forming a coherent new organization. Chapter 3 reveals how a combination of popular indignation at slaveholder aggression and savvy maneuvering by Illinois's anti-Nebraska leaders combined to create a state Republican Party, conservative in temperament and limited in its goals. That party's mixed performance in the 1856 elections offered a path forward for opponents of Stephen A. Douglas and forced the state's Democrats to recalibrate their own message.

Chapters 4 and 5 explore how infighting on both the state and national levels plagued both of the major political parties as each sought to seize the political center and draw former Know-Nothings into their own camp. The struggle over the Lecompton constitution revealed the fluid nature of realignment in Illinois as voters and party leaders alike struggled to distinguish the motivations and goals of each party. In Lincoln and Douglas's famous series of debates, each candidate aimed to present himself as the champion of a conservative center and frame his opponent as a radical threat to the constitutional order.

Chapter 6 traces the 1860 presidential campaign, as Lincoln crafted an antiextensionist narrative that promised to restore the vision of the Founders that appealed to the broad political center in his home state and across the North. Hampered by a divided national party, Douglas saw his own hopes for the White House evaporate even as he argued that he, and not Lincoln, would restore the Union to its proper balance.

Finally, chapter 7 examines how and why, despite rancorous partisanship throughout the secession winter, Illinois Republicans and Democrats united in defense of the Union following the Confederate attack on Fort Sumter. Even as Douglas and his Democratic supporters frantically worked to stitch together a compromise and avoid civil war, their underlying commitment to the Union compelled them to make common cause with their Republican rivals after secessionists fired on the national flag.

CHAPTER 1

PROLOGUE

"Whatever party may prevail, hereafter, the Union stands firm." So concluded Daniel Webster of Massachusetts shortly after the passage of the vaunted Compromise of 1850. A giant of the Senate, Webster had controversially abandoned his support of the anti-extensionist Wilmot Proviso to endorse the compromise measures in a famous address on March 7, 1850. Webster had paid a heavy political price for this decision as antislavery constituents lambasted their senator as a traitor. By the time the compromise measures passed in September, however, "Black Dan" had been elevated to the position of secretary of state, and the wider public echoed his sigh of relief. The citizens of Washington, DC, flocked into the streets as "the hearts of all . . . leaped with joy, that the factious spirit of Northern and Southern ultraism was crushed, and the danger that they had brought upon the Union, had subsided and passed away." After nine months of heated debate in Congress, the nation seemed to have resolved the quandaries raised by the Mexican Cession of 1848. Within the newly acquired territory, California would enter the Union as a free state, Texas would cede its claims to lands in New Mexico in exchange for the federal assumption of its debt, and white settlers in Utah and New Mexico would decide for themselves whether to allow slavery within their borders. Back east, two separate measures restricted the slave trade within the District of Columbia and strengthened the federal government's fugitive slave law.[1]

Thus, after years of sectional strife and nine months of heated debate in Congress, the compromise promised relief to a country that had come dangerously close to the precipice of civil war. Although the "Great Compromiser,"

Henry Clay, had crafted the formula for this resolution, the aging Kentucky Whig had been unable to secure the majorities necessary to enshrine these measures in law. That honor instead went to Stephen A. Douglas, Democrat of Illinois, known popularly as the "Little Giant" for his short stature and outsized personality. Douglas had craftily broken up the compromise into its constituent parts, rallying sectional majorities along with a handful of bisectional compromisers to pass each measure in turn.

Many American voters appreciated the pivot to the center made by these figures. Operating within a political culture that, despite the power of political parties, retained a reverence for antipartisanship, Webster, Clay, and Douglas's effort to move beyond partisan and sectional labels won plaudits from those conservative Whigs and Northern Democrats who occupied the broad middle of the political spectrum. Far more attached to the Union and their faith in American republicanism than to their party label, these voters held the balance of power in national politics. They also played an important role in the state politics of Illinois.[2]

While tension over the new territories had gripped Douglas's home state in the preceding years, with many formerly Democratic voters in northern Illinois defecting to the renegade Free-Soil Party in the canvas of 1848, the Compromise of 1850 met with the approbation of both established political parties. From Springfield, the Democratic *Illinois State Register* celebrated the "flood of light [that had broken] upon the republic, like the mellow morning sun upon the ship, long tossed by tempests and driven amidst threatening rocks." Across town, its Whig counterpart, the *Illinois Journal,* "rejoice[d] with others in the settlement of the slave question," while further downstate, the Whig *Alton Telegraph and Democratic Review* united "in rejoicing, and returning thanks to God, for having averted us from the evils which lately threatened all we hold dear as a people."[3]

Long a rising star in the national Democracy, Senator Douglas had added a peacock's plume to his political cap by pushing through the Compromise of 1850. Born in rural Vermont in 1813, Douglas had migrated west to Illinois in his early twenties. Soon thereafter, he entered the political arena as a supporter of President Andrew Jackson, winning a seat in the Illinois State Assembly. After serving as Illinois's secretary of state and justice of the Illinois Supreme Court, Douglas won a seat in Congress in 1842 and in 1847 was elected by the state legislature to the US Senate. While relatively young within that chamber of elder statesmen, Douglas had quickly established himself as a leading Democratic voice. His role in ushering through the compromise measures in 1850 solidified his reputation as a Democrat of national preeminence. Celebrating with the rest of Washington society in the aftermath of the bill's passage, the Little Giant undoubtedly indulged his penchant for whiskey when "it was declared the duty of every patriot to get drunk." But as he greeted the following day's inevitable hangover, a sober Douglas might have reflected on all that the compromise failed to resolve. While he and many of his fellow citizens hoped that the Compromise of 1850 represented the "final settlement" of the slavery question, the future remained uncertain in both the nation at large and Douglas's rapidly changing home state.[4]

Nationally, both major parties emerged from the crisis weakened by internal divisions. The Whigs especially suffered, as a cohort of Northern Whigs expressed their displeasure with the compromise while the party's base of support in the Deep South all but evaporated. In Massachusetts, many of Daniel Webster's Whig constituents lambasted Black Dan for repudiating the Wilmot Proviso and surrendering to the South. In the years that followed, citizens of the Bay State proved particularly hostile to enforcing the Fugitive Slave Act. Among Southern Whigs, the crisis prompted the defection of key leaders, including Alexander H. Stephens and Robert Toombs of Georgia, and contributed to the party's decline in Alabama and Mississippi. While most of these Southern ex-Whigs committed themselves to preserving the Union in the aftermath of the Compromise of 1850, they remained deeply estranged from their erstwhile allies in the North. While Northern Democrats began a process of reconciliation with their Free-Soil brethren, many Southern Democrats began to distance themselves from their Northern counterparts. As Fire-Eaters like William L. Yancey of Alabama continued stoking the of disunion, they received implicit support from extreme states' rights men like Jefferson Davis of Mississippi. Davis and his ilk argued that only a Southern-dominated Democratic Party could safeguard the slaveholding interests of the South within the Union and began making plans to reshape the party in their own image.[5]

Meanwhile, on the state level, Illinoisans found themselves at the heart of a region rapidly transforming from a culturally homogenous and locally oriented frontier zone into a heterogeneous and market-oriented "heartland." These changes proved both exhilarating and terrifying. Most white Illinoisans, Whigs and Democrats alike, seemed ready to set aside the divisive economic questions of decades past to join hands in building up their state as the core of the "Great West" with its metropolis at Chicago. By facilitating the rise of railroads and banks, the twin engines of economic development, the state's political leaders hoped to secure prosperity for their citizens and power for themselves.

Over the course of the 1820s, 1830s, and 1840s, increasing numbers of Northerners devoted greater proportions of their time and energy to the production of commodities for sale rather than household consumption. This transition, facilitated by improvements in transportation, communication, and finance, also coincided with bifurcated mass migration from the established farming communities of the New England and the Middle Atlantic states. As young men and women left their small family farms, many migrated to rapidly growing cities, such as the coastal entrepôts of New York and Boston, or to inland centers of manufacturing like Lowell and Rochester. But others turned their faces westward in search of opportunities. In contrast to the region's first settlers, who had hailed from the Upper South, these Yankee migrants to the Old Northwest had no intention of distancing themselves from the prevailing economic and cultural forces of the East. Instead, they sought to establish themselves as Western agents of the market, cashing in on the agricultural and commercial expansion. As a result of this migration, along with a major influx of German and Irish immigrants, Illinois's population would swell from a modest 157,000 in 1830 to more than 1.7 million in 1860.[6]

These migrations created sharp geographical and cultural lines within the state. In southern Illinois, also known as "Little Egypt," the state's earliest settlers, migrants from Virginia and Kentucky, and their families mistrusted the new arrivals. Having spent decades scraping out a hardscrabble existence on the frontier, southern Illinoisans shifted only gradually from subsistence farming to market-oriented agriculture and mistrusted financial institutions. Many subscribed to an extreme backwoods variant of the high Calvinism that their ancestors had brought from Ulster and Scotland. With predestination as their watchword, they perceived moral reform efforts as intrusive and misguided, an offense to God's sovereignty. In contrast, the "Yankees," who migrated to northern Illinois in increasing numbers from greater New England throughout the 1840s and 1850s, carried the zeal for Christian perfectionism sparked by the Second Great Awakening. Preaching a postmillennial faith that, while not always explicitly Arminian, stressed free will, they enthusiastically supported the development of civically oriented institutions like lyceum societies and morally oriented social movements such as temperance, Sabbatarianism, and education reform. Culturally blended central Illinois occupied a position somewhere between these extremes. Its citizens came from a variety of backgrounds, though a cohort of well-to-do ex-Kentuckians had helped to create the state's lone Whig stronghold. While religiously heterogenous, the well-established Methodist, Episcopal, and Presbyterian churches predominated.[7]

Although the native-born predominated throughout Illinois, the state also contained an increasingly influential population of immigrants. By 1850, they accounted for 13 percent of the state's population. Motivated to emigrate by both economic and political factors, German-language speakers generally came from middling backgrounds and had sufficient capital to establish farms, workshops, and stores throughout the state. Although predominantly Roman Catholic or Lutheran in their faith, a small contingent of free-thinking intellectuals and professionals, exiled after the failed Revolutions of 1848, would emerge as important leaders in this divided community. Impoverished Irish Catholics, however, migrated en masse to work as canal diggers and settled in Chicago, where they emerged as one of the Democratic Party's most faithful constituencies.[8]

In the minds of native-born Protestants, the cultural, political, and economic threats posed by this influx of immigrants necessitated a decisive response. Suspicion of immigrants, especially of Roman Catholics, had a long history in Illinois. Elijah Lovejoy, the antislavery editor murdered by an antiabolitionist mob in Alton in 1837 and brother of future radical Republican Owen Lovejoy, had ranted against "the hordes of ignorant, uneducated, vicious foreigners" who under the guidance of the Catholic Church were "calculated, fitted, and intended to subvert our liberties." Yet in the 1850s, as the number of foreign-born Illinoisans swelled well beyond anything Lovejoy might have predicted, the nativist imperative to check the influence of immigrants would take on a new urgency.[9]

The state's demographic expansion and economic growth had come at the expense of the state's Indigenous inhabitants. Unwilling to cede their lands without a fight, an intertribal alliance of Sauks, Meskwakis, Kickapoos, Ho-Chunks, and Potawatomis had launched a defensive war against American settlers in the spring of 1832. Led by the Sauk leader Black Hawk, a veteran warrior who had fought against the United States during the War of 1812, the allies raided white settlements throughout the Upper Midwest and fought several pitched battles in northern Illinois. Responding with overwhelming force, a unit of US Army soldiers and volunteer state militiamen pushed Black Hawk's warriors back toward the Mississippi River, decisively defeating the Indian allies in the Battle of Bad Axe on August 2, 1832. Although relatively brief, the conflict offered young white men a chance to display their martial prowess and leadership skills. The state's aspiring politicians filled the ranks, among them John T. Stuart, Joseph Gillespie, Orville H. Browning, and a twenty-three-year-old captain named Abraham Lincoln. These American conquests opened northeastern Illinois for unrestricted white settlement for the first time. Indeed, the forcible displacement of the region's Indigenous inhabitants by Lincoln and his comrades led directly to the incorporation of Chicago in 1833.[10]

Members of the state's small Black population also found themselves marginalized amid the rapid development. Although a free state under the law, Illinois had a history of slavery dating back to the colonial period, when European colonizers had adapted traditional practices of bondage to the environment of the American interior. Emerging in the 1730s as a strategic halfway point between Quebec and New Orleans for the French Empire, the Illinois Country required few settlers. Nevertheless, the French Canadian *coureurs de bois* who occupied the region enslaved both Africans and American Indians and traded these slaves back and forth with their native allies. With the white population dedicated to the fur trade, Black and Indigenous slaves produced vast quantities of grain for shipment downriver to New Orleans. The transfer of the region to the British Empire in 1763 led to a small increase in the enslaved population, as Anglophone settlers from nearby Pennsylvania and distant Jamaica brought their slaves to further develop the grain potential of the territory. Having augmented the fur trade with a successful slave-based staple economy, few settlers—Francophone or Anglophone—believed the new US government should outlaw the institution.[11]

Although both the Northwest Ordinance of 1787 and Article VI of the original Illinois Constitution of 1818 had prohibited "slavery and involuntary servitude," African Americans throughout the state remained in official or quasi-bondage. A grandfather clause granted slaveholders the right to keep so-called French Negroes in bondage and made their status heritable so that several hundred African Americans remained legally enslaved in Illinois into the 1840s. In addition, the Illinois Constitution of 1818 enforced indenture contracts of up to ninety-nine years, keeping many Blacks brought to the state by Anglo-American settlers from Virginia, Kentucky, and Tennessee in de facto slavery. This variant of vassalage so alarmed antislavery forces in Congress that several northeastern representatives voted against Illinois's admission to the Union out of a fear that the state would formally adopt slavery within several years. This concern almost came to fruition in 1824, when a proslavery state legislature had placed a referendum before the people that would likely have led to the adoption of slavery in Illinois. Although voters decisively defeated this, the state's rejection of de jure slavery did little to improve the material conditions of African Americans. In 1819, the state had adopted a Black code that prohibited three or more people of color from "assembling," "dancing," or partaking in any "revelry," and the legislature had added further restrictions in 1827, 1829, 1831, 1833, 1841, and 1845 to minimize the social, economic, and political rights of Black residents.[12]

Beginning in the 1830s, many of those who remained enslaved began to challenge their legal status. Assisted by a handful of white abolitionists, like the Maine-born Congregational minister Owen Lovejoy, these bondspeople found attorneys and brought their enslavers to court. In 1841, Nance Cromwell, a Maryland-born slave held under long-term indenture in Illinois secured her freedom from the Illinois Supreme Court with the help of a young Springfield lawyer named Abraham Lincoln. Another emerging politician, Lyman Trumbull, successfully litigated the end of slavery for "French Negroes" in the 1845 case of *Joseph Jarrot, a colored man v. Julia Jarrot*. Arguably, these decisions turned Illinois into the free state it claimed to be, but they did little to improve the social circumstances for the small Black communities of Alton, Springfield, and Chicago.[13]

In general, however, free Blacks in Illinois lacked reliable political allies. While a few individual Whigs and Democrats proved sympathetic to the plight of African Americans, indifference or hostility toward Blacks characterized the attitude of most men in the major parties. Support for the colonization movement, which advocated a gradual elimination of slavery and the deportation of African Americans to Africa or some other distant locale, remained the primary outlet by which Illinoisans in the political mainstream spoke out against slavery. Even some of the lawyers who defended enslaved Illinoisans or fugitive slaves from other states did so out of professional obligation rather than genuine sympathy for Blacks. For example, in 1847, James Matson retained Lincoln's legal services to help him recover a woman and four children he held in bondage, while the enslaved employed Orlando B. Ficklin, a Democratic congressman from Coles County who loathed abolitionists and described African Americans as "miserable, imbecile, and wholly worthless."[14]

Illinois had also drafted a new constitution in 1847. Principally to address issues of state finance, a few tepid Whigs from northern Illinois introduced measures that would have improved the status of the state's four thousand Black residents. A proposal to grant free Black men voting rights received a paltry eight votes, while a bipartisan majority of 137 voted against the measure. A furious cohort of reactionary delegates then took advantage of the opportunity to constitutionally prohibit the migration of free persons of color into the state. Despite opposition from the state's abolitionists, such as the mixed-race tailor John Jones, who published a rejoinder to the measure in Chicago's antislavery newspaper, the *Western Citizen*, voters endorsed this provision for Black exclusion the following spring by a margin of more than 2–1. In 1853, after several years of squabbling over the law's details, the state legislature would formally criminalize the immigration of free Blacks, imposing a fine of $50, or labor commensurate to that sum, on those who ignored the statute. Indiana and Oregon later followed Illinois's lead and formally excluded free Blacks from migrating to their states. According to the *Anti-Slavery Bugle*, with the passage of this act, Illinois could only be "factiously called a *free* state." From his printing office in Rochester, New York, abolitionist leader Frederick Douglass denounced the measure as "inhuman and barbarous legislation" imposed on Black citizens by "the offspring of wolves and tigers," while the abolitionist *National Era* of Washington, DC, suggested that the people of Illinois deserved "the scorn and abhorrence of Christendom" for such a law.[15] A Repeal Association of free African Americans repeatedly lobbied the state legislature to restore rights to the state's people of color, but to no avail. The measures would remain in force throughout the state until late in the Civil War.[16]

Following the adoption of the 1850 Fugitive Slave Law, the state's small but determined Black population resisted with a ferocity that surprised many and inspired a response in pockets of northern Illinois.[17] Following a meeting organized by Black leaders in Quin Chapel, Chicago's African Methodist Episcopal (AME) Church, white and Black abolitionists organized a Liberty Association and vigilance committees to protect people of color from slave catchers and pressured the Chicago City Council to take a stand on the measure, which it did a week later, denouncing the measure as unconstitutional. The council later softened its resolutions, which Douglas and other Democrats condemned as equivalent to nullification, but continued to insist that city officials would play no role in returning fugitive slaves. Despite a tacit endorsement of the Fugitive Slave Law by most of the state's leading politicians, Chicago alone hosted seven identifiable stations on the Underground Railroad. Even as Black abolitionists, like John Jones, helped fugitives escape to Canada, the city's tiny community of color would dwindle over the course of the 1850s from nine hundred residents to only three hundred, as the threat of kidnapping by slave catchers compelled many free-born and formerly enslaved Black residents to follow fugitives to safety under the British flag beyond the Great Lakes. Still, throughout the decade fugitive slaves continued to pass through Chicago, often via Underground Railroad stations in Quincy, Alton, or Princeton if escaping from Missouri and onward to Canada. Although some radical white politicians like Owen Lovejoy actively participated in their escapes, and slavecatchers' callous disregard for local authority and the rights of free Black citizens led some, including Abraham Lincoln, to call for a reform of the law, most mainstream opponents of slavery's extension distanced themselves from these fugitives.[18]

Throughout the period, Black abolitionists, such as Henry O. Wagoner, a Chicago entrepreneur and activist, worked tirelessly to improve the conditions of the state's citizens of color, believing, as Wagoner would write to Frederick Douglass in 1853, "that the great work of our redemption, rests with ourselves." Yet this work often appeared futile as white Illinoisans violently resisted any effort by Blacks to assert their social equality, as in 1854, when whites forced Joseph Spencer, a Black resident of Cairo, onto a burning barge and left him to die following a confrontation in the city's courthouse. The marginalization of Black activists from mainstream partisan politics and overt acts of hostility against Black Americans would remain constants throughout the antebellum period. Even as more white Illinoisans became concerned by the potential extension of slavery into the West, African Americans remained personae non gratae.[19]

Largely indifferent to the plight of Black Illinoisans, the state's white farmers focused their attention on technological improvements that would help propel the Prairie State toward unprecedented prosperity. Two technologies: the steel plow and the mechanical reaper, both widely adopted in the mid-1850s, helped to turn the state into the nation's breadbasket. The steel plow, developed and perfected by John Deere of Moline, allowed farmers to cut through the state's notoriously dense sod and open millions of additional acres to cultivation. The mechanical reaper, produced in Chicago by Cyrus McCormick, took the place of a scythe in the field, saving labor and increasing efficiency at harvest time. With the machine's perfection in the mid 1850s, farmers throughout the state adopted the technology at an astonishing rate, leading one leading historian to label the mechanical reaper "a necessity of rural life" by 1860. Adopted in tandem, the steel plow and mechanical reaper helped increase Illinois's production of wheat from 9.4 million bushels in 1850 to 23.8 million in 1860.[20]

Simultaneously, the rush to construct rail lines to transport these bountiful harvests reconfigured traditional political alliances as some Democrats embraced a program of internal improvements and national development that the Whigs had long championed. Increasingly, the potential benefits of such a transit network outweighed midwesterners' lingering suspicions of government interference in commercial affairs. Identified by historian James L. Huston as the "commercial Democrats," members of a new Western cohort within the party distanced themselves from Jacksonian-era agrarian policies and instead sought to foster economic development as a complement to territorial expansion. For men such as Douglas, fulfilling the nation's manifest destiny required enhanced economic activity as well as the conquest of the continent. For this generation, the sight of a locomotive soaring across the prairie seemed nothing less than "a force of nature, a geographical power so irresistible that people must shape their lives according to its dictates."[21]

The push to integrate central Illinois into the national economy through internal improvements had begun decades before. An ambitious system of roads, railroads, and canals championed by many young state legislators, including Abraham Lincoln, had flopped in the wake of the Panic of 1837. Aside from the Illinois & Michigan Canal (completed in 1848), connecting Chicago to the Illinois River, the state had little to show for its infrastructural ambition and had taken on more than $13.6 million in debt. Still, this rising generation of Illinoisans remained determined to transform the state into an economic powerhouse. Stephen A. Douglas envisioned Illinois as the economic and geographic center of a continental republic, connecting the Great Lakes to the vast Mississippi Valley. In pursuit of this dream, he repeatedly introduced federal legislation to fund the Illinois Central Railroad, a line that would bisect the state and range nearly five hundred miles from Cairo to Chicago in the northeast and branching to Dunleith—just across the river from Dubuque, Iowa—in the Northwest. After a failed effort in the Thirtieth Congress, Douglas successfully passed the bill in the wake of the Compromise of 1850, securing a grant of 2.5 million acres in federal land to fund the Illinois Central.[22]

The Little Giant's success in funding this unprecedented project simultaneously dampened criticism from Free-Soilers and jumpstarted a railroad frenzy that would stretch the total track length of the state from fifty miles in 1850 to twenty-five hundred miles by 1860. New lines appeared, including the Chicago & Alton, the Wabash, and the Galena & Chicago Union, which integrated Alton, Belleville, Springfield, Galena, and many more small towns into a vast network. The development of the "Great West," as Illinoisans envisioned it, would overcome sectionalism by modernizing the whole country. The "Steam Horse," would draw "the boundless and exhaustless riches" of the "fertile prairie land" on to "the great commercial marts of the East and South." Although the railroad ultimately tied Illinois and the rest of the Midwest closer to the Northeast than to the South, most saw the new technology as a complement, rather than a replacement, to the great waterways that had long linked them to the Gulf of Mexico.[23]

This vision of a free modernizing West modernizing transcended the partisan divide. In April 1852, Whig congressman Richard Yates declared the beginning of a "new era" for the United States in which "wherever the iron horse travels, he will carry, not only the rich productions of our soil, but our laws, our liberty, and our religion." Having reclaimed the land "from the savage and the solitude of the wilderness," Western fortitude and new technology would harness the region's boundless natural resources and create centers of manufacturing, producing opportunities for all white men. Indeed, Yates believed the project had advanced so far that "the fears of disunion growing out of the increased extension of territory no longer alarm the patriot." Expansion, when coupled with improvements in commerce and communication, would only bind the states of the Union closer together in the ties of mutual interest.[24]

Indeed, in the aftermath of the Compromise of 1850, Illinois Whigs eagerly embraced elements of the Democratic Young America movement, endeavoring to "spread liberal government throughout the world and to increase social mobility at home . . . through collective, majoritarian effort." In Bloomington, the *Western Whig* affirmed that "civilization, in its unceasing progress, is ever moving westward" advanced by the "determined energy, untiring perseverance, willingness to labor" and other "impressive characteristics of Western Men." The hearty workingman, "the tiller of the broad and beautiful prairie and the maker and builder of the useful," constituted "the real aristocracy of the land" as he advanced an empire of liberty and harvested the fruits of his labor. This endorsement of elbow grease as a path to prosperity hinted at the emerging Northern consensus on the virtues of free labor and the growing support for a homestead bill—providing free land to anyone who would settle a parcel and farm it for a period of years—among all northwesterners. Practical, industrious, and egalitarian, this Western Whig vision championed many of the qualities traditionally associated with the Democracy even as their opponents took up elements of the old American System.[25]

Although Democrats had traditionally opposed funding internal improvements, Douglas and his fellow commercial Democrats embraced railroads, river and harbor improvements, and the construction of telegraph networks throughout the country. Early in his career, Douglas had bucked party orthodoxy to support federal funding for river and harbor improvements in Illinois. Frustrated by the failure of inadequately funded federal programs, he began to advocate for state-led infrastructure projects and proposed that Congress grant states the power to levy tonnage duties to fund them. Such a scheme squared Douglas's faith in local self-government with his commitment to internal improvements. As the leader of a new generation of Democrats, Douglas sought to blend the best of the Jacksonian tradition with demands of a nation reshaped by the market revolution. While some traditional Democrats found him "too closely associated with the steamship, the railroad, and all sorts of stock-jobbing enterprises," many found Douglas's vision inspiring and lauded his advocacy of "progress all over, in every direction, and in every thing."[26]

In their effort to advance the country, some commercial Democrats in Illinois proved willing to make peace with the greatest of monsters for Jacksonians: banks. While a new state constitution in 1848, drawn up by a Democratic convention, had taken a decidedly antibank position, prohibiting both a central state bank and requiring a statewide referendum on corporate bank charters, the development of an integrated marketplace connected by a sophisticated rail network required credit. Within a few short years, the state legislature adopted, and voters approved, a free banking system—by which any qualifying party could operate a bank with corporate privileges—and vastly expanded the number of banks throughout the state. The system passed over the veto of Democratic governor Augustus C. French and generated a strenuous backlash among orthodox Jacksonians. One such stalwart, writing in the *Rock Island Republican*, lamented how banks would subject the state "to the fluctuations, the panics, and the extravagant and unprincipled speculations induced by the facilities for obtaining money." But as he wrote from Washington back to editor Charles H. Lanphier of the *Illinois State Register*, Douglas emphasized democracy and progress over established party dogma, reminding his friend that all "good democrats are forced to submit to the will of the people when expressed according to the forms of the constitution." Whatever the ideological scruples of diehard Jacksonians, most Illinoisans wanted access to banks and needed them to do business, and recent scholarship confirms the importance of such banks in the railroad boom of the 1850s.[27]

Of course, differences between the two parties remained. To sidestep questions of constitutionality, Democrats preferred for the states to manage improvements and fund these projects through tonnage duties approved by Congress rather than authorize them directly. In addition, many Illinois Democrats remained leery of out-of-state banks, fearing their small denomination paper notes would sap the state of specie. But beyond these policy differences, political persona and rhetorical style emerged as the greatest gulf that still separated Democrats from Whigs. The Democrats continued to rally their faithful using the memory of Andrew Jackson and castigating Whigs as neo-Federalist naysayers, holding back America's democratic destiny. The Whigs, meanwhile, continued to paint Democrats as corrupt intriguers spoiling after public offices. For the most dedicated party members, politicians, and newspaper editors, party affiliation tied them to past triumphs and affirmed their identity as righteous warriors in the ongoing struggle for power.

Thus, although the flaming controversies of the previous thirty years had diminished to a few crackling embers, the fires of partisanship continued to burn in many hearts.[28]

In 1852, the Democrats scored a major coup in the national elections as their presidential candidate Franklin Pierce overwhelmed his Whig rival, Winfield Scott, by a stunning margin of 254 to 42 electoral votes, while Whig candidates for Congress lost in more than 70 percent of the seats they contested. Critically weakened by defections in the South and internal squabbling in key Northern states like New York, the Whigs looked less and less like a viable national party. Yet the magnitude of the Democratic victory prompted discord within the vast coalition. With the old Jacksonian financial issues moribund and their opponents prostrate before them, Democrats took to squabbling among themselves. Following the inauguration of President Pierce in early 1853, Stephen A. Douglas found himself on the wrong side of intraparty patronage battles and looked on with dismay as rival Democratic factions in New York engaged in an all-out civil war. Discouraged but not disheartened, Douglas wrote to an Illinois advisor that they needed a new policy issue to snap the party out of its "distracted condition" and "perpetuate its principles." Near the end of this letter, Douglas fatefully mentioned that "the Pacific Railroad" might provide just such an issue.[29]

While his forecast ultimately proved a disastrous miscalculation, Douglas hoped his push to integrate the vast West into the wider body politic would draw support from the broad middle of the political spectrum. With many Whig and Democratic voters in Illinois seemingly in accord on matters of policy, whichever party could outline a compelling vision for national development would reap vast political dividends. By securing the fertile prairies beyond the Mississippi River for the children of Illinois's free white men, Douglas expected to launch himself into the national limelight yet again. Despite the supposed "final settlement" of sectional tension, the question of slavery in the West lingered uncomfortably in the background, ready to disrupt the best-laid plans.

CHAPTER 2

A HELL OF A STORM

Staring intently at the map before him, Stephen A. Douglas traced with his finger the future route of a transcontinental railroad across the vast expanse of the West. Connecting the Great Lakes to the distant Pacific, the line would bind the Union together, ensuring prosperity for untold generations of Americans. Douglas trusted that his bid to secure an eastern terminus for this epic railroad in Illinois would invigorate the Prairie State and secure his national reputation. But in single-mindedly pursuing this goal, he overlooked how other changes occurring across the state and the nation would fracture the political order beyond repair.

The Kansas-Nebraska Act, intended as the first step in securing this railroad for Illinois, provoked a partisan meltdown. While most white Illinoisans endorsed the marginalization of the state's small Black population, the potential expansion of slavery into the western prairies filled many with trepidation. Disturbed by growing Southern intransigence on the issue of slavery's extension, many in Illinois came to see the Kansas-Nebraska Act's repeal of the Missouri Compromise as a repudiation of a sacred national compact and the first step toward a tyrannical government headed by Southern aristocrats and doughface demagogues. In the minds of some, this misrule had been made possible by the migration of startling numbers of foreign-born voters, especially Roman Catholics. These immigrants, who had ventured to the Prairie State in search of economic opportunity, had until this moment loyally backed the Democratic Party and its pro-immigrant policies. As a result, for a moment at least, the anti-slaveholder and antiimmigrant causes merged into a concerted opposition. A muddled host of self-identified conservatives, the anti-Nebraska coalition deemed itself the defender of freedom, the Constitution, public order, and the Protestant faith. Douglas and his allies battled back with their own appeals to the conservative center, defending the hallowed principles of majority rule and white male democracy. To the dismay of many, the conflict between Douglas's supporters and the "anti-Nebraska" challengers upended the existing political organizations. While one Illinois paper blamed "uneasy politicians" for distributing the peace of the "tranquil masses," the events of 1854 and 1855 demonstrated that party leaders and voters alike were uneasy in their struggle to find order within a rapidly changing world.[1]

A Western Railroad

The Little Giant had not foreseen such turmoil from his place in distant Washington when he introduced the measure. Despite what some historians have argued, Douglas's decision to introduce the Kansas-Nebraska Act sprang not from deference to the Southern wing of his party but from his immense ambition and his aspirations for the American West. Aware of a growing consensus among voters on the major economic issues of the Jacksonian era, Douglas hoped that his vision of Western development—territorial expansion coupled with a homestead act and federally funded transportation improvements—might reinvigorate the Democratic Party. If all went well, the Free-Soilers, who had broken away in 1848 to support the third-party campaign of Martin Van Buren, would return to the Democratic fold, and a more expansive vision for economic development might even bring along a few Whigs. Should that course propel him to the top of the Democratic ticket in 1856 and win him the White House, all the better.[2]

Originally, Douglas hoped to sidestep the thorny issue of slavery's extension, but the insistence of Southern senators on a program of popular sovereignty for the newly organized territories coupled with an explicit repeal of the Missouri Compromise seemed like nothing more than a speed bump on the road to national preeminence. Popular sovereignty had formed the basis of the 1850 Compromise measures, the "final settlement" to the slavery question that Douglas had worked so hard to enact. As a committed Jacksonian advocate of local self-government, Douglas sincerely believed that local majorities ought to decide this important question. He also believed that the settlers of the Great Plains would ultimately choose free labor out of economic self-interest, just as settlers in Illinois had done when reconsidering their state constitution in 1824.[3]

The Kansas-Nebraska Act represented the first step in building a transcontinental railroad that would turn his home state into the nation's commercial center. While some might balk initially, the railroad would serve as a balm for all wounds. After all, Douglas had done this before, pressing through a congressional land grant for the Illinois Central Railroad in the immediate aftermath of the Compromise of 1850. The great railroad victory had overpowered hostility to popular sovereignty and had made Douglas stronger than ever. But by seeking to repeat the scheme on a grander scale, Douglas inadvertently jeopardized the future of his party and catapulted the North's anti-Democratic forces into the national spotlight.[4]

First proposed in 1844 by the eccentric New Yorker Asa Whitney, the railroad to the West Coast promised to connect the distant Pacific Ocean to the Mississippi Valley. At the time, California was a Mexican province, and Great Britain contested American claims to Oregon. Nevertheless, Douglas wrote to Whitney that he had no doubt "necessity will make the road." Anticipating that "a hardy and industrious population" would soon occupy the region and begin transporting goods east, Douglas saw the railroad as a matter of course. The eastern terminus for the route across the vast interior would become a major commercial center, the metropolis where East met West, and Douglas hoped to secure the honor for Chicago. To pave the way for settlement and the railroad, he needed to organize the territory west of Missouri: Nebraska. With the establishment of a territorial government there, the federal government could displace the territory's Native peoples, attract white settlers, and begin awarding land grants for the Pacific railroad.[5]

Douglas had tried and failed to organize the Nebraska Territory in 1844 and 1848, but he returned in April 1852 with a memorial from his constituents that demanded that Congress take up the measure to protect settlers moving overland to the West. When his colleagues moved to quash the bill later that summer, Douglas erupted in frustration, explaining that it "did not require the spirit of a prophet to foresee that it is utterly impossible to preserve this Union—that it is utterly impossible to preserve that connection between the Atlantic and the Pacific, if you are to keep a "wilderness of two thousand miles in extent between you." In the second session of the Thirty-Second Congress in the winter of 1852–53, Douglas tried a different tack, by having an ally in the House, Congressman William A. Richardson of Illinois, introduce a measure organizing Nebraska.[6]

During the subsequent debate on the organization in the House, a small group of Southern congressmen, apparently intent on blocking the construction of the transcontinental railroad along a central route, became the unexpected allies of the territory's Native peoples. Representative Volney Howard of Texas, a former Mississippian who had also served as attorney general of the Republic of Texas, expressed a newfound sympathy for the territory's Panca, Omaha, Pawnee, Oto, Kansa, Kiowa, and Osage inhabitants, as well the Native nations forced westward into the region by the US government. Taking the floor, he denounced "a clear violation" of treaties that ought to be kept in "good faith" as it had been "expressly guaranteed that these people might maintain their separate political existence." Introducing evidence from eighteen separate treaties between the Federal government and Indigenous nations, he argued, "The foregoing provisions constitute a compact with these tribes in relation to these lands which it is not competent for this congress to violate, and which it ought not to disregard, if it had the power." The cynicism of the Texan's appeal appeared obvious to his colleagues as the Missouri Democrat Willard P. Hall sarcastically congratulated Howard and "his constituents and the country at large, upon the wonderful change which . . . has taken place in Texas in regard to the rights of Indians." The discussion reveals that, far from swallowing the myth of a wide-open Western frontier, prominent politicians recognized that American expansion came at the cost of Indian peoples. Fortunately for Douglas, a majority in the House was unwilling either to acknowledge the rights of Indigenous peoples or pander to the material interests of the Texans, and the body passed the bill to organize Nebraska by a vote of 107–49. But to Douglas's dismay, the bill to organize the territory subsequently went down to defeat in the Senate, by 23 to 17.[7]

Never one to abandon a challenge, Douglas returned to Washington in December 1853 for the first session of the Thirty-Third Congress, bound and determined to push the Nebraska bill through the Senate by any means necessary. Writing to constituents back in Illinois, Douglas asserted that "the tide of emigration and civilization must be permitted to roll onward" into Nebraska and toward the Pacific. The railroad had become a matter of necessity because no man could "keep up with the spirit of this age" by traveling "on anything slower than the locomotive." Yet, this unstoppable force of progress would soon encounter the seemingly immovable barrier of the slavery controversy.[8]

The Death of a Compromise

The initial roadblock to passage appeared in the institutional force of the so-called F-Street Mess. Composed of Senators James M. Mason and Robert M. T. Hunter of Virginia, Andrew P. Butler of South Carolina, and David R. Atchison of Missouri, the four occupants of 361 F Street formed an influential Southern voting bloc. In his recent effort to introduce the Nebraska Bill, Douglas had enjoyed the support of Atchison, who had close ties to St. Louis Railroad interests. But in the subsequent months, Atchison, facing political assaults from his predecessor and Missouri rival Thomas Hart Benton, decided to bolster his reputation among the state's slaveholding interest. Although Congress had explicitly tied Missouri's admission to the Union in 1821 to antislavery guarantees in the territory to the state's west, Atchison now feared that another free soil neighbor would pose a mortal threat to the perpetuation of slavery in Missouri. Reversing course, he "damned to oblivion the Missouri Compromise and any Nebraska Bill that did not repeal it." Supported by his messmates, President Pro Tempore of the Senate Atchison threatened to derail Douglas's bill the moment he introduced it.[9]

Already facing the opposition of several eastern senators, Douglas recognized that he would need to make concessions to his Southern colleagues to propel his plan forward. For a solution, he reached back to the principle of nonintervention, or popular sovereignty, codified in the Utah and New Mexico Territories as part of the Compromise of 1850. By discarding the restrictions imposed by the Missouri Compromise and allowing the new territory's settlers to decide the issue of slavery for themselves, Douglas could reaffirm his commitment to local democracy and allow his Southern colleagues to save face. Given the region's climate and the prospective demographics of the settler population, Douglas did not expect slavery to spread into Nebraska. He anticipated the Democracy to rally around "the naked question as a matter of principle" and decide "whether the people shall be allowed to regulate their domestic concerns in their own way or not." Douglas mistakenly believed the Compromise of 1850 had established noninterference as a general principle and concluded that the Democratic landslide of 1852 confirmed Northern acceptance of popular sovereignty. Still, he recognized that the annulment of the Missouri Compromise would "raise a hell of a storm" in the North and proved reluctant to provoke controversy with such aggressive language.[10]

Nevertheless, Douglas buckled after Kentucky Whig Archibald Dixon introduced an amendment to that effect. Hoping to outflank Southern Democrats in their defense of slaveholders' rights, Dixon's amendment explicitly repealed the Missouri Compromise. The amendment also divided the region into two territories—Nebraska to the north and Kansas to the south—and declared that each would decide the question of slavery for itself. To opponents of the bill, this partition seemed to preemptively surrender Kansas to slavery. As Douglas reworked the measure's final language, a small group of antislavery radicals, led by Ohio's Senator Salmon P. Chase and Representative Joshua P. Giddings, issued the *Appeal of the Independent Democrats*, which denounced the Nebraska Bill as a plot by the aristocratic slave power to "permanently subjugate the whole country to the yoke of a slaveholding despotism." Although this conspiratorial language would evolve and gain popularity in the months and years to come, most mainstream opponents of the Nebraska bill initially rejected it on the conservative grounds that it trampled on a sacred national compact.[11]

This instinct to rally behind the historic accord appeared almost immediately in Springfield's premier Whig paper, the *Illinois Journal*, which on January 16 called the Nebraska bill a "movement to nullify the Missouri Compromise." By invoking the sectional crisis of 1832–33 and framing Douglas and his supporters as latter-day Calhounites, the *Journal* sought to bolster its own pro-Union credentials. The author, likely the editor Simeon Francis, held it "to be the obligation of the country to sustain the Missouri Compromise with equal sincerity and fidelity" as "the compromise of 1850" and voiced complete opposition "to disturbing these compromises" while announcing his support for all of them "as a unit." A subsequent issue of the *Journal* explained that although they were never sectional in their outlook, the freemen of the Northwest would "resist, when as in this case slavery becomes aggressive, and would break its barriers through stipulated compacts." Explicitly invoking the memories of nationalist heroes Henry Clay and Daniel Webster, the *Journal* emphasized the patriotic, pro-Union, and nonpartisan motivations of the anti-Nebraska position. One of these editorials appeared alongside procolonization reports from Liberia, reflecting the weak antislavery and antiabolitionist consensus that continued to dominate the region.[12]

Elsewhere in the state, the initial Whig response varied, fluctuating between alarm over the repeal of the Missouri Compromise and skepticism of the bill's lasting import. While the *Alton Telegraph* denounced Douglas's bill as a "bare-faced cheat" to give over Nebraska "to the pestilent influences of slavery, and to legalize it, where, by a solemn compact, it ought never to exist," another Whig editor in Carlinville wrote to Richard Yates that he would take no stand on the Nebraska bill and lamented the "the present disorganized and lethargic state of the party." The *Quincy Whig* doubted that the provisions on popular sovereignty would remain in the final bill, given the supposed opposition of some Southern Whigs, but it nevertheless lamented "the political agitation of the slavery question." Another of Yates's correspondents objected to the Free-Soilers' "great inconsistency" in opposing the repeal of the Missouri Compromise in 1854 after having attacked compromise efforts in 1850. Still, he advised the congressman to assert that the Missouri Compromise "must be observed as a compact by both parties forever."[13]

Such dedication to the Missouri Compromise as a cause worthy in and of itself has received scant attention from scholars. The Missouri Compromise loomed large in the minds of many Illinoisans in the 1850s. Midwifed by Henry Clay, Abraham Lincoln's "beau ideal of a statesman" and the pride of the Whig Party for decades, the accord had seemingly appeased both sections while reinforcing the principle of congressional exclusion of slavery first established by the Northwest Ordinance. In the succeeding three decades, the free-labor North had upheld its half of the bargain by respecting the establishment of slavery in both Missouri and Arkansas. But now it appeared as if Southern slaveholders would have their cake and eat it too. Such a repudiation of the tradition smacked of despotism and threatened the United States' apparently unique commitment to republican moderation.[14]

Meanwhile, radical Black abolitionists throughout the nation framed the conflict over the Kansas-Nebraska Act as a moral emergency threatening the lives of thousands of enslaved men, women, and children. Back in December 1853, Chicago's Black abolitionists had passed a series of resolutions endorsing *Frederick Douglass' Paper* and promising to distribute the organ widely in their community. In the following months, these loyal subscribers read co-editor William J. Watkins's denunciation of Stephen A. Douglas and the Illinois senator's resolution "to ride into power over hecatombs of the dissevered limbs, and bleeding hearts of the millions of his fellow country men, whom God has made a little lower than the angels." While Illinois's white conservatives urged calm, Watkins prophesied a revolution, announcing that "the clacking of the chain is heard. The slave will yet be free. His morn will yet appear . . . and sweep the monster of slavery into the dark abyss of ruin, as though a whirlwind had breathed upon it." By no means naïve, Watkins knew Black Americans would need allies in their struggle and hoped the Nebraska bill would at least "awake the slumbering North to consciousness of the fearful aggression" of the slave power and make such a transformation possible.[15]

But such a reaction was not forthcoming. As the debate over the measure stretched through the winter and the full implications of the bill became clear, both Democrats and Whigs in Illinois sought to frame their position as a defense of the status quo. The Democratic *Illinois State Register* claimed that the Kansas-Nebraska Act merely reaffirmed the Compromise of 1850 and represented "an embodiment of the spirit, meaning and object of that compromise," a position echoed in the *Ottawa Free Trader,* which demanded "the support of every true democrat upon the ground that it re-enacts and re-affirms the principles of the Compromise of 1850."[16] In a terse exchange, former Illinois governor Edward Coles and Stephen Douglas debated whether Congress or the people had initially excluded slavery from Illinois. Responding to Coles's claim that the Northwest Ordinance had kept slavery out of Illinois, Douglas reminded the former governor that in fact "slavery existed there in defiance of the prohibition and was recognized and protected by territorial legislation." Thus, the practice of popular sovereignty, and not a congressional prohibition, had ultimately excluded slavery from Illinois and other portions of the Old Northwest. As such, the Kansas-Nebraska Act merely continued a long-standing practice of allowing the citizens of a territory to debate the question of slavery themselves.[17]

Democratic organs endorsed this interpretation and heralded the free soil potential of popular sovereignty. The *Quincy Herald* noted that Illinois and Indiana needed to include prohibitions on slavery in their state constitutions despite the Northwest Ordinance and insisted, "It is because these States *were not* protected from the 'blight of slavery' by that ordinance, or by any thing else that induced the people to protect themselves!" The *Salem Advocate* confidently proclaimed, "It is perfectly apparent . . . the introduction of slavery has a blighting and benumbing tendency" and concluded that the people would exercise "good sense" and employ popular sovereignty to make "a prudent and just decision." Indeed, the *Quincy Herald* editor subsequently argued the "people of Illinois will enact laws to protect slavery, quite as soon as the people of Nebraska will enact laws to authorize and protect it there." In short, popular sovereignty already functioned to protect free territory from slavery, and those who pretended otherwise promoted such sophistry for political gain.[18]

Meanwhile, in a March 28 address before the House, Richard Yates invoked the memory of Henry Clay, author of both the Missouri Compromise and the Compromise of 1850, as he denounced Douglas for having "thrust the firebrands of discord into [Congress's] peaceful councils." He furthermore defended the Northwest Ordinance as the "Great Charter of Freedom for the Northwest" and insisted that "no brighter jewel glittered in the coronet which decked the brow of Jefferson." Such arguments disturbed even steadfast Democrats. The *Salem Advocate,* a nominal supporter of the measure, admitted that while it regarded "the principles of the Bill as essentially correct," it found "the present agitation of the principal question . . . both inexpedient and unnecessary."[19]

Despite the defection of some of their own members, including John E. Wentworth of Chicago, the Democrats passed the Nebraska bill with strong support from Southern Whigs. By insisting that all loyal Democrats support the measure, President Pierce had seriously weakened the party's position in the North, as a sizable cohort of anti-Nebraska Democrats found themselves alienated from their fellow partisans. Lifelong Democrats, such as George T. Brown of the *Alton Courier,* found themselves dismissed as traitors for attempting to maintain neutrality in the struggle. It would take months, and sometimes years, for these men to stop identifying themselves as Democrats, but with Douglas firmly in control of the state party apparatus, they could exercise little influence while they remained within the state organization.

For Douglas, the massive effort necessary to push through the Nebraska bill resulted in a pyrrhic victory. Although popular sovereignty reigned in two new federal territories, the Little Giant had failed to secure the homestead bill and river and harbor measures meant to complement this expansion into the West. Rather than unite Democrats around a program of national expansion and Western economic development, Douglas's initial push for a transcontinental railroad had fractured his party and earned him the ire of Northerners across the political spectrum. Having earlier expressed his expectation that Northern Democrats would choose to "stand with the Democracy" rather than "rally under Seward" and other such contemptible Northern Whigs, Douglas must have felt frustrated and bewildered by the hostile reception he received throughout the North as he made his way back to Illinois late in the summer.[20]

Though the Whig Party had fractured cleanly along sectional lines, many hoped to reunite the national organization. David Davis blamed Northern Democrats, rather than the Southern Whigs, for the Nebraska Bill and lamented "the movement on this question of slavery—being really afraid that a sectional issue" such as the repeal of the Missouri Compromise would prove "disastrous to the good feeling of this country." But Davis also mentioned the brightening prospects of another committed Whig, Abraham Lincoln, whom he thought could win in a statewide contest against Douglas.[21]

Born in Kentucky in 1809 and raised in southern Indiana, Lincoln had spent his youth performing the constant manual labor required of subsistence farmers on the frontier. Eager to rise above his humble roots, Lincoln relocated to central Illinois and worked as a surveyor and postmaster before becoming a lawyer. Following a stint as a militia captain during the Black Hawk War, he entered state politics as a Whig, serving four terms in the state legislature. An ardent supporter of Henry Clay's American System, Lincoln championed internal improvements, a national bank, and a protective tariff as instruments of economic growth and development. In 1846, Lincoln was elected to the US House of Representatives. While admired by many of his peers in Congress, Lincoln made himself unpopular at home by his strident opposition to the Mexican-American War and did not seek a second term. After failing to secure a satisfactory patronage appointment within Zachary Taylor's administration, he largely stayed out of politics until drawn back into the fray by the fracas over the Nebraska bill. While it would take several more months after Davis's letter for Lincoln to publicly denounce Douglas and the Nebraska bill, Davis's remark confirms the speculation of historians that Lincoln "saw early on the political opportunities that Douglas's dangerous measures had opened up." Indeed, the breach in the state's Democracy's ranks offered a golden opportunity for Davis, Lincoln, and other Whigs long accustomed to minority status in Illinois to reassert themselves.[22]

Still, as Davis's earlier remarks suggest, the agitation also created anxiety. Many Illinois Whigs traced their roots to Kentucky, including former Whig congressman John F. Henry, who wrote to Davis that while he did not oppose the anti-Nebraska movement per se, he could not "wish its success, coupled as it would be with the triumph of abolitionism." For men disturbed by any sectional agitation, the disruptions caused by Douglas's bill appeared dangerous to the country while favorable for their party. In the months to come, these conservative Whigs would grapple with the implications of political realignment, as a spate of other issues, raised alongside the Nebraska Bill, alienated former allies, and opened the door to form new coalitions.[23]

The Nativist Impulse

The political inferno ignited by the Kansas-Nebraska Act further inflamed Illinois's deep cultural divisions. Within an ever more diverse state, these ethnic and sociocultural tensions manifested themselves in four separate arenas in Illinois in the mid-1850s. First, evangelical Protestants sought to squelch cultural aberration among immigrant groups by imposing strict Sabbath ordinances that would prohibit the feasting and drinking popular among Irish Catholics and Germans of all denominations. Closely connected to such efforts was an attempt to adopt prohibition, or the Maine Law, and ban the production and sale of intoxicating spirits. Some nativists also sought to check the influence of the foreign-born at the ballot box by imposing restrictions on naturalized citizens holding public offices or lengthening the waiting period for naturalization. Finally, and most obliquely, many nativists supported the establishment of public schools throughout the state, equipped with the Protestant

King James Bible as a textbook, to encourage the use of the English language among Germans and check the growth of Catholic parochial schools. The rapid emergence of the American, or Know-Nothing, Party in the aftermath of the Nebraska bill served as the political engine for most of these measures.[24]

Within months of the bill's introduction, Illinois's long-dominant Democratic Party began to splinter over slavery extension and cultural tensions. Although settled largely by those of "Yankee" stock, northern Illinois had remained competitive for Democratic candidates, even after defections to the Free-Soil ticket in 1848. The Kansas-Nebraska Act, by opening free territory to the extension of slavery, permanently alienated many of these onetime Jacksonians from the Democracy. At the same time, Yankee Democrats had begun to join their Whig cousins in expressing nativist views and campaigning on issues such as temperance and anti-Catholicism. The dramatic success of the *Chicago Tribune* as an antislavery and anti-Catholic organ during this period reveals the compatibility of these positions in the eyes of many readers. Such a trend appeared elsewhere in the state, as anti-Nebraska Democrat George T. Brown of Alton championed temperance and Sabbatarianism before becoming a firm opponent of the Kansas-Nebraska Act. As such, anti-extensionist immigrants, such as German Democrat Gustave Koerner, found themselves, for a time, alienated from both the national Democracy and the new anti-Nebraska coalition.[25]

As such, the process of realignment remained anything but straightforward. Ethnic, religious, and cultural identities operated within a complex milieu of partisan affinities and policy positions. On the one hand, some antiextensionist Whigs, such as Abraham Lincoln, felt nothing but antipathy for political nativism even as they maintained close alliances with Know-Nothings. On the other hand, there were champions of temperance, nativism, and free schools who ultimately became loyal Douglas Democrats, such as Theodore S. Bowers of the *Mount Carmel Register*. Throughout the debates of the following years, party leaders of all stripes, as well as advocates of social reform, would try to activate these various identities to mobilize the electorate in their favor. Although the question of slavery extension would come to shape politics more than any other issue, this was not apparent to those living through the events of 1854. No clear path forward existed amid the political tumult that defined the months after the passage of the Kansas-Nebraska Act, as all factions sought to bolster their conservative credentials and restore a semblance of order, whether by reasserting the supremacy of the people through popular sovereignty, restoring the Missouri Compromise as a "sacred compact," or reimposing the cultural preeminence of Protestant Anglo-Saxons.[26]

Of course, the latter goal preceded the introduction of the Nebraska Bill. In November 1853, George T. Brown's Democratic *Alton Courier* had featured an editorial denouncing the indifference of German immigrants to American observance of the Sabbath. For Brown, the United States was "superior to Germany in very many respects," with the "general observance of the Sabbath as one instance of that superiority." A subsequent convention of Sabbatarians held across the state in White County declared that "the continued prosperity of [the] nation, in civil and religious liberty, are dependent upon the recognition and sanctification of the sabbath." While such sentiments might appear hyperbolic for twenty-first-century Americans, for believers in a sovereign God, the dangers posed by violating the Fourth Commandment appeared all too apparent. Indeed, in late 1854 another Sabbatarian convention would announce that such "a fearful amount of Sabbath desecration" as occurred in their midst was "calculated to bring down the judgments of Heaven; not only upon individuals but upon the nation at large." By dishonoring the Sabbath with drinking, carousing, and feasting, immigrants posed an immediate threat to the United States' covenant with Divine Providence.[27]

Liquor dealers facilitated these Sunday shenanigans, as well as darker scenes of perpetual drunkenness and inebriated violence that haunted the poor of all backgrounds. Reformers took aim at grog sellers using the same language of republicanism that antiextensionists had applied to Southern slaveholders. In March 1854, the *Mount Carmel Register* attacked liquor sellers as "the aristocracy of America," acting with impunity in their own interest against the will of the community. The *Chicago Tribune* denounced the "Whiskey interest" that profited off of vice and their intoxicated allies in the Democratic Party, who created an "engine to perpetuate drunkenness and crime." Widespread support for temperance among the "respectable" middle classes put pro-liquor Democrats on the defensive, and they did their best to separate temperance from partisanship. The pro-Nebraska *Rock Island Republican* objected "to the spasmodic efforts of defunct whiggery to galvanize itself into motion by hanging on to the tails of the temperance men." The *Republican* rightly feared that members of the opposition had garnered support from their stance on temperance, but liquor's most fervent opponents did not rally under the Whig banner.[28]

Instead, they took up the cause of the Know-Nothings, also known as the Native Americans or the American Party, who emerged as a political force from the shadows of semisecret fraternal lodges. These political nativists linked immigration, drunkenness, and sabbath-breaking together as part of a grand antirepublican conspiracy formulated by the Roman Catholic Church.

According to such nativists, the Roman pontiff sought to undermine Protestantism and liberty throughout the United States through mass immigration. Supposedly, the Catholic laity remained utterly enslaved to their diabolical priests and would carry out the instructions of the clergy without the slightest hesitation. As such, according to Springfield's Know-Nothing organ, the *Capital Enterprise,* "no American who employ[ed] an Irish servant [was] beyond the reach of Jesuitical spies." Drawing on a tradition of Anglo-American anti-Catholicism that dated to the colonial period, the Know-Nothings insisted that Catholicism encouraged idolatry, superstition, and devotion to a rigid hierarchy that would undermine rational Protestantism and Anglo-Saxon liberty. The Roman Church's "treacherous and devilish" lackeys would stop at nothing for "the advancement of the papal power" and inevitably bring about "the downfall of the liberties of the people." Historian Richard Hofstadter has rightly placed such rhetoric within the framework of a "paranoid style in American politics." Although the Roman Catholic Church remained a prominent force of reactionary antirepublicanism in Europe, American Catholics worked hard to balance the commitments of their faith with their duties as American citizens. Absolutely no evidence existed of a coordinated plot by the Church's hierarchy. But beyond its religious bigotry, the new nativist party also tapped into a strain of antiparty partisanship that resonated with a broad swath to the electorate.[29]

By calling themselves the "American Party," the Know-Nothing members signaled their intention to rise above the partisan squabbles that had driven the country to the brink of disaster. Winfield Scott's effort to court Irish American voters in the presidential election of 1852 had appalled nativist Whigs, while the waning of Jacksonian-era economic disputes and a perception of complacency and corruption within the Democracy fueled a sense of alienation among some Northern Democrats. As the national bonds that had held Whiggery together snapped, many hoped nativist patriotism could cleanse American republicanism of its profane heresies. Opposed to both the Southern Fire-Eaters and the immigrant profligates who stood poised to dominate the nation politically, the Know-Nothings hoped to "purify the politics of country," "refine its nationality," and foster "true patriotism." As aptly explained by one historian of Northern Know-Nothingism, the party "insisted that only ignorant foreigners could be duped by the outrageous promises of this cunning new breed of politician" who had emerged from the slaveholder-dominated Democratic Party.[30]

The Mixed Results of 1854

Yet, in Illinois at least, it would take the Know-Nothings time to distinguish themselves as an independent political force. Throughout 1854, the incipient Know-Nothings joined forces with other opponents of the Kansas-Nebraska Act in a loose "fusion" movement. In the one statewide contest for state treasurer, the fusion ticket backed James Miller, a Know-Nothing and fierce opponent of slavery. In other places throughout the state, the Know-Nothings backed anti-Nebraska Whigs. Abraham Lincoln managed to secure the endorsement of Benjamin S. Edwards of Springfield, Sangamon County's leading nativist, to support Richard Yates's bid for reelection to Congress. Although not a Know-Nothing, Yates expressed frustration with the existing party system and forwent the usual party convention process. Yates may have taken this cue from his correspondents, such as one formerly Democratic Baptist minister who argued that "the large portion" of the electorate would "vote without reference to party distinction" as "honesty, integrity, and capacity" would trump "mere party influence." Unfortunately for Yates, the gambit backfired when English settlers in Morgan County became convinced that Yates had joined a Know-Nothing lodge. Their dissatisfaction at his supposed bigotry, combined with vigorous push in the final weeks of the canvass by Democrat Thomas L. Harris, gave this once reliably Whig district to the Democracy.[31]

Throughout the state, the fusion movement received broad support from voters but remained fractured politically. In the state's Second Congressional District, which included Chicago, the race featured a regular Democrat running against an anti-Nebraska Democrat, an anti-Nebraska Whig, and a Republican. This new party muddied the waters for antiextensionists, as any connection to abolitionism would threaten their conservative credentials. In October 1854, the Reverend Owen Lovejoy and his fellow abolitionist Ichabod Codding attempted to organize a statewide Republican Party at a convention in Springfield. Former members of the Liberty Party, the two had traditionally linked their political and economic critiques of slavery with a moralistic denunciation steeped in the language of evangelical Christianity. Their condemnation of slavery had often extended to the Constitution's compromises with the institution, and while they never adopted the Garrisonian "covenant with death" perspective, the Liberty Party explicitly annulled the Fugitive Slave Clause as incompatible with God's law. As a result of this radical reputation, Lovejoy and Codding failed to attract the support of central Illinois's moderate anti-Nebraska Whigs like Lincoln, who left town to avoid any connection to the gathering. Although the platform proved moderate relative to previous abolitionist responses to the Kansas-Nebraska Act, this Springfield convention further alienated conservatives after the pro-Douglas press falsely reported that the convention had called for a repeal of the 1850 Fugitive Slave Act.[32]

The failure of these first Republicans to secure a base of support outside of northern Illinois reflected a dilemma encountered by antislavery politicians throughout the country. In the East, proto-Republicans faced an uphill battle as some antislavery leaders, like William H. Seward, remained loyal to the old Whig organization, while others rallied the rising Know-Nothing movement. In Ohio, Iowa, and Indiana, various anti-Democratic factions managed to unite for the 1854 contest but agreed on little aside from their opposition to the Kansas-Nebraska Act. Ohio's Free-Soil senator Salmon P. Chase, for instance, found the state's People's Party platform, which did not include a plank against the fugitive slave law, too conservative for his taste. In Iowa and Indiana, meanwhile, leading opposition figures injected strong doses of prohibitionism and nativism, respectively, into their contests. In the long term, these issues threatened to divide the anti-Democratic vote even as they rallied more mild opponents of slavery extension. Only in Michigan, where the Know-Nothings proved weak, and Wisconsin, with its large base of Free-Soil and immigrant voters, did a unified opposition take on the label *Republican*.[33]

This divided opposition serves as an important reminder of the role of contingency within the process of realignment. While historians have often drawn a clear line between the passage of the Kansas-Nebraska Act and the fully formed Republican organization that emerged in 1856, at the time, such a path appeared unlikely. Lingering divisions from the Second Party System; personal rivalries among prominent politicians; and the competing questions of slavery, Union, and culture produced an overwhelming sense of uncertainty. Rather than boldly strike out on new paths, political leaders emphasized the familiar and framed their responses as attempts to restore some sense of normalcy.[34]

In Illinois, Abraham Lincoln, at this moment still very much a Whig, sought to stake out a position as a firm defender of the Founding Fathers and of sectional parity. In a September address in Bloomington, Lincoln made it clear that he did not seek to interfere with slavery in the states or condemn slaveholders as sinners but rather challenged their repudiation of a sacred compact. Citing the legacy of Jefferson as the author of the Northwest Ordinance while he retold the stories of the Missouri Compromise and the Compromise of 1850, Lincoln accused the "slaveholding power" of trying to snatch away the "half of the loaf of bread" promised to freedom. Equality in the Union and respect for the framer's intentions demanded that Nebraska remain free soil. Building further on these themes in a direct rebuttal to Douglas at Peoria in October, Lincoln emphasized how the Midwest had become "what Jefferson foresaw and intended—the happy home of teeming millions of free, white, prosperous people, and no slave amongst them." He emphasized that the reinstatement of the Missouri Compromise would "restore the national faith, the national confidence, and the national feeling of brotherhood," whereas the "final destruction of the Missouri Compromise, and with it the spirit of all compromise" would "embolden" the South and embitter the North. Firmly rejecting Douglas's accusation that Henry Clay and Daniel Webster would have accepted the Nebraska Bill, Lincoln brandished his Whig credentials and turned the tables on the Little Giant, insisting that he had turned to help from dead enemies as his living friends deserted him.[35]

Lincoln's favorite organ, the *Illinois State Journal* of Springfield, took an even more conservative tack in a scathing attack on Douglas published in mid-October. Comparing Douglas and the "'n—' democrats" to the radical Thomas Paine and Revolutionary France, the *Journal* supposed that these "fools and hypocrites" would void the Constitution and the Bible along with the Missouri Compromise if they advanced their position to its logical conclusion. Appropriating the Democrats' favorite racial epithet in its attack, the *Journal* argued that far from guaranteeing the rights of the majority of white men, Douglas had aligned himself with "Garrison, Phillips, &c." and had begun their work of "tearing down all compacts." Douglas and his allies would need to pay such violations of the public faith, and the *Journal* called on those committed to "National Honor, National pledges,—the existence of the great Compromises on which our Union rests" to go to the polls and "give to demagogues a lesson never to be forgotten."[36]

Meanwhile, further south, Lyman Trumbull, a former justice on the Illinois State Supreme Court and lifelong Democrat, had made ripples of his own. Born into a prominent family in Colchester, Connecticut, Trumbull had received a classical education at Bacon Academy. His father, Benjamin Trumbull, owned a midsized farm and used his legal education to secure a position as a local judge. Still, the family's modest income could not keep pace with Yale's tuition, and so at the age of twenty, Trumbull, like many other educated New Englanders, took a post as a teacher in a private Southern academy to fund his own legal education. As a teacher and law student in Meriweather County, Georgia, Trumbull developed a lifelong distaste for the institution of slavery and the elite Southerners who maintained it. Firmly committed to the dignity of white labor, Trumbull adopted the political philosophy of a Jacksonian

Democrat and moved to Illinois shortly after his admission to the bar. Although "opposed to the immediate emancipation of the slaves and to the doctrine of Abolitionism," Trumbull denounced the mob that killed Elijah Lovejoy in Alton in 1837. Throughout the 1840s, he worked to close proslavery loopholes in the state's laws, serving as pro bono counsel for the Black plaintiff in the noted case of *Jarrot v. Jarrot*. Establishing a place for himself within the Illinois Democratic Party as a state legislator and judge, Trumbull ardently defended the interests of Illinois's ordinary white farmers against the elites of Northern cities and Southern plantations. After the passage of the Kansas-Nebraska Act, Trumbull came to believe that the latter posed a greater threat to the integrity of the Union and the dignity of white labor.[37]

Following a bitterly divisive Democratic Convention for the Eighth Congressional District, Trumbull emerged as the anti-Nebraska candidate running against Douglas supporter Phillip B. Foulke. With the endorsement of George T. Brown's Democratic *Alton Courier*, Trumbull made good on his immense popularity in Madison County, gaining bipartisan support for his bid by the support of the Whig *Alton Telegraph* and the endorsement of the area's leading Whig, Joseph Gillespie. Election returns indicated that Trumbull managed to secure the votes of thousands of Democrats who voted against the anti-Nebraska candidate in the race for state treasurer, an illustration of how muddled many felt in this year of political turmoil. Indeed, as pro-Nebraska Senator James Shields wrote from the district only a few days before the election, "all is perfect chaos." Throughout the state, the anti-Nebraska coalition won some 55 percent of the vote statewide in the congressional contest, securing five of the state's nine districts, but lost the contest for state treasurer. Trumbull did not disavow his association with the Democracy, despite his strong opposition to Douglas and the Nebraska Bill.[38]

Indeed, in the election's immediate aftermath, Trumbull appeared intent on repudiating Douglas and slavery extension from within the Democratic Party. Writing to state senator John M. Palmer, an anti-Nebraska Democrat, Trumbull made clear his desire to secure "the triumph of Freedom over Slavery" but also insisted that he could only support an anti-Nebraska Democrat, such as Gustave Koerner, in the coming election for US senator. Trumbull had no desire to see Shields secure reelection and recognized that the pro-Nebraska element intended "to have war to the knife." The anti-Nebraska men in the legislature, although overwhelmingly Whig in membership, could not secure a majority without the cooperation of the anti-Nebraska Democrats. Trumbull's conservative outlook at this moment showed through as he prayed that "our Northern friends will only stop at the proper point without urging us too far" and instructed Palmer to remind the anti-Nebraska Whigs of the "importance of concession" to "save themselves from utter defeat." As the new year approached, Trumbull remained willing to cooperate with the anti-Nebraska Whigs in an effort to repudiate Douglas and his policies, but he hoped that by doing so, he would ensure his own faction's survival within the Illinois Democracy. Although he buried his ambition beneath a veil of modesty in his words to Palmer, Trumbull had hopes of securing the seat. He sought not only the distinction that elevation to the higher chamber would bring him but the relished opportunity to go head-to-head with Douglas in the Senate chamber. Writing to his brother in December, Trumbull noted that while he "cared very little" about any office, he did "feel an interest in trying to prevent the spread of slavery" and of sustaining the will of the "strongly Democratic" voters he represented despite Douglas's claim to a popular mandate.[39]

At the same time, Lincoln had become engrossed in his own campaign for Shields's senate seat, noting, "It has come round that a whig may, by possibility, be elected to the US Senate; and I want the chance of being the man." Like Trumbull, Lincoln still saw himself firmly attached to his party and remained apprehensive that the political tumult might force him into taking extreme positions. "Things look reasonably well," he reasoned, but he projected, "Some will insist on a platform, which I can not stand upon." Working fervently to bring together the diverse elements of the anti-Nebraska coalition, he lobbied northern Illinois's Whig congressman Elihu B. Washburne to advocate on his behalf. Lingering suspicions between the northern and central portions of the state hindered Lincoln's bid, as did his rejection of a place on the nascent Republican Party's Central Committee, yet in the end, Lincoln locked in the support of forty-five legislators, leaving him only five votes short of a majority. His path to the office, however, still appeared dubious.[40]

The pro-Nebraska Democrats of Illinois, though reeling from their rebuke at the polls, still hoped to salvage the situation. With his senate seat and his political future on the line, James Shields sought to out-organize the opposition and apply pressure on those who had strayed from the party line. Writing to Charles H. Lanphier at Springfield, he encouraged the editor to list the anti-Nebraska Democrats in his paper as regular Democrats and pretend no break had occurred. By shifting their focus from slavery extension, Shields hoped to snatch victory from the jaws of defeat. Such reasoning might appear far-fetched, but Douglas also hoped to move on from the territorial debacle. Although less than sanguine about the junior senator's prospects for reelection, he demanded that his supporters "stand by Shields to the last and make no compromises." He deemed the battle over Nebraska "over" and declared Know-Nothingism "the chief issue in the future." As such, Douglas hoped to take advantage of Shields's Irish birth to frame the contest as a question of Democratic tolerance against fusionist nativism. Though he suspected that the anti-Nebraska Democrats might back William Bissell, the recently retired congressman from the Eighth District, rather than return to the fold, he planned to blame Shields's defeat on the Whig's bigotry. In what seemed the best scenario to Douglas, if the anti-Nebraska element remained divided, the legislature would deadlock, leaving the seat vacant until the next legislative election, when a reinvigorated regular Democracy could again put up Shields for the seat.[41]

Other regular Democrats, however, proved more willing to abandon Shields in order to retain the seat. Acknowledging that "all hope of electing Shields is gone" and recognizing a postponement of the election might also prove "hazardous," James W. Sheehan of the *Chicago Times* advised that the caucus might instead nominate Governor Joel Matteson. Having kept mum on the Nebraska issue publicly while retaining close ties to Douglas, Matteson could potentially attract the support of those anti-Nebraska men who squirmed at the prospect of voting alongside Princeton's newly elected representative Owen Lovejoy. The stigma of abolitionism, or "any of the allied isms," as Douglas referred to the alliance of abolitionism, Free-Soilism, Know-Nothingism, Prohibitionism, might drive a cautious opponent to reconsider. Indeed, such inhibitions might have resurfaced in the opening weeks of the session as the handful of radicals in the legislature introduced measures to protect Black rights. Lovejoy introduced a bill to repeal the state's Black Codes, while Representative Benjamin Hackney, a Republican from Kane County, introduced a measure to allow an African American to testify in court. Representative Wesley Diggins of McHenry County, an erstwhile conductor on the Underground Railroad, even offered a resolution to provide public schools for Black children. Although ready and willing to disavow popular sovereignty, endorse the Northwest Ordinance, and demand a restoration of the Missouri Compromise, most anti-Nebraska legislators would not countenance any attempt to undermine white supremacy in Illinois and quickly sidelined these proposals. Such intransigence led the Black physician and abolitionist James McCune Smith to declare that Illinois was "covered with deeper infamy in caste than any other state." Watching such proceedings at his home in New York, McCune Smith could see few redeeming qualities in the nominally free Prairie State.[42]

The senate election would amplify the widespread sense of political uncertainty that swirled like the winter snow over the lonely prairie at Springfield. Following a series of delays, the balloting in the state legislature began on February 8, 1855. After the first ballot, Lincoln led Shields forty-five to forty-one, with five ballots cast for Trumbull, one for Matteson, and a handful of votes for alternative candidates, including the German anti-Nebraska Democrat Gustave Koerner and the aging Whig Cyrus Edwards. Over the course of the next several ballots, Lincoln's strength waned, and on the seventh ballot, the regular Democrats abruptly threw their weight behind Matteson. On the ninth ballot, Lincoln's tally had dwindled to just fifteen determined supporters compared to thirty-five for Trumbull and forty-seven for Matteson. Unwilling to allow pro-Nebraska Democrats to steal the seat, Lincoln reluctantly directed his supporters to vote for Trumbull. Thus, in an unexpected coup, the anti-Nebraska Democrats had secured the prize for their own candidate, despite underwhelming numbers and limited influence within the anti-Nebraska movement. The choice proved satisfactory for those most intent on frustrating Douglas, and the *Chicago Tribune* claimed that Trumbull's election was "hailed by conservative men of all parties." Still, the affair disappointed Lincoln and left many other Whigs "a good deal mortified." Historians have long noted that Lincoln's magnanimity toward Trumbull and his allies ultimately served him well, but few could have guessed at the time that this same cohort would later propel him to the Republican nomination in 1860. Indeed, as the ice thawed in the spring of 1855, the tenuous anti-Nebraska coalition seemed poised to shatter as a resurgence of ethnocultural issues reignited long-standing animosities.[43]

Know-Nothings in Power

Although Douglas's assertion that the Nebraska question had passed out of public consciousness seems ridiculous in hindsight, the political questions that preoccupied Illinoisans throughout the first half of 1855 appeared to support his opinion. The surge among political nativists and moral reformers evident in the preceding months reached a crescendo as this conservative force, having voiced its support for the Missouri Compromise, sought to restore order and evangelical morality in the face of immigrant opposition. Although by no means a monolith, the pro-temperance and anti-Catholic Know-Nothings proved sufficiently organized at the local and state levels to rapidly advance their legislative agenda. Chicago's Lager Beer Riot, the passage of a statewide public-school law, and the narrow failure of a prohibition referendum showcased further divisions within Illinois's body politic. Although many voices would still cry out against slavery extension, it appeared as if the anti-Nebraska fusion men would be forced to either side with the politically powerful Know-Nothings or the state's significant German population, which had largely opposed the Kansas-Nebraska Act.[44]

The Chicago municipal elections of March 1855 offered the city's energized political nativists a chance to flex their newfound political muscle. A year earlier, they had lamented how "the Whiskey Party," aided by the "enemies of Free Schools and Political and Religious Liberty," could triumph over "Morality and Religion." Now, by electing their candidate for mayor, Levi Boone, over the Democratic incumbent, along with a slate of other city officials on a prohibitionist and nativist platform, the Know-Nothings hoped to realize their vision of a virtuous Christian society. Indeed, in his inaugural address, Boone promised to ensure that the city would "become as eminent for its moral characters as it is for the commercial facilities and material resources with which the lavish hand of a beneficent Providence has crowned it." Explicitly excluding Catholics from his vision of the city's new birth, he denounced the Church as "a powerful politico-religious organization" devoted "to the temporal, as well as the spiritual supremacy of a foreign despot" that sought "universal dominion over this land . . . by coercion and at the cost of blood itself." Boone made the reorganization of Chicago's police force a top priority, putting uniformed cops on the streets for the first time as he built an army for his moral majority that could crack down on the city's immigrant-dominated saloons, beer halls, and gambling houses.[45]

In April, this effort to restore law and order led to a violent civil disturbance throughout the city. Although Boone had voiced his opposition to issuing any liquor licenses and supported the looming statewide referendum on prohibition, the city government initially pursued a policy of limiting access to alcohol by raising the cost of liquor licenses and closing by-the-drink establishments on Sundays. As Boone said in his inaugural, the city had "long been disgraced and the holy Sabbath profaned" by Sunday liquor sales. But the Know-Nothing administration underestimated the ferocious opposition it would meet from the city's immigrant population, particularly the Germans, who regarded drinking beer on Sunday as a perfectly respectable activity. On April 21, an angry crowd of Germans gathered in front of the city's Clark Street courthouse to demand the release of nineteen saloonkeepers imprisoned for either failing to pay the new fee or for continuing to serve alcohol on Sundays. In response, Mayor Boone called out the city's new police force of eighty native-born officers to break up the crowd and deputized 150 more men to reinforce them. The clash that followed, the Lager Beer Riot, left at least one immigrant dead and dozens severely injured. The police arrested a group of sixty men, mostly working-class Germans, and Boone mustered the militia and placed the city under martial law.[46]

The press throughout the state reacted divisively to the violence along both cultural and partisan lines. The *Chicago Tribune* castigated the "Lager Beer swilling and Sabbath breaking Germans" and hailed the effort to enforce the law "against their low, drunkard, pauper making whiskey and beer shops." Downstate, George T. Brown's *Alton Courier*, though still identifying as a Democratic paper, labeled the riot "the fruits of the agitation which the Chicago Liquor dealers have been so industriously and unscrupulously endeavoring to raise." The prohibitionist and anti-Catholic *Moline Workman* also applauded the "bravery of the policemen" in the face "of a most disgraceful riot." The pro-Douglas *Daily Republican* of Rock Island, in contrast, blamed "know nothing rowdies and Maine Lawites" for their "relentless war of proscription and persecution," which represented a "tide of fanaticism and treason." The *Republican*'s editor, John B. Danforth, called on the "sober, right-minded people, who love their country and the principles of their fathers" to stem the tide of dogmatic bigotry. Less bombastically, the *Dewitt Courier* blamed the violence on "the over officiousness of the city officers." These and many other accounts tied the events in Chicago to recent legislation passed in Springfield that promised to implement a free school system throughout the state and enact a prohibition law, pending the result of a statewide referendum.[47]

State support for prohibition and public schools marked a triumph for evangelicalism. By drying out the state and herding ignorant immigrant children into schools infused with a strong dose of Protestant theology, the legislators hoped to restore order to a society overtaken by idleness and debauchery. Catholic immigrants and many native-born Illinoisans with Southern backgrounds staunchly opposed both measures as a coercive overreach by Yankee idealists. A host of others, including Protestant immigrants and less pious voters born in the free states, tended to support public schools but waffled on the so-called Maine Law. The new Free School law required localities to provide tax support for common schools instead of allowing each county to decide the issue for itself. Since many areas of Northern Illinois already featured competition between locally established public schools and Catholic parochial schools, southern Illinois voiced the strongest opposition to the measure. Yet, given that similar legislation had easily passed throughout the other free states, the measure provoked little controversy relative to the prohibition measure. The June referendum on that issue galvanized many voters, including the Democrats who had sat out the previous fall's congressional elections out of frustration with the Kansas-Nebraska Act. Although support for liquor consumption, per se, remained rare, opposition to prohibition's enforcement, or as the *Cairo City Times* put it, to the creation of a "tyrannical, dangerous, or cruel police authority" whose excesses might match "the decrees of Robespierre and his associates of France," appealed to those skeptical of replacing a familiar problem with an unknown evil. In the end, a coalition of Southern and Illinois-born voters united with nearly all eligible Irish and German immigrants to decisively defeat the measure, with 54 percent of voters opposing a dry Illinois.[48]

Though the defeat of prohibition owed as much to a lack of enthusiasm among some of the native-born as to the machinations of either immigrants or alcohol dealers, the *Moline Workman* bemoaned that Illinois was "no longer the land of milk and honey—but of whiskey outrage and murder" as a "great ocean of rum" had overwhelmed the state. Deeply frustrated by the result of the vote, temperance advocates would abandon prohibition efforts for the foreseeable future. The nativist coalition that had rallied in support of the measure would also begin to fracture. Illinois Know-Nothings divided as a "Know Something" wing dedicated to anti-Catholicism but more tolerant of Protestant immigrants emerged. But their brief moment in the sun had immeasurably complicated the task of building a permanent coalition in opposition to slavery's extension.[49]

As political factions split, realigned, and split again, adversaries became allies, then became adversaries again. Each party and sub-party hoped to preserve its own vision of American liberty in the face of a radicalized opposition, but in mid-1855, few could point out which of the radicals posed the greatest threat. Within a landscape of contested conservatism, politicians, newspaper editors, and ordinary voters underwent a crisis of confidence. As the old parties crumbled, whom could one trust to maintain the integrity of the Union, the principles of the Constitution, and the rights of free white men?

Indeed, although it seemed apparent that both the Whig and Democratic establishments had undergone a tremendous shock in the previous eighteen months, no one in Illinois could say for certain what sorts of coalitions might face off in the next year's statewide elections. Many anti-Nebraska Democrats like Trumbull remained committed to their Jacksonian identity and believed they represented "true" Democrats, while old Whigs like Lincoln and David Davis were equally hesitant to abandon their traditional label. Although the most radical opponents of slavery had secured some support in northern Illinois under the Republican banner, they competed with the Know-Nothings and a host of other half-baked anti-Democratic factions for the support of a moderate electorate. In October, Douglas crowed that the tide had turned and the "allied army of isms is bound to be routed & annihilated" amid a resurgence of the regular Democracy. To prove him wrong, opposition leaders needed to set aside their differences and unite on a coherent platform that could promise conservative voters an end to the present turmoil.[50]

CHAPTER 3

THE COMMON CAUSE

"I set it down as a fixed fact that an organization will be affected somehow but when or how no one can tell." With this final line, newly sworn-in US senator Lyman Trumbull set down his pen and read over his letter to fellow anti-Nebraska Democrat John M. Palmer. While the sentence referred specifically to the House of Representatives for the Thirty-Fourth Congress, which had yet to elect a speaker a month into its first session, it reflected Trumbull's broader sense of ambiguous optimism for the future of the anti-Nebraska movement.[1]

Despite a year of continuous agitation against the extension of slavery, Illinois's anti-Nebraskaites remained factious and divided along old partisan and sociocultural lines. Recognizing that competing tickets would result in disaster, a group of self-identified conservative leaders began to lead a movement to unite on their mutual antipathy toward slavery's expansion into Kansas. They sought to capitalize on their state's antiextensionist consensus while maintaining an authentically conservative defense of the Constitution and the Union. For these men, a free-soil agenda did not represent an aggressive first step toward national abolition but a defensive response to the noxious "ultraism" of slaveocrats and abolitionists alike. Bolstered by the recent attacks on Lawrence, Kansas, and Senator Charles Sumner of Massachusetts, Illinois's conservative opponents of the Kansas-Nebraska Act overcame their differences at the Bloomington Convention in May 1856. These newly minted Illinois Republicans took a defensive posture, framing their movement as a defense of the rights of free white men against Southern aggression.

Douglas and his Democratic supporters rejected the Republicans as incendiaries willing to risk disunion for free soil and maintained that popular sovereignty provided a reasonable solution—offering a democratic outlet for free-labor settlers to make their choice known without embarrassing the South. Undecided voters, wavering Democrats and ex-Whigs alike, balanced their genuine dislike of slave labor with suspicion of abolitionist agitation and fear of disunion. Ultimately, the more radical national Republican platform proved too extreme for many skeptics in central Illinois. Nevertheless, the Illinois Republicans' local successes with ex-Whigs in this same region provided a path forward for the party as the conservative defenders of the Union and emphasized to Douglas the necessity of distancing himself from Southern extremists and presenting himself as an independent statesman.

The Barriers to Fusion

Even as the Know-Nothings began to falter in Illinois and divided over the question of slavery at their national convention, the prospects for a formal unification of Illinois's anti-Nebraska elements still appeared dim to Senator Trumbull. Writing to the abolitionist minister and state representative Owen Lovejoy, Trumbull noted the disdain among his supporters in southern Illinois for fusion and insisted that only a convention of antiextensionist Democrats could secure support in his part of the state. Such a scheme would soon appear naive, given the dominance of Douglas's supporters in the state organization, who, as one pro-Nebraska loyalist pledged, would keep "the Democratic party pure and uncontaminated" from "all traitors, abolitionists, Know Nothings, etc." by firmly endorsing popular sovereignty in the coming year's state convention. Yet even as the important election year approached, Trumbull's close allies expressed their desire "not to lose our identity as Democrats" and insisted on a separate organization, even at the cost of losing the election, in order to avoid the "abolitionizing tendencies" of the Fusion movement.[2]

Rightly confident in his party's underlying doctrinal unity, Stephen A. Douglas turned his attention to his presidential aspirations as the new year began. The Democratic National Convention of 1856 was set to assemble in Cincinnati in June, giving Douglas and his partners six months to secure pledges of support among the prospective state delegations. Douglas faced two principal opponents for the nomination: the incumbent president, New Hampshire's Franklin Pierce, and Pennsylvanian James Buchanan, an experienced statesman then serving as the American ambassador to the Court of St. James's. Confiding to *Chicago Times* editor James W. Sheahan, Douglas wondered whether they could "combine the whole North West as a unit" behind his nomination. In his recent Annual Message to Congress, Pierce had staked out a pro-Southern position by condemning antiextensionists as disunionists "engaged in plans of vindictive hostility" against slaveholders. Douglas expected that Buchanan, who had thus far avoided the question of slavery extension thanks to his diplomatic post, would need to take a similar position to maintain his base of support in the South. With Pierce and Buchanan squabbling with each other, Douglas hoped to consolidate his support in his home region and present himself as the most viable national candidate and the true champion of popular sovereignty.[3]

In Washington, the victors of the 1854 midterm elections belatedly assembled as the Thirty-Fourth Congress in December 1855.[4] The Democrats maintained control in the Senate but had lost their majority in the House, sparking a protracted battle for the speakership as the various strands of the opposition: Northern and Southern Know-Nothings, Southern former Whigs, and Northern anti-Nebraskaites wrangled for the speaker's chair. The contest ended only in early February 1856, with the election of Nathaniel P. Banks, an antislavery Know-Nothing from Massachusetts. Affairs in Kansas soon captured legislators' attention as the settlers' attempt to exercise popular sovereignty turned violent. In January, free-soil elements in the state had voted to form their own government in defiance of the officially recognized proslavery government elected the previous March. At that time, thousands of proslavery Missourians had crossed the border into Kansas to vote illegally, a violation clear to all through election returns in which a voting population of 2,905 had managed to cast 6,307 ballots. The failure of Federal officials to intervene had given the free-soilers good reason to reject the legitimacy of the territorial government, and over the course of the fall and winter of 1855–56, proslavery and free-soil settlers engaged in a series of violent clashes. Rather than blaming the situation on voter fraud and calling for new elections, President Pierce denounced the supposed rapacity of the small number of abolitionists who had migrated to Kansas with the help of the Massachusetts Emigrant Aid Company. Douglas, meanwhile, had been confined to bed for the better part of three months by a severe case of bronchitis. Upon his recovery in mid-February, he took a similar line, employing his position as chairman of the Committee on Territories to draft a report that, although it denounced extremists on both sides of the issue, suggested that New England had violated Kansas's constitutional right to popular sovereignty.[5]

These developments infuriated anti-Nebraskaites, Trumbull not least among them. For months, Trumbull sat frustrated in Washington, unable to take his seat as a pro-Nebraska challenge to his eligibility for office delayed his entry into the Senate. Under the Illinois Constitution, state officers could not seek any other office until one year after their term expired. While Trumbull had resigned his position as a state judge, pro-Nebraska Democrats claimed he remained ineligible throughout his nine-year term. The Senate ultimately confirmed Trumbull's membership on March 5, 1856. In the meantime, he wrote to his brothers of his sense of isolation, noting how many Northern former Whigs mistrusted him while Southerners and pro-Nebraska Democrats denounced him as an abolitionist. Although historian Rachel A. Shelden has shown that many members of Congress maintained amicable social relations with their partisan and sectional opponents amid a tense atmosphere, Trumbull received a decidedly icy welcome to the Capitol, noting that "it augurs badly that men sent here to legislate for the good of a common country should not be on familiar and pleasant terms socially."[6]

Despite skepticism among some ex-Whigs, Trumbull proved steadfast in his anti-Nebraska convictions. When given a chance, the new Senator immediately locked horns with Stephen Douglas over the Committee on Territories' majority report. Renouncing the epithets of *abolitionist* and *Know-Nothing* hurled at him by Douglas's supporters, Trumbull seized the populist traditions of the Democracy for his own side on the debate over slavery's extension. By ignoring the will of the majority of Kansans, the free-soilers, and validating "an assembly of usurpers" that had "been imposed on them by violence," Douglas invalidated popular sovereignty. Trumbull challenged his senior colleague's judgment and integrity on the floor of the Senate, detailing the acts of intimidation and violence committed against the innocent free-soil settlers of Kansas by their proslavery Missouri neighbors. Denouncing the Kansas-Nebraska Act for a lack of "fixed and certain principle," which contributed nothing "except for evil in consequence of its vagueness" in this three-hour speech, Trumbull urged the Senate to return to "the doctrine of the fathers of the Republic" and govern the territory as the common trust of the American people. Horace Greeley's *New-York Tribune* lauded the address as comparable to the orations of Patrick Henry and Daniel Webster, and it argued that it positioned Trumbull as Douglas's "natural antipode" on the national stage.[7]

Indeed, Trumbull's resolute defiance in the face of Douglas won him Whig converts in Illinois as well. Writing "on behalf of the old disbanded Whigs," the Belvidere attorney Stephen A. Hurlbut praised Trumbull for maintaining that "just medium where the sober citizenship of the country can stand unbroken." Equally impressed by Trumbull's rejection of the "radicalism and anarchy" that adherents promoted to "a higher law" and the "southern madness made rampant by political success," Hulbert encouraged Trumbull to "hold fast" to the "sound national constitutional basis" he had assumed in his debates with the Douglas Democrats. Such an endorsement may have heartened Trumbull, who had earlier lamented that being scorned by both Whigs and Democrats, he was "pretty much in a gang by myself." With the endorsement of Hurlburt and others like him, Trumbull began to more seriously consider the potential of political ecumenism.[8]

Meanwhile, although out of office, Lincoln continued to exercise political influence. At a gathering of prominent anti-Nebraska newspaper editors at Decatur on February 22, 1856, Lincoln employed a mixture of folksy charm and hardnosed pragmatism to reframe the question of slavery's extension on conservative terms. Setting the stage for a fusion of anti-Nebraska activists into a single statewide party, the Decatur resolutions ensured respect for slavery within the slave states and acknowledged their constitutional obligations to honor the Three-Fifths Compromise, return fugitive slaves, and suppress domestic violence (i.e., slave revolts). Indeed, the journalists instead focused their resolutions on unifying policies such as restoring the Missouri Compromise, protecting naturalized citizens, and eliminating graft within the state government. Writing to an editor back home, Illinois congressman Elihu B. Washburne thought the platform captured the spirit that "seems to animate the great northern mind" against the "complete and unchecked control of" the government by the "slave power." George T. Brown, the *Alton Courier*'s anti-Nebraska Democratic editor, endorsed it as "a very good platform" but still hoped the anti-Nebraska Democrats might nominate one of their own for president in 1856, perhaps the Missourian Thomas Hart Benton or Speaker of the House Nathaniel P. Banks, who had only recently departed the Democrats for the Know-Nothing Party.[9]

Indeed, despite the concessions offered at Decatur, many anti-Nebraska Democrats remained reluctant to unite on a common platform with the likes of Lovejoy. Although the editors in Decatur had made significant overtures to conservatives by acknowledging the Constitution's proslavery compromises, their broad denunciation of "property in man" and assertion that slavery violated the Constitution's essential principles alarmed skeptics who remained primed for abolitionist dog whistles. Furthermore, in addition to their call to restore the Missouri Compromise and ensure a free Kansas, the Decatur Resolutions opposed the entry of any additional slave states. Seemingly inconsequential in hindsight, this distinction remained important for expansion-minded Democrats hesitant to limit the nation's growth southward.[10]

Trumbull, however, infuriated by the violence in Kansas, had become determined to "unite the anti-slavery extension sentiment of the North." To further this work, he began a targeted mailing campaign designed to galvanize conservative voices and marginalize the abolitionists at the state anti-Nebraska convention, set for late May in Bloomington. Circulating his own speeches as well as the works of other anti-Nebraska conservatives to small-town newspapers, Trumbull hoped to rally moderately antislavery ex-Whigs and Democrats to his cause while also combatting pro-Douglas propaganda, which labeled him as a radical. But amid the chaotic collapse of the Second Party System, some southern Illinoisans began to mistrust their local editors. Having always identified as Democrats, many gravitated toward Douglas, who franked hundreds of pro-Nebraska tracks to the region. Encouraged by local leaders such as Lewis Brown, who instructed him to "fight the devil with his own weapons," Trumbull mirrored Douglas's use of the franking privilege for political ends. Armed with lists of anti-Nebraska men throughout the state, Trumbull sought to maintain his own Jacksonian bona fides, employing what historian Jean H. Baker has called the "habits, instincts, and traditions" that had defined the Democracy for many Northerners and distributed tracts to local Democratic groups as far south as Massac County. These pamphlets stressed protections for white farmers and the restoration of the Missouri Compromise as the central goals of the "true Democracy."[11]

The anti-Nebraska Democratic label might also prove more appealing to the German voters of Chicago. Although many opposed slavery's extension and the Kansas-Nebraska Act, the city's Germans had spent the previous year grappling with anti-Nebraska Know-Nothings intent on suppressing their culture and stripping them of their political power. In March 1856, they overwhelmingly voted for the pro-Nebraska mayoral candidate, though more out of a concern for liquor licenses than to affirm popular sovereignty. According to the anti-Nebraska Democratic state senator Norman B. Judd, the "free soil Germans" had difficulty distinguishing between a candidate "*being* a know nothing and *being* supported by know nothings." Overcoming such prevalent ethnocultural tensions would prove an immense challenge in constructing any durable antiextensionist coalition.[12]

Perhaps influenced by such obstacles, the anti-Nebraska Democrat supported by Lincoln for governor at Decatur, former congressman William H. Bissell, remained decidedly pessimistic. Although Bissell's name had drawn support early from his fellow anti-Nebraska Democrats, such as the former state senator Ebenezer Peck, and Bissell had earlier pledged to prevent Illinois from "joining the ranks of the slavery supporting and slavery propagandizing states," the endorsement of those outside his old party left him uneasy. Writing to Trumbull less than a month before the scheduled Bloomington Convention,

Bissell acknowledged that in "a different state of things [he] should have no objections to running," but given his opinion that anti-Nebraska Whigs and radicals remained firmly in control of the proceedings, he could "see no sort of inducement to mix [himself] up with them" and intended to decline the nomination. Acknowledging that altered circumstances might convince him to reconsider, Bissell prayed that providence might intervene "in time for us to save the state."[13]

Even with these fears, other anti-Nebraska Democrats recognized Bloomington as an opportunity to seize control of the movement and redefine the antiextension battle. George T. Brown reminded Trumbull that their chance of retaining any influence among pro-Nebraska Democrats had evaporated at the Democratic Party's state convention at Springfield. There, the pro-Douglas delegates had adopted a resolution that condemned Trumbull as a "black republican" who won his office "against the unanimous voice and wish of the democracy of Illinois." Organizing anti-Nebraska men of both parties throughout central Illinois "to make the Bloomington affair as respectable as possible," Brown hoped to use the convention's platform to frame Trumbull as the "true representative of the state." With promises of support from the anti-Nebraska Democratic lieutenant governor Gustave Koerner and former Whig congressman Richard Yates, Brown was now "satisfied that [Bloomington's] proceedings [would] be conservative." In an *Alton Courier* editorial, Brown outlined the choices facing voters. He identified four parties: "the Douglas slavery party," the "Know Nothing party," "the abolition party," and the "the great Anti-Nebraska party, the party of the people, to which all [the] union-loving, constitutional and conservative men belong." Brown maintained that with proper support from the right men, that party would have "the honor of saving this glorious Union, and bringing back the administrative policy of the government to its true and original position." Of course, the Radical Abolition Party enjoyed only the most marginal base of support in Illinois, with most members belonging to the state's small Black community, who remained disenfranchised under state law. This small group of supporters included Black Chicago abolitionist Henry O. Wagoner, who, despite his inability to vote organized a meeting for the party. Surprisingly, this gathering went on to endorse anti-Nebraska Fusion candidates rather than the national ticket led by Gerrit Smith. But as the campaign unfolded, this group came to realize that they remained profoundly unwelcome in the anti-Nebraska fold.[14]

The prospect of a conservative convention also held immense appeal for those Whigs left homeless by their party's collapse. Former state legislator Orville H. Browning of Quincy balanced his optimism with deep fears for what the meeting might yield. Writing across old partisan lines to Trumbull, Browning explained how he hoped "to keep the [anti-Nebraska] party of this state under the control of moderate men, and conservative influences" but lamented that "if rash and ultra counsels prevail all is lost." Many of the Whigs who had joined Know-Nothing lodges wondered whether they could maintain their opposition to the Kansas-Nebraska Act and still succeed on the state and national levels as an independent nativist party. In 1855, the state Know-Nothing Party had called for a restoration of the Missouri Compromise, but in February 1856, the Know-Nothing national convention had bypassed the slavery question and nominated former president Millard Fillmore, a champion of the Compromise of 1850 and the last Whig to hold the nation's highest office. Fillmore had little interest in nativism, and this ambivalence, combined with his failure to call for a repeal of the Kansas-Nebraska Act, led many Northern Know-Nothings to reject his candidacy.[15]

But others, unaffiliated with the Know-Nothings and distraught by the collapse of the Whig party, believed Fillmore might revive the party of Henry Clay and Daniel Webster. Upon hearing the news, William H. Bailhache, the new coeditor of the *Illinois State Journal,* wrote to his father with satisfaction, "Fillmore has always been my choice." Bailhache, along with Edward L. Baker, would follow his predecessor's pattern of using the *Journal* to cooperate closely with Lincoln, and he had recently endorsed the meeting at Decatur. But like many Whigs in central Illinois, Bailhache retained a profound distrust of the more radical anti-Nebraska elements. Indeed, even as he reflected fondly on the prospect of a "Union ticket" headed by Fillmore for president and Bissell for governor, he admonished the Republicans for "their violence on the 'n——' question."[16]

Douglas and his allies hoped to capitalize on the confusion and consolidate their strength both within the state and at the upcoming Democratic National Convention in Cincinnati. As early as the fall of 1855, the Illinois Democracy had begun to make appeals to oldline Whigs, encouraging the downstate followers of Henry Clay to reject the Know-Nothings, Republicans, and fusionists in favor of the only party that intended to advance "the general interests of the country." Claiming the conservative mantle as defenders of the Revolution's great legacy, the Constitution, Illinois Democrats positioned themselves as the only party that could "safely pilot the ship of state through the present crisis." Congressman Thomas L. Harris, a close Douglas ally, concluded that Fillmore's nomination would inspire disagreement among Whigs in Illinois but also strengthen Douglas's hand at the Cincinnati Convention. Fillmore's reputation as a nationally minded statesman might dissuade Democrats from nominating a figure closely associated with the South and sway delegates toward the nationally oriented Douglas. In an effort to further muddy the waters, Harris encouraged the editor of the *Illinois State Register*, Charles H. Lanphier, to spread a rumor that Trumbull had joined the Know-Nothings in order to undermine his support among German voters. He hoped to also tar other anti-Nebraska Democrats, such as Palmer and Bissell, with similar charges. In the weeks before the Bloomington Convention, Douglas's allies sought to undermine support for the gathering by distributing a broadside authored by "an Old Line Whig" who denounced the gathering as a convention for "a contemptible Abolition Party," which would likely be headed by "some renegade Democrat."[17]

As late as the spring of 1856, factionalism threatened to undermine the anti-Nebraska movement. Dedicated to preserving essential elements of their long-held political faiths, whether on matters of economics, race, religion, or ethnicity, anti-Nebraska Democrats, Whigs, and Know-Nothings eyed one another skeptically. Barring the political bombshells that followed, a series of violent events that no one could have predicted, it remains doubtful whether a successful state ticket could have come together to contest the November elections.

United in Indignation

In fact, it was a series of distant events in Kansas and Washington, DC, that fundamentally altered conditions on the ground for Illinois's anti-Nebraskaites. The proslavery raid on Lawrence, Kansas, and the caning of Senator Sumner galvanized anti-Southern feelings throughout Illinois and empowered conservative anti-Nebraskaites to take control of the Bloomington Convention. Reacting against the violence and disorder of the Slave Power, Trumbull, Lincoln, and their compatriots sought to unite conservative Illinoisans on their common commitments to the Constitution and the Union. Advancing the popularly held Northern conception of restrained masculinity, they framed the assault on Lawrence and Sumner as attacks on free white labor and the freedom of speech for white men.[18]

Battling back against the electoral interference of proslavery Missourians, the free-soil settlers of Kansas rejected the legitimacy of the federally recognized regime and adopted a free-state constitution for Kansas in a separate convention at Topeka in the fall of 1855. In late November, a politically charged land dispute at Hickory led to bloodshed as a proslavery settler from Missouri murdered a free-soil man from Ohio. In retaliation, a group of free-soil vigilantes burned down the home of the murderer and, for good measure, torched several other proslavery homesteads. The situation quickly spiraled out of control as proslavery Missourians formed militias, some of them nominally recognized by the proslavery territorial government, and began to harass free-soil settlers. When one of these groups murdered another unarmed free-soil settler in December, the territory degenerated into an undeclared civil war. Throughout the winter of 1855–56, free-soil forces gathered weapons in earnest and formed their own military companies under the authority of a free-soil shadow territorial government committed to the Topeka constitution.[19]

The federally appointed territorial governor, Wilson Shannon, and the Pierce administration resolutely supported the proslavery territorial government fraudulently elected by Missouri interlopers in March 1855. While Democratic leaders in Washington did their best to frame the violence as the product of abolitionist agitation, pointing to the Massachusetts Emigrant Aid Society as a hotbed of radicalism, in reality, most of the free-soil settlers had only a mild distaste for the institution until provoked by proslavery Missourians. The increasingly organized nature of each faction allowed small disputes over land and parochial matters to escalate into political clashes. As historian David M. Potter has observed, when a settler found himself opposed in a land claim or on some other minor matter "not merely by another squatter like himself but by an organized adversary group, the effect was to polarize and organize all the diffused and random antagonisms, which might otherwise have remained merely individual and local." Across the free states, meanwhile, the promise of popular sovereignty appeared weaker and weaker as fraud and bullets, rather than legitimate ballots, shaped the course of events in Kansas.[20]

This sentiment only intensified after May 21, 1856, when proslavery border ruffians from Missouri attacked the free-soil settlement of Lawrence, Kansas. Burning the Free State Hotel to the ground, the raiders ransacked private homes and businesses before destroying the printing presses of two antislavery newspapers. Although merely one in the series of violent episodes that created the infamous "Bleeding Kansas" image, the raid on Lawrence received widespread coverage in the Northern press. Anti-Nebraska editors seized on the incident as proof of the folly of popular sovereignty and framed the raid as an attack on the principle of free labor and the manhood of ordinary white Northerners.[21] In the national press, Horace Greeley's *New-York Tribune* identified the "charred and blackened waste" of Lawrence as proof that two years of so-called popular sovereignty had transformed the territory "into a breeding-ground and fortress of Human Slavery." Illinois's anti-Nebraska *Alton Courier* described the raid as an outrageous exhibition of "mob law" characteristic of a new era of "brute force" that had superseded the Constitution and order in the territories. The *Freeport Journal* directly tied the "heap of smoldering ruins" at Lawrence to the Bloomington Convention and called on citizens to use the gathering as a platform to defend "all that is dear to American freemen."[22]

The sense of disorder created by the attack on Lawrence escalated further with the following day's attack on Senator Sumner. Perhaps the most radical antislavery member of the Senate, Sumner had delivered a searing five-hour admonishment against Southern aggression in Kansas on May 19 and 20. His tirade specifically targeted several of his colleagues, including Senator Andrew Butler of South Carolina. This insult provoked Congressman Preston Brooks, Butler's cousin, to assail Sumner with a cane on the floor of the Senate on May 22 with the help of Congressman William Barksdale of Mississippi. Beating Sumner to a bloody pulp while onlookers watched helplessly, Brooks received praise throughout the South for defending his kinsman's honor. Northerners, meanwhile, interpreted the assault as an attack on free speech and the rights of ordinary white men.[23]

Although most Northerners considered Sumner an obnoxious extremist and recoiled at his demands for racial equality, Brooks's actions seemed to confirm their worst fears about the Southern Slave Power. No longer content to dominate Black slaves alone, the despotic Southern slaveholders now hoped to make slaves of white Northerners, stifling voices of dissent with the rod. Such an egregious act of violence on the floor of the Senate, an offense unbecoming of a man according to Northern standards of restraint and self-discipline, also revealed the South's antipathy for order and good government. As historian Michael E. Woods notes, the events in Washington and Kansas "stirred fierce and pervasive indignation by dramatizing the threat that proslavery Southerners posed to the lives and liberties of free Northerners." Throughout the free states, men who otherwise abstained from passionate outbursts indulged in this righteous anger. The choice left for Northerners, as Horace Greeley framed the issue in the pages of the *Tribune,* was between civilization and barbarism, between freedom and slavery for white men, because "so long as our truly civilized communities succumb to the rule of the barbarian elements in our political system, we must be judged by the character and conduct of our accepted masters."[24]

The press throughout Illinois echoed these sentiments. The *Chicago Democrat* announced "there should be indignation meetings everywhere where the spirit of liberty is not extinct." In Bloomington, the anti-Nebraska *Pantagraph* declared that under the proslavery regime, "no man, in private or public life, who has the manhood to express the sentiments worthy of a freeman, is safe from the attacks of cowardly scoundrels!" In Springfield, the *Illinois State Journal* wondered aloud: what "are matters coming [to] in this free land? Can the north no longer raise her voice in the halls of Legislation, without being outraged and insulted?" The *Freeport Journal* noted, "Conservative men all over the north, men who have never sympathized in the least with Abolitionists, but have always stood diametrically opposed to them, are now standing up to the shameless aggressions of the Slave power." Notably, even the fiercely pro-Douglas *Ottawa Free Trader* declared, "Unquestionably, the attack [on Sumner] must be regarded as a shameful and brutal outrage." Throughout the state, regular Democratic papers tended to emphasize Sumner's radical abolitionism, but none could defend Brooks's assault on a sitting US senator and chastised Southerners for their unrestrained aggression.[25]

Such denunciations went beyond the partisan presses and became the central concern for the politically engaged anti-Nebraska men of all backgrounds. Indeed, as documented by Senator Trumbull's incoming correspondence, ordinary Illinoisans reacted ferociously against the Slave Power in the days following the attacks on Lawrence and Senator Sumner. Writing to Trumbull on May 23, businessman E. W. Hazard of Galesburg denounced the brutality of the South and Stephen Douglas for having "sold the freemen of the North for office." Another constituent, the ex-Whig lawyer Abraham Jonas, labeled the Lawrence attacks "a Second Glencoe" after the seventeenth-century Scottish massacre made famous by Sir Walter Scott's poem of treason and pitiless "Southern clemency." Ebenezer Peck, an anti-Nebraska Democrat from Chicago, characterized the assault on Sumner as "an assault upon freedom and free speech everywhere." Joseph Gillespie, a state senator from southern Illinois associated with the Know-Nothings, wrote that his constituents shared his belief that "the Union is in great danger" as a result of "these ruffianly proceedings" and noted a growing "aposition to the repeal of the Missouri Compromise" among those previously apathetic to the slavery question. With a dramatic flair, the Reverend Benjamin Franklin Lemen, a Baptist minister from Marion County, called on Trumbull to summon the "moral courage" to stand up to "the ghostly deformed image of iniquity" in "these dagger days— in these secret midnight banditti days."[26]

This moment also allowed anti-Nebraska activists to attach specific individuals to the seemingly faceless Slave Power conspiracy. Preston Brooks exemplified the tyranny inherent in Southern aristocrats' code of "chivalry." Brooks's "attempt to crush out free speech by brutal violence" revealed that Southern honor amounted to nothing more than "sheer cowardice" and "fiendish malice."[27] But the attack in the Senate, when coupled with the sack of Lawrence, also highlighted the Northern-born targets of Sumner's "Crime against Kansas" speech. Following Sumner's lead, outraged Illinoisians lambasted President Pierce and Stephen A. Douglas as champions of the border ruffians and proslavery mob rule. Both appeared to have betrayed the interests of their free-labor constituents in a quest for power. The violence now directed at free-soil men in Kansas made Douglas "worse than Benedict Arnold" and "Frank Pierce and his myrmidons . . . murders and traitors . . . [responsible for] all the blood shed there."[28] The anti-Nebraska press substantiated these charges by emphasizing the pair's close relationship with former Missouri senator David Atchison. Atchison, who had pressured Douglas to introduce the Kansas-Nebraska Act back in 1854, now led hordes of proslavery Missourians in cross-border raids and served as a dastardly figurehead for the otherwise anonymous vigilantes.[29]

The powerful force of collective indignation lay at the heart of these critiques of Southern aggression. As an emotion associated with the abolitionist movement, indignation on behalf of the enslaved had long failed to stir Northern hearts. Despite their own distaste for slavery, mainstream party men like Trumbull, Lincoln, and other self-identified conservatives had readily acquiesced to protections for slavery within the Compromise of 1850, including a revised Fugitive Slave Act. But for this same cohort, the attacks on Lawrence and Senator Sumner revealed that the Southern Slave Power now sought to dominate the free men of the North.

Already alarmed by the repeal of the quasi-sacred Missouri Compromise, conservatives were compelled by such overt acts of violence to acknowledge the radical threat posed by the slaveholding class of the South. Far beyond securing the right to slavery within their own states, Southern slaveholders now hoped to subordinate proponents of free labor as their vassals, depriving them of their right to representation in the government and their freedom of speech. In his examination of emotion and antebellum sectional conflict, Michael E. Woods captures the profound implications of this moment: "Northern indignation was more than an ephemeral outburst of passion. It directly promoted political realignment, bringing former opponents into the Republican camp." Indeed, to the amazement of many, a fusion of former Whigs, Democrats, and Free-Soilers crystalized in Illinois one week later at Bloomington.[30]

Although Richard H. Sewell has argued that these twin assaults strengthened the hand of the radical anti-Nebraskaites, other scholars have pointed to this moment as a turning point for conservatives in Illinois.[31] For moderates, the raid on Lawrence and the attack on Sumner seemed to prove that the greatest threats to law, order, and the Constitution came not from abolitionists, but the Southern Slave Power and their dough-faced Northern abettors. Compelled to build a new political coalition to defend the rights of Northern whites, they hoped to unite anti-Nebraska men on the principles of perpetual Union, free speech, and majority rule. Maintaining a defensive posture, they only insisted on restoring the Missouri Compromise. This goal, the lowest common denominator within the proto-Republican ranks, fell far short of the aggressive goals of political abolitionists. Indeed, the delegates who assembled at the Bloomington Convention had no intention of surrounding the slave states with a "cordon of freedom." Rather, as captured by a sympathetic Springfield editor, they had gathered "for the purpose of rolling back the black tide which [had] swell[ed] upward from the South and threaten[ed] to snatch away the liberties of the free inhabitants of the North."[32]

Finding Common Ground

On May 29, some 270 anti-Nebraska men from throughout Illinois convened at Major's Hall on the corner of East and Front Streets in downtown Bloomington. The three-story brick building was a product of the economic and demographic surge that would swell the city's population from fewer than sixteen hundred in 1850 to more than seven thousand by decade's end. The once sleepy prairie town now bustled as mills, machine shops, and locomotives harmonized to create the commercial vibrancy that Illinois' boosters had long promised. Located in the center of the state and at the intersection of two major railroads, Bloomington proved the perfect place for delegates to meet in the middle—both geographically and ideologically. The *Illinois State Journal* promised its readers that the convention would "not be a of a partisan character" but would instead "reflect the views and opinions of the conservative, freedom loving voters of all parties in the State." The gathering's organizers hoped to capitalize on this sense of a common cause and overcome the lingering barriers of conflicting ideologies and former partisan allegiances.[33]

The platform the delegates adopted made no mention of the classically divisive subjects of banking, internal improvements, or the protective tariff. Nor did it protest the Ostend Manifesto, a plan proposed by James Buchanan and other American diplomats to wrestle away slaveholding Cuba from Spain, or the Fugitive Slave Act. Instead, the resolutions focused on the Southern Slave Power's recent aggressions in Kansas and in the halls of

Congress. The convention unanimously adopted a stance against the Pierce administration's "propagation of slavery and its extension into Territories heretofore dedicated to freedom" and denounced its role in forcing slavery into Kansas "against the known wishes of the legal voters of that territory."

Although Trumbull remained in Washington, his ally George T. Brown made sure to bolster his standing among the delegates. He encouraged the adoption of a resolution that endorsed Trumbull's conduct in the Senate with "unqualified approbation." Furthermore, the delegates declared themselves "devoted to the Union" and the Constitution, promising "to the last extremity, [to] defend it against the efforts now being made by the disunionists of this administration to compass its dissolution."[34]

In his address to the convention, Orville H. Browning reflected that the "strange company . . . [of] Democrats, Whigs, Free Soilers" gathered together at Bloomington. Long a proud Henry Clay Whig, Browning insisted that he remained one and suspected that his new compatriots retained their own identities. They now "met to defend their common liberties" not because they had apostatized themselves from their old parties but rather because "*others had changed.*" They met under the old assumptions that Congress could, and should, legislate to keep slavery out of those territories already designated free. Their opponents had abandoned these doctrines in favor of the interests of the elite Slave Power. Drawing on the foundational principle of majority rule, he urged a united front so they would not "by an increase of slave States . . . come to be governed by a meagre minority."[35]

In his so-called Lost Speech at the convention, Lincoln hammered away at these same themes. Trumpeting the importance traditional statesmanship and the inviolability of majority rule, he denounced the perfidy of Southern disunionists. A rousing speech, the address was praised by all and yet recorded by none in its entirety. Nevertheless, listeners would recall years later how the speech compellingly connected the recent aggressions of the Slave Power in Kansas with the threat of Southern secession.[36] In an uncharacteristically animated tone, Lincoln boldly declared, "SOUTHERN DISUNIONISTS, We won't go out of the Union, and you SHAN'T!"[37] According to Lincoln, these radicals had seized control of the Democratic Party, forming a "Black Democracy" that had announced itself "in favor of white slavery"—by which he meant the subordination of free labor to slave labor. As he finished, Lincoln implored his former Whig colleagues to reject the Democrats' demagoguery and instead return to the moderate and constitutional positions of Henry Clay, now championed by the anti-Nebraska ticket.[38]

In such rhetoric, the color black served a dual purpose by alluding to both the Democracy's apparent support for enslaved Black labor over free white and its inherent villainy. These allusions to racial competition—and the possibility of racial dilution—had proven a successful tactic in the earlier Free-Soiler campaigns and resonated among many Border North voters. In a letter to Trumbull four days before the convention, former Illinois attorney general Wickliffe Kitchell described pro-Nebraska Democrats as "Mongrels—a Mulatto Party" committed to "Black autocracy." This type of language suggested that racial amalgamation would become a standard talking point within both major parties and foreshadowed the centrality of racism in coming campaigns.[39]

The convention sought to further broaden its base of support by balancing its nominations among the various anti-Nebraska factions. As the *Peru Chronicle* surmised, the organizers hoped to draw in "every man not opposed to freedom" and thus proceeded "with the greatest harmony and concession." Despite his earlier reluctance, Bissell communicated via a letter to Brown that he would accept the convention's nomination for the governorship. Universally endorsed as the strongest candidate, the former Democratic congressman and Mexican War hero from southern Illinois was promptly nominated by the convention to lead the statewide ticket. Curiously, the fact that Bissell had converted to Catholicism in 1854 never drew the attention one might have expected. Carefully balancing the demands of antislavery German Americans— mainly Protestants and free-thinkers—who had settled in northern and central Illinois and ex-Whig nativists, they nominated German-born Francis A. Hoffman for lieutenant governor and four native-born ex-Whigs for the remaining statewide offices.[40] James Miller, the convention's candidate for state treasurer, had already been nominated by the state's American (Know-Nothing) Party but declined in favor of campaigning on the slavery question with the anti-Nebraskaites. His choice reflected the weakness of the Americans' statewide organization and the priorities of their would-be candidates, including their gubernatorial nominee William B. Archer, who instead became a delegate to the Republican national convention.[41]

Owen Lovejoy, who distanced himself from abolitionism in his own address to the convention, also received an appointment to the national convention as a concession to the radicals. Despite the distinctly conservative disposition of the convention's platform and nominations, most of the radical Free-Soilers readily embraced the united party. Jacksonville abolitionist Jonathan B. Turner manifested the willingness of the radicals to support a more moderate platform in a series of notes drafted for the convention. Although employing more aggressive language than that which the convention eventually adopted, Turner, a defender of Black rights in other contexts, recognized that the convention ought "to fight for the freedom of the 20 millions of white men" against "treason, anarchy, & ruffianism." By agreeing to frame the question as a defense of the free white men of the West, rather than "the freedom of the negroes of the South," the radicals had made a significant step toward the antiextensionist mainstream.[42]

While many moderates remained unwilling to use the name "Republican" on the state level because of its radical associations, the "Anti-Nebraska Ticket" or "People's Party" had overcome significant internal disputes to form a united front. Adopting a conservative platform dedicated to protecting the rights of free white men, they formed, as the formerly Whig *Illinois State Journal* described the group, "one common brotherhood to war against the allied forces of nullification, disunion, slavery propagandism, ruffianism and gag law." Thus, "shorn of its radical image," the state's proto-Republican party had finally organized and united on a common platform which it could advocate nationally in the Philadelphia Convention, scheduled for mid-June.[43]

The Bloomington Convention, according to former Democratic congressman John E. "Long John" Wentworth of Chicago, had left the people "all wide awake, and resolved to put an end to the damnable acts of violence equally disgracing Washington and Kansas."[44] Galvanized by their indignation, organized by perceptive moderates, and united on a conservative platform, these new Republicans seized the political offensive.[45] Casting themselves as defenders of white labor and the Union, the state's Republicans faced off against a Democratic Party bewildered by defections. Taking advantage of the public's focus on Kansas, the Republicans labeled popular sovereignty a sham doctrine, a proslavery measure conceived by the Slave Power—represented by Preston Brooks—and advanced by their Northern cronies: President Pierce and Stephen A. Douglas. As a result, Douglas and his followers faced the difficult task of negotiating a position that could draw indignant Illinoisans back to the national party without breaking ranks with the Southern Democracy.[46]

Popular Sovereignty, National Union, and Freedom

Convening at Cincinnati on June 2, delegates to the Democratic National Convention sought to reaffirm their commitment to popular sovereignty in Kansas and form a united front against the rising tide of "black republicanism." The three major candidates, Pierce, Buchanan, and Douglas, each entered the convention with a solid bloc of supporters. In accordance with the prevailing custom for active candidates to absent themselves, Douglas avoided the convention but sent a loyal lieutenant, Illinois's Democratic gubernatorial candidate William A. Richardson, in his stead. Douglas rightly recognized that Buchanan would emerge as his primary rival. Mature, experienced, and seemingly untainted by the fallout from the Kansas-Nebraska Act, Buchanan had a base of support in the key states of Virginia and New York and managed to siphon off some of Douglas's support in the Northwest, winning the endorsement of Indiana senator Jesse D. Bright. Pierce had a strong core of supporters from New England and the Deep South, but Douglas believed that these delegates would shift to support his candidacy once it became clear that the president would fall short of the mark. This prediction proved only half-right. Most of the northeastern Democrats recognized that Douglas, as the chief architect of the Kansas-Nebraska Act, had alienated many onetime Democrats in their states. In a series of events that seem ironic in light of what was to come over the next four years, the Deep South states of Alabama, Mississippi, Arkansas, Florida, and Texas backed Douglas to the end while Northern delegations deserted him. For these delegates, Buchanan, unsullied by the fight over the Nebraska Bill and the violence in Kansas, appeared a safer bet to bring wayward Northern Democrats back into the fold. Many interpreted the decision to pass over Douglas as an attempt to reframe the question of slavery extension. Even Illinois Republican congressman James Knox viewed Buchanan's nomination as a rebuke to the South, writing privately that "the Pennsylvanian" had "bullied & cowed Douglas's and Pierce's Southern allies." In another act that would seem incongruous four years later, the convention gave the vice presidential slot to thirty-four-year-old John C. Breckinridge of Kentucky, then an ally of Douglas, to ease bitterness among the Little Giant's supporters.[47]

The Democratic platform highlighted the bisectional composition of the party and stressed ideological continuity and a respect for precedent in an effort to appeal to conservatives of all stripes. Claiming the mantle of the Jeffersonian tradition, Democrats denounced their opponents as neo-Federalists bent on destroying state sovereignty by promoting banks, tariffs, and sectional discord. The irony in such an accusation, quickly identified by the Republican press, was that Buchanan had begun life as a Federalist, abandoning the party only after its political disintegration at the end of the War of 1812.[48] Despite this, the Democrats endorsed the Kentucky and Virginia Resolutions of 1798 to demonstrate their opposition to both centralization and nativism, characteristics the party identified with the neo-Federalist "fusionists." Although many of their planks—denouncing banks, federal funding of internal improvements, and high tariffs—appealed to traditional Democratic voters, the party's claim to "fellowship with ... all who regard the preservation of the Union under the Constitution as the paramount issue" in the sectional crisis marked an effort to bring ex-Whigs into the fold.[49]

This plank proved especially valuable to the Illinois Democrats, who needed to secure a proportion of the ex-Whig vote to secure a majority under the conditions imposed by the recent realignment. Although they had reason to hope that many of the traditional Democratic voters in central and southern Illinois who had absented themselves in 1854 would return to vote for Buchanan, the party's weakness within the state's antislavery northern counties remained apparent.[50] Deprived of these votes, Douglas and his allies would have to secure the support of ex-Whigs from central Illinois and begin to emphasize the connection between popular sovereignty and the Compromise of 1850, originally drafted by the Whig hero Henry Clay and famously endorsed by the conservative stalwart Daniel Webster. Declaring itself "the only national-Union sustaining party of the country," the Illinois Democracy framed its policy of popular sovereignty as a defense of old-fashioned statesmanship and compromise in the face of a radical opposition.[51]

Crucially, such a position did not preclude antislavery conservatives from supporting the Democrats. With the state's conservative Republicans firmly in control of that party, Illinois's Democrats could ill afford direct ties to the Slaveocracy. Douglas himself could not frame popular sovereignty as an antislavery measure without alienating his Southern colleagues, but many other Illinois Democrats operating on the state level argued that the policy would achieve an antislavery outcome. In fact, careful parsing of the Illinois Democracy's campaign rhetoric reveals that most Illinois Democrats retained their commitment to white free labor. Indeed, their faith in free labor's superiority allowed them to discount Republican outcry against the Southern Slave Power as paranoid propaganda. The Illinois Democrats perceived slavery as an undesirable institution but argued that a true commitment to the Constitution required local autonomy and popular democracy. Although such a course could, in theory, allow slavery to expand, demographic and economic trends favoring free labor discounted such an outcome in practice. As summarized by Adam I. P. Smith, the Illinois Democracy hoped "to navigate a political path toward a free West while respecting, as the Founders had done, the divergent interests of North and South."[52]

Democratic Illinois editors frequently advanced the practical antislavery implications of popular sovereignty while denouncing their opponents as extremists bent on disunion. The *Ottawa Free Trader* spoke for most Northern

Democrats when it argued that under popular sovereignty, "the territories, are by nature free; and that slavery, being an institution of purely municipal creation, and congress having no power to either make or unmake a slave, or delegate such a power, slavery cannot be established in any territory that came into the possession of the Union free, until it shall become a sovereign, independent state." Such sentiments seem to echo the principles of "Freedom National"— freedom as normative and slavery as the aberration—while emphasizing the people's ultimate sovereignty in forming a new state. This same column took the argument a step further, declaring that, contrary to the Republicans' campaign rhetoric, the vital question of the campaign "concerns no issue involved in reference to the slavery question." According to editor William Osman, both Northern Democrats and Republicans acknowledged that it would be better for the people of Kansas to vote down slavery since each professed to defend the principles of Jeffersonian democracy. This, in turn, rendered the question of congressional interference an abstract dispute stressed for political advantage by the Republicans while actually making the spread of slavery more likely by agitating the South and endangering the Union.[53]

The indecision that paralyzed ex-Whig and Know-Nothing Benjamin S. Edwards of Springfield perfectly illustrates the state Democracy's allure to self-identified antislavery conservatives. Writing to Trumbull in the midst of the summer campaign season, Edwards identified himself as "an antislavery man" firmly "opposed to the extension of slavery." While he would vote to make Kansas a free state, he questioned whether a congressional edict would permanently resolve the matter and had grown "tired of the agitation of the slavery question." He asked whether it would "not be better to withdraw this question from Congress . . . [and] leave the whole matter to be settled in time and peaceably by the people themselves?" Such an action would allow the natural course of demographics and economics to resolve the question and relieve the nation of this "political strife" that threatened to destroy the Union.[54]

Attacking the issue from another angle, the *Salem Advocate* argued that the Democrats' opposition to congressional interference with slavery mirrored their opposition to laws prohibiting adultery or requiring observance of the Sabbath. By this account, a free society relied on the virtue of the people, rather than the compulsion of law, to repress evil. Such evils included drunkenness, infidelity, sabbath-breaking, and slavery. The Democracy's opposition to formal prohibitions did not imply acquiescence to such evils. Rather, Democrats opposed the heavy hand of the state imposing morality on a free people.[55]

At other times, Democratic editors bolstered their antislavery credentials through hyperbole or shameless falsehoods. The *Rock Island Argus* vigorously defended James Buchanan as a man "who never owned a slave, or lived in a slave state, or whispered a sentence in favor of its extension, or cast a vote by which any honest man could construe a wish to support the institution." Some went even further and accused the Republican presidential candidate John C. Frémont of secretly owning slaves and hiding them away at a home in St. Louis.[56] While completely unfounded, these assertions proved a serious headache for the Republicans throughout the campaign. Indeed, Republican activists in Illinois found the charges sufficiently plausible that nationally prominent officials like Trumbull received requests for clarification from loyal foot soldiers, and Republican organs such as the *Freeport Journal* felt repeatedly compelled to repudiate the accusations in print. Frémont's ultimate weakness as a candidate in southern and central Illinois highlights the distinctions which emerged between the Illinois Republicans and the national Republican Party during the Philadelphia Convention of June 17–19.[57]

Fighting for a Conservative Candidate

In the three weeks preceding the Philadelphia Convention, the cohort of newly united conservative Illinois Republicans worked to secure a national platform and presidential nominee that reflected their moderate principles. Sensing Fillmore's appeal among many Northern conservatives, Congressman James Knox had written to Richard Yates, "Unless the Republicans nominate and *unite* in supporting a *conservative* man, I think we are beaten." Having planned to take the current administration to task on the national stage, Buchanan's nomination in Cincinnati further complicated the Republican campaign strategy. As G. D. A. Parks, a delegate at Bloomington from Will County, explained to Trumbull, Buchanan's power derived "not from any inherent strength, but by reason of his exemption personally from the causes which made Pierce and Douglas so fearfully odious." To win, the Republicans would need to nominate someone equal to Buchanan in "age, experience, moderation of views, and integrity of character." In other words, Parks believed the Republicans "must make a nomination conservative down to the last degree."[58]

For Trumbull, and many of his supporters in Illinois, Supreme Court Justice John McLean perfectly matched these criteria.[59] A friend of Trumbull's, Justice McLean had served as a US representative from Ohio and postmaster general to both James Monroe and John Quincy Adams before Andrew Jackson elevated him to the Supreme Court in 1829. Since then, McLean's views had shifted across the political spectrum toward Whiggery as he consistently espoused a firm yet conservative opposition to slavery's westward expansion. A long-standing member of the political establishment who could relate to moderate Republicans of all backgrounds, McLean could match Buchanan's experience as a statesman and reputation for civil moderation. But McLean's supporters recognized two major flaws as they floated his candidacy. First, at seventy-one, he could hardly inspire the faithful through youthful vigor, and the potential political consequences of dying in office had become apparent in the aftermath of John Tyler's and Millard Fillmore's presidencies. More importantly, the party's radical wing, including Salmon P. Chase and Benjamin Wade of McLean's home state, opposed McLean for his conservatism on the slavery issue and his flirtations with Know-Nothingism.[60]

Despite these obstacles, Lincoln begged Trumbull to secure McLean's nomination for the sake of Illinois. In an early June letter that revealed the full extent of both his shrewdness and his trust in Trumbull, Lincoln framed the stakes of the Philadelphia nomination in no uncertain terms. Still integrated among the oldline Whigs of central Illinois, Lincoln believed that these undecided conservatives would "go heartily for McLean" but would support Buchanan "against, Chase, [Nathaniel P.] Banks, [William H.] Seward, [Francis P.] Blair, or Fremont." Confident that Bissell's nomination and the Bloomington platform had secured a victory in the gubernatorial contest "by a very large majority" and recognizing that Trumbull's influence would "be greater than that of any other Illinoian," Lincoln implored Trumbull to bolster the conservatives. Should Trumbull fail, Lincoln feared the state would inevitably go to Buchanan as conservative Whigs split their ballots three ways, among Buchanan, Know-Nothing candidate Millard Fillmore, and the more radical Republican nominee.[61]

Unfortunately for the pair, McLean failed to secure the nomination, and the national Republican Party that emerged from Philadelphia presented a substantially more radical agenda for the nation than the goals approved by the Illinois anti-Nebraska delegates at Bloomington. Although careful to avoid controversial and divisive issues such as the Fugitive Slave Act of 1850 and instead harness the Northern public's indignation over Kansas, the national platform's language reflected the influence of radical leaders like Salmon P. Chase. Framing the extension of slavery as a violation of the Fifth Amendment, the Philadelphia platform advanced a controversial interpretation of constitutional law. Rather than adopt the defensive stance maintained by the Bloomington Convention, which emphasized the need to restore compromise, sectional balance, and Union, the delegates framed the Constitution as a distinctly antislavery document. The platform expressly denied the "authority of Congress . . . to give legal existence to Slavery in any Territory of the United States" under the constitution and attacked slavery as a "relic of barbarism." Chase and his fellow radicals rejoiced at their triumph. "I can hardly believe that the majority understood what broad principles they were announcing," marveled the Ohio governor. In another blow to the conservatives, Chase's Ohio supporters also blocked McLean's nomination despite his strong support among the other Border North delegations.[62]

Instead, the convention elevated Mexican War hero John C. Frémont, a wildcard who had enjoyed support from New Englanders and the powerful Blair family of the Border South. Aside from a brief stint in the Senate, where he had represented California as a Democrat, Frémont had no substantial political experience. A military adventurer best known for his exploits in the trans-Mississippi West, the "Pathfinder" garnered support for less substantive reasons. Born in Georgia and married to the daughter of the influential Missouri senator Thomas Hart Benton, Frémont appeared bisectional, and his relative youth (at the age forty-three), dashing appearance, and history of daring exploits seemed to make him just the man to stand up to the Slave Power. In reality, Frémont carried significant baggage. Vain and arrogant, Frémont had a propensity toward insubordination that had ended his career in the army. Since then, he had failed in his reelection bid to the Senate and had made few concrete contributions to the Republican cause. Indeed, his rapid ascendency speaks more to the political abilities of his wife, Jessie Benton Frémont, than to his own leadership skills. The potential for scandal further hindered Frémont. Although both American-born Protestants, John and Jessie Frémont had eloped in 1841 with the help of a Roman Catholic priest, a fact that—along with John Frémont's French Canadian heritage—alarmed nativists crucial to the Republican coalition in battleground states like Pennsylvania. Finally, his influential father-in-law, Senator Benton, an early opponent of the Kansas-Nebraska Act, endorsed Buchanan rather than break ranks with the Democrats.[63]

Although disappointing in many respects for the Illinois delegates—Trumbull, disgusted by his experience, determined to avoid all future national conventions—Philadelphia offered one promising foretaste for moderates from the Prairie State. In an unexpected move, the Illinois delegation asked John Allison of Pennsylvania to nominate Abraham Lincoln for the vice presidency. State legislators Judd and Palmer, who had blocked Lincoln's 1854 senate bid, now led the charge for his nomination. Outmaneuvered by the supporters of the New Jersey ex-Whig William Dayton, Lincoln's backers nevertheless garnered 110 votes, a strong second-place finish that boded well for the future.

This unexpected result demonstrated how far the competing factions of Illinois conservatives had come toward reconciling their earlier differences.[64]

"The Political Cauldron Is Boiling, Boiling, Boiling!"

The subsequent campaign season highlighted the advantages of the Illinois Republicans' conservative stance while confirming the public's skepticism toward radical attacks on slavery. The absence of a viable Know-Nothing candidate for governor produced a contest directly between Bissell and Richardson. While Richardson's close ties to Douglas made it impossible for him to separate himself from the repeal of the Missouri Compromise, Bissell's long history in the state as a Democrat and war hero protected him from any association with abolitionist radicalism.[65] Thanks to their candidate's discretion and Anglo-Saxon surname, the Republicans also largely avoided discussing Bissell's Catholic faith.[66] Unfortunately for the party, Frémont's inexperience and innate bellicosity made it difficult to cast him as a moderate figure. In addition, persistent false rumors of Frémont's Catholicism in the national press dampened support among nativists. As previously discussed, Buchanan had no direct ties to Douglas or the Kansas-Nebraska Act, allowing erstwhile opponents of Douglas to support him in good faith. Finally, the candidacy of ex-president Millard Fillmore, nominated by the Know-Nothings and the last vestiges of the national Whig Party, offered oldline Whigs a means of avoiding both the potential radical and Jacksonian Democrat.

Facing an uphill battle for the state's electoral votes, Illinois Republicans worked to frame the race as a battle between reasonable conservatives devoted to the Union and rabid proslavery radicals bent on destroying Northern freedom. By reprinting incendiary pro-Buchanan and pro-disunion excerpts from Southern newspapers such as the *Richmond Enquirer* and *Charleston Mercury,* the *Chicago Tribune* highlighted the relationship between Southern Democracy and secession. Northerners faced a choice either to "aid those who deliberately avow such treasonable designs" or to support Frémont, "who is for maintaining the Union." By this same account, the Republicans represented "the only National party" and "the Constitutional party" because of their unwavering support for compromise and Union. The *Alton Courier* endorsed Frémont as "the only conservative candidate before the country" committed to equality for the North within the Union. Highlighting a recent speech delivered by Fillmore, which seemed to acknowledge the right of secession, the *Courier* framed both Fillmore and Buchanan as hopelessly beholden to Southern extremists.

Republican moderation, in the words of the *Belvidere Standard*, represented "the true policy of men who love the Union—conservative, businessmen, who hate turmoil, and bloodshed, and internal struggles, and wild excitement." This period of Southern aggression required "a bold, decided, manly front" against the slaveocracy to restore sectional balance.[67]

While the Republicans largely succeeded in swinging the Know-Nothings of northern Illinois into the Republican column, local leaders recognized that central Illinois would determine the election's outcome and worked tirelessly to co-opt conservative ex-Whigs inclined toward Fillmore. In Greene County, William Herndon—Lincoln's law partner—and ex-congressman Richard Yates negotiated a truce with Know-Nothing activist Jim Matheny so that both factions would advocate for antiextension policies. Lincoln himself wrote to many leading Fillmore supporters urging them to throw their support behind Frémont. Presenting a pragmatic plan for limited cooperation, Lincoln explained that by supporting the Republicans and depriving Buchanan of Illinois, the Know-Nothings could potentially send the election to the House of Representatives—where Fillmore might emerge triumphant as a compromise candidate.[68]

In a case that highlighted a generational divide among former Whigs, William H. Bailhache of the *Illinois State Journal* sought to convince his father, John Bailhache, the former editor of the *Alton Telegraph* to shift his support from Fillmore to Frémont. The younger Bailhache acknowledged that he too "would have preferred Fillmore as a candidate" as would have "a large number of the delegates" to Philadelphia, but he insisted that Frémont's "record is a good one" and hoped that the young hero might take on a role like Zachary Taylor, the last Whig to win the White House. Yet while the elder Bailhache wrote to his fellow oldline Whigs denouncing defections to Buchanan and would back Bissell for governor, he remained in Fillmore's camp. In an effort to cultivate goodwill, William Bailhache even assisted in the establishment of a pro-Fillmore newspaper in Springfield. He apparently believed the Fillmore campaign would do more harm to Buchanan than Frémont and, as evidenced in late October letters with his father, hoped that the Fillmore men would switch candidates at the last moment. Despite these efforts, ex–Know-Nothing William B. Archer recognized that "the friends of Fillmore [would] not come over" to the Republicans, thanks to Frémont's association with Catholicism and the increasing number of German-born Republicans.[69]

As discussed earlier, the Democrats took advantage of Frémont's relative obscurity to tar him with a variety of blatantly false and contradictory charges. Recognizing the tenuous and sometimes conflicting elements of the Republican coalition, they hoped to alienate at least one of the party's key constituencies through this campaign of misinformation. Thus, Democrats could accuse the Republicans of a plot "to degrade the alien-born white man" and also lambast them for "laying drunk in beer saloons . . . to fool the ignorant laboring Dutchman." As a result, Republican organs found themselves in the strange position of simultaneously denying Frémont's status as "a Know Nothing or Catholic, an Abolitionist or a slaveholder."[70]

Fillmore supporters sought to step into the breach by making the case that their candidate offered the only hope for national reconciliation and revival. The Fillmore campaign paper William Bailhache had assisted, the *Conservative*, largely targeted the Democrats, denouncing "the present imbecile administration" for its "repeal of the Missouri Compromise" and its "reopening the slavery agitation which had been closed by the Compromises of 1820 and 1850." Yet, it also lambasted "Republican madness and folly" alongside "Locofoco corruption" and attempted to sow doubt into the minds of oldline Whigs leaning toward the Republicans by suggesting that the John McClean, the conservative favorite Supreme Court justice, favored Fillmore over Frémont. With the statewide Know-Nothing Party in disarray and resolved, with varying degrees of enthusiasm, to support Bissell in the gubernatorial contest, the Fillmorites claimed the mantle of disinterested patriots who stood apart from party. Drawing on a tendency among Whigs identified by Daniel Walker Howe "to think of themselves as nonpartisan defenders of reason against the passions of the crowd," the pro-Fillmore forces positioned their candidate as arrayed against "sectional parties" who represented "the wildest and most dangerous passions." In the campaign's final days, the *Conservative* appealed to the "many good and true men, whose every impulse is patriotic" who planned to vote for Frémont to reject the "designing demagogues" and "abolitionists" who led the Republicans at the national level in favor of "Fillmore and the Constitution."[71]

Meanwhile, after battling Democratic attempts throughout the summer to admit Kansas to the Union prematurely, Trumbull took to the stump in September in support of Bissell and Frémont. Drawing on his Democratic roots to infuse the campaign with the popular energy sometimes lost amid conservative rhetoric, Trumbull accused Douglas and his followers of acting as "political chameleons." Such Democrats would take up proslavery policies at one moment and antislavery at another to suit their own desires for power. Trumbull's public speeches throughout the state stressed the continuity of principles and his dedication to compromise. Focusing his attention on the repeal of the Missouri Compromise, Trumbull also spoke directly to would-be Fillmore voters. Citing the hopelessness of Fillmore's prospects, he appealed to their shared desire to bring order to Kansas "and to save the country from anarchy and blood, from the spread of odious institutions." A vote for Frémont, would, as paraphrased in the *Chicago Tribune,* mark "the first step towards bringing back the policy of the government to the days of Washington and Jefferson."[72]

In Springfield, the *Illinois State Journal* urged its readers to support "True Conservatism" in the face of "the black folds of demagogueism" that sought to "declare Slavery National" and "Freedom Sectional." Bailhache and Baker emphasized the "peace and quiet" that the country had enjoyed prior to the Democratic destruction of the Missouri Compromise and insisted that conservatives would not "be so blinded by the sophistry of politicians" to believe the Kansas-Nebraska Act in any way represented the intentions of the Founders. The true heirs of the Constitution knew "that Freedom is the national principle, and as such . . . it is the duty of every true conservative man to labor for its development, extension and perpetuity."[73]

Critically, however, such support for Freedom National did not entail any support for abolitionism, as the *Illinois State Journal* made clear by denouncing Gerrit Smith's National Liberty Party campaign as evidence that "the abolitionists of the North avow precisely the same doctrines as the n——drivers of the South" by calling for "disunion, the separation of the North from the South, and the destruction of the Constitution and the Bible." Further downstate, another prominent Republican organ made it clear that the party rejected the moralizing tendencies of abolitionism by reminding readers, "We have nothing to say of the morality of slavery, except so far as it puts its grasping hand under our very noses, to snatch from us the soil of freedom." Although the accusation by conservative Republicans that the abolitionists "would rather see Buchanan elected than Fremont" distorted the position of even the most ardent abolitionists, the state's radicals found themselves in a precarious position.[74]

Recent works, most notably those by James Oakes and Sean Wilentz, have engaged closely with the idea of an antislavery reading of the Constitution, which allowed Americans from 1787 onward to reject the legitimacy of "property in man." This view of the Constitution as allowing slavery without condoning it adds a necessary layer of nuance to any examination of the document and antebellum constitutionalism. The prevailing consensus among historians that the nation's foundational document was explicitly and entirely proslavery reflects the views of some historical actors, like John C. Calhoun and William Lloyd Garrison, but completely ignores how ordinary white Northerners interpreted the Constitution. Yet, in his examination of the Republican Party, and especially Lincoln's Republican Party in Illinois, Oakes offers a misleading assessment of the organization's commitment to universal human rights. Early Republicans in Illinois sought to restrict slavery's growth but would have bristled at Oakes's assessment that there were "substantial overlaps" between themselves and abolitionists. Rather than seeing themselves as the pragmatic allies of radical antislavery actors who stressed the plight of the enslaved, Illinois Republicans viewed themselves strictly as the defenders of white freedom in the territories and Northern rights in the Union.[75]

Those abolitionists within the state Republican Party, like Owen Lovejoy of Princeton, faced significant hostility from the dominant conservatives. Nominated as the Republican candidate for the Third Congressional District over the conservative Leonard Swett, Lovejoy confronted a third-party challenge from Judge T. Lyle Dickey, a former Whig and a delegate to the Bloomington Convention. Though Swett's defeat had turned Lincoln "blind" with fury, he advised his confidants to let Lovejoy stand unopposed. Eventually, Judge David Davis got Dickey to withdraw from the race, correctly recognizing Lovejoy's popularity in the district and knowing that a split vote among anti-Nebraskaites would hand the seat to the Democrats. But he managed to do so only after Dickey had done his best to embarrass Lovejoy in the press, and Lovejoy's allies continued to accuse Davis of undermining their candidate through the last days of the campaign. Lovejoy subsequently spent the campaign emphasizing the plight of the free-state people of Kansas and his pragmatic concerns in relieving them from the violence of proslavery forces.[76]

Lovejoy's candidacy marked the outer bound of what most Illinois Republicans would accept, and the organization pushed the state's small cohort of Black abolitionists out of the fold. A brief burst of optimism had led the Radical Abolition meeting that abolitionist Henry Wagoner organized to endorse Frémont over their party's candidate, Gerrit Smith. H. Ford Douglas of Chicago, a notable abolitionist and proponent of Black emigration had also endorsed the Republicans but within a few months had come to regret the decision. Speaking to a state convention of "Colored Citizens" in Alton shortly after the election, he called the Republican Party's platform "that Freedom is National and Slavery is sectional . . . destructive and fatal to American liberty." Ford Douglas argued that acknowledging that slavery could exist legitimately anywhere in the Union, the Republicans and the abolitionists who supported them, including Frederick Douglass, sought to "break up the throne of God and spit in the face of the deity." Born enslaved in Virginia in 1831, Ford Douglas had escaped to Ohio in the mid-1840s and worked as an abolitionist lecturer there before moving to Illinois in 1854. Following a brief stint as a newspaper editor in Canada, he settled permanently in Chicago. Although he expressed sympathy for the Garrisonian abolitionists, who held that the Constitution wedded slavery to the republic, Douglas espoused a rare variant of antislavery constitutionalism. First popularized by the abolitionist Alvan Stewart, this view held that the federal government had every right, indeed the duty, to abolish slavery everywhere, including the states where it already existed. In essence, this interpretation shared the Republicans' core conviction of that slavery was inconsistent with the principles of the American Revolution. Unlike the Republicans, however, Ford Douglas and his fellow Black abolitionists at Alton remained convinced that "true anti-Slavery" abjured any concessions to the institution as a local matter. Standing fast by this radical position, Douglas and allies like Wagoner remained beyond the pale of mainstream partisan politics in Illinois.[77]

The alienation of the Black abolitionist went beyond constitutional interpretations, as racist rhetoric flourished throughout the campaign. Indeed, the overwhelming prejudice against African Americans among Illinois's white voters fueled demagogic race-baiting by all parties. Democrats regularly labeled the Republicans as "n——-worshipers" bent on extending equal civil and political rights to African Americans alongside radical abolitionists.[78] Republicans responded by labeling their opponents "n——-loving Democrats" and by accusing the Democrats of degrading white laborers by arguing "that n——s were more honorable than poor whites." According to the *Belvidere Standard,* Democrats endorsed "n——ism" and had produced a "n—— aristocracy" to defeat ordinary white republicanism. Even the *Chicago Tribune,* which at times appeared sympathetic to abolitionism, presented the issue in starkly racial terms, asking its readers, "Are you for the freedom of the white Anglo-Saxon, or are you in favor of making slaves of us all? Are you in favor of the white man or are you for the slavery of him and his posterity forever?" The Republicans, the editors argued, had taken a bold stand against the "Black Democracy" in favor of free white labor, while their opponents facilitated "the onward march of the Southern despotism."[79]

A Victorious Defeat?

The final results of November's vote marked what some contemporaries and scholars have labeled a "victorious defeat" for the Republican Party.[80] Hampered by unfavorable districts, the Republicans in Illinois still secured four of nine state's congressional seats. Owen Lovejoy emerged among the victors, securing a majority of six thousand votes. While never fully abandoning his abolitionist views, Lovejoy would nevertheless prove a loyal ally of more moderate Republicans and apply the energy of the radicals to the party's shared goals. In addition, voters elected the entire Republican state ticket, with Bissell securing the governorship by more than two points. As expected, the Republicans performed remarkably well among Yankee-born voters in northern Illinois, with Frémont winning 74 percent of the vote in that region. The efforts of Koerner and other leading German American Republicans paid dividends as German Protestants voted for Frémont throughout the state. Irish immigrants remained overwhelmingly Democratic, except in several Chicago wards long dominated by Wentworth.[81]

Unfortunately for the Republicans, the most cautious ex-Whigs could not bring themselves to vote for Frémont and split their tickets to vote for both Bissell and Fillmore. Fillmore secured 15 percent of the vote throughout the state, with 37,595 to Frémont's 96,185 and Buchanan's 105,526. While Frémont won large concentrations of voters in densely populated northern Illinois, he struggled further downstate, and Fillmore outperformed Frémont in forty-five counties. As a result, Frémont won only 37 percent of the vote in central Illinois and trailed behind Buchanan for a plurality by four points. Southern Illinois, predictably, firmly rejected Frémont by a margin of three to one, and small pockets of German Americans proved the only reliable Republicans in the region.[82]

Fillmore's base of support reflected the strong desire for continuity among some former Whigs as well as the continued relevance of nativism. Although willing to back a former Democrat for governor, a significant number of voters preferred a reliable former Whig president to a glamorous adventurer with a Catholic-sounding surname. Nevertheless, translating the success of Bissell's gubernatorial campaign into future contests would become a top priority for Illinois Republicans. By focusing their appeal on the rights of free white men, steering away from charges of abolitionism, and reminding voters of their commitment to the government of the Founders, they could win the Prairie State.

The results of the election in Illinois reflected important trends in national politics. Frémont solid majorities in Illinois's northern counties mirrored the Pathfinder's convincing victories throughout the Upper North. Yet, just as Frémont struggled in the Prairie State's central counties, he also underperformed in the Border North states of Indiana, Pennsylvania, and New Jersey. Scholars have often framed the 1856 presidential election as two parallel contests, one between Frémont and Buchanan in the North and the other between Fillmore and Buchanan in the South.[83] Fillmore's strong showing in central and southern Illinois complicates this narrative and underscores the importance of the split-ticket Bissell and Fillmore voters to Republican fortunes at both the state and national levels. Instead of dismissing Fillmoreism as "a reactionary sentiment clothed in moderation," historians should seriously consider how Fillmore voters' own sense of moderation shaped the political trajectory of the Republican Party in Illinois and beyond.[84]

On the Democratic side, Buchanan's relative distance from the Nebraska controversy and the antiextension potential of popular sovereignty prevented many Northern conservatives from crossing over to the Republicans despite their opposition to Southern aggression. Stephen A. Douglas and other Northern Democrats could, for a moment, celebrate the public's faith in a united Democracy in the face of the violent outbursts in Kansas and Washington. Nevertheless, the political path forward for Douglas remained unclear. The defeat of Richardson, his close ally, in the gubernatorial contest stung deeply, and although the Little Giant had soldiered loyally for "Old Buck" in the fall's campaign, Buchanan disdained Douglas and distrusted his wing of the party. Writing to a trusted ally in the election's aftermath, Douglas emphasized the importance of promoting "a common cause" among all the "Constitutional-law-abiding-Union-loving men" and bringing them into the Democratic fold. The events of the past year had shown the power of rallying politically adrift Illinoisans to a defense of the Union and the rights of free white men in the face of sectional aggression. Douglas hoped that in the coming months, he could redirect this conservative instinct against "Fremont abolitionism." Yet the challenges of the coming year would make Douglas's task a Herculean endeavor.[85]

CHAPTER 4

NO MAN'S LAND

The mud squelched underfoot as Charles H. Lanphier crossed Adams Street and trudged toward his office. A January thaw had replaced the bitter cold and snow of the preceding days, shrouding the nearby statehouse in a layer of mist. The fog covering Springfield reflected the murky political horizon that clouded Lanphier's mind. The thirty-six-year-old editor of the *Illinois State Register* had been enmeshed in Democratic politics since his arrival in the state as a printer's apprentice two decades earlier, and he had seen his share of intraparty squabbles. Still, the recent letter from Congressman Thomas L. Harris, dated January 20, 1857, troubled him. Rumors in Washington suggested that the *Chicago Times* would have its government printing contracts, a vital subsidy for partisan newspapers, cut off. Other pro-Douglas organs, the *Peoria Union, Quincy Herald, Alton Democrat,* and *Cairo City Gazette,* might follow. Harris was right. The Douglas men would need to "clinch and grapple" to maintain their power both in Washington and at home.[1]

Distinguished historian Kenneth M. Stampp has rightly characterized the United States in 1857 as "a nation on the brink." The first year of James Buchanan's presidency, marked by the Dred Scott decision, the Panic of 1857, and the congressional battle over Kansas's Lecompton constitution, deepened sectional tensions and threatened to realign the political system yet again. Following an extended effort to accommodate President Buchanan and his pro-Southern administration, Douglas and the vast majority of Illinois Democrats ultimately broke with their president, casting themselves into the no man's land of national politics in the name of the "great principle" of popular sovereignty. Illinois Republicans, meanwhile, having rallied together in opposition to Buchanan, Douglas, and the Taney court, found themselves in turmoil at the end of the year as the Panic of 1857 revived old economic questions, and their greatest enemy took their side in the debate over Kansas. For those ex-Whigs and Know-Nothings who had voted for Fillmore the previous November, the political horizon appeared as murky as ever as their independent political organizations faltered and their rivals appeared to converge. As they struggled to distinguish friend from foe and mired themselves in conspiracies, Illinois's partisans worked to stake out a centrist position as true conservatives—as defenders of the Union and free white labor.[2]

A New Year of Uncertainty

As the new year dawned, the *Illinois State Journal* editors encouraged a tempered optimism among their Republican readers. Looking back on the setbacks of 1856, William Bailhache and Edward L. Baker encouraged Illinoisans to remember that "a first disappointment should never dishearten" and to "not suppose that momentary difficulties, or even a year's misfortunes are without their uses." Their perspective reflected the mixed result of the 1856 elections, in which the Illinois Republicans garnered sufficient support from conservative Know-Nothings and ex-Whigs to win the gubernatorial contest even as the state's anti-Democratic vote split between Millard Fillmore and John C. Frémont in the presidential race. Although enough to win the state's electoral votes, Buchanan's 44 percent plurality did not compare favorably to Franklin Pierce's majority of nearly 52 percent in 1852. A path to victory appeared open for the Republicans in the statewide contests of 1858 and 1860, but only if they could consolidate anti-Democratic voters into a single party.[3]

Yet, in recognizing that the fledging party had benefitted immensely from the popular outcry against slaveholder aggression in Kansas and Congress, one might reasonably have wondered whether popular agitation over slavery's extension might fade in the succeeding months. Should Kansas enter the Union as a free state under the provisions of popular sovereignty—an outcome that seemed likely, given the preferences of the territory's actual settlers—the Northern public might dismiss further antiextensionist rhetoric as aggressive abolitionism rather than a principled defense of free expression and free white labor. While the new Republican governor, William H. Bissell, offered some token support to the state's Black population, petitioning Louisiana authorities for the release of a free Black Illinoisan held in New Orleans as a fugitive slave,

Henry O. Wagoner and other Black abolitionists in Illinois recognized the profound limitations on the Republican's antislavery position and organized in January for their own convention of Radical Abolitionists. In early 1857, Douglas's organ, the *Chicago Times,* reminded its "republican neighbors" that "in less than one year from the present time, Kansas, Minnesota, and Oregon will be admitted into the union as free states, and shortly afterwards Nebraska and Washington will be admitted in the same manner." Illinois Democrats, with some justification, believed these victories for free labor would vindicate popular sovereignty and put an end to agitation over slavery's extension. Republican leader David Davis agreed, writing with frustration that he "[took] it for granted that the Democratic Party [would] always be in power" as they had "no settled principles of action" and could adjust their policies to the whims of voters, even if it contradicted their earlier intentions.[4]

In the wake of the national Democratic triumph that had secured the White House and majorities in both houses of the Thirty-Fifth Congress, one might have expected that Douglas and the Illinois Democrats would also project optimism heading into 1857. Yet, as president-elect Buchanan prepared to take office, the prospects for Douglas and his Northwestern supporters appeared bleak. Deeply hostile to Douglas both personally and politically, Buchanan passed over the Little Giant's favorite for a cabinet post, former congressman and defeated gubernatorial candidate William A. Richardson, and opted for a slate of Southerners and anti-Douglas Northerners. In a letter to Lanphier shortly after the new year, Congressman Thomas L. Harris had gloomily noted that "the weight of the cabinet is against us," and while he hoped it would not "hurt D[ouglas] at all," the slight would "create a fuss in the country that we cannot afford to stand." Directing the Northwest's patronage toward friends of the avowedly pro-Southern Indiana senator Jesse D. Bright, Buchanan had all but declared war on the party's Douglas wing. Always ready for a fight, Douglas pledged that he would "return every blow they may give" and would "neither ask nor give quarter." But it remained unclear how Douglas could deliver such blows without further jeopardizing his standing in national Democratic circles. No doubt Douglas did his best to temper his frustration with the outcomes of 1856 with his hopes for 1860 when he hoped control of the Democratic Party might finally pass from the old-guard Jacksonians to the champions of an economically vibrant and territorially expansive Young America.[5]

Popular Sovereignty's Free-Soil Potential

In the lame-duck session of the Thirty-Fourth Congress, Douglas turned his attention to westward expansion, championing enabling acts for the Minnesota and Oregon Territories. For Douglas and boosters of Chicago, the rapid development of Minnesota's agriculture promised to help make the city "the great commercial mart of the northwest," and the Democratic *Ottawa Free Trader* praised the territory as having the "finest soil in the United States" for farmers and also noted the bright prospects for artisans in the rapidly expanding river towns of St. Paul, St. Anthony, and St. Peter. In short, Minnesota's qualities—fertile soil for industrious yeomen, customers for tradesmen, and commerce for merchants and manufacturers—made good on the promises of the West for ordinary white men.[6]

Yet, in the debate over Minnesota's enabling act, these same features drew the ire of Kentucky senator John B. Thompson. A Southern Know-Nothing eager to display his proslavery credentials to his constituents and embarrass his Democratic rivals, Thompson argued that Minnesota, as a portion of the Louisiana Purchase, ought to remain open to slavery and that if it did not—as it would not—then Congress should refuse to admit it. Utterly disgusted with "free soilism," Thompson urged Congress to dismiss the desires of Minnesota's free white settlers and instead "rule them as Great Britain rules Affghanistan, Hindoostan and all through Punjaub, making them work for you as you would work a negro on a cotton or sugar plantation." Denouncing Minnesotans as latter-day Huns, he insisted, "They are that same northern race which ... overran the Roman Empire" and would, like "prairie wolves," eventually "invade the South" and abolish slavery.[7]

In his response to Thompson, Douglas took the opportunity to detail the democratic and constitutional nature of popular sovereignty, arguing that the entry of Minnesota or any other free state into the Union did no wrong to the South so long as the actual settlers chose to abolish slavery. Fiercely denouncing the idea that the nation needed to balance free states and slave states, Douglas called the demand for a sectional equilibrium "contrary to the principles of the Constitution" and "to the principles of state equality and self-government." The Little Giant asserted that Thompson had "no more right to insist upon having slavery tolerated in Minnesota, than [Douglas had] to insist on having slavery abolished in Kentucky." To deny free white people their just rights because more of "the territory acquired by our ancestors by the Revolution" had "been devoted to free labor than slave labor" violated every tenet of white male democracy. Douglas, like most of his constituents, could tolerate Southerners enslaving Blacks in their own states, but he would not allow slaveholders to force the institution onto the free white men of the North. In a fair test of the two systems, free labor had triumphed over slavery. It might well do so again in every other territory, but as long as Congress did not impose its will on these distant regions, Southern slaveholders had no grounds to cry foul.[8]

The exchange between Thompson and Douglas produced few headlines, with most editors dismissing the Kentuckian's hyperbole as bluster. In a sign of the persisting importance of nativism, many more newspapers focused on whether the new state would allow unnaturalized foreigners to vote.[9] Still, their arguments foreshadowed fiercer debates. While many recent historians have labeled Douglas as proslavery, his tolerance for Black bondage extended only so far. In the minds of many Southerners of both parties, freedom could not exist without Black slavery as the right to property, including property in man, superseded all other rights. But for Douglas and most Northwestern Democrats, imposing Black slavery on a community without popular support among free white men violated white freedom. Closer in this sense to their Republican enemies than to their Southern copartisans, Douglas Democrats resented the presumption of slaveholders to restrict white freedom in the West. In early 1857, this resentment among Northwestern Democrats had not risen to a level sufficient to overcome their deep hostility to the Republicans, but the tension undoubtedly existed, simmering uneasily on the back burner of national politics.[10]

For the time being, however, most partisans focused on President Buchanan, who took the oath of office on March 4, 1857. Despite the friction between Douglas and the president, Illinois's Democratic press heartily praised Buchanan's inaugural address. Unwilling to acknowledge a potential sectional division in their own party, the state's Democrats heard only what they wanted to hear in the president's first public address. Although Buchanan had announced in his speech that he favored the South's more limited interpretation of popular sovereignty, allowing the people of a territory to vote to restrict slavery only when "the actual number of settlers in the Territory shall justify the formation of a constitution," the *Rock Island Argus* nevertheless thought that the address confirmed the Northern interpretation of popular sovereignty and promised that "the people of a territory, like the people of a state, shall be protected in the exercise of their rights, against all outside interference." In another selective reading of the address, the *Randolph County Democrat* believed Buchanan had confirmed their argument "that the Democratic party, as a party, could not truly be charged with favoring the extension of slavery." Predictably, the state's Republicans espoused a dourer view of the new chief executive, with the *Chicago Tribune* bitterly denouncing Buchanan as "servile and compliant" and "subservient to Southern dictation" as he selected a cabinet of "contemptible calibre." The *Pantagraph* of Bloomington found in the president's address, "the craftiness of the practiced diplomat in almost every paragraph, loopholes of escape from embarrassing conclusions very plentifully provided."[11]

The Dred Scott Decision

Buchanan's duplicity appeared even more apparent to Illinois Republicans following the announcement of the Supreme Court's decision in *Dred Scott v. Sandford*. Enslaved by an army surgeon named John Emerson, Dred Scott had followed his enslaver to his posts in the free state of Illinois and in the free territory of what would become Minnesota. Bringing suit against Emerson's widow in 1846, Scott argued that his residence on free soil had freed him and his family. Gradually working its way through the court system in the succeeding decade, Dred Scott's case had placed profound questions of Black rights and the constitutionality of slavery in the territories before the Supreme Court. In an infamous majority opinion issued just two days after Buchanan's ascension to the presidency, Chief Justice Roger B. Taney not only denied that Scott had a right to sue in Federal court on the basis of his race but claimed that any congressional restriction of slavery in the territories violated the rights to property enjoyed by all US citizens under the Bill of Rights. Ignoring decades of precedent and brazenly dismissing public opinion, Taney retroactively nullified the Missouri Compromise of 1820 and declared the Republican Party's chief plank unconstitutional. Taney added that territorial legislatures, as the creations of Congress, could not act against slavery either. Only when a territory drafted its state constitution and applied for admission to the Union could it choose to restrict, limit, or prohibit slavery. Overtly partisan and sectional, the decision cut down the positions of both the Republicans and most Northern Democrats in one fell swoop.[12]

The sharp racial boundary defined by the decision inspired a sustained reaction only among Illinois's small group of radical abolitionists. Eager to point to the absurdity of Taney's argument that "the negro might justly and lawfully be reduced to slavery" and "treated as an ordinary article of merchandise and traffic," a Chicago attorney cleverly embraced the decision as he argued a case in April claiming that his clients, fugitive slaves arrested in the city for stealing poultry, could not face punishment as "the defendants being chattels, not *persons,* are consequently incapable of committing crime." Though the court rejected this argument and continued to prosecute the fugitives, the local jury ultimately found them not guilty of larceny.[13]

The Illinois Republican press, while shocked by Taney's audacity and appalled by the decision's implications, interpreted the Dred Scott decision as an overt attempt by slaveholders and their Northern lackeys to establish slavery throughout the West. The *Belvidere Standard* argued that by extending the reach of slavery, Taney had reversed "the policy of the brave and liberty-loving spirits who founded this Republic." Convinced that Buchanan, who had alluded to the decision in his inaugural address, had influenced the decision, the *Chicago Tribune* railed that "by this conspiracy . . . the leaders of the sham Democratic party" had despoiled the Constitution and left "its very life-blood sucked out of it." Reflecting its Jacksonian heritage, John E. "Long John" Wentworth's *Chicago Democrat* saw the decision as a dangerous step toward centralization, an "encroachment upon State rights and State sovereignty" animated by "the spirit of federalism." Some former Whig papers also understood the decision as a threat to Northern state sovereignty, darkly forecasting that a future decision of the court might extend slavery into all states. As the *Pantagraph* of Bloomington explained, "one little step only remains; to decide all *State* prohibitions of slavery to be void," thus completing the "enslavement" of the free white North to the Slave Power.[14]

Although no evidence existed to support the Republican claim that the South hoped to extend slavery into the free states, their fear appears more rational when placed into a broader context. Even as they took up elements of the so-called paranoid style, indicting their opponents as conspirators set on undermining the Constitution and American liberty, Illinois Republicans believed they had good reason to fear the encroachment of slavery. In a few short years, the repeal of the Missouri Compromise, the disintegration of the Second Party System, and the violence of Bleeding Kansas had overturned decades' worth of sectional accommodation. As territory reserved for freedom became a domain for slavery, and as slaveholders asserted their "rights" by shedding the blood of white Northerners on the plains of Kansas and in the halls of Congress, Republicans felt increasingly under siege.

While they viewed the political system as under threat from forces within the government, as conservatives, Republicans needed to walk a fine when denouncing the decisions of the highest court in the land. Committed to preserving the constitutional order, if not the current status quo, some in the party dismissed Taney's ruling on slavery in the territories as mere obiter dictum. They claimed that the first half of the Dred Scott decision, which contended that Scott, as a Black man, had no right to file suit, had fully resolved the case. Having thus decided against Scott, Taney could not consistently rule on the territorial issue. Such an interpretation allowed Republicans to reject the most uncomfortable aspect of the case for Northern white men without assaulting the authority of the Supreme Court.[15]

Yet, most Illinois Republicans also recognized that to regain control of the court and reverse the decision, they would need to enlarge their coalition and win victories at the ballot box. Without a change on the high bench, George T. Brown of the *Alton Courier* predicted that the Supreme Court would continue to advance the "grand conspiracy against freedom" and "in any future controversy before their tribunal" would "carry the doctrine of the supremacy of slavery much further." In Springfield, the editors of the *Illinois State Journal* hoped that this Democratic overreach might draw Fillmore voters into the Republican fold, gleefully noting "a revolution among the American Party papers" in the East as previously mild opponents of the Kansas-Nebraska Act now firmly committed themselves to prevent slavery's extension. The *Waukegan Gazette* noted that with slavery effectively nationalized by the Supreme Court, "nothing but public sentiment now hinders the slaveholder from going into any of the territories or States of this Union, and holding his slaves there." The state's Republicans could only hope that public outrage would continue to run hot and "melt the mass of the people into one great irresistible party of freedom."[16]

Illinois's Democrats also placed their faith in public opinion, though they interpreted the situation through a radically different lens. According to Douglas and his allies, the people of Illinois could revel in the decision as "an entire condemnation of sectionalism . . . in favor of a broad, conservative, constitutional nationalism." Although the ruling might generate a "last dying kick of fanatical sectionalism," from their Republican rivals, their efforts would ultimately come to naught. A combination of misinformation, racial bigotry, and misplaced faith in the power of free labor allowed the state's Democrats to embrace the Dred Scott decision, despite that it appeared as if Taney's expansive interpretation of the Fifth Amendment had struck down their understanding of popular sovereignty in the territories alongside congressional restriction. The *Ottawa Free Trader* admitted that it would have preferred "if the supreme court had decided that the territories were by the law of nature free, and that congress could neither establish nor prohibit slavery in them" but urged citizens to submit and reminded them that "practically . . . the decision amounts to nothing" as ultimately "the people of the territories shall regulate this subject for themselves." The people of the free states had nothing to fear from Dred Scott because free labor would ultimately triumph, thanks to the laws of political economy.[17]

Indeed, juxtaposing themselves with the shrill warnings of the Republicans, Illinois Democrats argued that white Northerners could relax and allow nature to take its course. The *Mount Carmel Register* explained that even as the Dred Scott decision might establish "the theoretical expansion of slavery North and West," it would never expand the institution's actual boundaries. To the contrary, the paper observed that "free labor is marching with a very tangible step into the heart of the strongholds of slavery" and predicted that the migration of free farmers and artisans to the border slave states would soon extinguish the institution in Delaware, Missouri, Kentucky, and even Virginia. Adding a dash of humor to the column, the editor noted that it would "take a good many Supreme Courts to reverse a law of nature" and concluded that the Supreme Court could afford to respect the Constitutional rights of slaveholders because "practically, slavery is doomed, and must give way before the march of free labor." Even deep in Little Egypt, the region with the most cultural and political affinity for the slaveholding South, Cairo's Democratic *Times and Delta* thought slavery would wilt away in time. In fact, it blamed radical abolitionists, rather than their support for Southern rights, for undermining gradual emancipation in the slaveholding border states, suggesting that "if, during these last twenty-five years, slavery had been let alone as it had been before—to be treated as it was treated in Jefferson and Madison's day—Missouri, Kentucky, Delaware, Virginia and Maryland would have now been free states." The "self-interest" of the citizens of these states would lead them to adopt free labor as soon as the abolitionists abandoned their misguided crusade.[18]

Creatively repurposing the rhetoric of national expansion, Illinois Democrats claimed, "The manifest destiny of Virginia is to be a free state." Utterly contemptuous of William Lloyd Garrison and "his colleagues who disgrace themselves" without advancing the "cause of human freedom one hair's breadth" by their railings against the South, they insisted that the white laborer's "superior industry and intelligence" would displace enslaved Black labor wherever the climate allowed. The gradual migration of free white Northern labor into states like Virginia would "accomplish a great and glorious reform, a reform, which, sooner or later, must take place." Given this fact, an experience authenticated by the North's own gradual abolition of slavery several decades before, Illinois Democrats believed abolitionists and Republicans had a hidden agenda driving their attack on the abstract rights of slaveholders, and the particulars of the Dred Scott decision seemed to offer some hints.[19]

Reviving an accusation from the campaign of 1856, some Illinois Democrats argued that the Republicans latched onto public prejudices, whether against slavery, immigrants, or alcohol, simply to seize power and that they, in fact, lacked any genuine commitment to these causes. In the case of Dred Scott, the Democratic press took advantage of the fact that the widow of Scott's original owner, at one time the defendant in the case, had married a Republican congressman from Massachusetts named Calvin C. Chaffee. The *Randolph County Democrat* implied that Chaffee had manipulated Scott by refusing to manumit him and instead pressured the Supreme Court into a controversial ruling in order to bolster the prospects of his party in future elections. Far from serving as their friends, Republicans merely used African Americans as props in a political drama. A few months later, the *Ottawa Free Trader* leveled a similar critique against Republicans at the Minnesota state constitutional convention, inquiring why they had denounced "that part of the Dred Scott decision which declares that negroes are not citizens as an outrage" only to then "refuse themselves to confer citizenship on negroes in Minnesota" by limiting suffrage in the state to white men. Of course, the alternative of awarding civil and political rights to African Americans horrified most white men of both parties throughout the Northwest. Although it challenged their claim to Republican opportunism, Illinois Democrats also rallied against Republicans as closet abolitionists covertly intent on racial egalitarianism.[20]

In a June 12 address in Springfield, Stephen A. Douglas focused on the first portion of the Dred Scott decision, denying that Black Americans had any rights that "a white man was bound to respect." Reveling in the racism of his audience, Douglas harangued Republicans for including Blacks in the Declaration of Independence's pledge that "all men were created equal" and insisted that as each of the thirteen colonies had permitted slavery in its borders at the time of the Declaration's adoption, none could have intended to include "the negroes and all other inferior races" in the promise of universal equality and self-government. In deference to his audience's dislike of slavery, Douglas quickly added, "It does follow by any means that because the negro race are incapable of governing themselves that therefore they should become slaves and be treated as such" and endorsed the "wise and just policy of Illinois" in prohibiting slavery. Indeed, by excluding Blacks altogether, Illinois avoided any intermixture of the races, whereas the elevation of African Americans to citizenship would inevitably lead to "amalgamation" in social and political contexts. Douglas insisted that all reasonable white Americans could agree that the mixing of the races constituted a "degraded, demoralizing disease" and could therefore agree that any effort to include African Americans in the body politic would poison, rather than complete, American freedom.[21]

Even as he sought to focus the attention of his audience on its racial animosity, Douglas could not avoid the questions surrounding the nature of popular sovereignty created by the Taney ruling. For years, Douglas had promised Illinoisans that the people of the territories would decide whether to allow slavery in their midst. Now, Taney's ruling appeared to open all of the federal territories to slavery at all times, limited only by the adoption of a free-state constitution at the end of the territorial stage of government. Seemingly poised to run aground on the shoals of slaveholders' constitutional rights, Douglas navigated around the issue by insisting slavery existed only through positive law. As such, he argued that although Southerners might retain the abstract right to bring the enslaved into the federal territories, it "necessarily remains a barren and a worthless right, unless sustained, protected, and enforced by appropriate police regulations and local legislation." As a result, the people of a territory retained their right to settle the issue of slavery on the basis of popular sovereignty, as any such regulation "must necessarily depend on the wishes of the people of the territory" and could "only be prescribed by local legislatures." Although this peculiar interpretation of Dred Scott would outrage Southern Democrats in the months and years ahead, at the time, it created more headaches for Illinois Republicans.[22]

By maintaining that even under the Dred Scott ruling, popular sovereignty could still produce a free-soil outcome and redirecting the public's attention to the issue of racial equality, Douglas forced Illinois Republicans to refine their critique of the decision. Responding directly to Douglas's speech in Springfield in his own address before the town two weeks later, Lincoln argued that the Declaration of Independence's promise of universal rights included all men, irrespective of race, but he also emphasized that it could never create equality among Blacks and whites in the United States. The declaration declared a universal right for people to rid themselves of tyrannical authority. Intended to inspire a movement for self-determination and personal freedom around the world, it promised equal access to "certain inalienable rights, among which are life, liberty, and the pursuit of happiness" and checked despotism. According to Lincoln, the declaration recognized that slavery, like the rule of kings and lords, infringed on these fundamental rights and declared the truth nonetheless. They could "not confer it immediately" but instead sought to "set up a standard maxim for free society, which should be familiar to all . . . even though never perfectly attained." Slavery had existed within the original states, and the Founders had allowed it to remain, for fear that the cure might prove worse than the disease, but they did not intend to allow the malignancy of bondage to expand unchecked.[23]

Yet, as Lincoln then emphasized, this equal commitment to "life, liberty, and the pursuit of happiness" by no means made men "equal in color, size, intellect, moral developments, or social capacity." Noting the horror Douglas expressed at the thought of interracial sex, Lincoln "agreed—a thousand times agreed" but countered that "a separation of the races is the only perfect preventative of amalgamation but as an immediate separation is impossible the next best thing is to keep them apart where they are not already together." Thus, those who sought to check slavery's extension also hoped to prevent any inappropriate intercourse between whites and Blacks. Adopting the solution of Thomas Jefferson and Henry Clay, Lincoln advocated for a program of voluntary colonization and argued that once the government had removed the financial incentive of selling the enslaved westward, masters might find it in their self-interest to fund deportation to Liberia.[24]

Such a position made perfect sense to the white men of Illinois in 1857. Having internalized the idea of equality and fair play within their democratic society, few would argue for the inherent merits of slavery. Setting the enslaved aside, the institution created a quasi-aristocratic class hostile to republicanism. Thus, even for those most concerned with maintaining the rights and sovereignty of the slaveholding states, the containment of slavery seemed desirable. Nevertheless, their racial prejudice, based, in their own minds, on the dictates of natural science, Divine law, or both, automatically excluded the possibility of a functional biracial democracy. As such, only a program of containment and deportation would "liberate" free white men from the dual threat of slavery and racial integration.

On June 27, the day following Lincoln's address, Lyman Trumbull sought to further distance his party from social radicalism and focused instead on the threat posed by the Slave Power. Although some Republicans in northern Illinois fostered sympathy for the enslaved and sought to elevate Blacks, in the tradition of New England radicals, Trumbull and the mainstream of the Illinois Republican Party had no such interest. Confident his audience would agree, Trumbull said he would not argue "with Judge Taney or any one else, as to the degradation of the negro race" and rejected any association with the "repulsive notions" of "allowing intermarriages between the races" or "placing negroes . . . on a level of the white race." Such ideas formed "no part of the Republican creed," as the party's only goal remained to protect "free white men from contamination with negro slavery, by keeping it out of the territories." Trumbull then sought to turn the tables on Douglas by intimating that his proposal for popular sovereignty under Dred Scott would inevitably lead to racial anarchy. He mocked this "precious right" that would "permit negro slaves to run at large, uncontrolled by local legislation." He insisted that if forced to accept Black slavery in their community, any reasonable white person would "greatly prefer having proper police regulations in their midst," and he presciently questioned whether slaveholders would "thank one of their colaborers for intimating that they are not entitled to such protection." For this reason, America's "Revolutionary ancestors" had given Congress "complete power to prevent [slavery's] introduction into the territories" so as save them from the evils of slavery while still maintaining "the peace and good order of society."[25]

Warming to his theme, Trumbull insisted that preserving the West for freedom represented the Founders' true intent, a sound and conservative policy that "the self-styled Democracy" now hoped to undermine by "making the extension of African slavery the grand object and end of the government." Slavery ought to remain "a local Southern institution, as it was considered by all parties prior to 1854." In an appeal true to his Jacksonian roots, Trumbull called upon "the People" directly as "a power and higher and above" the Supreme Court to protect "the rights of white men" against the Slave Power and the influence of "ten thousand federal officers feeding upon the treasury pap" that had corrupted the free states. These conspirators would not stop until the voters of Illinois vindicated their rights and restored order to the country. Far from bringing about disunion, Republican triumphs in future elections would restore sectional balance to the Union and safeguard the nation's future.

It is important to note that the racism of Trumbull and his constituents had dire consequences. Several weeks after the speeches, the *Illinois State Chronicle* of Decatur reported on a group of twenty white citizens in Cairo who had attacked local free Blacks, intending to kidnap and sell them into slavery in neighboring Missouri or Kentucky. They succeeded in carrying off at least two people of color to Missouri, though one man subsequently escaped and returned to Cairo, wandering into town "naked as he was born, and horribly mangled about the head." In a tremendous act of courage, the small local Black population resisted, firing on kidnappers with pistols as they attacked a Black home, and wounded one of the assailants. The *Chronicle*, a Republican paper, did condemn Cairo's overwhelmingly Democratic citizens for their actions but noted that "there was no question of the supremacy of the white man" at stake. Rather than taking a stand against racism, the editor objected to "midnight rioting" and violating the laws. Reflecting the underlying temperamental and racial conservatism of mainstream Republicans, the *Chronicle* presented the suffering of free people of color as secondary to the question of whether "the laws of the State of Illinois should be upheld, and the peace of the people secured."[26]

Within their respective addresses critiquing the Dred Scott decision, Lincoln and Trumbull launched a more pointed attack on Douglas by gesturing toward the glaring failures of popular sovereignty in Utah and Kansas. In the former territory, Mormon settlers, under the leadership of Brigham Young, had created a theocratic regime hostile to religious dissenters (so-called gentiles). Although polygamy ("plural marriage") had emerged as a practice among Mormons before the sect's migration to the Great Salt Lake, the Latter-Day Saints' Reformation of 1856–57 promoted such marriages and increased their prevalence within the community. This surge in Mormon piety further alienated outsiders, and by the spring of 1857, the Mormons had ousted federal officials and seemed on the verge of open rebellion. In response, Douglas had called for repealing Utah's territorial status and the implementation of a coercive policy to bring the Mormons back under federal control. As Lincoln noted, this stance clearly undermined the Democrats' "much vaunted doctrine of self-government for the territories." Public opinion throughout the Union would not allow the Mormons to practice polygamy unchecked, and so the federal government would intervene to block it. If Douglas could admit this, why could he not apply the same principle to slavery in Kansas?[27]

While Lincoln questioned the underlying logic of popular sovereignty through the example of Utah, Trumbull offered a forceful critique of the doctrine as applied in Kansas. Although open hostilities in the territory had subsided since the chaos of 1856, Republicans still objected to the territory's proslavery legislature, which had installed itself through fraud and maintained its legitimacy by the threat of force from either Missouri border ruffians or federal troops. With his own roots in the populist Democracy, Trumbull recognized the appeal of popular sovereignty as an assertion of local autonomy. Detailing the fraught experiences of Kansas's actual free-state settlers, he hoped to flip Douglas's argument on its head. Trumbull insisted that the Kansas-Nebraska Act had not empowered Kansans but instead had disenfranchised them and exposed them to violent intimidation. He blasted "an administration and a party which can enforce laws to protect slavery, but refuses to enforce those which protect freemen." The struggle in Kansas between the officially recognized territorial government and the free-state party's shadow government went beyond merely the future status of slavery there. According to Trumbull, the infringements on civil liberties and voting rights by proslavery partisans had made the question: "Shall the white population be permitted to assert their rights, or shall they be enslaved by a cunningly devised system of fraud and violence?" In light of the upcoming Kansas Constitutional Convention, this question had taken on a new urgency.[28]

Several weeks earlier, the free-state men in Kansas had boycotted the election of delegates to the convention, scheduled to meet in Lecompton in September, so as not to recognize the legitimacy of the proslavery territorial legislature. This outcome disappointed Illinois Democrats, who had hoped that the free-state men, many of whom had been Democrats before moving to the territory, would appeal to the "aid of the free state sentiment among the masses of the national democracy" rather than pursue "the no-voting, do-nothing policy of the abolitionists." Indeed, the *Rock Island Argus* had boasted that the Republicans were "terribly exercised by the fear that [Kansas] will become a free state" should everyone participate in the election and thus rob them of a campaign hobbyhorse. Yet, despite the setback, Illinois Democrats felt little trepidation about the eventual entry of Kansas into the Union as a free state. Since they believed that any state constitution drafted by the Lecompton body would have to be approved by the people in a general referendum, as promised by the new territorial governor, Robert J. Walker, it seemed reasonable to believe that the free-state majority of actual settlers would assert itself at that time. Indeed, even after the botched election for seats at the convention, Illinois Democrats believed they could rest easy as some of the Southern Democratic papers appeared to write off any chance of securing Kansas for slavery.[29]

Illinois Republicans, meanwhile, continued to sound the alarm that the Buchanan administration had slated Kansas to enter the Union as a slave state, regardless of the will of its actual settlers. A *Chicago Tribune* correspondent fretted, "if the [Lecompton] Constitution is to be submitted to the people, we wish to know WHAT people it is to be submitted to." After all, had not the Democrats represented the previous elections as the "will of the people," regardless of what proportion of the population had actually voted? A correspondent of Trumbull similarly suspected that the new administration would try to foist slavery upon the territory, noting that "Buchanan is doing up his dirty work finely, doing every thing for the South, and entirely disregarding the interest of the North." He hoped that in such an event, the Northern Democrats would "finally be convinced that the whole policy of Government is administration with a view to the interest of the South" and would unite with Republicans "in defence of the rights of the North," but he could not count on it.[30]

According to the Republican press, this covert effort to assist in slavery's expansion marked a profound shift away from the intentions of the Founding Fathers. As framed by the *Illinois State Journal,* when the United States adopted the Constitution, "slavery was universally acknowledged to be a great moral, social and political evil." Still, since the states lacked the resources necessary to bring about a peaceful end to the institution, "slavery in a land of freedom was explained and justified only upon the plea of necessity." The Southern states might still lack the resources to end slavery within their own borders, and the Republicans would not force them to do so. Nevertheless, the Republicans would oppose the "ultra creed of Calhoun" that sought "to carry out a universal *extension of slavery*" as it represented "a radical change" in the institution's protection under the Constitution. Although it might have "been necessary to *tolerate* slavery in the union, it was plainly not necessary to *extend* and spread out the evil." In a similar vein, the *Chicago Tribune* noted that it pitied but did not judge the "Christian slaveholder [who] weeps and prays over an intuition, of which they see all the evils." The editor believed that such men, like Washington and Jefferson, could "[be held] neither ... responsible nor accountable" for having such a burden thrust on them. Yet, he heartily condemned "those men of the North who meekly apologize for and who labor actively for the spread of this work of Satan." For Illinois Republicans, American slavery remained an unresolvable dilemma but one that ought to remain confined, as the frames of the Constitution intended, to those regions that it had already contaminated.[31]

Yet, it seemed to Republicans that the Southern slavocrats and their Northern lackeys would stop at nothing to spread slavery. When Buchanan's choice for Kansas's territorial governor, Walker, promised a fair vote up or down on slavery in the territory in his inaugural address, Democrats in Mississippi—the state Walker had represented in the US Senate—denounced the speech as "dictatorial intermeddling" and "unjust and uncalled for discrimination against the rights and interest of the proslavery party in Kansas and throughout the Union." The Republican *Central Transcript* of Clinton suspected that Walker or Buchanan would soon equivocate on that promise and find "some hole through which to creep and get back fairly upon Southern ground, and slave favor." Convinced that Fire Eating Southerners could drive the Northern Democrats to a submissive humiliation, Illinois Republicans found "the present silly shuffle" by the administration both "foolish and dishonest."[32]

Furthermore, by presenting this case, Republican leaders hoped to convince wavering Douglas Democrats that popular sovereignty was a fraud. Having long suspected that Democratic commitment to majority rule would prove hollow, they all but welcomed the opportunity to show misguided Illinois Democrats the error of their ways. Once awakened to the hollowness of popular sovereignty, some of these voters might join them and block the attempts of "ultra" slaveholders to undermine republican government.

A Fair Vote for Kansas

Douglas felt confident in Walker and the Democracy's commitment to popular sovereignty in Kansas. Whatever his differences with the Buchanan administration, Douglas thought Walker, an expansionist Young American and longtime ally, recognized the importance of popular sovereignty and of bringing Kansas into the Union as a Democratic state. He believed that free- state Democrats in Kansas would let bygones be bygones so long as they could fairly vote to approve or reject their new state constitution. The *Ottawa Free Trader* agreed, writing, "By the aid of the free state sentiment among the masses of the national democracy, they [free-state Kansans] can effect more than by pursuing the no-voting, do-nothing policy of the abolitionists." Writing to Walker, Douglas acknowledged that the Lecompton Convention contained an unrepresentative body of delegates, but he insisted that they would "adopt some just rule upon this subject [of voting qualifications] and form such a constitution as a majority of the people will ratify" as they surely realized that "it is all important that constitution shall make such a constitution as the people will ratify, and thus terminate the controversy." Given the territory's demographics, the free white men of Kansas would adopt a constitution that prohibited slavery if given a fair vote, and this inevitable outcome had apparently caused some consternation in the South. Yet Douglas insisted that the malcontents "were in fact dissatisfied with the national administration" on matters such as "the formation of the Cabinet and the distribution of patronage" rather than with popular sovereignty and white men's democracy. After all, Douglas also had his own disagreements with Buchanan, but that would not prevent him from resolutely standing on the promise made to the white men of Kansas in the Cincinnati Platform of 1856.[33]

The state's Democratic press seemed equally sanguine, as the *Ottawa Free Trader* praised the territorial governor's conduct and dismissed the Southern Democratic opposition to Walker as "a contemptible minority" that had "always been a dead weight on the democratic party." The *Rock Island Argus* called Walker's course "eminently just and fair" and turned its attention back to their Republican opponents, dryly remaking that in such an "emergency something must be done by the [antislavery] agitators, or Kansas would become quietly a free state." Eager to distinguish between those in favor of a free state and the ardent backers of the Topeka government, the *Argus* concurred with a Kansas paper and noted that the "majority of the people [of Kansas] belong to no political organization, and are simply in principle, in favor of securing the admission of Kansas into the Union as a free state." Such an outcome could, and it appeared, would occur, especially after a convention of free-state men agreed to participate in that fall's upcoming election for a new territorial legislature, accepting Walker's contention that the election originated by an act of Congress rather than a resolution of the "bogus" proslavery territorial legislature that had governed the state for the past two years. This development found favor even in Republican journals, as the *Quincy Whig* approvingly reprinted the resolutions. Although a confrontation between Walker and the free-state municipal government of Lawrence in late July dampened spirits temporarily, it still seemed to most that Kansas would enter the Union as a free state under the auspices of popular sovereignty.[34]

Within this environment, as Douglas and the Democrats seemed poised to welcome Kansas into the Union as a free state with the consent of the South and emerge as champions of the Union, some Illinois Republicans felt the need to reassure themselves of their own moderate credentials. In a letter to Joseph Gillespie, Governor Bissell wondered whether publishing a note sent to him by Henry Clay during the crisis of 1850 and endorsed by the pro-Compromise Whigs Daniel Webster, John J. Crittenden, and John Bell would relieve "those who thought and acted with [him] from the charge of being abolitionists." Two days later, the *Illinois State Journal* reminded the world that "the Republican party is essentially a conservative and defensive party—that it was born and it lives to prevent innovations, not to make them." The *Journal*'s editors, perhaps believing their readers might lose interest in the contest, insisted that the political struggle in Kansas would not end "until the Democracy abandon their novel claims and fall back upon their old position and policy [of free soil], in which the honest and considerate and truly conservative masses can consistently sustain them." In addition to this appeal to political conservatism, the *Journal* bolstered its racial conservatism by dismissing charges made in the Democratic *Illinois State Register* that it promoted "negro equality" and sought to "hurl the charge back in its face," as only "the Register's own Southern friends" sought racial equality by being "the only amalgamationists in the country." Such diatribes also appeared in northern Illinois. The *Chicago Tribune* held that "the only appreciable difference between the amalgamation doctrine held by the n——-making Democracy and the doctrines held by the Garrisonians" was that "Garrison and his friends believe that before amalgamation begins, marriage should unite the amalgamating parties." By accusing the Democrats of promoting illicit interracial sex, the Republicans reasserted their claims of moral superiority and white supremacy simultaneously.[35]

Mainstream Republicans throughout Illinois perceived themselves as squarely in the center of the political spectrum. In making their claim to represent the conservative mass of ordinary voters, they worked to discredit "ultras"—whether abolitionists or proslavery Democrats—who, in their minds, threatened to tear the country apart. While historians have often pointed out that Republicans engaged in racist demagoguery less frequently than did their Democratic opponents, the evidence reveals that party leaders would lash out when they felt threatened by Democratic success.

The Republican reassertion of racial conservatism frustrated Illinois's few abolitionists and alarmed some Democrats, who always hoped to capitalize on the state's strong racial prejudice. The abolitionist *Congregational Herald* of Chicago lambasted Republican members of the legislature for voting for "Freedom in Kansas" while preserving "Slavery in Illinois" by refusing to "expunge the Black Laws" that pressed free people of color into bondage if they entered the state illegally. The Democratic *Ottawa Free Trader,* though acknowledging that many Republicans recognized "that this is a nation of white men and not of divers colors" and would prefer Blacks to "keep at quite a respectful a distance from their parlors as their hen roosts" suggested that the party might soon come under radical influence. Pointing to the "old-line abolition" wing as an "indomitable and cunning faction" within the Republican Party, the editor speculated that the Republicans would embrace Black social equality within a year. Yet, for most Republicans, as for most Illinoisans, the rights and privileges of free white men, whether in Kansas or Illinois, superseded any concern for African Americans.[36]

Indeed, Black abolitionists in Illinois became increasingly pessimistic about the prospects of achieving any measure of racial equality in the face of bipartisan prejudice. Following his repudiation of the Republicans in late 1856, H. Ford Douglas left Illinois and emigrated to Canada West, where he hoped to attract more African Americans to depart from the "miserable, contemptible despotism" of the United States. While most of the state's Black residents continued to reject emigrationism, their goal of securing equal social and political rights within Illinois seemed an impossible dream. John and Mary Jones, two of Chicago's most prominent Black abolitionists, might have kept their spirits up by maintaining contact with prominent advocates of Black freedom like Frederick Douglass, Wendell Phillips, and the fiery John Brown, but events at home must have appeared grim as the Republican press reminded them that they were "emphatically the white man's party" and that the "government was made for free white people, and should be wielded for their benefit." The long-standing movement by Colored Conventions to repeal the state's discriminatory statutes stalled in the face of hostility and indifference of white politicians. Early in 1857, a small group of abolitionists petitioned the state legislature, controlled by a Democratic majority, to reconsider the state's Black Laws. Unsurprisingly, the legislators balked at the petition, and, with Republican support, they dismissed the proposed measures without formal debate. Although the Democrats would continue to accuse the Republicans of favoring racial equality, the reality on the ground throughout Illinois proved otherwise.[37]

Panic!

As the weather cooled, the confidence in popular sovereignty that had risen up among the state's Democrats throughout the summer of 1857 crashed unexpectedly alongside the nation's economy. As the nation's banks foundered and the Western railroad bonanza fizzled, the Buchanan administration yielded to the South's most extreme proslavery elements. Illinois Democrats, feeling alarmed by the financial panic and betrayed by Buchanan, took a stand that fractured the national party. The events of the fall and winter also threw the Republicans into confusion as the resurgence of old economic issues and the potential of an alliance with their greatest enemy, Douglas, created immense anxiety among the state's leading figures.

Although scholars continue to debate the precise trigger of the Panic of 1857, all recognize that a series of Philadelphia and New York bank failures in August and September jolted the national economy. After a decade of economic growth fueled by the rapid construction of railroads and loose credit, the sudden suspension of specie payments by banks in each of the nation's major financial centers shook investors and led to a rapid decline in the value of Western land and railroads. The price per share of the Chicago & Rock Island Railroad dropped 10 percent in four days while the Illinois Central Railroad dropped by 20 percent in the same period, much to the chagrin of stockholders like Stephen A. Douglas, whose own income dropped sharply in the succeeding months. Many initially suggested that the curtailment of credit would only affect reckless speculators. In September, Bloomington's *Pantagraph* protested against "unnecessary alarm" and was "not convinced that speculation [had] been carried to a very dangerous extent in Illinois." Yet, the ripple effect quickly drew in Illinois's farmers as the value of wheat throughout the West dropped from $1.92 per bushel in July to $1.37 in October. Matters grew worse as St. Louis businessmen briefly stopped accepting notes from Illinois banks, cutting downstate Suckers off from their principal entrepot, casting doubts on the value of the state's currency, and creating a rush for gold in anticipation of the suspension of specie payments.[38]

Seeming to forget their own reckless boosterism of the past years, some Democratic and Republican papers blamed speculation and greed as the source of the panic and advocated for fiscal conservatism. The Republican *Quincy Whig* sadly concluded that "inflated with supposed wealth," many Americans had sunk themselves into poverty in order "to buy the glitter and tinsel and gewgaws of life" and concluded that personal "moderation must now naturally and necessarily be the curative." A week later, the same paper castigated the nation's investment in railroads, concluding that the "rushing dashing reckless speed of the railway train" represented "a fast, reckless age" of loose credit. The Democratic *Rock Islander and Argus* employed a similar tone as it scolded individuals and the country as a whole, noting that "the men in trouble now are the men who owe and must borrow" and insisted that "Americans, in our haste to get rich, forget the old proverb, that a bird in the hand is worth two in the bush." While unhelpful as economic assessments, these invectives reflected the tensions created by the region's rapid economic growth. While exhilarated by the potential riches made available by the growth of the railroad and the financial instruments of industrial capitalism, Illinoisians also feared the fragile networks and dependence this new economy created.[39]

Unsure of the ultimate outcome, one might have expected a concerted effort to turn back the clock and reanimate the economic debates of the 1830s and 1840s. Indeed, the revival of questions surrounding banks, tariffs, and internal improvements would have made sense to the political generation that had emerged from the Panic of 1837. Yet, with the coalitions of that period now scrambled beyond recognition by the question of slavery extension and Kansas still at the forefront of national affairs, the new alignments held. Thus, while the *Illinois State Journal* ranted against "the free trade system" as "the rock upon which we are splitting" and the *Rock Islander and Argus* reveled in the people's renewed interest in specie as a return to "Democratic money," the Panic of 1857 did not immediately shift the party associations that had emerged in the year before. Instead, all eyes remained fixed on the convention that had assembled at Lecompton to draft a state constitution for the troubled territory of Kansas.[40]

Gathering for the first time on September 7, the proslavery delegates at Lecompton adjourned four days later to await the results of the state election scheduled for early October. For the first time since the "Border Ruffian" election of 1855, free-state Kansans turned out to vote, decisively electing their candidate for Congress. Curiously, it initially appeared as if the proslavery forces had retained their strength in the state legislature, but Governor Walker's careful review of the votes revealed that two southeastern counties had submitted a tally of more than twenty-eight hundred ballots despite the fact that fewer than thirty eligible voters resided in either. In a galling act of electoral fraud, proslavery partisans had copied the names of the "voters" directly from a Cincinnati directory. When Walker threw out the fraudulent ballots, proslavery forces wailed in protest over undue electoral interference by a federal official, a view members of Buchanan's cabinet shared. Reassembling in Lecompton on October 19, the convention delegates resolved to protect slavery in Kansas despite the will of the territory's voters. Although the convention's president, John Calhoun, a longtime ally of Stephen A. Douglas in Illinois, worked to moderate the convention's effort to impose slavery on Kansas, the delegates pressed ahead. Presenting their handiwork to the public on November 7, the delegates refused to allow a popular vote on the constitution as a whole. Instead, they would only allow voters a chance to prohibit the further introduction of slaves into the state. The 450 enslaved people already in Kansas, and their descendants, would remain in bondage. Based on the failure of similar provisions in Kentucky and elsewhere in the slaveholding South to limit slavery's expansion, the free-state party rejected the referendum as no choice at all. As the *Alton Courier* quipped, the proslavery party had agreed to flip a coin under the terms of "heads we win—tails you lose." Determined to boycott the referendum sponsored by the convention, the newly elected territorial legislature proposed its own referendum on the Lecompton constitution, giving voters a chance to reject the document in its entirety. President Buchanan rejected this second referendum as illegal and bordering on sedition, setting up a major battle in Congress when the proslavery faction easily secured ratification of the constitution with slavery in their official referendum on December 21.[41]

This repudiation of popular sovereignty, in spirit if not in form, shocked Illinois Democrats, who had just weeks before expressed their unbounded confidence in the wisdom of the Lecompton delegates and the Buchanan administration. Writing in the aftermath of the October territorial election, the *Rock Islander and Argus* declared, "Kansas must be a free state, even those person in the territory who are known as 'pro-slavery' men, must recognize in the late election a decision which must not be slighted or put at defiance." In the same vein, the *Ottawa Free Trader* smugly asserted, "Kansas will be a state in less than a year, and a free state if the New England politicians will let her alone." Yet in the aftermath of the constitution's release, that same publication declared the document should "not [be] regarded as worth the paper it was printed upon." Joining the *Chicago Times*, Douglas's primary organ, nearly every Democratic paper in the state voiced its opposition to the "Lecompton Fraud." Those few Illinois Democrats who stood by Buchanan would become a thorn in Douglas's side over the coming months, but from the outset, it seemed clear that a majority of the party would not oppose Kansas's admission to the Union as a slave state. As Douglas put it, "trickery and juggling have been substituted for fair dealing" in Kansas. He insisted that the free white men of Kansas had exercised popular sovereignty by voting for free-state candidates and that the Democratic Party must "stand on this principle and go wherever its logical consequences may carry [it]." Douglas may have been reluctant to openly break with a president of his own party, having stuck by the administration over the past year despite numerous slights, but his Illinois constituents would never support such an affront to local autonomy by Southern slaveholders.[42]

By taking a stance against Lecompton, Douglas Democrats in Illinois could frame themselves as moderates, consistent in their principled devotion to both popular sovereignty and opposition to extremism in both sections. As historian Adam I. P. Smith has aptly noted, the break with the Buchanan administration allowed Douglas's supporters "to support again a political movement in what they saw as the real Jacksonian tradition—opposing centralization, meddling, and fanaticism, and supporting localism and states' rights." Indeed, one Illinois Democratic editor denounced Southern claims that the Constitution "carried slavery into every state of the Union" as a "violent and unreasonable perversion" of the document and a violation of the "Democratic doctrine of State Rights, as defined by the immortal Virginia Resolutions of 1798." As the heirs of Madison and Jefferson, the Douglas Democrats presented their program as a conservative defense of republican government, which was equally at odds with radicals and disunionists in both the North and the South. Thus, the *Illinois State Register* could condemn the "sophistry" of the administration's defense of "the precocious Lecompton contrivance" and, in the same breath also castigate the Republicans for their "new born zeal" for popular sovereignty, a principal "they so bitterly combatted" the year before. In keeping with their constituents' general distaste for slavery, Illinois Democrats had long denied Republican charges that popular sovereignty was merely a ploy of Southern slaveholders to extend their influence into the free West. Instead, they insisted that popular sovereignty granted local self-government, the essence of American democracy, to the free white settlers of the territories. Geography, climate, and economic self-interest, not congressional restriction, would keep slavery out of the West while preserving state equality within the Union. With the people of Kansas clearly in favor of entering the Union as a free state, Illinois Democrats hoped to prove their sincerity to the voters.[43]

In response to the news of Douglas's stand, local party activists lauded the Little Giant as the "Champion of Popular Rights." One such supporter urged Douglas to press on, warning him that a retreat now would surrender "the principles contended for in the terrible struggle of 1856" by the "masses of the party" who "all ways do right." James W. Sheahan of the *Chicago Times* assured Douglas that "the party here is unanimous" and emphasized, "the justice of [their] position, to say nothing of the sound policy of consulting Democratic sentiment in Illinois above all things at this time." From Galesburg, George C. Lanphere, another loyal Democrat, crowed to Douglas that "not even in this abolition town" would a single man dare "to raise his voice against [Douglas's] present course." He hoped that the people might now see how the Republicans had "been just as inconsistent as the South" and would support popular sovereignty on its merits as a sound national policy.[44]

Writing Lanphier, the editor of the *Illinois State Register,* Douglas announced that the pair would "nail [their] colors to the mast and defend the right of the people to govern themselves against assaults from all quarters." Undaunted and self-righteous now that the confrontation had come, he would, as Illinois congressman Harris observed, "make the greatest effort of his life in opposition to this juggle." Douglas thought of himself as an advocate of fair play who would yield sectional interests—like his constituents' dislike of slavery—in order to preserve popular self-government within a white man's republic. The South seemed to agree to this principle by adopting the Kansas-Nebraska Act. But as the *Quincy Herald* explained, Southern Democrats now showed "by their conduct that while Douglas was fighting for principle, they were fighting for slavery and not for principle!" Under such circumstances, Douglas and his allies could not back down without becoming the doughfaces that the Republicans had always accused them of being. The time for sectional conciliation for the sake of party unity had passed. Just as the South had deserved protection from the fiercest abolitionists, the *Rushville Times* proclaimed, "The north now needs . . . the same intrepid, deliberate defender of its constitutional rights." The Little Giant would stand against those who had, with impunity, "violently and dangerously" assailed the "great doctrine of popular sovereignty."[45]

Such determination to defend popular sovereignty, while the norm among Illinois Democrats, alarmed the most reactionary members of the party in the Northeast. President Buchanan's powerful patronage network kept Pennsylvania's Democracy in line with the administration while the fiercely pro-South Hard Shell faction of New York exercised considerable influence in the Empire State. The widely read *New York Herald* made a case for Northern Democrats to "martyr" themselves on the issue by claiming that the future of the Union depended on "the prestige of Southern rights and the time-honored principle of Northern concessions." Reflecting the antidemocratic inclinations of the Southern Democrats and their doughface allies, the *Herald* feared that with the rejection of Lecompton, "the law of the strong arm will supersede those fraternal obligations" between the two sections and "the organic law of the South will be the law of submission—absolute submission—to the will of an overwhelming Northern majority." Of course, for Douglas Democrats, this argument made little sense. The majority of free white men in Kansas had voted against slavery in the new state. Although the broader demographics of the Union—a considerable majority of white men lived in the free states—had influenced who had migrated to Kansas, the local majority, those actually inhabiting Kansas, had made the decision. Firing back at the *Herald*, the *Illinois State Register* rejected the call for Northern martyrdom and exclaimed that the Union faced no danger "except in the divisions of the democratic party, caused by a repudiation of solemn pledges." The *Register* recognized "the right of the majority of the people to rule" as the "first great principle" of the Democratic Party. Moreover, that commitment to majority rule resonated far beyond the bounds of the party.[46]

The defiance of Douglas and his Democratic allies in opposition to Lecompton represented both a principled stand for popular sovereignty and a keen understanding of the political reality in Illinois. While some proportion of Douglas Democrats may have proved willing to forsake popular sovereignty at the command of their chief, many would have balked. While willing to give

Southern slaveholders their right to express their views in a fair vote, they would never surrender the right of the free white majority to rule. By standing up to the haughty extremists of the South, just as they had to the radical abolitionists of the North, they sought to maintain the integrity of republican government and majority rule, the pillars of the American constitutional order.

Douglas at the Helm

Douglas's break with the Buchanan administration and the Illinois Democracy's claim to conservative moderation inspired respect within the state's undecided political center and a sense of alarm among partisan Republicans. Knowing that they would need the support of voters who had split their tickets between Fillmore and Bissel in 1856 if they ever hoped to secure Illinois in a presidential contest, the Democrats' pivot to the center posed a serious threat to the Republican Party and its leadership. By taking the side of Free-Soilers in the Lecompton controversy, Illinois Democrats presented popular sovereignty as a pragmatic antiextensionist solution. For Illinoisians deeply concerned by the Slave Power's aggression in Kansas but alarmed by sharing a party with abolitionists like Owen Lovejoy, anti-Lecompton Democrats appeared to occupy the sensible center. Should Buchanan and the South drive them from the Democratic Party entirely, they might become the dominant block in a new antiadministration coalition. Indeed, even among those who had supported Frémont in 1856, Douglas's rejection of Lecompton held immense appeal. The Republican *Rockford Register,* for instance, explained that while it did not "propose to accept Mr. Douglas as a member of the Republican Party . . . without a much longer probation," it did "not know of another man so well qualified to lead the opposition of the ultraists of the Senate" in the battle against the Lecompton constitution.[47]

Horace Greeley's *New-York Tribune,* the leading national Republican paper, seemed to think such a fusion possible and desirable. Reporting on Douglas's defiant return to Washington, the *Tribune* gushed that the Little Giant was "as firm as a rock . . . not boastful, but quietly certain of ultimate triumph." The editor believed the South's effort to take over the Democratic Party had not only alienated Douglas but marked "something more radical and fundamental," as "the Northern section of the Democratic Party" would not "see itself converted into a mere makeweight" for the South and would resist "the usurpation of the slaveholding interest." The misleadingly named *Missouri Democrat,* a Republican paper in St. Louis, voiced its support for the courage of the *Chicago Times* and other pro-Douglas papers while it lambasted the local pro-Lecompton paper as a "profligate or fanatical press" that had "arrogate[d] to itself the title of conservative." Perhaps the moment had finally come when Northerners of all parties would rally in defense of the prerogatives of free white men. Indeed, many eastern Republicans seemed to agree with Greeley that they should welcome Douglas and his followers with open arms. A disgruntled *Chicago Tribune* inadvertently revealed the potential in such a fusion when it insisted that Douglas's opposition to the Lecompton constitution, "because it has not been submitted to the people," put him "on ground that is common to all parties—the American, Democratic, and Republican parties alike."[48]

For Republican leaders in Illinois, however, an enduring alliance seemed out of the question. Having battled Douglas and his cronies head-to-head for years, they felt little inclination to yield now. Party managers subsequently oscillated between suspicions that Douglas soon enough bow again to Southern interests and bewilderment as to what a permanent break in the national Democracy might mean.

Leading Republicans in Chicago, Douglas's adopted hometown, expressed their skepticism with a special ferocity. Norman B. Judd wrote to Trumbull that he suspected the whole ordeal had been concocted to break up the Republican Party. He thought that amid the confusion over the Panic of 1857 and Kansas, the Democrats hoped that "old Whig element in the Republican Party will revive the Bank and tariff question and thus drive off or render neutral the old democrats" who might then willingly return to an anti-Lecompton Illinois Democratic Party. Judd's intraparty rival in Chicago, Wentworth, another former Democrat, came to a similar conclusion insisting that "the bait, thrown out for Republican support comes from a tricky fisherman." He explained the break as a personal feud between Douglas and the president, insisting Douglas was "fighting James Buchanan, not James Buchanan's party principles." This illusion of opposition made Douglas "more dangerous to the principles of the Republican party than [Buchanan]" and the Southern Democrats. Across town, *Chicago Tribune* editor Charles H. Ray prompted Trumbull to beat Douglas to the punch and introduce a new Kansas enabling act, as he feared he would "get a good deal of capital out of his late movement if he is not headed off." Charles L. Wilson of the *Chicago Journal* also insisted to Trumbull that Douglas had opposed Lecompton only to save his senate seat and did "not merit endorsement or absolution for an act which after all is but one of self-preservation."[49]

Meanwhile, in Washington, Senator Trumbull initially echoed his allies back in Illinois, but as the confrontation between Douglas and the president escalated, he admitted that Douglas might cross the proverbial Rubicon into opposition with the Republican Party. Writing to Lincoln in early December, Trumbull characterized the break as an intraparty feud, noting that he did "not think the 'Rumpus' among the bogus Democracy [would] amount to much, except to help us a little with the people." Trumbull believed Douglas had driven him out of the Democratic Party with a whip borrowed from the Slave Power, and it seemed impossible to him that the Little Giant might now find himself subjected to the same lash. Perhaps, Trumbull mused, Douglas would posture for a bit on the Lecompton question in order "to save himself at home," but he remained confident that he would not "do any thing which will cut him off from the South and the administration." By Christmas, however, with Douglas now on record as an opponent of the administration's policy in Kansas, Trumbull vocalized his uncertainty in a second letter to Lincoln. He now thought it "useless to speculate on the future course of Douglas or the effect it is to have in Ills & other states." As a rebel within the Democratic Party, Douglas might face opposition from both the Democratic establishment and the Republican opposition. How long Douglas could maintain such an awkward stance remained an open question, but he did not have time on his side. Trumbull did not believe Douglas sought to join the Republican Party, yet he noted that "if the Kansas question should be kept open for a few months, he may be forced into that position" as "the African Democracy may drive him from among them." Although Illinois Democrats had for the most part stuck with Douglas thus far, would they continue to operate without their eastern and Southern allies and lose all access to patronage and favor from the national party? If not, they could either return meekly to the fold or strike out on their own. Trumbull feared the latter.[50]

Deeply distrustful of Douglas and resentful of his role in destroying the Second Party System, Trumbull feared Douglas and his partisans might now make their appeal as a third way to moderate voters opposed to slavery's extension but fearful of abolitionists. Following the path Trumbull and his fellow anti-Nebraska Democrats had blazed three years earlier, Douglas might draw support from disaffected Democrats, oldline Whigs, and conservative Republicans to form a new party based around bringing Kansas into the Union as a free state. With the anti-extensionist potential of this policy on full display, those who had opposed the repeal of the Missouri Compromise might finally make their peace with popular sovereignty. Indeed, in Indiana, where the Southern-born proslavery Senator Bright emerged as a common enemy, such a coalition did form, with Republicans standing shoulder to shoulder with Douglas Democrats on the basis of the "true and ever living principle States rights and popular sovereignty."[51]

This possibility also alarmed Lincoln, who feared such a realignment would undermine both any future claim of Congress to regulate slavery's extension and his own ambition to replace Douglas in the US Senate. Lincoln seethed with frustration at the willingness of many eastern Republicans, especially former Whigs, to make common cause with the Little Giant. In a tone that bordered on despair, he asked Trumbull, "What does the New-York Tribune mean by it's constant eulogising, and admiring, and magnifying Douglas?" He believed that if Greeley's paper spoke for the national party and concluded "that the republican cause, generally, can be best promoted by sacrificing us here in Illinois," the state party might as well fold. Although no one in his circle had jumped ship thus far, he thought that if "the Tribune continues to din his praises into the ears of it's five or ten thousand republican readers in Illinois, is more that can be hoped that all will stand firm." Lincoln believed the Founders had sought to contain the cancer of slavery and had entrusted Congress with the power to enforce their plan for a free West. Embracing popular sovereignty and a permanent coalition with the wily Douglas would surrender that conservative ground for antiextensionists. Of course, Lincoln also had much to lose personally from a Republican embrace of Douglas. Having fallen short in his 1855 bid for the Senate, the ever-ambitious Lincoln could not stand the thought of deferring to Douglas, his principal antagonist. He had spent the last two years building a new political party from the ground up to oppose Douglas, popular sovereignty, and slavery's extension and understandably believed he deserved recognition for this feat.[52]

Trumbull shared this frustration and assured Lincoln that he would support his bid for the Senate, regardless of the national party's agenda. Douglas's dramatic stand against Lecompton had taken all Republicans "somewhat by surprise" as they "did not believe he would go so far as to offend the South till he did it." The events of the past year had transformed the political landscape in unexpected ways, and although Douglas might yet reconcile with the president, neither Trumbull nor Lincoln could predict his course with any degree of certainty. Still, Trumbull promised Lincoln he would "continue to labor for the success of the Republican cause in Ills—& the advancement at the next election to the place now occupied by Douglas of that *Friend*, who was instrumental in promoting [his] own." In the face of ignoble intransigence among anti-Nebraska Democrats in the winter of 1854–55, Lincoln had graciously yielded to Trumbull. This sacrifice earned the Springfield attorney an unusually high level of respect from his former opponents, especially Trumbull. Historians have long recognized that nineteenth-century political parties existed primarily as state organizations that united into national coalitions for presidential contests. Although personal disputes among state and local actors often created fissures, the intimacy of these networks also fostered deep loyalty. Trumbull recognized that Lincoln's goodwill and devotion to the common cause had proved instrumental in his own election. He now pledged to return the favor in 1858.[53]

As revelers throughout the United States once again welcomed the new year, antiextension voters in Kansas took to the polls to vote in the election called by the new territorial legislature. Although the six thousand proslavery voters who had recently cast ballots in favor of Lecompton sat out the contest, the ten thousand free-state voters firmly rejected the Lecompton constitution and proved once and for all that the majority of actual settlers in Kansas disapproved of slavery's extension. On hearing the news, Douglas telegraphed the *Illinois State Register* with a rallying cry: "Let the voice of the people rule." The Democratic Party stood on the verge of self-immolation as Buchanan remained determined to approve the Lecompton constitution with slavery. The contest's final result remained anyone's guess.[54]

Old Dilemmas and New Anxieties

By January 1858, the hopes and frustrations of early 1857 had yielded to a whole new set of expectations and anxieties. Although the economy had begun to recover from the fall's financial crisis, the sudden crash following a decade of unprecedented prosperity had alarmed many throughout the West. For Illinois Republicans, the Dred Scott decision appeared to confirm the Democrats' sycophancy to the Slave Power, depriving both Congress and local settlers of the right to restrict slavery's extension into the national territories. This departure from the established understanding of both the management of the territories and the role of the Supreme Court signaled an ascendant radicalism within the Democracy that alarmed an opposition composed mainly of self-identified conservatives. Nevertheless, the state's Democrats continued to cling to their own conservative credentials by ignoring the inconvenient truths of the decision, instead reveling in Taney's repudiation of Black rights and bludgeoning their opponents with accusations of racial egalitarianism. Though Douglas and his allies took exception to the repeated slights of the national administration, they retained their faith that

President Buchanan and his Southern allies would stand by the Cincinnati Platform, a creed they believed enshrined the right of self-government for white men throughout the West. Illinois Democrats thought the combination of climate and economic self-interest would guarantee a free Kansas while a fair vote on the issue recognized the rights of the South. The battle over Lecompton revealed that they had overestimated their clout within an increasingly Southern-dominated coalition. Now, Illinois Democrats and Republicans awkwardly found themselves working for the same end. It would take considerable time and energy to disentangle the motivations and implications of this congressional battle and reestablish party distinctions for an electorate confused by the sudden shift in national allegiances. That process, as played out over the following months, would ultimately produce the most memorable set of debates in American political history.

CHAPTER 5

THE GREAT DEBATES

Stephen A. Douglas had arrived at the executive mansion on December 3, 1857, prepared for a confrontation. In the preceding weeks, it had become clear that President Buchanan would support federal approval of the fraudulent Lecompton constitution. This interview, scheduled for the day after Douglas's return to Washington from Chicago, confirmed the president's position. Buchanan coolly explained that he expected Douglas to fall in line on Lecompton and work for the measure from his position as chairman of the Senate Committee on Territories. The Little Giant boiled over in a rage, incensed that the president would commit to such a policy without so much as consulting him. Loudly protesting the injustice of foisting a sham constitution on Kansas, Douglas prepared to leave. As he turned to go, Buchanan reminded Douglas that "no Democrat ever yet differed from the Administration of his own choice without being crushed." Unphased, Douglas spat back that Buchanan ought "to remember that General Jackson is dead." While the founder of the Democracy might have held sufficient clout to purge Washington of his enemies, "Old Buck" was no "Old Hickory."[1]

In the aftermath of this decisive split of the Democratic Party into pro-Douglas and pro-Buchanan wings, the contours of national politics appeared once again in flux. Less than four years after Douglas's advocacy of the Kansas-Nebraska Bill divided the Northern Democracy and permanently sundered the Whig Party, the Little Giant had again thrown partisans into confusion. For once, finding themselves on the same side of an issue as their nemesis, Illinois Republicans wondered whether they might coopt Douglas and feared that he might do the same to them. The Lecompton crisis had revealed the uncomfortable truth that, despite profound animosity toward one another, Illinois Republicans and Democrats could seek the same political end. Centrist voters in Illinois would support whichever party would defend the rights of free white men while respecting the Constitution and maintaining the Union. Although some voices in the state party seemed amenable to a merger, leading figures like Abraham Lincoln balked at any permanent alliance with Douglas and his followers.

Thus, after uniting to defeat the Lecompton constitution, Illinois Republicans and Democrats struggled to reassert their independent partisan identities while simultaneously capturing those centrist voters, especially former Whigs and Know-Nothings, who would ultimately decide whether Douglas would retain his Senate seat. The Republicans, in particular, feared defections as Douglas's supporters brandished his leadership on Lecompton to refute charges of proslavery toadyism. Following his formal nomination for the US Senate, Lincoln allowed his idealism to cloud his political judgment, and he committed a series of blunders that forced him and his party to play catch-up through much of the campaign. Nevertheless, both sides articulated coherent arguments that led to an exceptionally close election. Although Douglas emerged the victor by the skin of his teeth, he could hardly claim the unconditional loyalty of Illinois's moderate electorate.

"Democrats, Let Us Have a Full Turn Out"

Stephen A. Douglas faced a serious dilemma as he walked away from the White House, now the declared enemy a president he had helped to elect. In his own mind, of course, Douglas had acted consistently throughout the previous decade, dutifully advocating for the right of the white men of the West to decide the fate of slavery in 1850, 1854, and now again in 1858. But for President James Buchanan, Douglas's stand epitomized base treason, a nearly unprecedented challenge to the president and his party. Arrayed against the administration, the Southern Democracy, and those Northern Democrats who—largely to the dismay of their constituents—stayed loyal to Buchanan, Douglas and his allies stood shoulder to shoulder with their Republican adversaries. Did this political convergence signal a partisan realignment that would unite Douglas Democrats and Republicans on a moderate free-soil platform? Republicans had long maintained that Douglas had sold out Kansas to the Slave Power in 1854, but it now appeared that a defense of popular sovereignty would secure freedom for that territory. In Illinois, a bewildered

Republican leadership sought to craft a coherent response even as Douglas's allies braced themselves for a Democratic civil war.²

From the outset, a majority of Illinois Democrats joined with Douglas and stood opposed to admitting Kansas under the Lecompton constitution and denounced the document as an undemocratic fraud imposed on the territory by imperious Southerners. With the results of the territorial legislative elections and the referendum of early January clearly before the people, the *Quincy Herald* resolved that "those who now advocate for the admission of Kansas under [the Lecompton] Constitution, simply contend for the right of the minority to rule." Since the adoption of the Kansas-Nebraska Act, Illinois Democrats had insisted that popular sovereignty—by which free white men governed their own affairs—represented the only practical, national, and constitutional solution to the slavery question. Lecompton represented a grave overreach of congressional power, granting power to a favored minority in defiance of the will of the majority. Illinois Democrats might have expected such a stance from "Black Republicans," but they could hardly believe their own national organization would endorse such a measure. Confused by their sudden alignment with their interstate rivals, the *Randolph County Democrat* insisted that, far from abandoning their principles, Illinois Democrats had remained consistent and that it had been the Republicans who had "come over to us so far as they give their assent to the right of the people of Kansas to settle their own affairs." Indeed, as alluded to in the previous chapter, a number of Republicans had begun to express a more positive view of popular sovereignty, a development that quickly drew the ire of party leadership in Illinois.³

Strikingly, the small contingent of pro-administration Democrats in the state, soon to be christened *Danites*, seemed to confirm the pro-Douglas wing's suspicions of abandoning self-government and embracing centralized tyranny. Kept loyal to Buchanan by a combination of ideological commitment to a pro-Southern policy, promises of federal patronage, and resentment of Douglas's dominance within the state party, this small but influential cohort of Illinois Democrats tried to lead the rank and file back into the fold. Yet, they struggled to find a way to control popular outrage over Lecompton. The editor of the *Peoria Democratic Union* discouraged Democrats from organizing meetings to discuss the administration's policy and publicly despaired as local meetings repudiated Lecompton and endorsed Douglas. In a misguided appeal to the conversative base of the party, the *Democratic Union* asked voters to support the president as a means of maintaining order, insisting that they preserve federal authority in Kansas even if it required enslaving "every free white man, woman, and child, in the state of Massachusetts," as the repudiation of the Lecompton convention would mark the "first step taken in a path terminating in chaos, such as is now witnessed in the republics south of us on the western continent." Whatever ill will Illinois Democrats held for New England Yankees in general, the editor gravely miscalculated his readership's commitment to white freedom. The tone of the *Democratic Union* might have appealed to some of the most aristocratic Southern planters, but it hardly matched Illinois Democrats' commitment to individual liberty in a white man's republic. In an equally bizarre ploy, Cairo's *Times and Delta* brazenly propagated the idea that the majority of Kansas settlers actually favored slavery and that only Yankee abolitionists opposed the state's admission under Lecompton. Ignoring months of violence, fraud, and political turmoil, the *Times and Delta* insisted that "the case is as plain as daylight," for if the Free-Soilers "were in the majority they might have voted slavery out of the constitution." All too aware of the electoral irregularities and the overwhelming Free-Soil vote in January's referendum after months of national coverage, only the most ignorant or stubborn Egyptian Democrat could have found such an appeal convincing.[4]

Although habituated by partisanship and unionism to excuse the South and the evils of slavery, pro-Douglas Illinois Democrats began to vent their frustration with their estranged Southern brethren and drifted, somewhat unintentionally, closer to the ground maintained by conservative Republicans. As the debate over the Lecompton constitution reignited in the aftermath of President Buchanan's February 2 call for the speedy admission of Kansas as a slave state, the *Illinois State Register* applauded Thomas L. Harris's anti-Lecompton resolution in the House, claiming it would "be made the test of strength of the two parties." Although it might appear trifling at first glance, the decision by editors, and Democratic stalwarts, Charles H. Lanphier and George Walker to frame the battle as fought between "Lecomptonites" and their opponents marked a shift from a neat dichotomy of Democrats and Republicans. Indeed, though the pair had long disdained sectional labels, they now used the occasion to specifically chastise those "northern members" supporting Lecompton who were "acting in opposition to the will of their constituencies" and violating the Northern public's trust. The pair might have felt more comfortable doing so, having received correspondence from Harris that proclaimed "war to the knife" against Lecompton. In a separate letter to former Democratic congressman John A. McClernand, Harris announced his determination to stand firm against "Southern dictation" and prevent "covert disunionists in the South" from undermining the republic.[5]

Throughout the state, other pro-Douglas Democratic editors struck similar notes as they sought to draw support from moderates who had supported

Fillmore or Frémont in 1856. Following a drunken scuffle in Congress, the *Ottawa Free Trader* castigated South Carolina's Representative Lawrence M. Keitt, Preston Brooks's accomplice in the 1856 caning of Charles Sumner, as "notorious" and "a representative of the ruffian phases of Southern chivalry" and called on the House to expel him. Sounding almost like a conservative Republican paper, the *Quincy Herald* defended the ordinary people of the South but targeted elite Southerners as it denounced the "politicians of the south" who remained "unquestionably wrong" in their attempt to force "Kansas into the Union under a constitution which they know to be obnoxious to the people of Kansas." Softening its stance on antislavery activism, the *Islander and Argus* of Rock Island disparaged Republican Francis P. Blair's colonization proposal as unrealistic but still saw the need "for a manly and vigorous attempt to grapple with and conquer the difficulties of the great problem of African slavery" and remained confident that the "problem will some day find its solution." Though they vigorously maintained their Democratic identity, these editorial concessions hinted at broadening political horizons.[6]

The Republican press in Illinois, for its part, also softened its critique of Douglas Democrats in February, though they appeared to do so in the hope that the anti-Lecomptonites would later find their way into the Republican fold. In rejecting Buchanan's demands for a speedy admission of Kansas as a slave state, the *Waukegan Gazette* of deeply Republican Lake County adopted the language of popular sovereignty as it appealed to the "high-minded, right thinking, plain spoken men of both parties" to combat this "great crime against self-government." Although they would likely not have admitted to the fact, the editors of Springfield's *Illinois State Journal* echoed the approval of their crosstown rivals at the *Illinois State Register* when they praised Representative Harris for "boldly declar[ing] that he is for 'the rights of white men, which are in danger,' and against the despotism of the South." Another Republican organ, the *Central Transcript* of Clinton, hailed the redemption of the Douglas Democrats, awarding "all honor to the twenty-one democrats in the House of Representatives who acted and voted with the Republicans in support of the Harris Resolutions." Still, further downstate, George T. Brown's *Alton Courier* hinted that the shift in partisan allegiance had already occurred, noting "the secession of Northern Representatives" from the Democracy and hoping that as a result, the Republican strength in Congress has gained sufficiently to prevent" the adoption of Lecompton. Of course, the votes cast in favor of Harris's resolution and against Lecompton did not constitute a formal realignment but merely a bipartisan vote. Still, as Lincoln's alarm back in December had indicated, Illinois's Republican leaders thought it might become one.[7]

For both Republicans and Douglas Democrats, the word *Lecompton* came to represent, as written in the Democratic *Illinois State Register,* a whole host of "frauds and villainies." The clear violation of the rights of free white Kansans confirmed the worst fears of Republicans about popular sovereignty and evidenced a shocking breach of faith among Illinois Democrats committed to the policy. Douglasites had defended the actions of the Democratic Party and national government in the territory since the passage of the Kansas-Nebraska Act, insisting that free white Kansans would receive a fair vote on slavery and that it would inevitably enter as a free state if only the abolitionist agitators would cease their griping and submit to the constituted authorities. Now, however, as the Buchanan administration feebly acquiesced to Southern extremists in the face of massive electoral fraud, only the most obsequious Illinois Democrats could continue to defend the powers that be. Not only had the administration abandoned the loyal Robert J. Walker, but they had abetted corruption and deceit in the territorial government while reneging on the basic promises of popular sovereignty. Suddenly, Southern proslavery extremists had become just as dangerous, if not more threatening, to the right of white self-government.[8]

Recruiting among the Enemy

Like their journalist allies, Republican Party leaders in Illinois hoped to draw in disaffected Democrats if they could do so on their own terms. Yet, the danger remained that if the parties converged too quickly, Douglas and his defectors might win over former Know-Nothings and even some Republicans. Initially, Ozias M. Hatch, the Republican Illinois secretary of state, felt confident that Douglas Democrats would soon add to his party's strength, noting in a late January letter to Lyman Trumbull that the anti-Lecompton Democrats of Springfield believed "that they shall soon be classed as Republicans" and had "entirely ceased to use hard names" toward Republican leaders. Another of Trumbull's correspondents echoed this sentiment, gleefully anticipating that if the Lecompton constitution was approved by Congress, then "the Democratic Party would be busted 'wide open'" and "there would not be a grease spot left of Douglas in Illinois." Yet within a few weeks, the Prairie State's junior US senator received more concerning news as a downstate correspondent reported that "the friends of Douglas here are busy beating up recruits" and hoped "to secure the assistance of those" Republicans and Know-Nothings "upon whom a short time since they were hurling their political anathemas."

The Old Whigs and ex-Know-Nothing Republicans of southern Illinois, deeply devoted to the Union and eager to embrace an opposition movement that would stand on national, rather than sectional, principles, seemed vulnerable, especially after the principal leader of downstate conservative Republicans, Joseph Gillespie, praised Douglas's stand on Lecompton.[9]

Another indication of the Republican leadership's sense of uncertainty came in its speculations on the power of the pro-Lecompton Democrats in the state. Knowing the power of party patronage and disposed to see their rivals as unprincipled hypocrites, leaders believed many Democrats would ultimately favor Buchanan. In Quincy, one Republican partisan jeered, "Let a few removals be only made—and Lecompton anti-Douglas men will spring up like mushrooms." In Chicago, Norman B. Judd expected that a third of all Illinois Democrats would break for Buchanan in the end. Revealing the contempt many Republican insiders felt for Douglas, Judd insisted that he could not blame them, for if he "had to chose [he] would sooner serve in the ranks of the administration because villainy is not masked by hypocrisy." Others still struggled to understand the extent of the breach between Douglas and the pro-Lecompton Democrats. In the midst of Chicago's municipal elections in March, another prominent Republican, Mark T. Skinner, insisted that the Democratic factions would reconcile and unite behind Buchanan, but after Republican victories, he noted with some confusion how "The Presd. & his faction, are quite jubilant on occasion of the defeat of the Democratic ticket" headed by Douglas supporters. This new reality of Democratic division put partisan Republicans in a strange position, in which the most dogmatic proslavery men in Illinois might tip the balance of elections in favor of the Republicans.[10]

Indeed, President Buchanan and his advisors hoped to undermine Douglas and his supporters in Illinois. In Washington, pro-Lecompton Democrats had stripped Douglas of his chairmanship of the territorial committee, but his supporters back in Illinois found themselves out of a job entirely. Having initially slighted Douglas back in early 1857, the Buchanan administration now systematically purged pro-Douglas federal officials in Illinois. The president controlled dozens of lucrative positions in the postal service and federal land office, and without the need to placate Douglas, Buchanan happily turned over these offices to his toadies. Most notably, he replaced Chicago postmaster William Price with Isaac L. Cook, a corrupt saloon keeper who had fallen out with Douglas over a dispute with James W. Sheahan at the *Chicago Times*. Simultaneously, proadministration forces began to funnel funds to establish new pro-Buchanan newspapers to try to bolster support for Lecompton within the state. By the end of February, Douglas could write with perfect sincerity that "the administration is more anxious for my distruction than they are for the harmony & unity of the Democratic Party." Douglas's pro-Lecompton correspondent insisted that Douglas need only to "submit gracefully to your political friends" and abandon his "attitude of factiousness," but it had become clear to all that such submission would violate Douglas's principles and render him impotent as a political leader.[11]

Thankfully for Douglas and his allies, both Buchanan and the Republicans had grossly overestimated the extent of Danite strength in the state. As debate on the Lecompton constitution continued in the Senate through March, reports continued to flood in that Douglas's stand on Kansas remained popular with rank-and-file Illinois Democrats. From Griggsville in west-central Illinois, one party activist assured Lanphier, "There are not a dozen Buchanan Democrats in the county." In Christian County further to the east, another Democrat reflected that out of the nine hundred voters who cast ballots for Buchanan in 1856, "there is not one with him on Lecompton." Buchanan's obsequiousness toward the South seemed especially perverse in light of the boldness of Southern extremists. In early March, South Carolina senator James Henry Hammond asserted the economic and moral superiority of slave to free labor and proclaimed cotton as a "king." While Hammond's speech was a fiercely sectional statement, what flabbergasted the Christian County activist was not the implicit disunionist sentiment in the address, but the fact that Hammond had "said *minorities* ought to rule; that laborers were slaves only dif between Negroes was the coler & that they were the mudsills of society." Such a position undercut the commitment of Illinois Democrats to majority rule and equal opportunity for free white men. In the minds of nearly every white Illinoisian, to compare the independent white laborer with a Black slave insulted the dignity of labor and implicitly threatened white men with bondage. Few in Illinois could swallow such sentiments. Indeed, by early April, even the Democrats of Cairo, Illinois's most pro-Southern town, had asserted their solidarity with the Little Giant in a mass meeting, declaring Douglas "the faithful and bold champion of popular rights."[12]

Republican leaders, meanwhile, worked to overcome divisions within their own coalition and cling to the conservative ground they had staked out in the 1856 contest without surrendering their party to the proponents of popular sovereignty. A variety of challenges emerged throughout the spring as ideological and old partisan tensions flared in anticipation of the campaign season. Owen Lovejoy, the radical Republican congressman from Illinois's Third District, continued to irk the party's more conservative leaders. Sensing trouble after a visit to Lovejoy's district, Lincoln warned him to "guard most vigilantly" as he feared that the "democracy would wheedle some republican to run against you without a nomination, relying mainly on democratic votes." In light of Douglas's anti-Lecompton stand, it seemed plausible that a coalition of Douglas Democrats and renegade conservative Republicans would work to unseat Lovejoy by offering a centrist alternative. In fact, though neither of them could know it, one of Douglas's supporters would urge the Little Giant to form a permanent centrist alliance with New York's William H. Seward and Kentucky's John J. Crittenden to create "a party dominant in the Union and overwhelming in Illinois." While Lincoln was more conservative than Lovejoy and remained close to David Davis, one of the congressman's prime antagonists, he knew that any such move would alienate radicals, a small but enthusiastic wing of the state party, and simultaneously hand substantial power to Douglas Democrats. Whatever the alternate candidate's political identity at the beginning of the campaign, he would end the contest beholden to thousands of Democratic voters. At the same time, Lincoln advocated the nomination of James H. Matheny, a close friend but also a vocal Fillmore supporter in 1856, for Congress in his home district. As Lincoln explained to Richard Yates, "we must have some one who will reach the Fillmore men, both for the direct and incidental effect." Thirty percent of the Sixth District's voters had cast ballots for Fillmore in 1856, so the nomination of a conservative former Whig would hopefully secure their support and counterbalance Democratic charges that local Republicans were closet abolitionists.[13]

The prospect of fusion with Douglas simultaneously became more real and vexing to Illinois Republican insiders as the Lecompton debates reached a climax in Congress. In March, Charles H. Ray of the *Chicago Tribune* wrote that party activists had become discouraged by the news, convinced that their "hard work [would] result only in helping to warm the place for him who we all hate." Around this time, Sheahan of the *Chicago Times* became something of a diplomat for Douglas in Illinois Republican circles and began floating various propositions to try to salvage the careers of Douglas and his allies. Although Trumbull and Judd remained thoroughly unconvinced, some Republican leaders, such as Jesse K. Dubois, seemed interested in Sheahan's offer to give up Douglas's Senate seat in order to retain anti-Lecompton seats in the House. By April, Ray began to question his opposition to uniting with the anti-Lecompton Democrats. He noted in a letter to Lincoln that another Democratic emissary had proposed that Douglas would drop out of the Senate race if allowed to run uncontested as the anti-Lecompton candidate for Congress in Chicago. Indeed, the Little Giant not only pledged to block slavery's extension in Kansas but also promised to oppose the acquisition of slaveholding Cuba by the United States. Although none of these plans ever matured beyond initial talks, the fact that many Republican leaders discussed them indicates that both they and Douglas's operatives seriously considered some sort of fusion conceivable, if not necessarily desirable.[14]

For Lincoln, however, fusion with Douglas Democrats remained out of the question. Motivated by his principles and ambition for a senate seat, the Springfield lawyer believed that an alliance with the anti-Lecompton men would dilute the Republican platform and elevate Douglas within the coalition at his expense. While some might have forgotten Douglas's desecration of the Missouri Compromise, Lincoln had not. Writing to Illinois secretary of state Ozias M. Hatch, he insisted "We must never sell old friends to buy old enemies" and made it clear that he thought the party should endorse a slate of Republicans rather than succumb to "strange and new combinations." At the time, Lincoln felt quite good about the party's chances of winning over ex-Fillmore voters and believed this coalition could win without the anti-Lecompton Democrats. As such, he continued to push for Republicans downstate to nominate old Whigs and Know-Nothings for Congress, suggesting to Republican leaders in the Seventh Congressional District that they "take some good reliable Fillmore men into conference" as "it may appear expedient to select a Fillmore man as the candidate." He also worked to keep straying Republicans in line, tactfully admonishing First District congressman Elihu B. Washburne for his flirtations with the Douglas faction. Although Lincoln would face further challenges in the months ahead, notably convincing Republican ex-Democrats that ex-Fillmore men could serve as reliable allies, the talk of fusing with Douglas diminished precipitously in late spring.[15]

The failure of Illinoisans to form an enduring cross-party alliance in the wake of Lecompton speaks to the power of personality in partisan politics, the limits of pragmatism in the face of ideological conflict, and the intrinsic challenges posed by a two-party system. Although many rank-and-file Republicans and Democrats throughout the Prairie State had applauded the bipartisan impetus to squelch Lecompton, the Republican leadership remained hostile toward Douglas, resenting his long dominance in state politics and distrustful of his true intentions. Each side retained a distinct justification for opposing the proslavery constitution. Although it was hard to see in 1858 how conflict over the spread of slavery might arise outside of Kansas, rendering the contest between popular sovereignty and congressional exclusion a moot point, both sides stubbornly clung to their conflicting viewpoints. Confined by the winner-take-all stakes of the first-past-the-post electoral system, leading figures in the two parties could not easily share power. Although former

Whigs and anti-Nebraska Democrats had overcome this challenge between 1854 and 1856 through a common commitment to antiextensionism, without a shared vision for the future and the cooperation of leadership on both sides, an enduring alliance between Republicans and Douglas Democrats was doomed to failure. A weaker Republican Party in Illinois might have followed Horace Greeley's advice and adopted popular sovereignty as a free-soil policy, as their compatriots in Indiana would do. But after two years of organizing, the Illinois Republicans believed they had a chance to seize full power, and they had no intention of ceding this authority back to Douglas.

Back in Washington, the crisis generated by Lecompton reached an uneasy conclusion. In late March, Douglas had passionately voiced his opposition to the adoption of the "fraudulent" constitution only to see it pass the Senate on a vote of thirty-three to twenty-five. The two dozen Douglas Democrats in the House, led by Illinoisan Harris, proved more successful in resisting the measure, and with a coalition of Republicans and a handful of Southern Know-Nothings blocked the bill's passage. Instead, the House coalition insisted that Kansans should have an opportunity to vote on the entire Lecompton constitution in a carefully monitored referendum. Deadlocked, the administration allowed Representative William H. English, a pro-Buchanan Democrat from an Indiana district brimming with anti-Lecompton sentiment, to introduce a compromise bill. Unwilling to acknowledge the propriety of resubmission on the slavery question, the English Bill cut the federal land grant to Kansas requested under the Lecompton constitution and returned the document to the people of Kansas on that basis. The legislation also detailed that if Kansas voters rejected the smaller grant, they would have to wait for statehood until their population reached ninety thousand inhabitants. As such, Southerners would not need to fear the immediate admission of a free Kansas should the voters reject Lecompton and statehood. Although Douglas and the Republicans remained in opposition, enough anti-Lecompton Democrats conceded to pass the English bill on April 30, thus opening the door to Kansas's rejection of the Lecompton constitution 11,300 to 1,788 in an August referendum.[16]

Although Douglas and his supporters made some tentative efforts to reconcile with the Danites in the weeks following the resolution of the Kansas question, President Buchanan's determination to oust Douglas made such efforts futile. Throughout the 1858 election cycle, Douglas Democrats would face opposition from a determined, if marginal, group of pro-Buchanan dissidents who considered the Little Giant "a traitor to everything except himself." At the end of April, when Douglas Democrats met in Springfield to nominate candidates for state treasurer and state superintendent of public schools (the only two statewide offices on the ballot), the Danites organized their own "National Democratic" convention and nominated their own slate of candidates. This group hoped to syphon off enough votes in legislative races throughout the state to deny Douglas his seat, even if it meant electing a Republican. To that end, the National Democratic leader Cook of Chicago schemed with Republican renegade John E. "Long John" Wentworth to combine Republican and National Democratic votes in the legislature and boost Wentworth into office.[17]

Racial Resentment and Party Politics

As the tremors from the Lecompton debacle began to subside over the course of the late spring, both Douglas Democrats and Republicans worked to promote regularity within their own party ranks while securing the support of undecided voters and drawing off the most sympathetic members of the opposition. For any Illinois Democrats left confused as to the difference between his party and the Republicans, the *Freeport Bulletin* reminded its readers that while the "'Douglas Democrat' asks only to know what is the will of the people; the 'Republican' insists that the people, their wishes to the contrary, must shape their laws and institutions to meet his ideas of right." Douglas Democrats remained confident that the wisdom of the masses would secure economic opportunity and political equality for the white men of the republic. Any effort to restrain the people, whether by slaveholding aristocrats or abolitionists moralizers, could only end in disaster. Although this policy theoretically allowed for the expansion of slavery, most Illinois Democrats thought it better to allow the people to make a mistake than to limit their rights. To demonstrate their consistency, the *Bulletin* even admitted, "While we believe that the people of Kansas ought to reject every proposition of the kind, we must say, that if they think that the negro is their equal, let them make him so." Since the average white male voter in Illinois detested both slavery and racial equality and valued his own common sense, the Douglas Democratic argument for popular sovereignty remained potent.[18]

In fact, the appeal went so far as to force Illinois Republicans to concede its wisdom in matters aside from the extension of slavery into free territories. While they continued to insist that the hand of the Slave Power tipped the scales against ordinary white men and pointed to the Lecompton crisis as proof, they acknowledged the policy's wisdom in matters of race relations.

On May 5, as the Senate debated the admission of Oregon to the Union, Republican senators Seward of New York and William P. Fessenden of Maine spoke out against the provision in the Oregon state constitution that prohibited the immigration of free Blacks to the state. Although Trumbull objected to Oregon's admission on the grounds of its population, he made it clear that he did not share the racial views of his northeastern counterparts. Instead, he insisted that while he continued to oppose slavery's extension into the territories, he would "by no means assent to the doctrine that negroes are required by the Constitution of the United States to be placed on an equal footing in the States with white citizens." Instead, sounding very much like a Douglas Democrat, he insisted that he had "no power to prevent Oregon . . . or any other state, dealing with her black population as shall seem to her best." The New England states that allowed Blacks the franchise could extend this "privilege" at their own hazard, but they could never expect their fellow states to submit to such an odious political experiment.[19]

This sharp dissent from leaders within Trumbull's own party not only reflected his personal prejudice but also made political sense, considering the racial views of Illinois Republicans. Although sometimes downplayed in the historiography, as matters stood in the spring of 1858, while some Republicans in Northern Illinois supported basic rights for Black Americans, many of Trumbull's supporters throughout the state would have found more to laud in the words of a downstate activist who promised that "you may consider me a Republican till the last 'n——' leaves our shores." The fight against the Slave Power represented a battle against both aristocratic white Southerners and the Black men and women whose labor built their empires while "degrading" the honest work of ordinary white men.[20]

Later in the debate, Douglas highlighted the convergence of Illinois Democrats and Republicans in matters of race as he echoed the views of his state's junior senator. Douglas agreed with Trumbull that the people of Maine had every right "to confer just such privileges as they think proper in that state, under their local constitution upon the colored population" but insisted that other states, such as his own, retained the right to decide otherwise. He reminded Seward and Fessenden that the Topeka Constitution, drafted by Free-Soilers in Kansas and backed by Republicans in Congress as the legitimate will of the people of Kansas, contained similar language restricting the migration of free people of color into the proposed state. Drawing on themes he would return to consistently throughout the coming campaign season, Douglas emphasized his own constitutional consistency and lambasted the Republicans for their apparent malleability.[21]

Eager to take advantage of the public's prejudice, Illinois Democratic newspapers leveled charges of racial egalitarianism against the Republicans. That Trumbull had repudiated his northeastern compatriots made little difference, and several publications falsely printed that Trumbull had concurred with Seward and Fessenden. Even when confronted by the transcript of the debates, the *Illinois State Register* insisted that Trumbull had offered only a halfhearted defense of white supremacy and opened the door to racial equality. In frustration, Trumbull wrote to John M. Palmer that he had only spoken out to "disavow the objection" of these men, knowing that "such a position could not be maintained in [Illinois]" and hoped that the local Republican press could "set [him] right in the matter." Trumbull had sought to frame a centrist position that appealed to the prejudices of his constituents, opposed both to slavery's extension and to Black rights, but instead found himself tarred with the brush of radicalism. Trumbull's subsequent vote against Oregon's admission, though justified on the grounds of insufficient population, left him further exposed to such attacks as that in the *Illinois State Register,* which mocked him for refusing to add "another free state to the galaxy of the Union" and standing instead with "the abolition ultraes and the ultra southern senators" who blocked the westward progress of white Americans by their obsession with enslaved Blacks.[22]

As if to highlight their racial animus, that same month, white Illinoisians in the solidly Republican town of Bloomington attempted to lynch Josiah Brown, a Black Springfield resident accused of assaulting a little girl. Although Brown escaped the angry mob with the assistance of local marshals, as the parties raced to the steps of the town jail "one man attempted to throw a rope around his neck," and "he received a powerful blow, from a powerful man, on the side of his head." While the city's Republican organ, the *Pantagraph,* condemned the vigilantes, it made it clear that it "did not have the slightest sympathy for the guilty criminal." Instead, employing distinctly conservative language, it denounced "the mob spirit" that it found reminiscent of the "Jacobin tribunal of revolutionary France" and announced its "resolute determination to sustain the law and its officers, at all hazards, to the fullest extent, against all opposition." The threat that mobs posed to white citizens, and especially private property, disturbed the editors far more than the assault against a Black man. Indeed, they took it on themselves to remind their readers that in other cities, attacks that had originally only intended to destroy "'abolition' halls and negro dwellings . . . grew in a few years into mobs against banks and railroads." By their account, mobs might commence their struggle with righteous anger such as when they attacked "disreputable houses" (i.e., brothels) or Black criminals. In the end, however, the madness of an unrestrained mob would ultimately target wealth and threaten those "gentlemen of property and standing" who had originally acted alongside the rowdies.[23]

Beyond distancing themselves from charges of racial egalitarianism, Illinois Republicans sought to establish themselves as the conservative defenders of free soil battling against a vacillating demagogue. Although a chasm remained between Douglas Democrats in Congress and the administration—indeed, Trumbull believed by late May that Congressman Harris would never reconcile with the party's pro-Southern wing—the Republican press painted Douglas and other Democrats as meekly returning to the fold. Deliberately misconstruing peace gestures by Douglas as an act of submission, the *Illinois State Journal* encouraged anti-Lecompton Democrats to formally cross the aisle for principle's sake. The paper confidently declared that "the main body of the anti-Lecompton Democrats through the country cherish no thought or dream of stultifying themselves," and however Douglas and his organs may shift and back and fill and dodge and waver," honest anti-Lecompton Democrats would not "be intimidated by the cry that they are affiliating with the Black Republicans, when sacred and fundamental principles are sacrificed." Confident that the Lecompton crisis had revealed the venality of the Buchanan administration, the Illinois Republicans hoped to peel away Douglas's supporters by hinting that he would inevitably submit to the dictations of the pro-Southern party leadership.[24]

In contrast, the state's leading Douglas Democrats expressed renewed confidence that they could draw many conservative Republicans into a new centrist coalition. Writing to Douglas at the end of May, Sheahan of the *Chicago Times* acknowledged that while Douglas Democrats could not "expect a single Republican leader to join" them, they might yet "obtain large accessions from the rank & file" of that party. Responding to a call by its rival, the *Illinois State Journal*, to publish Douglas's latest speech, the *Illinois State Register* chortled that it was "pleased to see that the Journal finds a demand for Douglas' views among its readers" and expected that the Republicans merely sought to "steal Douglas' thunder" in order "to justify their efforts to supplant him" in the Senate. The *Register* correctly recognized that Douglas's stand against his party's Southern leaders distinguished him in the minds of wavering voters as a leader rather than a lackey.[25]

Balancing their distaste for domineering Southerners with a fear of sectional discord, conservative former Whigs, even those who had supported Fillmore or Frémont in 1856, saw an appeal in Douglas's middle way. Despite his earlier missteps with the Kansas-Nebraska Act, Douglas could build a coalition that would protect the interests of free white Northern men without destroying the Union and Constitution, the ultimate safeguards of their rights.[26]

To prevent such defections, some Republicans pushed to purge the party of its most radical leader, Congressman Lovejoy. Having reluctantly consented to Lovejoy's nomination in 1856, Davis of Bloomington now worked behind the scenes to draft an alternative candidate who could beat Lovejoy in the district's convention. The full extent of the scheme remains unclear, but on May 25, Davis confided to Ward Hill Lamon, "Unless our friends are all woefully mistaken in their calculations, somebody other than Mr. Lovejoy will be nominated." Having apparently taken Lincoln's advice to heart, Lovejoy simultaneously had his own allies working for his renomination, and at the close of the congressional session in June he wrote to his daughter to assure her he had recently received a dispatch that "settles the matter of my nomination." What exactly this dispatch contained remains unclear, but two days after Lovejoy drafted his note, a distressed Lamon wrote to Lincoln that Lovejoy's nomination would put "this Congressional District irredeemably in the hands of the Abolitionists" and that many conservative Republicans expressed their preference to back Douglas and his men rather than continue in such an organization. Lincoln stoically replied that he considered Lovejoy's "renomination a fixed fact" and believed that running an independent candidate would "result in nothing but disaster all round" as it would split Republicans on the state level and might easily hand a safe Republican seat to the Democrats. Furthermore, he believed that he intended "to run with patience" the chance that some fellow Republicans might go over to Douglas. With his eyes squarely fixed on the impending race for the Senate, Lincoln believed the Republicans could not afford to upend their fragile coalition. Instead of guiding another realignment that would exclude the abolitionists, Lincoln hoped to downplay the radicalism of his allies while bolstering his own conservative credentials and positioning Douglas as either a dupe or covert agent of the Slave Power.[27]

"A House Divided against Itself Cannot Stand."

The Republican state convention in Springfield, scheduled for June 16, 1858, marked a chance for the party to rally on a common platform and, in an unusual move, on a candidate for the US Senate. As it had in the case of Trumbull and all US senators prior to the adoption of the Seventeenth Amendment in 1913, the state legislature of Illinois would choose the state's next senator. Given the indirect method of election, the battle for a Senate seat usually occurred after the popular election, as it had in the contest between Shields, Trumbull, Matteson, and Lincoln in early 1855. But in 1858, with the state's Republican leadership unanimously in favor of Lincoln and the challenge of unseating the indomitable Little Giant clear to all after the Lecompton affair had tipped so many eastern Republicans in Douglas's favor, the convention chose to formally announce that Lincoln was "the first and only choice of the Republicans of Illinois for the United States Senate."[28]

Beyond the choice of candidates for state treasurer and state superintendent of public schools, the convention adopted a declaration of principles, drafted primarily by Orville H. Browning, that fiercely denounced the Dred Scott decision as judicial overreach and lambasted the Buchanan's administration's "corrupt, unjust, and undignified" actions in Kansas. They also adopted a plank that lamented "the rapidly increasing expenditures of the General Government, which . . . threaten the country with national bankruptcy" and pledged to enact "a thorough and radical reform in the Administration of the government finances" should they win power. This measure furthered the cause of partisan consolidation by simultaneously appealing to the fiscal conservatism of former Jacksonians and the reform impulses of ex-Whigs. According to the *Illinois State Journal,* these declarations proved that the Republican Party was not a sectional clique but rather "eminently national" in its outlook and pledged to principles that "commend themselves to all conservative and patriotic men." Reflecting on the party's political journey since the Bloomington Convention, the *Chicago Tribune* celebrated the spirit of unity that prevailed at Springfield and believed its resolutions demonstrated that "the Republican party is the true, and only conservative party of the nation" and the vehicle for "that triumph for which the opponents of slavery and the friends of white men and free labor have contended." Recognizing the document's popular appeal, the *Illinois State Register* could only argue that Browning had "smothered" the "actual position of his party" by taking such conservative ground. Radical abolitionists lamented the document's conservative tendencies and hoped "the honest friends of freedom" would no longer "delude themselves with the idea that a party" that defended the rights of the slave states could, in fact, warrant antislavery support. As such, as Lincoln took the stage at the close of the convention, he had a golden opportunity to cement his campaign as a conservative quest to protect the rights of free white Northerners.[29]

In the address that followed, however, Lincoln inadvertently exposed himself to charges of radicalism, a stigma his campaign would carry until the close of the 1858 contest. The so-called House Divided speech has lived on in popular memory as a prescient prediction of the impending sectional struggle and a statement of Lincoln's determination to cleanse the nation of slavery. This interpretation, although understandable for twenty-first-century readers focused on the Civil War and for contemporary Southerners primed to see abolitionist conspiracies, seriously misunderstands the speech's message and more closely matches the misreading propagated by Lincoln's partisan opponents than his actual intent. The confusion arises from the undue emphasis placed on the address's opening lines:

- In *my* opinion, it *will* not cease, until a *crisis* shall have been reached, and passed.
- "A house divided against itself cannot stand."
- I believe this government cannot endure, permanently half *slave* and half *free*.
- I do not expect the Union to be *dissolved*—I do not expect the house to *fall*—but I *do* expect it will cease to be divided.
- It will become *all* one thing or *all* the other.
- Either the *opponents* of slavery, will arrest the further spread of it, and place it where the public mind shall rest in the belief that it is in the course of ultimate extinction; or its *advocates* will push it forward, till it shall become alike lawful in *all* the States, *old* as well as *new*—*North* as well as *South*.

At first glance, Lincoln appeared to predict the coming storm in which Northern arms would defend the Union, extinguish slavery, and reunite the divided nation on the basis of freedom. It is possible he intentionally deployed these lines as a calculated effort to broadcast his antipathy for slavery to radical members of the party. Yet, as historian William W. Freehling has pointed out in his recent biography, *Becoming Lincoln,* it was the critical following sentence—"Have we no tendency to the latter condition?"—that served as the speech's thesis. For the remainder of the address, Lincoln outlined the efforts of Southern slaveholders to extend the institution of bondage into the free territories and free states. In a theme that would reappear throughout the campaign, Lincoln caricatured Douglas as either the pawn or dupe of powerful slaveholders. Largely ignoring Lecompton, Lincoln attacked Douglas for his support of the Kansas-Nebraska Act and the Dred Scott decision, policies that had put Northern free-soil advocates on the defensive. He argued that contrary to the Founders' intentions, freedom had become the exception rather than the rule. He warned, "We shall *lie down* pleasantly dreaming that the people of *Missouri* are on the verge of making their State *free;* and we shall *awake* to the *reality,* instead, that the *Supreme* Court has made *Illinois* a *slave* State." Far from an outline for ridding the South of slavery, Lincoln's speech was a rallying cry to protect freedom in the free states.[30]

While the remainder of the address clearly framed Southern slaveholders and not Northern Republicans as the sectional aggressors, by invoking Mark 3:25 and hinting at the "ultimate extinction" of slavery, Lincoln offered his opponents all the ammunition they needed to tar him as an abolitionist. In Lincoln's mind, the Founders had begun the process of arresting its progress and gradually excising the institution from the body politic, a project the Republican party, as the conservative national party, sought only to renew. Lincoln had borrowed the phrase *ultimate extinction* from Henry Clay, who had written of his desire to see a gradual end to slavery in his home state of Kentucky back in the early 1840s. The North's gradual emancipation laws—which had liberated the enslaved at a snail's pace (and, in fact, were still under way in New Jersey in the 1850s)—served Clay and Lincoln's model for efforts to end slavery. In the years since Clay's letter, however, radical abolitionists, including William Lloyd Garrison, had referred to slavery's "extinction" within an immediatist framework. Indeed, except for its rhetorical flourishes, Lincoln's address spoke more to the ideals of the Kentucky statesman than to those of the New England abolitionist. Nevertheless, the speech's Manichean framework and ambiguous phrasing proved deeply unsettling for moderates who hoped to preserve sectional harmony as well as the rights of the free states.[31]

Within a few days, Lincoln began to recognize his words' unintended implications. John L. Scripps, a friendly editor from Chicago, wrote to Lincoln congratulating him on his address but warning him that "his Kentucky friends who want to be Republicans, but who are afraid we are not sufficiently conservative" objected to the "ultraism" of his promise to set slavery toward "ultimate extinction" and believed it "an implied pledge of behalf of the Republican party to make war upon the institution in the states where it now exists." Lincoln, "much mortified" that his words had taken on such a radical bent, immediately sought to clarify his position. He repeated, as he "had declared a thousand times," that "neither the General Government, nor any other power outside of the slave states, can constitutionally or rightfully interfere with slaves or slavery where it already exists" and that his word simply reflected his commitment to "head off" the introduction of slavery into the territories and "into the free states themselves." It seems Lincoln genuinely believed that Douglas would willingly resubmit the yoke of slavery whenever it proved politically expedient. But this theory discounted Douglas's significant role in blocking Lecompton, a display of political independence voters would not soon forget. As such, while Lincoln's words would ring prophetic for future generations, they struck a dissonant chord in the context of 1858 Illinois.[32]

Indeed, the *Illinois State Register* quickly exploited this oversight, rebuking Lincoln's characterization of Douglas as "a dead lion" by asking their readers if "the lion who stood in the pathway of Lecomptonism [was] dead when he bid the entire power and patronage of the government defiance and forbid the consummation of that iniquity." To use a different metaphor, Douglas had successfully rebranded himself as a political maverick, breaking definitively with the administration while maintaining his Democratic identity. This sort of independence allowed him to claim the mantle of the disinterested statesman, a relic of eighteenth-century republicanism, and an appealing trait for former Whigs who remained suspicious of political parties in general. Although now despised by many Southern Democrats, Douglas had retained the support of a few Southern leaders and organs, bolstering his claim to national, as opposed to merely sectional, support. The *State Register* eagerly pointed out that even "a number of republicans . . . think that in a struggle for the defence of the state, and of the constitution, and of the north, good sense would dictate [the election of] a senator who can command support and power with the entire people of the Union." Within this narrative, Douglas emerged a fierce defender of the Union who stood against sectional extremists, assailing proslavery men from the South as fiercely as abolitionists from the North.[33]

In a letter to Palmer shortly after the Springfield Convention, Trumbull correctly recognized that Douglas would "claim great credit for independence" in his opposition to the Lecompton constitution and "appeal to the masses of all parties to sustain him for the great good he has done." Indeed, one of Douglas's correspondents proudly identified himself as "an anti-Lecompton anti-slavery Douglas Democrat." In Washington, as the Senate's session wound to a close, Trumbull delivered the disturbing news that Kentucky senator Crittenden, a Know-Nothing and one of a handful of Southern officials who had opposed both the Kansas-Nebraska Act and the Lecompton constitution, now voiced full support for Douglas. The Kentuckian, widely seen as Clay's political heir, had recently approached Trumbull in the Senate chamber and told him that he "ought to have no controversy with Douglas" because "he was opposing the administration too." Should Crittenden publicly endorse Douglas, his influence would likely sway many of the Fillmore men in Illinois, who might interpret Crittenden's bipartisanship as the foundation for a new national conservative Union coalition.[34]

Douglas thus benefited immensely from his renewed claim to the political center. Having distanced himself from overtly proslavery Southern Democrats, Douglas could convincingly rebuff Republican claims that he was a mere tool of slaveholders. By defending popular sovereignty and the integrity of the electoral process, Douglas struck a chord with conservative defenders of constitutional order and republican government. Furthermore, by building bridges with Southern former Whigs, like Crittenden, Douglas could claim to have transcended both party and section, an alluring prospect for voters who still yearned to recreate the supposed unpartisan atmosphere of the Founding era. Thus, while Douglas's break with Buchanan and the South had come at a considerable political cost on the national level, it vastly enhanced his stature among conservative Illinois swing voters.

Appealing to the Conservative Masses

Despite such advantages, Douglas still faced a difficult campaign season. While he might have erred in his House Divided speech, Lincoln was a worthy opponent, and on learning the news of his nomination, Douglas told his colleague John W. Forney, "I shall have my hands full.... If I beat him my victory will be hardly won." Beyond facing the opposition's best stump speaker, the Buchanan administration cut off all the normal Democratic fundraising channels, and Douglas had to journey north to ask for money from Cornelius Vanderbilt and other disaffected New York Democrats once Congress adjourned. Circumstances eventually required Douglas to mortgage his real estate in Chicago for $80,000 to finance the campaign, a sacrifice the two-term incumbent could not have imagined a year before.[35]

Although he had intended to wait until after he met with the Democratic state committee to begin his campaign, upon his return to the Windy City on July 9, Douglas extemporaneously responded to Lincoln's accusations in a speech delivered from the balcony of the Tremont House. To no one's surprise, the address centered on popular sovereignty. Douglas colored his "great principle" with a shade of white supremacy that appealed to the state's farmers, tradesmen, and laborers. In a statement that would have resonated with a vast majority of white men in both parties, he promised to "extend to the negro and the Indian and to all dependent races every right, every privilege, and every immunity consistent with the safety and welfare of the white races" but would never take "any step that recognizes the negro man or the Indian as the equal of the white man." He defined popular sovereignty as "the right of every community to decide for itself, whether a thing is right or wrong, whether it would be a good or evil for them to adopt it." As such, Douglas insisted that social evils, whether slavery or intemperance, could not and should not be regulated from on high. Instead, local communities of free white men should decide how to regulate these evils. Douglas maintained that the South had as much right to impose slavery on Blacks as the New England states had to enfranchise them. He believed both choices foolish and endorsed Illinois's decision to both exclude slavery and deny Blacks social and political rights. Still, he asserted that only time, experience, and the will of the people would bring about the moral uniformity the Republicans seemed so eager to impose from above. Douglas also accused the Republicans of forming a secret alliance with the Danites to unseat him. Such charges were not without merit. Although Lincoln himself would have nothing to do with the Buchanan Democrats, Danite managers had begun corresponding with Republican leaders early in the year and would continue to do so throughout the campaign, pragmatically recognizing that sharing information with the enemy of one's enemy could serve a productive purpose.[36]

The speech highlighted Douglas's bid for a broad centrist coalition to fight against the two extremes of abolitionist Republicans and proslavery Danites. The *Mount Carmel Register* framed the address as an invitation for wayward Democrats with free-soil proclivities to return to the fold, noting that Douglas had shown how he would "equally resist the proslavery aggressions of Southern Hotspurs, and the fanatical intolerance of Northern biggots," and thus the "thousands of good Democrats" who in 1856 "left the party and voted with the Republicans, under the full belief that popular sovereignty would extend slavery" could "now see their error" and rejoin their old comrades. The *Islander and Argus* of Rock Island built on this theme and made the connection to free soil even more explicit as it appealed directly to "the men who make their bread by the sweat of their brow—the honest day laborer, the industrious mechanic, and the hard-fisted farmer." The *Islander and Argus* urged those in the Republican ranks to "see the error of their way" by reminding them that they too hoped "that every state which comes into the Union for the next century may be a free state" but that the decision remained in the hands of the people of those states, as they, like free men everywhere "are abundantly able to take care of themselves." Such an interpretation of popular sovereignty spelled trouble for Lincoln and the Republicans, as Douglas appeared to offer both a free West and an end to sectional agitation on slavery.[37]

It would take several weeks before Lincoln and Douglas would agree to share a platform for a set of formal debates, and in the meantime, Lincoln revived his practice of trailing Douglas on the campaign trail and offering rejoinders when the opportunity arose. Present in the audience for Douglas's Chicago address, Lincoln replied to the Little Giant the following day at the same venue. After disclaiming any connection with the Danites, Lincoln argued that popular sovereignty, a fraud from the beginning, had become a moot point after the Dred Scott Decision. Since territorial legislatures could not constitutionally prohibit slavery, it was mere sophistry to argue that the people of that territory retained the right to govern the institution. Lincoln knew that Douglas had addressed this issue back in 1857 by arguing that the people could still exclude slavery by failing to pass positive laws protecting the institution, a position that would become known as the Freeport Doctrine in the debates to come, but felt the point contributed to his portrayal of Douglas as the dupe of proslavery forces. Disgusted by Douglas's preening on Lecompton, Lincoln reminded his listeners that the Republicans had provided most of the votes against the constitution and had opposed the fraud with as much vehemence as had Douglas or any other Northern Democrat.[38]

Yet, despite these attacks, Lincoln took up a largely defensive posture, seeking to clarify his position on slavery's "ultimate extinction." He said that he had "made a prediction only," and "it may have been a foolish one" that slavery would ultimately wither away but claimed that by doing so, he merely professed the faith of the Founders. He in no way sought to interfere with slavery in the states but rather believed that the institution would recede if blocked from the West and claimed that through this means, "the great mass of the nation have rested that slavery was in course of ultimate extinction" until the trend reversed itself via the Kansas-Nebraska Act. Recognizing the allure of Douglas's appeal to white supremacy, Lincoln insisted that the Republicans remained committed to "the settlement of free white laborers who want the land [of the West] to bring up their families upon" and that "no one wants to deny" Douglas's assertion "that this government was made for white men." Regarding race relations, Lincoln insisted that "as God made us separate, we can leave one another alone, and do one another much good thereby." In closing, he offered his most convincing argument for undecided listeners by claiming that the Republicans sought only to protect the Declaration of Independence's assertion of egalitarian republicanism against the assault of an entrenched aristocracy. He held that the Republicans echoed the Founders by rejecting "the arguments that kings have made for enslaving the people in all ages of the world," by upholding the dignity of labor.[39]

Yet, before he finished, Lincoln punctuated this point with a phrase that, while it rings true in the twenty-first, amounted to a costly gaffe in the nineteenth century. In concluding his point on the promise of the Declaration of Independence, Lincoln asked his listeners to "discard all this quibbling about this man and other man—this race and that race being inferior . . . and unite as one people throughout this land, until we shall once more stand up declaring that all men are created equal." As he had already asserted his conservatism on matters concerning slavery and white supremacy, one should not understand this passage as evidence of the Springfield lawyer's underlying commitment to racial egalitarianism. His opponents, eager to capitalize on any hint of radicalism, would read it this way, but Lincoln intended only to clarify that the questions of race paled in comparison to the principles of republican government. Still, by asking his listeners to disregard the question of race, even for just a moment, Lincoln again opened himself up to the charge of favoring Black equality. As such, the *Illinois State Register* gleefully reprinted the speech in full, claiming it revealed Lincoln's "bald-faced abolitionism," and Douglas twisted the language to argue that Lincoln believed "that the Almighty had made the negro equal to the white man . . . [and] that the negro is his brother." Lincoln's immediate reaction to such accusations remains unknown, though his later remark from an undated manuscript— "Negro equality! Fudge!!"—likely captures his feelings at the time.[40]

Already on the defensive following Lincoln's House Divided speech, Illinois Republicans sought to distance themselves from any form of radicalism. Reviving its Whig identity as it claimed Clay's mantle, the *Illinois State Journal* explained, "There is a vast and illimitable difference between Abolitionism and Republicanism." While the former demanded adherence to radical dogmatism, the latter only sought to restore the status quo of the Revolutionary Fathers. The *Olney Times* built on this theme, explaining to its readers that while "there are a few abolitionists that have voted for the Republican ticket . . . [it] only proved that they lay down their abolitionism and give in their adhesion to the conservative doctrine of Republicanism." Democrats would repeatedly claim that the abolitionists had established the "Black Republican Party" to serve their radical ends, but Republicans insisted that, if anything, they had turned some abolitionists into solid constitutional conservatives. Encapsulating the admixture of antislavery, anti-Southern, and anti-Black sentiment that characterized mainstream Illinois Republican thought, the *Waukegan Gazette* insisted, "Republicans believe that there are other rights and interests to be fostered and guarded aside from slavery. That white men have rights which negro-drivers and negro-breeders are bound to respect."[41]

As the campaign season intensified, the Illinois Republicans mustered their full strength for an all-out battle. Unlike most of the Illinois congressional delegation, Trumbull had postponed his homecoming after the end of the congressional session in June and displayed some reluctance to take the stump. One historian has attributed this reticence to a lack of enthusiasm for Lincoln and his candidacy, a view informed by the pair's 1855 senate contest and past partisan affiliations. It is true the two never developed a close friendship, and Trumbull may have feared playing second fiddle to Lincoln in the senate. Nevertheless, Trumbull deeply respected Lincoln and acknowledged his essential role in forming the state Republican Party. Committed as any Illinois Republican to bringing down Douglas, Trumbull had pledged to support Lincoln's bid for the senate months before the Republican convention at Springfield. It seems more likely that Trumbull was expressing authentic fatigue when he wrote to his brother that he was delaying his return out of a combination of exhaustion and a desire to avoid the sweltering heat of the Illinois summer. Trumbull was never completely comfortable in front of large crowds, and the prospect of a relaxing vacation with his extended family in New England must have seemed more appealing to him than tramping the dusty roads of the Prairie State. Still, at state party leaders' urging, he traveled back to Illinois in time to change the course of the campaign.[42]

Arriving in the state in late July, Trumbull delivered his first canvass speech on August 7 in Chicago. In a passionate address sprinkled with populist flair, Trumbull sought to create a clear distinction between the Republicans and Democrats in the minds of voters. Like Lincoln, he sought to blur the line between Buchanan and Douglas and frame the contest as a battle between the corrupt forces of slavery extension and the righteous defenders of free labor. But appealing to his audience's fiscal, constitutional, and racial conservatism, however, Trumbull's address proved more palatable to moderate voters than Lincoln's House Divided speech.

Determined to "cram the truth down an honest man's throat until he cannot deny it," Trumbull insisted that "the ruling dynasty" had appropriated millions of taxpayer dollars and "squandered [it] upon partisan favorites" through a wasteful expansion of federal bureaucracy that amounted to nothing less than a "plundering [of] the public treasury." By denouncing the Buchanan administration as corrupt and fiscally irresponsible, he sought to appeal to both the longstanding Whig preoccupation with executive overreach and the Democratic desire for strict economy in matters of federal spending. In another clever attack on the administration, Trumbull harangued President Buchanan and the Supreme Court for their efforts to force slavery into the territories via the Dred Scott Decision, announcing that "despotism is despotism, whether practiced by crowned heads or men in gowns" and promising to appeal the ruling "to a power higher than presidents . . . whose name is the people." Again, by attacking executive overreach and framing resistance as a bottom-up response, Trumbull appealed to constituents of both old political parties simultaneously. In his most damning accusation, Trumbull tied Douglas to Buchanan's Lecompton policy and insisted Douglas had prevented an up or down vote in Kansas on the Lecompton constitution by blocking an amendment to that effect when Congress had authorized Kansas's constitutional convention. Douglas's subsequent turn against Lecompton amounted to nothing more than a cowardly act of political self-preservation. More committed to power than to principle, Trumbull hinted that Douglas would soon return to his old ways of gratifying corrupt slavocrats.[43]

As such, Trumbull told his audience that it faced a clear choice, that despite what Douglas said, "no middle ground," "no third party," and "no Douglas party" existed. Instead, a moderate core of former Democrats and Whigs had rallied to the Republican standard while corrupt extremists stood by "the self-styled Democratic party." Far from occupying radical ground, Republicans proposed to leave the slavery question "exactly where the men who framed the Constitution left it" and merely block its advance because, like Jefferson and Washington, they thought "it better for the white race that there should be no slavery [in the territories]." Rather than promote Black rights or racial "amalgamation," Trumbull promised that the Republican Party would allow states and territories "to deal with their black population as they shall think best, for we have no power then to interfere with it." Appealing to the baser prejudices of white Illinoisians, Trumbull mocked enslaved people, who were "black as the African, with flat noses, thick lips and wooly heads," and degraded free white labor by their presence. Eager to show that the Republicans exhibited as much enthusiasm for white supremacy as their opponents, Trumbull insisted that "I want to have nothing to do, either with the free negroe or the slave negroe. We, the Republican party, are the white man's party." By giving moderate white male Illinoisians a chance to vote simultaneously against slavery and against Blacks as devotees of the Founders, Trumbull struck a chord that would have resonated with many voters throughout the state.[44]

Illinois Republican organs heartily endorsed such sentiments. The *Waukegan Gazette* rejoiced that Trumbull had made clear that he and the Republican Party merely sought "to bring back the Government to the economical and freedom-fostering condition it occupied during the times of Jefferson and Madison, and to stay and set back the tide of slavery-propagandism." The *Illinois State Journal* praised the state's junior US senator for exposing Douglas's "treachery and hypocrisy" on the Lecompton question and reminding voters of the failure of popular sovereignty. The speech even drew the attention of the press outside the state. The *Louisville Journal*, Kentucky's premier ex-Whig and Know-Nothing organ, hailed Trumbull's address as the beginning of a new chapter in the Republican Party's history, commending Trumbull's position "as the doctrine of the Constitution and the fathers of the Constitution." While the *Chicago Press and Tribune* believed the *Journal* had made a mistake in reading Trumbull's address as an innovation, it remained glad that it had discovered that the Republican Party "is a truly conservative organization based upon the principles of the federal constitution."[45]

Such an endorsement by a voice of border state Whiggery proved especially welcome as the Republicans reeled from a cutting betrayal. As it had become increasingly clear that Lovejoy would coast to renomination in the Third Congressional District, Republican leaders expressed concern that some sort of coalition between Douglas Democrats and the most vocally antiabolitionist Republicans might emerge. As late as August 2, Davis had written to Lincoln encouraging him to shift his support to a moderate candidate to avoid a split in the party. On August 9, T. Lyle Dickey, a former Whig originally from Kentucky and Lovejoy's prime Republican nemesis in the Third District, announced his support for Douglas in a letter to Benjamin S. Edwards—another former Whig and Know-Nothing who had defected to the Democrats following the Lecompton crisis—published in the *Chicago Times*. Dickey explained that the Illinois Republicans had come under the sway "of the revolutionary element of the old Abolition party," thus leaving Douglas "the representative of the conservatism of the country." To assuage those who had long opposed Douglas for repealing the Missouri Compromise, Dickey promised that Lecompton had chastened the Little Giant and that he "would not again be led astray in a foolish crusade on the errand of slavery propagandism." Dickey thus outlined the middle way that Trumbull denied in his Chicago speech: disgruntled Republicans, Know-Nothings, and Free-Soil Democrats could all unite behind Douglas and strike a blow against both the arrogant slaveholders and the fanatical abolitionists. Joining other prominent former Whigs like John T. Stuart, James Singleton, and Usher F. Linder, Dickey's endorsement of Douglas created a crisis for the Republicans in the key counties of central Illinois.[46]

Aware of Dickey's influence among the former Whigs, many of whom had split their tickets and voted for Fillmore and Bissell in 1856, key Republican newspapers sought to win over these voters through appeals to their deeply entrenched nativism and anti-Catholicism. Unwilling to alienate the many German Protestants who had become reliable Republicans, the party usually targeted the Irish in its attacks. The *Chicago Press and Tribune* denounced Democratic "demagogues" for their pursuit of "Catholic influence and Irish votes." Later, in its coverage of the debate between Lincoln and Douglas at Freeport, the *Press and Tribune* mocked Douglas's "bodyguard of five or six hundred Irish Papists," whom it saw "yelling and cheering at all he said, perfectly indifferent whether it was sound sense or wild raving." For its part, the *Illinois State Journal* claimed, "Popery and Slavery have been the hard masters of the American people" and this insidious force would "proscribe and beat down Americans because they were born on American soil, and because they would not yield allegiance to those of Rome." As such, the paper subsequently argued that it would welcome the "overthrow in the councils of the nation of the now ascendant and intolerant Catholicism of the Irish" in support of "the further progress of the white man's party to which we belong." To make the ethnocultural and political split even more apparent, the *Central Transcript* of Clinton lambasted "the attempt of the Senator and his friends to honeyfuggle the Americans, while surrounding themselves with, and depending upon the votes and shillealahs of the Tipperary and Galaway democracy." Such a revival of the rhetoric of 1854, framing the Democrats as the party of slavery, Catholicism, and rowdiness, would have forced Douglas-leaning former Know-Nothings to take stock of their priorities.[47]

Indeed, while nativist sentiments had waned since the Know-Nothing surge of 1854–55, ethnocultural factors continued to play a role in the ongoing realignment. While former Fillmore voters heartily appreciated Douglas's effort to push back the tide of extremism from both sections, they continued to distrust the Irish Catholic laborers who served as the Democracy's foot soldiers in Chicago and other commercial centers. The working-class sons of the Emerald Isle had acquired a reputation for disorderly behavior and corruption. Such characteristics, combined with supposed superstition of their faith, made former Whigs and Know-Nothings think twice before joining forces. Disturbed as they were by the abolitionists and the threat of disunion, these men recoiled from the prospect of selling their republican—and Protestant—birthright for a mess of Irish pottage.

Although the results among swing voters proved mixed, the push to establish the Republicans' conservative bona fides did persuade some. While not an intentional strategy, the Republican appeals to white supremacy, nativism, and anti-Catholicism, along with the party's insistence that it would leave slavery at peace in the states where it already existed, disgusted the state's small cohort of radicals and drew denunciations from national voices of abolitionism. Such rebukes clearly distinguished the Republicans from radical antislavery activists and indirectly assured conservative voters of the party's soundness. For instance, Seth Paine, a radical white abolitionist from Chicago, insisted "this Republican party has no principle to carry it along" and complained that "old-fashioned abolitionism is totally ignored even among the old staunch friends of freedom." He took special aim at Lovejoy, the preeminent "radical" Republican, and claimed that by tempering his rhetoric to suit voters, he had lost "the old fire that reached the soul when there was no chance of his going to Congress." Watching the contest from afar, Frederick Douglass agreed, explaining that "just this kind of cowardice, this shortsighted expediency, this time-serving policy, which has been adopted in Illinois ... if generally adopted, would shut up the mouth, not only of the editor of this paper, but of every earnest, honest Abolitionist in the country."[48]

Schemes and Debates

At the opposing end of the political spectrum, the proslavery Danites offered the Republicans some indirect assistance through their attempts to siphon off most unabashedly partisan Democrats as well as those few Illinoisans with pro-Southern outlooks. Danite newspapers emphasized that Douglas had unliterally cast longtime party leaders, such as former governor John M. Reynolds, out of the fold while appealing to the party's enemies. The *Times and Delta* of Cairo defiantly exclaimed that Douglas "may enlist Know Nothings and other outsiders under his new banner, but the true old Democracy believe that the party exists for some other purpose than to merely send Stephen A. Douglas to the United States Senate." The eccentric editor and Republican mayor of Chicago, Long John Wentworth, had earlier pushed Democrats toward the Danites through similar accusations of a cult of personality, explaining the "the Douglas faction in this State ... has no distinctive principles of its own—Douglas is the Alpha and Omega of its creed. Let Douglas die to-morrow and the faction would melt away like the morning dew."[49]

Months after any hope of a real coalition between the Republicans and Douglas had collapsed, the Danites also continued to insist that the rivals had consummated such a union and as eagerly pointed to one local Republican convention in southern Illinois that refused to nominate candidates to oppose the pro-Douglas Democrats. In an astounding display of submissiveness to

Southern interests, one Danite of Little Egypt attacked Douglas in the pages of Cairo's *Times and Delta* for acknowledging the right of New England states to permit Black suffrage. Although Douglas had repeatedly stated his opposition to Black voting, he affirmed the right of the people to make such a "mistake" out of deference to traditional Democratic commitments to states' rights and local self-government. Not so, according to the author of this letter to the editor, who demanded federal intervention in the North to prevent "the perverted tastes" of Yankees "to kill our votes in the election of President of the United States." Such a position ventured beyond the pale for most Illinois Democrats, who, in the words of historian Michael E. Woods, recoiled when Southern interests "threatened white men's vaunted self-rule." Still, the point would have rung true with the most extreme pro-Southern radicals, who, like radical abolitionists, peered inward from the margins of the state's political community.[50]

The Danites ultimately hoped to retain a voice in a divided legislature to thwart Douglas, but even the faction's leaders sometimes doubted they could achieve such an end. Back in June, an administration supporter in Chicago had diplomatically informed President Buchanan, "The Democratic Party in this state is peculiarly situated" before explaining how Illinois Democrats overwhelmingly supported Douglas. Later in the summer, the Danites convinced former US senator Sidney Breese to enter the race as their candidate, but in a telling note, a longtime Breese admirer warned the candidate that he should not expect more than two hundred votes in his county, even though it had given Buchanan more than five thousand in 1856. Still, optimists like Cook of Chicago wrote "Although not successful we shall hold without doubt the balance of power." Although the proadministration vote totals would fall far short of such a goal, the Danites gave the Douglas Democrats enough trouble to prompt the *Illinois State Register* to attack those "sallow looking people, the majority of whom suck at the 'government teats'" and accuse them of serving as "the guerillas of the Republican Party." Furthermore, the possibility of defections among particular state senators in exchange for national patronage positions continued to trouble party leaders like Harris and Lanphier well into the fall.[51]

Historians have devoted oceans of ink to the seven joint debates held between late August and mid-October in Ottawa, Freeport, Jonesboro, Charleston, Galesburg, Quincy, and Alton, and some have sought to identify individual winners and losers of each meeting. A scholarly consensus has emerged that Lincoln grew increasingly comfortable throughout the debates and shined brightest in the final contests. This analysis recognizes Lincoln's disadvantage in entering the contest because of his blunders earlier in the summer and that despite his activism in the state party, he remained a marginal figure in comparison to Douglas. By avoiding serious missteps and maintaining a fierce energy on the campaign trail despite a grueling schedule, Lincoln likely gained more from the meetings than Douglas. A blow-by-blow account of each debate goes beyond the scope of this book, but several key features need to be addressed.[52]

First, as Lincoln and Douglas formally began their series of famous debates, the Douglas Democrats had set their sights on winning back the estimated two-thirds of Illinois German Americans who had defected to the Republicans since 1854. A series of reports sent to Douglas insisted that targeted support for the Democratic German-language press and adroit handling of the unpopular Dred Scott decision would swing the community back into the fold. Although Douglas needed to tread carefully as he sought to cultivate both Germans and nativists, Louis Didier, a former editor of St. Clair County's *Deutcher Demokrat,* thought that Douglas's position on Lecompton and Lincoln's apparent radicalism would "bring [Germans] over in squads."[53]

In an unsavory reflection of Douglas's political pragmatism, the Little Giant employed race-baiting to square the circle and appeal to both Germans and former Know-Nothings in the pair's first joint debate at Ottawa, where he attacked Lincoln as a proponent of racial equality and suggested that Lincoln would "turn this beautiful State into a free negro colony." Never one to shy away from demagoguery when it suited his needs, Douglas exploited Lincoln's earlier missteps to put the Republican on the defensive. Throughout each of their joint debates, Douglas would reiterate his argument that Lincoln's commitment to universal human equality, as expressed in the Declaration of Independence, would lead inexorably to Black citizenship and racial amalgamation. At Ottawa, Douglas also proposed that Lincoln and Trumbull had concocted a vast conspiracy to undermine the Second Party System and "abolitionize the old Whig Party and the old Democratic party." Unaware that Lincoln had avoided any association with the radicals who had formed the state's first Republican Party in 1854, Douglas ultimately overplayed his hand by accusing Lincoln of opposing the Fugitive Slave Law and of supporting unconditional abolition in the District of Columbia.[54]

Lincoln, of course, could honestly refute that he had ever held such positions and did so, but his statements from earlier in the campaign, intended to distinguish his position from Douglas's, had come back to bite him, and he spent copious time explaining that he could endorse the proposition that "all men are created equal" while simultaneously insisting, as he stated at Charleston in mid-September, "there is a physical difference between the white and black races which I believe will forever forbid the two races living together on terms of social and political equality."⁵⁵

Douglas recognized the tension inherent in this sentiment and repeatedly sought to exploit it but found himself limited by the fact that many listeners shared Lincoln's cognitive dissonance. While many white Illinoisans retained deep racial prejudices, they resented slavery's imposition on the West, a territory they thought the Founders had justly reserved for free white men. Lincoln believed slavery a great moral evil and repeatedly told his audiences as much, reminding them that Clay had articulated the same sentiment. Still, Lincoln's most effective appeals came when he distanced himself from the moral argument against slavery's injustice and framed his case in terms understandable to the most bigoted in his midst. He explained to his audience at Alton in October:

> How many Democrats are there about here who have left slave States and come into the free State of Illinois to get rid of the institution of slavery? . . . If the policy you are now advocating had prevailed when this country was in a Territorial condition, where would you have gone to get rid of it? Where would you have found your free State or Territory to go to? . . . Now irrespective of the moral aspect of this question as to whether there is a right or wrong in enslaving a negro, I am still in favor of our new Territories being in such a condition that white men may find a home-may find some spot where they can better their condition-where they can settle upon new soil and better their condition in life.⁵⁶

The extension of slavery into the West posed a severe crisis for free white men who hoped to settle the region, establish independent farms maintained by free labor, and connect themselves to the great commercial markets of the East. Lincoln's policy of congressional action guaranteed that the haughty slaveholders of the South would remain where they belonged, perpetuating their peculiar institution only in the peculiar climate of the South. Eventually, perhaps, slavery there too would fade away amid the progress of the age, but in the meantime, the free white men of the North would flourish, and the Union would remain united.

Republican operatives recognized that Douglas's supposed independence, combined with Lincoln's misstep in the House Divided speech, had forced them to play catch-up with the critical swing voters of the state's central counties. Lincoln had made a strong comeback. Historian Graham Peck has mischaracterized Lincoln's "antislavery nationalism" as radical in essence, but Peck rightly notes that the theme of a return to the policy of the founders held immense appeal among undecided voters. In his debates against Douglas, Lincoln argued that the Founders had recognized slavery's threat to republican government and the economic advancement of white men. As such, they had sought to limit its reach by confining it to those states where it had already taken root. The failures of popular sovereignty in Kansas and the continued aggression of Southern slaveholders in the territories demanded a firm response and a return to this earlier policy. By implementing the wisdom of the Founding generation, "the old conservative principle," as one of his supporters had put in an October 2 speech at Alton, Lincoln promised a return to normalcy and the end of extremist agitation.[57]

Douglas did his best to frame his own policies as the true middle ground for white Illinoisans. Although his so-called Freeport Doctrine—declaring that slavery could only exist in a region affirmed by positive law—merely reiterated a position he had expressed to Illinoisians since the Dred Scott Decision, its featured role in a contest of national interest would haunt him in his future sojourns to the South. Aware that many former Whigs and Know-Nothings still resented the court's ruling against the Missouri Compromise in Dred Scott, Douglas reframed the issue as a matter of law and order, arguing at Quincy on October 13 that Republican "attempts to stir up odium and rebellion in the country against the constituted authorities, is stimulating the passions of men to resort to violence and to mobs instead of to the law." Whatever their attachment to the compromise Clay had forged, reverence for the compact would not overcome these voters' respect for authority and fear of anarchy.[58]

Yet Douglas's most effective counter to Lincoln's claim that congressional action alone could stem the tide of slavery's expansion came through his historical framing of popular sovereignty. Dismissing the chaos in Kansas as an aberration and brandishing the prestige he had acquired by defending popular sovereignty's sanctity amid the Lecompton crisis, Douglas insisted that popular sovereignty had already secured national preeminence for the North and West and that the free white men of Illinois could rest easy, leaving the South to do as it pleased since no real threat existed. He spoke in his own appeal in their final meeting at Alton:

> How has the South lost her power as the majority section in this Union, and how have the free States gained it, except under the operation of that principle which declares the right of the people of each State and each Territory to form and regulate their domestic institutions . . . it was under that principle that the number of free States increased until from being one out of twelve States, we

have grown to be the majority of States of the whole Union, with the power to control the House of Representatives and Senate, and the power, consequently, to elect a President by Northern votes without the aid of a Southern State. Having obtained this power under the operation of that great principle, are you now prepared to abandon the principle and declare that merely because we have the power you will wage a war against the Southern States and their institutions until you force them to abolish slavery every where.[59]

Douglas remained ever careful not to insult Southerners or dismiss slavery out of hand, but his free-state audience would have recognized the underlying message. Douglas told listeners that no crisis existed because free labor had already demonstrated its superiority over time through the votes of the people themselves. Illinoisians should honor the constitutional guarantees awarded to the South and its slave system, taking comfort that the course of events had already made the region a junior partner in the Union and that history might continue to advance toward a free labor future.

As the campaign drew to a close, the Little Giant found himself hoarse and exhausted from the 102 speeches he had made throughout the campaign in Illinois. But to his good fortune, his campaign received a fourth-quarter boost in the form of endorsements by two national figures. As Trumbull had feared months before, Kentucky's Crittenden formally endorsed Douglas in October, as he allowed Dickey to circulate a letter he had written confirming his support for the Little Giant. Meanwhile, another Kentuckian, Vice President John C. Breckinridge, forgave Douglas's opposition to the administration and publicly endorsed his reelection bid on the eve of the election. The twin endorsements simultaneously boosted Douglas's prospects among former Whigs and Know-Nothings, especially those with roots in Kentucky and the Upper South, while also undercutting the Danite claim to legitimacy as the "National Democrats."[60]

The Republicans feebly attempted to rebut Crittenden's endorsement as a misrepresentation—insisting that he had meant only to praise Douglas's stance on Lecompton and would never follow Douglas into "the bottomless quagmires of his native Locofocism." But such protests fooled only the most gullible partisans. In doubt of the ultimate result, the Republicans also did their best to brace themselves for defeat and simultaneously bolster support from former Whigs and Know-Nothings by alleging election fraud. The Republican press insisted that Douglas planned to win the election by "imported votes," recruiting gangs of Irish laborers from Chicago and shipping them downstate. Even Lincoln, never a proponent of ethnic bigotry, noted his fear in a letter to Judd that "Celtic gentlemen, with black carpet-sacks in their hands" might appear throughout swing districts to steal the election.[61]

As the results came in on November 3, two things became clear. First, the Danite attempt to undermine Douglas's following in the state had failed, as John Dougherty, the pro-administration candidate for state treasurer, won only 5,071 votes out of more than 250,000 ballots cast. Second, despite Republican victories in the statewide contests for state treasurer and state superintendent of public instruction, Lincoln had lost his bid for the Senate. Although Republican candidates garnered nearly 52 percent of votes cast in open state house races and nearly 54 percent in the state senate contests, the combination of incumbent Democrats and southern Illinois's disproportionate representation in the state legislature gave Douglas's supporters a majority in both houses. Critically, Republicans lost several key swing districts in the old Whig counties of central Illinois.[62]

Historians have fiercely debated exactly how, why, and to what extent the party failed to bring over the Fillmore voters of 1856. Quantitative analyses have led to diametrically opposed conclusions. Employing a statistical regression to model the statewide results, Stephen L. Hansen has claimed that the Douglas Democrats picked up a significant proportion of Know-Nothing voters while the Republicans failed to attract former Fillmore men. In contrast, William E. Gienapp, using his own method, has asserted that 73 percent of Fillmore voters statewide swung into the Republican camp and that Douglas's limited success with old Whigs and former Know-Nothings occurred in just the right places. Of course, there is no way to accurately trace the ballots of individual voters from contest to contest, and as historians such as Allen C. Guelzo and Bruce Collins have demonstrated, local results reveal a medley of outcomes that defy simple explanations.[63]

Still, narrowing in from the state to the county level offers some insight into the extent of the Republicans' failure among central Illinois's conservative voters. Lincoln's home county of Sangamon, for example, had given 1174 ballots for Frémont in 1856, compared to 1612 for Fillmore, and 2475 for Buchanan. In 1858, the Republican candidate for state treasurer, James Miller, won 2726 votes in Sangamon; William B. Fondey, his pro-Douglas Democratic opponent won 3078; and Dougherty won a paltry 138. Miller's vote count closely matched that given by Sangamon voters to the Republican congressional candidate in 1856, indicating that in 1858, even as some Fillmore voters broke for Douglas, the Republicans largely retained the support of voters who split their tickets between Fillmore and the Republicans in 1856. Similar results appear in the neighboring counties of the old Whig belt. The only significant pickups for Douglas among former Know-Nothings occurred in thinly populated areas of Little Egypt, such as Williamson County, which had given Frémont only ten votes in 1856. As such, while Dickey's defection and Crittenden's endorsement of Douglas undoubtedly hurt Lincoln, they did not reverse the steady flow of Fillmore voters into the Republican Party. The decision of some, though by no means a majority, of Fillmore's former supporters in central Illinois to back Douglas only proved decisive because of the indirect nature of the election and the quirks of state house districts.[64]

"It Is Evident That the People Must Triumph in 1860"

From such a vantage point, one might conclude that the 1858 contest ended in a draw or something close to one. In the aftermath of Lecompton, both the Douglas Democrats and the Republicans needed to reestablish themselves as distinct political entities. This task proved challenging in a state with a heterogenous and ideologically moderate electorate. To borrow words from the *Chicago Journal,* the parties sought to prove they contained "nothing extreme—nothing sectional—nothing narrow or impracticable" but rather were "eminently patriotic, conservative, [and] national." Stressing both their aversion to Southern slaveholders and Black Americans, each party emphasized themes that resonated with most white Illinoisians and strategically employed sociocultural cues as they balanced nativist and foreign-born constituencies. On the one hand, while Douglas had retained his office and confirmed the support of his state's Democrats by fighting off the Danites, he had not drawn overwhelming numbers of conservative Republicans, or even Know-Nothings, into his coalition. On the other hand, despite errors that cost him the legislative districts he needed most, Lincoln had still run an effective campaign and gained national attention through his joint debates with Douglas. The narrow Republican majority in the state at large held immense promise for the presidential contest of 1860. Although he was still without an office, Lincoln would recraft his arguments to appeal to the broadest possible audience and use his notoriety to convince voters throughout the nation that he deserved a rematch against Douglas.[65]

CHAPTER 6

RACE TO THE WHITE HOUSE

Although the result had been all but certain for months, a certain nervous energy still hung in the hall as the doorkeeper was ordered "to clear the Galleries of all persons except ladies." The roll call labored on for several minutes, but when all hundred names had been called, the Democrats in the chamber breathed a bit easier. It was January 5, 1859, and Stephen A. Douglas had been officially reelected to the US Senate by a joint session of the Illinois legislature, 54 to 46. The outcome provided palpable relief to the Little Giant's supporters throughout Illinois, but the senator's future on the national stage remained uncertain. While a key cohort of national Democratic figures, including Vice President John C. Breckinridge, had endorsed Douglas as preferable to a Republican (in contrast to the Illinois Danites, who had covertly aided the Lincoln campaign), most Southerners remained deeply antagonistic toward the Little Giant. For their part, Illinois's Democrats, and Douglas Democrats more broadly, remained deeply bitter toward Buchanan and the Southern Democracy. As it crowed Douglas's triumph, the *Chicago Times* castigated the president and his "vindictive cabal" for their "facile stupidity" in opposing popular sovereignty and for entrusting "convicted knavery with the treasurer's key." In a vindictive coup, proadministration forces stripped Douglas of his chairmanship of the Committee on Territories in December 1858, a blow intended to humiliate the Little Giant and further marginalize his influence within the national party. Still determined to secure the nation's highest office in 1860, Douglas embarked on a mission to defeat both the Buchananites and the Republicans and reunite a victorious Democratic Party on his own terms. But with many Southerners decrying his Freeport

Doctrine as no better than "Black Republicanism" and the road to the White House running through a national convention at Charleston, South Carolina, the prospect for victory appeared grim.[1]

The Illinois Republicans faced their own set of challenges as they set their eyes on the 1860 contest. The great lesson of 1856 that moderate candidates and a conservative platform could carry the state appeared salient to all. But how to apply it was another matter. Abraham Lincoln, now a twice-defeated Senate candidate, had somehow caught the presidential fever. Although his debates with Douglas had put him on the national stage, at the beginning of 1859, he remained a bit player. Reasonable observers might have predicted an appointment for the Springfield lawyer in a future Republican administration, perhaps a diplomatic post or even a spot in the cabinet. The most optimistic might even have envisioned a nod for the vice presidency, should a western man be needed to balance the ticket. But for most in the party outside of Illinois in early 1859, the nomination of Lincoln for the presidency stretched credulity to the breaking point. In addition, over the course of 1859 and 1860, personal and ideological conflicts within the state Republican Party's leadership threatened to break apart the organization Lincoln had worked so hard to form in 1856 and keep together in 1858. For any chance of success, he would need to gather support from Republicans throughout the country, preferably entire state delegations, as well as retain the support of a firmly united Illinois state party. To that end, Lincoln took advantage of speaking invitations to stump for his party throughout the nation, offering notable addresses throughout the Northern states, most famously at New York City's Cooper Institute. In the process, he refined his own arguments against the extension of slavery to emphasize his essential moderation.[2]

Ultimately, Lincoln and the Republicans' pledge to redeem the nation from the domination of Southern slaveholders and the corruption of the Democratic Party would prove convincing to most Illinoisans and Northerners. Positioning themselves as a moderate voice of reason, Republicans committed to preserve both the rights of free white men and the Union. To be sure, the party had taken on a more militant edge in the years since the passage of the Kansas-Nebraska Act. Pushed too far too many times by Southern elites, many voters indifferent to the eradication of slavery now hoped to strike back against the slaveholding bullies. Thus, even as Stephen A. Douglas framed himself as the only candidate capable of reestablishing sectional harmony, voters sent Lincoln to the White House as a corrective to Southern intransigence and to restore slavery to its proper sphere as envisioned by the Framers. Nevertheless, Illinoisans remained as committed to the Union as ever. Far from manifesting a radical spirit of sectional subjugation, they simply demanded an honest and fair-minded government that would confine their slaveholding countrymen to the places designated for them by the Constitution.

Intraparty Divisions

In the aftermath of his Senate victory, Douglas took an extended trip to Washington, traveling via the Mississippi to New Orleans before boarding a steamer bound for New York City. This travel served a dual purpose; it provided the Little Giant with a vacation after a hard campaign, and it allowed him to renew political contacts in the South as he sought to regain control of the party. While in the South, Douglas would face immense pressure from advocates of territorial expansion bent on acquiring land from Mexico and annexing Cuba, as well as from proslavery forces determined to reopen the Atlantic slave trade and pass a territorial slave code in Congress. As a longstanding proponent of the nation's manifest destiny to expand throughout the western hemisphere, Douglas embraced the former group as a potential ally but had little patience for the latter, which he believed was as responsible for the sectional infighting as the Republicans. Shortly before departing from Chicago, Douglas privately told Republican editor Charles H. Ray that he would confront any congressional attempt to expand slavery and "hit it between the eyes precisely as [he] did Lecompton." Unfortunately for Douglas's strategy, many of the same Southerners who advocated expansion also favored reopening the Atlantic slave trade and the territorial slave code. Thus, while Douglas could boast, "It is our destiny to have Cuba . . . its acquisition is a matter of time only," he did little to raise his prospects in the Deep South.[3]

Indeed, within a few weeks of his return to Washington, Douglas had locked horns with Mississippi's Jefferson Davis over the issue of slavery in the territories. Determined to overcome the passive exclusion of slavery intimated by Douglas's Freeport Doctrine, Davis demanded the passage of a territorial slave code that would enable the federal government to offer "full and adequate protection" for the property rights of Southern slaveholders throughout the far West. Douglas believed Davis's proposal violated the spirit of popular sovereignty and offered a mirror image of the Republican's policy of federal exclusion. For the previous five years, Douglas had dedicated himself ceaselessly to "the principle of non-intervention." Just as Congress should not prohibit the introduction of slavery from its position in faraway Washington, it "ought not to force slavery on the people of the Territories against their will."

The free white men who entered the territories would decide for themselves, according to their own interests and sense of justice, whether slavery ought to receive the sanction and protection of local law. Over the course of the debate, Davis stated that he would withhold his support from any Democratic presidential candidate who refused to support a territorial slave code, throwing down a gauntlet that anticipated the party's formal disintegration.[4]

In Illinois, Douglas's allies backed his firm stance. The *Illinois State Register* denounced "the monstrous doctrine that congress shall protect slavery in the territories," while the *Quincy Herald* called on its readers to "disregard and spit upon the teachings of those professing Democracy who lead our party and our country estray" by abandoning popular sovereignty. For its part, the Republican *Chicago Press and Tribune* gloried in the "contradictory and irreconcilable opinions" now entertained by the Democrats of each section and announced, "The party is rent in twain, and the country is glad!"[5]

Indeed, the Republicans hoped that this split, if permanent, would enhance their political fortunes in the Thirty-sixth Congress. That body, elected in 1858 but not scheduled to assemble until late 1859, had a Republican plurality in the House of Representatives. With the remainder of the House split between Buchanan Democrats, Anti-Lecompton Democrats, and members of Southern Opposition (a regional label for former Know-Nothings and ex-Whigs), the Republicans stood a chance of blocking the election of a Democrat and elevating one of their own to the speaker's chair. Unfortunately for the party's leaders, events in subsequent months revealed divisions in Republican ranks, on both the state and national levels, that proved nearly as serious as the divisions in the Democracy. In fact, as early as January 1859, the *Chicago Times* confidently cackled that the Republican Party "is so rent by feuds and the rivalries of hostile aspirants, that it is entirely without reasonable hope, and must soon be frittered away."[6]

The first challenge faced by Illinois Republicans emerged from ethnocultural tensions outside of the state. In Massachusetts, the state where the Know-Nothing movement had made its strongest showing between 1854 and 1856, the Republican Party remained decidedly nativist in its outlook and passed a state constitutional amendment to prohibit immigrants from voting for two years following their naturalization as US citizens. The political wisdom of this measure seemed obvious to Massachusetts Republicans eager to strike a blow against the state's Democratic Irish Catholic vote, but this broad attack on the foreign-born threatened to overturn the delicate balance struck among northwestern Republicans between their nativist supporters and Protestant immigrants.[7]

Although Republicans in Illinois continued to indulge in Hibernophobia and anti-Catholic rhetoric to appeal to former Know-Nothings, they had carefully cultivated the sizeable Protestant German and Scandinavian populations within the state. Now Democrats eagerly pointed to the Massachusetts amendment as evidence of Republican antipathy for all immigrants. Ignoring their own appeals to former Know-Nothings in the last canvass, the *Islander and Argus* insisted that the Massachusetts measure provided "naturalized citizens . . . every evidence that can be required by intelligent beings, that the Republicans favor and stand by Know Nothingism." The measure generated a mixed reaction across the state in Republican circles. The *Chicago Press and Tribune* reacted cautiously, disavowing the specific provisions of the Massachusetts amendment but insisting that some reform in naturalization laws was necessary to prevent "abuses of the elective franchise" and protect "rational liberty." Gustave Koerner warned Lincoln that many German Republican newspapermen had declared that "unless this step is disavowed by the Republicans in the other states, they will leave the party." Alarmed, Lincoln urged the Illinois Republican Central Committee to adopt resolutions to distance itself from the measure, but others, including Lyman Trumbull, feared that an attack on the Massachusetts Republicans might do more harm than good and tabled the proposal. Lincoln, worried about alienating former Know-Nothings as he pursued the Republican presidential nomination, pacified his German allies through a carefully worded statement opposing such a measure's adoption in Illinois and by financially supporting the insolvent *Illinois Staats-Anzeiger* of Springfield.[8]

To further complicate matters, over the summer of 1859, a long-simmering feud between two of the most prominent Chicago Republicans, Norman B. Judd and John E. "Long John" Wentworth, erupted into open warfare. Although both were former Democrats who had split with the party over the Kansas-Nebraska Act in 1854, the two had loathed each other for years. Both now occupied positions of immense power within the state's Republican ranks, as Judd, a former state senator, had emerged as the chairman of the Republican State Central Committee, while Wentworth, a former congressman and editor of the *Chicago Democrat*, served as Chicago's first Republican mayor. Wentworth, now out of office thanks in large part to Judd's meddling, sought to undermine his rival's chances of securing the party's gubernatorial nomination in 1860. In the winter of 1858–59, Wentworth began to promulgate allegations that Judd with John M. Palmer and Trumbull had worked to undermine Lincoln's 1858 Senate race because they resented his old affiliation with the Whigs. Lincoln quickly disavowed any such notion, writing that he believed all three "were as sincerely anxious for my success in the late contest, as I myself," but this did not stop Wentworth's assault as he next accused Judd of colluding with the former Democratic governor William A. Matteson to defraud the state treasury. Although such accusations proved baseless, they delighted Judd's other intraparty enemies throughout the state, including Judge David Davis and Lincoln's law partner, William H. Herndon. In response, Judd's allies at the *Chicago Press and Tribune* replied with their own salvos, detailing Wentworth's checkered political past and further escalating the conflict.[9]

Farther downstate, gubernatorial contenders Richard Yates and Leonard Swett eyed the situation with interest. As longtime enemies of Wentworth and Judd, the pair, rivals, might have hoped the two Chicagoans would do enough damage to one another to open an avenue for a downstate candidate to seize the gubernatorial nomination. Already faced with the potential of a four-way battle royal for the governor, the *Central Transcript* of Clinton made matters even more complicated by injecting interstate sectionalism and ideology into the contest. The *Transcript* mocked the two Chicago candidates, lambasting northern Illinoisans as "ultra men . . . who boast of stealing Negroes, and violating the Laws of the land" and insisted that "no man of this class will suit the conservative, law-abiding, God-fearing Republicans of Central and Southern Illinois." Concerned by the power of radicals like Owen Lovejoy and his supporters within the state party, editor I. N. Coltrin hoped to bring the party back to its conservative antiextensionist roots. Lincoln responded with a letter chastising Coltrin for his "unjust and impolitic" editorial, reminding that each of the major Republican state officeholders came from downstate Illinois and that such attacks could not fail but "to weaken our party." Although northern Illinois did contain communities sympathetic to fugitive slaves and Black civil rights, most residents who voted the Republican ticket remained decidedly closer to their allies in central and southern Illinois than to radical Black abolitionists like Henry O. Wagoner.[10]

The Radicalism of John Brown's Raid

Despite his exclusion from electoral politics, Wagoner, and radical allies, did play a role in the events that followed in a bold strike at the heart of slavery, which further destabilized the Illinois Republican Party and put the state's Democrats on the offensive. Earlier in 1859, Wagoner and John and Mary Jones, also leading Black abolitionists in Chicago, had met with John Brown as he helped enslaved fugitives from Missouri make their way to freedom in

Canada. Brown had made a name for himself as a "captain" of free-soil settlers in Kansas when he butchered several proslavery settlers at Pottawatomie Creek in retaliation for the 1856 Sack of Lawrence. A radical's radical, Brown advocated not only the cause of free soil in Kansas but immediate abolition and racial equality. Devoted to the Calvinist faith of his Puritan ancestors, Brown had grown increasingly zealous throughout the 1850s and had taken on the tone and appearance of an Old Testament prophet, impressing both Black and white radicals with his sincere devotion to the cause of abolitionism. The details of Brown's meeting with the Chicago abolitionists remain obscure, but the group may have discussed Brown's evolving plan to bring a violent end to American slavery. Brown might even have invited Wagoner to join him in his attack on slavery, but if so, like Fredrick Douglass and most of Brown's Black abolitionist allies, Wagoner demurred. Nevertheless, in the aftermath of Brown's daring raid, Wagoner would praise him as the "noblest of God's heroes." As historian Kellie Carter Jackson explains, for increasingly militant Black abolitionists, "Brown was not leading black people into death, he was continuing and enhancing the work of black abolitionists who believed that violence was the only weapon that would overthrow the system of slavery."[11]

Late on the evening of October 16, 1859, a multiracial force of twenty-one radical abolitionists led by Brown attacked the US arsenal at Harpers Ferry, Virginia. The insurgents hoped to seize the weapons and munitions stored inside and use them to equip the enslaved, whom they believed would rally to their standard as they launched a guerilla war for immediate emancipation. After their initial success in seizing the armory, the raiders quickly came under siege from local militia and were eventually subdued by a contingent of US Marines led by the Brevet Col. Robert E. Lee of the regular army. Although Brown's raid on Harpers Ferry hardly constituted more than a skirmish and failed to launch the uprising Brown had hoped for, the attack chilled the blood of white Southerners and prompted a swift and vicious backlash. Within days, a wounded Brown was put on trial for treason and sentenced to die. The stoicism Brown displayed throughout his trial and subsequent execution won him laurels in many radical Northern circles and elicited sympathy even among some antislavery moderates.[12]

In Illinois, the raid added to a sense of political chaos as mainstream Republicans sought to distance themselves from Brown, and Democrats exploited the event as evidence of Republican bloodlust. Speaking for most Republicans, David Davis, Lincoln's close confidant and campaign manager, called the insurrection "a dreadful affair" and denounced "the wild fanatics" responsible for it, explaining in a letter to his son that slavery's power could only be subdued through "the peaceful mode of the ballot box." Some Illinois Republicans, however, especially those with New England evangelical backgrounds, praised Brown's "duty, humanity, and patriotism." Repelled by coverage in Northern Illinois papers that sympathized with Brown's plight, a Republican under the pen name "Union lover" wrote a letter to the *Chicago Press and Tribune* denouncing "ultraism" and begging his compatriots to "frown down all these attempts to convert the party into an abolition organization" and instead to honor the "truly patriotic, conservative feeling among the great body of the American people." Democrats eagerly labeled the raid as "Black Republican Theory in Practice" and the beginning of the "Irrepressible Conflict" outlined by Republican senator William H. Seward the previous autumn in Rochester, New York.[13]

The Democrats had an immediate need to make political capital out of Brown's raid as they contested a special election for the state's Sixth Congressional District. With control of the House of Representatives hanging in the balance, the unexpected death of Democratic representative Thomas L. Harris had given Republicans a second chance to win this key central Illinois district. In the runoff, the Republicans nominated former state senator Palmer to run against Democrat John A. McClernand, a longtime Douglas ally who had served in Congress from 1843 to 1851 as a representative from Little Egypt. Prior to Brown's raid, the Danites had again been working to sow dissension in Illinois Democratic ranks, and Douglas wrote McClernand of the imperative for his majority to "be, large, overwhelming, on account of its effects at this time on other States." Douglas knew he had a hard road ahead as he trudged toward the 1860 Democratic National Convention at Charleston and needed to display his strength at home to bolster the confidence of his allies across the North. The timing of Brown's raid provided the Democrats with an excellent cudgel, and the *Illinois State Register* insisted that "the doctrines taught by Seward and Lincoln, and echoed by Palmer and the lesser lights, tend to produce precisely what Brown attempted." The Republicans responded that Brown's attack represented Democratic popular sovereignty "practically applied, and is a mere continuation of its late bloodstained workings in Kansas." That rationale proved unconvincing for Sixth District voters, however, and McClernand handily defeated Palmer by a margin comparable to Harris's victory the year before.[14]

Meanwhile, whether motivated by genuine radical conviction or a desire to sow discord within a party he believed had turned on him, Wentworth sang Brown's praises in the *Chicago Democrat*. Many Republicans had long suspected Wentworth of lacking true commitment to the party and had predicted his defection from their ranks back to the Democrats or some third party. While such a defection would not occur until 1862, Wentworth's tone-deaf radicalism disquieted Republicans, who feared a further split in the party and delighted Democrats, who pointed to Wentworth's praise of Brown as evidence of Republican sympathy for violent abolitionism. On the eve of Brown's execution, Judd filed suit against Wentworth for libel. Wentworth responded audaciously by asking Lincoln to defend him in the lawsuit. Distraught by the turmoil within his party, Lincoln turned Wentworth down and suggested several compromises to bring about a truce. Eventually, Lincoln convinced Judd to drop his lawsuit and endorse Wentworth's bid for a second term for mayor of Chicago in the March 1860 election. Lincoln later repaid Judd by ensuring that he, rather than Wentworth, received a position as a delegate at large from Illinois at the 1860 Republican National Convention.[15]

In the aftermath of Palmer's defeat, conservative Republican newspapers, which had provided scant coverage of Brown during the actual events of the raid, trial, and execution, sought to purge the issue from the coming canvas. That some radical Republicans had approved of Brown's action, or at least made little effort to condemn it, produced immense discomfort within the party and threatened to undermine its moderate image. Democrats had gleefully exploited the issue and might have done even more with it if not for the ongoing struggle within their own national organization. Republicans hoped the passage of time would help voters forget the raid's embarrassing revelations and redirect their attention to the continued dysfunction of the national Democratic Party and the extreme demands of its proslavery Southern wing.

Events in Washington muddied the political waters further as a yet unorganized House of Representatives floundered throughout December. Still hoping to reunite the party under his leadership, Douglas had encouraged anti-Lecompton Democrats, led by the newly elevated McClernand, to hold out against the Republicans. The path to a compromise candidate for speaker seemed open as the Southern Opposition abandoned any inclination to form a coalition with Republicans following the Harpers Ferry raid. Republicans further infuriated Southerners by nominating John Sherman for the speakership. A generally moderate Ohioan, Sherman had drawn the special ire of Southerners by endorsing Hinton R. Helper's controversial book, the *Impending Crisis of the South*. Helper, a North Carolinian resentful of the planter class, offered readers a plethora of statistics to prove slavery's economic backwardness. Explicitly disclaiming "any special friendliness or sympathy for the blacks," Harper sought to convince his white Southern yeoman to abandon their support for slaveholders and embrace his vision of a free labor South. While such an argument readily aligned with the Republican worldview, it represented an existential threat to slaveholding Southerners. In private, Harper's work might have received tacit nods from Douglas Democrats skeptical of slavery's economic utility, but in public, the Little Giant's supporters kept mum.[16]

When members of the Southern Opposition and administration Democrats subsequently refused to cooperate with the Douglas men, tensions rose to a fever pitch. On December 27, President Buchanan delivered an annual message that explicitly endorsed federal protection for slavery in the territories, igniting a firestorm among anti-Lecompton Democrats. McClernand correctly recognized that the revival of the issue would "embarrass D[ouglas's] friends in the South" and severely hurt the Little Giant's chances at the Charleston convention. From the floor of the House, Congressman Isaac Morris of Quincy accused Southerners of attempting to "drive the last nail in the lid of the coffin of the great northwestern Democracy." Meanwhile in Illinois, Charles H. Lanphier declared the address "rank treason to democracy" and urged McClernand to "go to war on principles—and win" rather than submit to Southern dictation. Over the next few weeks, McClernand continued to fight on behalf of Douglas to secure an acceptable anti-Republican leader, reluctantly entering the speakership contest himself, but fell short of a majority as Southern members continued to oppose the selection of any Douglas supporter. Instead, the self-identified conservative Republican William Pennington of New Jersey, with the help of votes from several Northern antiadministration Democrats and New York's one remaining Know-Nothing, secured a bare majority on February 1, 1860.[17]

The outcome left Douglas's Illinois supporters feeling gloomy as Southern opposition to their champion cast further doubt on the chances of a united Democratic ticket in 1860. As reported by Republican Henry J. Atkins, the whole affair left them in "a very bad humor" and "wonderfuly disgusted by the course of things at the Capitol." Amid the speakership battle, Senators Jefferson Davis and Albert G. Brown, of Mississippi, offered a series of competing resolutions to employ federal power to protect slavery in the territories. While the Mississippians battled each other for leadership of the Southern Democracy, they both targeted Douglas and Northern Democrats for their insistence on popular sovereignty. In February 1860, the Mississippi state legislature, the body that had elected Davis and Brown, went so far as to declare that the election of any presidential candidate that did not support the protection of slavery in the territories—that is, both Douglas Democrats with the Republicans—would justify the state's withdrawal from the Union. Douglas felt no inclination to retreat from his position, a stance supported by one supporter Illinois who reminded him that his followers stood for "free territory for white men" and that he needed to ensure they were "free to make it free." Disturbed and disgruntled, Douglas supporters "utterly repudiate[d] . . . a Congressional slave code for the Territories" in their state convention and looked ominously ahead to the national convention at Charleston scheduled to convene on April 23, 1860.[18]

Lincoln's Appeal

As the prairie's winter frosts yielded to warm spring rains, Illinois Republicans could delight in their enemies' distress, but they still faced significant internal conflict. Although the consternation displayed in the wake of John Brown's raid had faded and the Judd–Wentworth feud appeared under control, state Republicans remained starkly divided on candidates for the 1860 gubernatorial and presidential races. The three-way race between Judd, Swett, and Yates divided the party leadership into rival camps, with the latter two representing downstate constituencies of former Whigs, like David Davis and Orville H. Browning, while Judd enjoyed the support of Northern Illinoisans and former Democrats. Among presidential candidates, although Lincoln enjoyed the state's "favorite son" status, many northern Illinoisans supported the national frontrunner, William H. Seward of New York, while residents of southern Illinois expressed support for former Know-Nothing Edward L. Bates of Missouri. Still, others hinted at their support for Pennsylvania's Simon Cameron or the Ohioans Salmon P. Chase or John McLean. To secure a united front from his state's delegation at the party's national convention, conveniently held close to home in Chicago, thanks Judd's work at a Republican National Central Committee meeting, Lincoln needed to bolster his national stature so as to assure friends and skeptics alike that he could win the nomination and the presidency.[19]

The Springfield lawyer's national star had been on the rise for months by the time the race for the nomination entered its final stretch in the late spring of 1860. Over the course of 1859 and early 1860, Lincoln embarked on a series of speaking tours, refining his 1858 arguments into a concise case against the extension of slavery grounded in the material concerns of ordinary white men and the intentions of the Founders. Dropping references to slavery's ultimate extinction and reframing his commitment to the principles of the Declaration of Independence, Lincoln crafted a conservative appeal for blocking slavery's march into the West that resonated with the average Northern voter's distaste for slavery and resentment of Southern slaveholders. As he crisscrossed the nation, Lincoln hoped to avoid the mistakes of his 1858 campaign and secure the loyalty of a broad constituency. Though some claim that Lincoln's pivot to the center represented a mere rhetorical shift to cloak his radical intentions, Lincoln never sought to deceive voters. Rather, by appealing to his audience's reverence for the Revolutionary generation and hopes for the West, he cogently articulated his sincerely held belief that the further extension of slavery violated the intentions of America's Founders and undercut the possibility of self-improvement for ordinary white men.[20]

This stand on slavery's extension, moderate in its outlook and conservative in its disposition, ultimately proved broad enough to unite Illinois Republicanism's diverse factions and regional antagonisms. While conflict between the northern counties and their central and southern neighbors would continue for decades (and remains a factor in Illinois politics to this day), partisan animus against slaveholder aggression and a common devotion to free labor and republican government for white men proved sufficient to overcome all other ideological questions. Although he lacked Seward's oratorical flair or Bates's regal bearing, Lincoln had proven trustworthy to all in the state party and made their common ground a more comfortable place to stand.

But even as the state party remained fractious, Lincoln began building his case to voters beyond Illinois by crisscrossing the Midwest in late 1859. Addressing a crowd in Columbus, Ohio, on September 16, he hoped to disabuse his audience of the idea that either he or his party hoped to radically transform the republic. Rather, he argued that the "chief and real purpose of the Republican party is eminently conservative," as it merely sought to "restore this government to its original tone in regard to this element of slavery, and there to maintain it, looking for no further change." The Northwest Ordinance of 1787, originally drafted by Thomas Jefferson, clearly reflected the Founders' intentions regarding slavery's future by excluding the institution from the territory ceded to the new nation by Great Britain in the Treaty of Paris of 1783. Lincoln explained that the residents of Ohio, Michigan, Indiana, Illinois, and Wisconsin enjoyed all the advantages of a free society thanks to this wise policy. He elaborated on this vision in a speech before Wisconsin's Agricultural Society as he explained that free society allowed wage earners, with nothing but their labor, to work their way to prosperity through thrift in industry. Such a system celebrated labor and "gives hope to all, and energy, and progress, and improvement of condition to all."[21]

Slavery posed an ominous threat to this system by which free men educated themselves and advanced their stations as the institution sought to reduce laborers to nothing but "mud-sills." That term, which South Carolinian James Henry Hammond employed in defense of bondage before the US Senate, reflected the slaveholders' desire to reduce a laborer to "a blind horse upon a tread-mill." As such, slavery not only violated the abstract spirit of free institutions but threatened to undermine the freedom social and economic freedom of ordinary white men. Lincoln assured a racially sensitive audience at Indianapolis that, whatever Democrats might claim, "if there were any conflict between the white man and negro, he would be for the white man as much as Douglas." But, according to Lincoln, no such conflict existed, as most "white men were injured by the effect of slave labor in the neighborhood of their own labor." The free white men of the North, and indeed throughout the country, therefore needed to guard against slavery's influence for their own sake.[22]

In October, Lincoln received an invitation to address an audience of New York Republicans at Henry Ward Beecher's Plymouth Church in Brooklyn later that winter. The venue shifted shortly before Lincoln's arrival to the newly constructed Cooper Institute, where on February 27, 1860, the aspiring candidate addressed fourteen hundred curious Empire State citizens. Lincoln recognized that to have any chance at gaining the nomination in May, he would need to impress this audience. Although most New York Republicans strongly supported Seward for the presidency, a notable group of dissidents, including editor Horace Greeley of the *New-York Tribune,* could become essential allies. Perhaps even more important, coverage of the address in the Eastern press could draw attention to him and secure support beyond his midwestern base.[23]

In a carefully crafted speech that read almost like a lecture, Lincoln made his case for opposing slavery's extension as a conservative defense of the Founders. While a poor example of historical scholarship, Lincoln's claim that an overwhelming majority of the original thirty-nine signers of the Constitution opposed the extension of slavery and approved federal restriction of the institution was a stroke of political genius. Although his analysis of the Founders lacked the nuance and ambiguity we associate with modern studies of the Constitution and slavery, this reflected Lincoln's deficiency as a historian rather than any intentional deception. Like many throughout the antebellum North, Lincoln genuinely believed that the framers of the Constitution had intended for slavery to remain localized and contained, an unfortunate aberration to be tolerated rather than an essential element of the Union. From this perspective, one could only blame Southern slaveholders and their Northern lackeys for sectional agitation. The Republicans merely sought to defend the status quo. Challenging those who labeled his party as radical, Lincoln asked his audience, "What is conservatism? Is it not adherence to the old and tried, against the new and untried?" If so, Lincoln argued, then the Republican Party alone could claim the mantle of conservatism as it sought to "stick to, contend for, the identical old policy on the point in controversy which was adopted by 'our fathers who framed the Government under which we live.'" The unanimous vote reaffirming Northwest Ordinance in the first Congress clearly confirmed his contention that the Constitution sought to marginalize and minimize slavery while reserving the West for free white laborers.[24]

In Lincoln's account, the so-called agitation of the slavery question arose only when slaveholding Southerners and politically subservient Northerners sought to reverse the course established by the Revolutionary Fathers and substitute a government friendly to slavery's expansion. The Southern argument that the Constitution expressly protected slaveholders' right to take their human chattels into the new territories broke down under a cursory glance at the document, as the "instrument is literally silent about any such right." The Northern Democratic insistence on popular sovereignty as the only constitutional solution also dissolved under scrutiny as it substituted an "innovation" of Lewis Cass's 1848 presidential campaign for the intentions of Jefferson and Washington. Frustrated by the "sophistical contrivances" flung at his party, Lincoln denied his party's "sectional" identity and denounced the Southern policy of "rule or ruin" instead urging any who would listen that if they "would have the peace of the old times," they needed only "readopt the precepts and policy of the old times." Far from occupying the position of conservatives, Southerners emerged as the real radicals, bent on subverting the order established at the nation's birth. In a final word to his Republican audience, Lincoln encouraged a moderate course, cautioning against acting out of "passion and ill temper" but insisting that they must, and would, stand firm in their duty against those who would invoke Washington only to "unsay what Washington said, and undo what Washington did."[25]

As the candidate had hoped, Republican approval of Lincoln's Cooper Institute speech extended far beyond the "frequent and irrepressible applause" that greeted his closing sentences. Although Horace Greeley nominally remained a backer of Bates, his *New-York Tribune* praised the speech as a throwback to "the days of Clay and Webster" and immediately reprinted the address as a campaign pamphlet. The *Tribune*'s endorsement quickly drew the attention of newspapers throughout the Northeast and won the candidate publicity for his subsequent campaign stops in New England. Even the thoroughgoingly pro-Seward *Poughkeepsie Eagle* acknowledged that the address proved Lincoln "one of the statesmen of the age," who would "soon take his proper position in the nation." Although still a second-tier candidate for the presidency, Lincoln's tour in the East had helped to make his campaign turn from a fantasy into a viable, if still arduous, political endeavor.[26]

The Cooper Institute address captured the essence of Lincoln's argument and revealed its broad appeal. For years, he had worked to build up a solid base of support without alienating any major faction of either the state or national party. Diplomatic and prudent, he had worked with all and schemed against none. Since his political reemergence in 1854, he had refined a case that the Founders had sought to limit slavery's reach and that restricting the institution's reach represented the only true conservative policy. This argument offered effusive praise for the Constitution, and the Union and was rooted in a reverence for the wisdom of the past. For voters convinced of the United States' exceptional place in history, it seemed a cogent, thoughtful, and balanced case that sought to revive the nation's republican institutions and protect the integrity of the Union for years to come.

A Battle in Charleston

Meanwhile, as the Democratic gathering at Charleston grew ever closer, Illinois Democrats became increasingly militant in their promotion of Stephen A. Douglas for the presidency. Although a tiny pro-Buchanan minority, represented by the *Chicago Herald* and a handful of other Danite newspapers, held Douglas "responsible for every calamity that has for the last three years befallen the Democratic Party," the popular roar for Douglas drowned out their appeals. Urging a united front among all Northern Democrats, the *Ottawa Free Trader* accused the Buchanan administration of having "determined by fair means or foul to defeat the nomination of Douglas at Charleston . . . by motives purely of personal spite." The paper accused Georgia's Howell Cobb, a favorite among Southern Rights men, of disloyalty to the Democracy by cultivating the leaders of the Constitutional Union movement, a collection of former Whigs and Know-Nothings who planned to nominate their own presidential candidate at a convention scheduled for early May. The *Rock Island Argus* insisted, "Douglas is already nominated in the hearts of the people" and demanded "only a ceremony" affirming that choice at Charleston and "the quicker it is performed, the better." The *Chicago Times* echoed this sentiment, declaring it regarded "the position of Mr. Douglas as impregnable as the fortress of Gibraltar." Reviving the old trick of antiparty partisanship, the *Olney Press* insisted that all patriots supported Douglas, with "each forgetting that they were Whigs, or were Democrats" as they united "upon one common platform—the preservation of the Union as it was and is." Whether assailed by extremism from the North or South, they argued that Douglas stood prepared to defend the sovereignty and rights of the American people.[27]

Behind the scenes in Washington, McClernand lobbied for the support of key Northern delegations at Charleston, writing back to Illinois with some frustration that while "eight out of the fourteen [New Jersey] delegates are for Douglas," he was "not confident" of rumors that the "the N. Y. delegation were also for him." He warned that the contest between "extensionists" and "Douglas and all conservative democrats" had grown "more and more vehement," and as "the fight is hand to hand," he and his allies could not afford to give quarter.[28]

Despite this rancor, Murray McConnel, an Illinois delegate from Morgan County, was still "surprised at the bitterness of some of our Southern opponents" upon his arrival in the "Queen City of the South." Writing to Douglas, who remained in Washington, on the eve of the convention, McConnel reported with frustration that the Southerners "call us abolitionists and say we had better stay at home and attend the Chicago convention." As partisans who reveled in decrying their Republican opponents as "abolitionists," Illinois Democrats reeled when Southerners foisted the epithet on them.[29]

Led by Alabama Fire-Eater William Lowndes Yancey, a determined core of Southern Rights radicals entered the convention determined to break up the Democratic Party and precipitate a national crisis that would produce an independent Southern confederacy. Alongside this group of avowed disunionists, a larger cohort of Southern Democrats purported to support the Union but insisted that the convention pass over Douglas and renounce his Freeport Doctrine by endorsing a federal slave code and prohibiting interference with the institution at any point before statehood, a position known as the Alabama platform. Such hardliners found ample support among the local population as the *Charleston Mercury* demanded "a distinct recognition of the rights of the South before her Delegates shall be called upon to act in common with the Northern delegates, in selecting a common candidate for the Presidency."[30]

As the convention opened on Monday, April 23, Douglas enjoyed the majority's support. Unlike in Congress, where Southerners had reigned supreme among Democrats since the elections of 1854, the Democratic National Convention allotted votes to states based on their relative weight in the Electoral College. Thus, the Democrats of reliably Republican Massachusetts could still outvote their counterparts in Mississippi by nearly two to one. Unfortunately for the Little Giant, Democratic Party rules required that the nominee receive the support of two-thirds of the delegates, not merely a majority. Douglas's backers achieved a victory early on when they secured an amendment to loosen the so-called unit rule, which prescribed that state delegations vote as a bloc. This change allowed the minority of pro-Douglas Southerners, concentrated mostly in the Border and Upper South, to cast votes for Douglas, whereas Southern anti-Douglasites could expect free-state votes only from reliably pro-Buchanan Pennsylvania and pro-Southern California and Oregon. Although this amendment did not prevent the selection of a pro-Southern doughface, Caleb Cushing of Massachusetts, for chairman of the convention on a separate state-by-state vote, pro-Douglas forces remained optimistic, claiming the 198–101 vote on the unit rule as a "triumph," which showed that they were in striking distance of nominating Douglas. Although a close ally of Douglas was aware that several Southern state delegations had agreed to work in concert to prevent the Little Giant's nomination, he maintained that their "cause is too desperate to apprehend any danger" and insisted that so long as "our friends of the North will but remain calm, but determined, all will result well."[31]

Yet all would not "result well," as the Douglasites underestimated the determination of Southern delegates to stand by their extremist position of federal protection for slavery throughout the national territories. Thanks to the fact that each state cast one vote in committee, Southern delegates, with the assistance of Californians and Oregonians, managed to pass the Alabama platform's slave code as the "majority" report of the platform committee by a single vote. When confronted with this proslavery platform on the convention floor, the pro-Douglas delegates balked, with Ohio's George E. Pugh, stating bluntly, "Gentlemen of the South, you mistake us—you mistake us—we will not do it." Douglas's supporters acknowledged that the rejection of the misnamed "majority" report could lead some Southerners, perhaps an entire delegation or two, to depart the convention in frustration. Yet they had not anticipated how their 165 to 138 vote against the "majority" report on April 30 would signal the departure of every Deep South delegation, along with that of Arkansas from the convention.[32]

Undoubtedly, many Douglas men welcomed the withdrawal of Yancey and his ilk, but the departure of so many delegates alarmed them, and the anti-Douglas Upper South delegates who remained appeared determined to stand their ground. With the support of the New York delegation, whose loyalty McClernand had been right to question, the remaining Southerners insisted the Douglas men would still need two-thirds of the original number of delegates rather than two-thirds of those still present to nominate their champion. In the coming days, the convention undertook a series of pointless votes in which

Douglas secured a majority but not two-thirds of the delegates. Exasperated with the process and sick of Charleston's pro-Southern strident atmosphere, Douglas delegates voted to adjourn until June 18, when they would reconvene in Baltimore. In the meantime, they hoped a new slate of pro-Douglas Southern delegates would be chosen to replace those firebrands who had withdrawn from the Charleston Convention.

As word spread of the events at Charleston among Douglas Democrats in Illinois, a spirit of frustration and defiance took hold. The *Ottawa Free Trader* lambasted the "awkward squad of about fifty sore-headed fire-eaters" who had walked out and "with a hundred understrappers and pimps" employed every "infamous engine" to "defeat the people's favorite—the true and tried statesman—Steven A. Douglas." Likewise, the *Salem Advocate* denounced the men of the "extreme Southern States" who had become "secessionists" and promised its readers that "there will be a day of reckoning. These men will be held to account." Nomination or no nomination, the *Quincy Herald* pasted "Stephen Douglas for President" on its masthead and declared him the Democracy's nominee "by the authority of THE PEOPLE." While committed to sending Illinois's delegates to the Baltimore Convention to secure Douglas's rightful place, the *Illinois State Register* warned that if Southerners should continue in their demand for a territorial slave code, "the delegates from the free states would have but one alternative, and that would be to retire at once . . . and adopt such measures for the future as the contingency might seem to demand." No longer willing to take orders from the Southern slaveholders who had pushed their party to the brink in the free states, Illinois's Democrats had determined to stand by popular sovereignty and nominate Douglas for president, one way or another.[33]

The confusion emanating from Charleston delighted Illinois Republicans who correctly recognized that "either the Northern Democracy must recant" and endorse a territorial slave code or "the permanent division of the party is inevitable." In either case, the Republicans could see a clear path to victory. A repudiation of Douglas would drive thousands of Illinois Democrats out of the party, while a division of the Democrats into warring parties would sink Douglas's chance of winning a majority in the Electoral College. This conclusion presupposed that the Constitutional Unionists, who would be in Baltimore on May 9, would play no significant role in the contest. Indeed, prior to that convention, Illinois Republicans dismissed the prospective ticket as a side show that would run an aged candidate pledged to a few old Whig and nativist "clap-traps" such as "'protection to American Industry" and 'Americans to rule America,' &c" while ignoring the pressing issue of slavery's extension.[34]

This prediction proved true as the Constitutional Unionists, led by Kentucky's John J. Crittenden and a cohort of former Whigs from the Upper South, effectively ignored both of their potential Northern constituencies in their nominations. As thoughtfully outlined by historian Michael Holt, the Constitutional Unionists might have appealed to a broad swath of former Whigs by nominating Bates or McLean. The former Missouri congressman and Supreme Court justice had the unique potential of appealing to the opponents of the Democracy in both sections through their Whig backgrounds, outspoken opposition to the Kansas-Nebraska Act, and impeccable unionism. Such a move would have placed the Republicans at the subsequent Chicago Convention in a delicate position. They would have needed to either accede to the Constitutional Unionists' nomination and soften their position on slavery's extension or else refuse and potentially split their own party. In the wake of the Charleston fiasco, the Constitutional Unionists might also have chosen to unite with Douglas Democrats by forming some sort of joint ticket and running a campaign against perceived extremists in both sections. The Democratic antecedents of Texas's Sam Houston, the perceived frontrunner for the nomination at the beginning of the convention, would have made such a ticket even more likely. In the end, however, the five hundred delegates who gathered in Baltimore chose to do neither and nominated two oldline Whigs, John Bell, an experienced but unremarkable senator from Tennessee, for president, and Edward Everett, a former senator from Massachusetts who had left office in 1854, for vice president. As the *Illinois State Journal* astutely observed, the ticket would "poll a respectable vote" in the South and "perhaps carry Maryland" but would "fail to rally around it more than a corporal's guard" in the Northern states. With the Constitutional Unionists effectively out of the picture throughout the free states, the Republicans enjoyed a free hand as their delegates wended their ways to the metropolis of the Prairie State.[35]

Republican Unity

Despite the intraparty squabbles in preceding months, the Illinois delegation arrived committed to the newly dubbed Rail Splitter's candidacy. The effort of reunifying the party had occupied Lincoln in the months following his address at Cooper Institute. The work, while delicate, was feasible thanks to Lincoln's exceptional position within the party. He had kept above the bickering between Judd and Wentworth and cultivated goodwill among the radical minority of the party through his defense of Lovejoy without alienating his conservative base of supporters. Uncommitted to any one faction but friendly to all, Lincoln tempered enthusiasm for Seward's candidacy in northern Illinois while coopting Bates's greatest supporter in the state, his old friend Browning.

The gubernatorial contest remained fractious, with northern Illinois and many former Democrats backing Judd's candidacy; Yates receiving popular support in central and southern Illinois; and Swett emerging as the favorite of other old Whigs of the region, including David Davis. When balloting began at the Republican State Convention at Decatur on May 9, a mere week before the national convention would begin at Chicago, Judd led with 255 votes, compared to Yates's 197 and Swett's 184, but in the succeeding ballots, the Swett backers steadily shifted into Yates's camp, sending him over the top on the fourth ballot with 363 votes to Judd's 237 and Swett's 36. As mentioned, a disappointed Judd enjoyed a consolation prize when he was selected as a delegate at large to the Chicago Convention and also the enjoyed schadenfreude of watching his archenemy, Wentworth, leave the convention empty-handed. With that unpleasant confrontation settled, the Republicans quickly balanced Yates, a former Whig with perceived connections to Know-Nothingism, with the German former Democrat Francis A. Hoffman.[36]

The enduring moment of the Decatur Convention, however, had come just before the balloting when Honest Abe received a second nickname. Announced by Richard J. Oglesby of Decatur, Lincoln entered the hall with thunderous applause. As the crowd roared its approval, John Hanks of Macon County, Lincoln's second cousin, brought forward two fence rails and a placard that declared "Abraham Lincoln, The Rail Candidate for President in 1860. Two rails from a lot of 3,000 made in 1830 by Thos. Hanks and Abe Lincoln." Although Lincoln reacted to his Rail Splitter designation with some embarrassment—the image of the towering lawyer mauling rails delighted the audience and proved invaluable for Lincoln's image as a self-made man. With near unanimity, the convention-goers declared Lincoln their choice for the presidency in 1860 and instructed their delegation to the Chicago convention to vote for Lincoln as a unit. The *Chicago Press and Tribune* delightedly proclaimed Lincoln's nomination and touted his restorative potential, noting that Lincoln would uphold "the doctrine of Henry Clay" and do more than any other man to "bring the country back to prosperous times, or to raise her character to what it once was."[37]

Upon arriving in Chicago, the Illinois delegates, led by Davis, touted Lincoln's appeal as a rugged westerner, an outsider to national politics untainted by the corruptions of office, and as a centrist moderate. Both Lincoln and

Seward had hoped to shake charges of radicalism springing from their 1858 House Divided and Irrepressible Conflict speeches. Indeed, only two days after Lincoln's speech at Cooper Institute, Seward softened his stance as he sought reconciliation between the slaveholding "capital States" and the free "labor States." But while many interpreted Lincoln's Cooper Institute address as a clarification of principle for the obscure westerner, Seward's moderate tone struck some as disingenuous backpaddling. Seward's moderation during his time as Lincoln's secretary of state would prove he was genuine, but his many years in the national spotlight and earlier his penchant for phrases like "a higher law than the Constitution" had made his candidacy a liability for Republicans in the Border North states of Pennsylvania, New Jersey, Indiana, and Illinois, whose voters disliked abolitionism nearly as much as slavery.[38]

Before gathering in the Wigwam, a new hall built especially for the Republicans' convention, the Illinois delegation invaded nearby hotels, promoting Lincoln's candidacy among the undecided and wavering delegates. While rival New York editors Thurlow Weed and Horace Greeley advocated on behalf of Seward and Bates, respectively, Davis stalked the halls of the Tremont House hotel, directing a team that included recent adversaries Judd, Yates, and Swett as well as State Auditor Jesse K. Dubois and Congressman Elihu B. Washburne. As alluded to, Browning, in an act of personal loyalty to Lincoln, also worked hard for the Rail Splitter's success, though he continued to secretly hope for Bates's nomination. Only Wentworth, so often a renegade, refused to lobby on Lincoln's behalf and slighted the candidate's chances in his coverage of the convention in the *Chicago Democrat*. Despite Wentworth's sabotage, the Illinois delegation secured first ballot support for Lincoln from the entire Indiana delegation. The Indiana Republicans took a decidedly moderate course on slavery's expansion, having formed a coalition with Douglas Democrats in the aftermath of Lecompton, and contained a substantial group of former Know-Nothings. The nomination of Seward, widely perceived as a radical noted for his antinativist views, would likely sink their chances of winning the governorship. With the Bates campaign floundering, Lincoln appeared as the ideal alternative. In addition to growing up in their state and sharing their midwestern Republican outlook, Lincoln would likely reward Indiana with a place in the cabinet.[39]

Thus, following two days of ordinary party business that included the adoption of a platform that—by abandoning the moralistic language of slavery as a "relic of barbarism"—appeared more moderate than that of 1856, the Illinois and Indiana delegations cast their united ballots for Lincoln on May 18. On the first ballot, as many states scattered their votes across all the candidates or backed a favorite son, Lincoln's command of Illinois and Indiana, along with strong support from the New Hampshire and Virginia delegations, placed him second behind Seward with 102 votes to the New Yorker's 173.5. More important, Lincoln easily outran each of the other Seward alternatives, more than doubling the tallies of Cameron, Chase, and Bates. By depriving Seward of a first-ballot majority and winning a large plurality of the anti-Seward votes, Lincoln's supporters had placed him in a strong position to pull ahead in subsequent ballots, especially since Davis had convinced Pennsylvania's delegation to back Lincoln after the first ballot. After the second ballot, Lincoln pulled within three and a half ballots of Seward, and the third ballot pushed Lincoln over the top, with several Chase backers from Ohio switching their ballots to give the Illinois Rail Splitter the nomination. While Chicagoans left the Wigwam triumphantly amid shouts of celebration, the convention neatly balanced Lincoln's nomination by selecting Hannibal Hamlin, a former Democrat from Maine, as his running mate. While the intense competition of the convention necessitated soothing bruised egos, especially among Seward's staunchest supporters, the Republicans adjourned their convention unified and enthusiastic for the contest ahead.[40]

As mentioned above, the 1860 Republican National Platform reflected the party's broader effort to reach out to undecided conservative Northerners without abandoning their fundamental opposition to the extension of slavery. In that spirit, they declared that they held "in abhorrence all schemes for disunion," promised to maintain as "inviolate . . . the right of each state to order and control its own domestic institutions," denounced the "reckless extravagance which pervades every department of the Federal Government," and promised "a return to rigid economy and accountability." Taking aim at both proadministration and Douglas Democrats, the platform attacked both the "infamous Lecompton Constitution" and the "deception and fraud" enabled by the "boasted Democratic principle of Non-Intervention and Popular Sovereignty." In its opposition to slavery in the territories, the platform cited the authority of "our Republican fathers" and declared the effort to extend slavery a "dangerous political heresy" at odds with the Constitution and thus "revolutionary in its tendency, and subversive of the peace and harmony of the country." This language of preservation and restoration served a dual purpose. It provided a counter to party opponents who denounced it as sectional, power-hungry, and radical, but it also reflected the genuine commitment of many delegates to return to an imagined past age in which republican statesmen governed honestly and preserved the common territory for future generations of the nation's free white citizens. Combined with the platform's allusions to tariffs and internal improvements (an incitement for former Whigs), support for the homestead act (popular among Northwestern Democrats), and commitment to maintaining the existing naturalization requirements (a nod to the party's German contingent), the platform opened the door to a "Big Tent" Republican Party as expansive as the Chicago Wigwam.[41]

In short, the party reflected the views of typical white Illinoisans like Charles Balance, who, writing to Trumbull at the beginning of May, explained the conservative position of his neighborhood in the following terms:

> With regard to general politics, our people are generally moderate men—opposed to extremes. We are neither abolitionists, nor nullifiers. We are all union men and are willing to be foiled in our prospects provided the union is safe—provided the country is quiet and prosperous. The majority of us are opposed to the fugitive slave law, but for the sake of peace we say let it be enforced, but when an attempt is made to open up the slave trade, or force slavery into the territories by holding to the Dred Scott decision, a slave code for the territories, there is no difference of opinion here. Whigs, democrats, republicans, abolitionist, all say "it shall not be."

This cohort of voters remained committed to maintaining the nation they believed they had inherited from the founding generation. While willing to tolerate slavery as a necessary evil, they could not condone its continued expansion and would resist the encroachments of an increasingly aggressive Southern planter class. Indeed, subsequent developments at the second Democratic National Convention in Baltimore confirmed Balance's portrait of a bipartisan consensus on this point.[42]

Unity in Illinois—Division in Baltimore

As the Democratic delegations prepared to reassemble in mid-June, Illinois partisans made it clear that their delegates needed to stand by Douglas to have any hope of victory in November. J. W. Maxwell of Bloomington, writing to Douglas in late May, insisted that nothing could be done to "save us in this state unless you head the ticket." Another party operative warned the Little Giant, "There are some professed Democrats who say . . . they will vote for Honest Abe if you are not the nominee." Echoing the public, the *Illinois State Register* insisted that the party must stand against "the reckless ferocity of ambitious and mischievous ultraists" of the South and "obey the democratic popular behest and nominate Mr. Douglas." This "Douglas or nobody" attitude reflected the anger of Illinois Democrats marginalized by Southerners and their sycophants since before the Lecompton crisis. On the defensive since 1854, the Illinois Democracy recognized that its very existence depended on a continued commitment to popular sovereignty. Its constituents would continue to allow Southerners to have a fair vote in deciding the question of slavery in the West as they would all other matters, but they would not surrender their own rights and interests to please a cohort of haughty slaveholders bent on disunion.[43]

The fate of this second Democratic Convention rested on whether the Southern delegates who had bolted at Charleston would return as delegates to the second gathering. While the entire South Carolina delegation avoided the national gathering and instead attended only the states' rights Democratic gathering held concurrently in Richmond, most Deep South delegates attempted to reenter the convention at Baltimore. Several Southern states sent competing pro-Douglas delegations, and as the convention came to order on June 18, the credentials committee faced a dilemma. Those Upper South delegations who had remained at Charleston now threatened to bolt the Baltimore Convention if the Northern delegates refused to seat the original Deep South delegations. Pro-Douglas Northern Democrats could either concede to Southern demands or divide their party along sectional lines. Faced with another broken convention, Douglas attempted to compromise, offering in a letter to William A. Richardson to withdraw from the contest if the convention would unite "upon some other non-Intervention and Union loving Democrat." Douglas hoped that this sacrifice would at least save his political legacy if not his career. But Richardson and Douglas's allies could not countenance backing down, and instead, McClernand telegraphed Douglas that the New York delegation would finally fall into line and sustain him. On June 22, the convention voted to reject the credentials of nearly all of bolters, triggering a second Southern walkout led by the Virginia delegation.[44]

With the damage done, the rival factions of the Democratic Party each claimed the title of the National Democracy and nominated rival candidates for the presidency. Most Northern delegates and a small minority of Southerners who remained at the original convention hall at the Front Street Theater voted to adopt a platform committed to popular sovereignty and nominated Douglas for president. Herschel V. Johnson of Georgia would eventually join Douglas on the ticket, but only after Benjamin Fitzpatrick of Alabama declined the spot. Back in Illinois, news of the Little Giant's nomination threw the state's Democrats into ecstasy, and the residents of Freeport rejoiced with "one hundred guns firing . . . flags & music [and the] greatest enthusiasm." Across the city, at Maryland Institute Hall, the revolting Southerners and pro-administration Northerners readopted the "majority" report of the Charleston Convention and nominated Vice President Breckinridge of Kentucky for the presidency and the pro-Southern Oregonian Joseph Lane as his running mate. The handful of diehard Fire-Eaters who had remained at Richmond seconded these nominations several days later. This irrevocable split in the Democratic ranks provided Douglas with only the narrowest path to the presidency. With a significant portion of the South lost at the outset, Douglas needed Northern majorities, especially the electoral votes of his home state.[45]

To rally the moderate majority to his side, Douglas implored Lanphier to "organize every County in Illinois thoroughly" and strike "boldly against the Northern abolitionists and Southern Disunionists, and give no quarter to either." By positioning himself as the conservative alternative between two extremes, he could construct an explicitly centrist coalition dedicated to protecting the rights of free white men. As such, Douglas further encouraged his advisor to "cultivate good relations" with Constitutional Unionists, "for they are Union men" and might be persuaded to come to Douglas's aid later in the contest. Douglas might have saved his ink, as Lanphier had already adopted this approach in the *Illinois State Register*, whose columns already denounced every form of "disunionism, whether the Fire Eaters of the south, or the abolition-blackrepublicans of the north." The *Ottawa Free Trader* concurred, arguing, "The only right course must be found in a medium between these extremes. That medium we find in the National Democratic and Douglas Position of Non-Intervention." The grassroots organizers also followed this moderate tone, with supporters of the Democratic Club of Rock Island declaring themselves members of "the only national, conservative and constitutional party in the country" and dedicated to "the preservation of the integrity and Union of these United States, in accordance with the constitution framed by our patriotic fore-fathers."[46]

Lincoln's Conservative Appeal

Yet the Douglas Democrats faced off against Republican opponents who claimed to occupy the same middle ground. The *Chicago Press and Tribune* announced to its readers that Lincoln's election would signal "no social or violent political revolution; only a constitutional effort to administer the government so that the Slavery question will cease to be a foot-ball of politicians." The *Illinois State Journal* likewise assured undecided readers that Lincoln was "a conservative, peace-loving man, and would use all the powers and prerogatives of his office to protect the rights of every State." Addressing a large crowd in McClean County, Oglesby insisted that the Republicans sought "to place the government on a conservative stand, where slavery shall not be the absolute idea." Even further downstate, in Little Egypt's Jefferson County, a host of speakers addressed mass meetings to demonstrate "the conservative position of the Republican party and satisfy the old-line Whigs and Fillmore men that their principles and duty placed them squarely in the ranks of the friends of freedom." Emphasizing their national orientation, thirty-three Republican women processed through Springfield accompanied by thirty-three horsemen, to represent each state in the Union. Alongside them, young men dawned matching oilcloth capes and marched in perfect order as Lincoln's Wide Awakes. Drawing on the anger of members of all parties toward the corruption of the Buchanan administration, the Republicans promised a clean slate under Honest Abe. A Lincoln presidency, according to another editorial, promised to "put an end to this double dealing upon the question of slavery ... and settle it by returning to the policy of the early days of the Government." Amid the tumult of the Democratic disintegration, the Republicans' united front and promise of order appealed to a broad base of voters vexed by political turmoil.[47]

This sense of unity drew from an Illinois Republican party that overcame its internal divisions, at least for a season, to secure a decisive victory at the polls. Following Lincoln's nomination, Davis, Judd, and other party leaders urged Browning to convince his favored candidate, Bates, to endorse Lincoln and the state's Republican ticket, confident that such an intervention would "emphatically settle the Fillmore men for us." Browning agreed, and his success in recruiting Bates helped to offset the blow the Republicans sustained when Fillmore endorsed the Bell and Everett ticket. A subsequent letter, sent from Seward's right-hand-man, Thurlow Weed, Swett, assured the Illinois party leaders of the "entire confidence reposed in Mr. Lincoln" by that faction and rallied his backers to the campaign. Locally, Davis employed Koerner to keep German voters in the Republican fold while simultaneously courting nativists who had voted for Fillmore in 1856. In a mark of further consolidation, Cyrus Edwards, a prominent former Whig who had quarreled with Lincoln since the late 1840s, pledged to "bury the hatchet" with the Rail Splitter and "cast all of [his] influence for the promotion of [Republican] success." Expanding well beyond their base in the northern counties and the usual battleground in the state's center, Davis and Swett embarked on a "Southern tour" to secure every ballot possible. With statewide votes for governor and the presidency, winning over former Fillmore supporters in districts otherwise uncompetitive for the Republicans made a real difference.[48]

Yet in their effort to create a broad coalition, Illinois Republicans further alienated the state's small corps of Black abolitionists. Deeply frustrated by the Republican Party's acquiescence to the constitutional status quo and promise to enforce the Fugitive Slave Act, many Black abolitionists would have concurred with the headline in William Lloyd Garrison's *Liberator* that denounced Lincoln as "The Slave-Hound of Illinois." H. Ford Douglas of Chicago, among the state's most prominent Black abolitionists, limited his criticism of Stephen A. Douglas and the Northern Democrats to only a few opening sentences when he addressed a crowd of Garrisonians at Framingham, Massachusetts, on July 4, 1860. Throughout the remainder of his speech, Ford Douglas sought to prove that "the Republicans of Illinois [are] on the side of slavery" and proclaimed Lincoln "just as odious to the anti-slavery cause and anti-slavery men as ever was John C. Calhoun." He could discern no difference "between the anti-slavery of Abraham Lincoln, and the anti-slavery of the Old Whig party" and proclaimed any such antislavery sentiment "barren and unfruitful." In Douglas's account, it was white abolitionists, not white conservatives, who fooled themselves by believing the Republican Party would pursue its interests once in power. In a subsequent speech delivered in Ohio, Ford Douglas elaborated further: "The Republicans say they are bringing the Government back to the policy of the fathers. I do not desire this; the policy of the fathers was not uncompromising opposition to oppression; and nothing less than a position far higher than they occupied, will ever make us worthy of the name of free men." So long as the Republicans remained committed to restoring the nation to its founding ideals, rather than transcending them African Americans had little to gain from the party. Therefore, according to Ford Douglas, the radicals, not the conservatives, would find themselves cast aside once the party obtained power.[49]

Ford Douglas's addresses likely would have infuriated Stephen A. Douglas, had he encountered them in print. To have any chance of victory, Senator Douglas needed the Northern public to believe that Lincoln and the Republicans presented a threat as radical and dangerous as that posed by the Southern planters and Breckinridge. While this was largely an uphill battle, the actions of a few zealous northern Illinois Republicans during the campaign did provide Douglas and his backers with appropriate ammunition. In October 1859, a Scottish-born abolitionist named John Hossack, along with several other residents of Ottawa, had assisted in the escape of a fugitive slave named Jim Gray. Convicted in October 1860 of violating the Fugitive Slave Law, Hossack boldly denounced the law as a desecration of "both the letter and spirit of the Constitution" during his trial at the US District Court in Chicago. The fiery oration drew praise from the Republican organs in northern Illinois most sympathetic to abolitionism, including the *Belvidere Standard*. The ever-controversial Wentworth attracted further attention by raising money to pay Hossack's fine. Delighted by the Chicago mayor's controversial action, the *Illinois State Register* proclaimed that it served as "proof that the republicans [of Illinois] are paying premiums to the abolitionists to rescue fugitive slaves and mob the courts." Flabbergasted, the editors of the *Illinois State Journal* and *Chicago Tribune* quickly distanced themselves and the Republican Party from the incident, insisting that Hossack was not a Republican but instead a member of Gerrit Smith's Radical Abolition Party and denouncing Wentworth as a traitor bent on rendering the Republicans unelectable. This panic and infighting, in turn, invited cackles from the Democratic press elsewhere in the state.[50]

Meanwhile, Douglas, convinced that he alone stood between the nation and a constitutional crisis, broke with precedent and openly campaigned on his own behalf. Leaving the contest in Illinois to his longtime allies, the Little Giant crisscrossed New England, Pennsylvania, and the Upper South before making his way home through the Northwest. Throughout the summer, Douglas remained firm that while he would sanction a coalition between his supporters and those of Bell in select states, he would not agree to such a union with Breckinridge's supporters. While Douglas was certain of his cause's righteousness, his hope began to fade over the course of the campaign as reports from the South revealed that he may not win a single slaveholding state. With the Republicans surging in the North, he faced catastrophe in the Electoral College. At home, the disruptive Danite movement, although still meager in strength, remained a thorn in Douglasites' side as the administration continued to target any Douglas man who benefited from party patronage. Deep in Little Egypt, the *Cairo City Gazette* urged the minority that sympathized with the Southern Democrats to recognize that "the Black Republicans consider the supporters of Breckinridge and Lane their special allies," but this small faction remained resolute in its obstinacy.[51]

Divided nationally and facing a Republican resurgence, some Illinois Democrats resorted to falsehoods and hyperbole in desperation. In the span of two columns, the *Quincy Herald* claimed that Lincoln supported Black suffrage, opposed the proposed homestead bill, and had for years sought to "betray the interests of [Henry] Clay and the Whig party in Illinois into the clutches of the abolitionists." A few days later, the *Rock Island Argus* argued that Breckinridge would not carry a single Southern state and that the Republicans hoped not only to liberate Blacks in the South but to replace them by condemning Germans and Irish immigrants to slavery. In Springfield, a Douglas supporter implausibly suggested that the state of Virginia, and not Congress, had restricted slavery's spread westward in the Northwest Ordinance of 1787 and that, as such, the Founders themselves vindicated popular sovereignty.[52]

In more cogent moments, Douglas's supporters emphasized their independence from the radical Southerners who had long dominated the national Democracy and touted their devotion to the Union. The *Ottawa Free Trader* denounced as an "outrageous falsehood" the Republican suggestion that by accepting the Dred Scott decision, Northern Democrats admitted that "the territorial legislatures cannot prohibit or interfere with such property in the territory." Douglas and his supporters had denied such an implication from the moment Taney released the decision and had devised the Freeport Doctrine to counter it. The same paper subsequently asked skeptical readers how "the Democratic party [could be] in favor of the extension of slavery, when it has admitted the three states—California, Minnesota, and Oregon—that gives the free states the preponderance in the Senate, and the majority of states in the Union." Believing their faction transcended the petty bounds of sectional interest that Lincoln and Breckinridge represented, the *Illinois State Register* urged its readers to "to fight with undiminished courage in defence not of the north, nor of the south, but of the Constitution and the Union."[53]

In the aftermath of Republican victories in the state elections of Indiana and Pennsylvania, however, Douglas recognized that Lincoln would win a majority in the Electoral College. These two states, crucial to Buchanan's 1856 victory, now gave the Republicans such decisive majorities to that none but the most obtuse partisans could doubt the outcome. With his own fate as a candidate sealed, Douglas embarked for the Deep South in the hope of softening the blow of a Lincoln presidency. Naively hoping that Southerners would come to their senses and recognize that Lincoln could do little damage without the support of the Senate or the Supreme Court, the two institutions where Southerners held decisive sway, Douglas encountered overt hostility as he traveled through Georgia and Alabama denouncing secession. His despair grew deeper still as he watched the fever of secession take hold of Mobile as the results poured in on the evening of November 6, 1860.[54]

Thanks to a well-disciplined national organization and the Republicans' broad appeal to moderates across the North, Lincoln won a decisive majority of 180 electoral votes. However, since Republican tickets did not even appear in ten slaveholding states, the Rail Splitter received only 39.8 percent of the national popular vote, with 1,865,908 ballots. Douglas ran second in the popular vote, with 1,365,976, but 88 percent of these ballots came from the free states, and his only electoral votes came from New Jersey, which he split with Lincoln, and Missouri, where he secured a meager plurality of 35 percent. Breckinridge polled third in the popular vote and second in the Electoral College with the support of all the remaining slaveholding states, save Kentucky, Tennessee, and Virginia, which went for Bell.[55]

In Illinois, Lincoln's narrow margin of victory closely matched that achieved by the two statewide Republican office-seekers in 1858. With 50.69 percent of the vote, Lincoln won 11,956 more ballots than Douglas, who secured 47.17 percent. The marginal candidacies of Bell and Breckinridge drew 1.45 percent and 0.69 percent, respectively. An examination of votes on the county level reveals that Lincoln won over most of the state's conservative Fillmore voters. Had these voters believed that Lincoln posed a threat to the Union or the Constitution, they might have cast ballots for Douglas, whose campaign eagerly courted their suffrages with continued appeals to the legacy of Henry Clay, or else thrown their support to Bell, the choice of Fillmore himself. Instead, the evidence indicates that these voters saw Lincoln as a moderate alternative who could check the fanaticism of Southern planters without giving in to the radicalism of abolitionists. In Bond County, for example, Fillmore's plurality of 46.4 percent of the vote in 1856 transformed into a 49.5 percent plurality for Lincoln in 1860. Similarly, in Edwards County, a 40.3 percent plurality for Fillmore turned into a Lincoln majority of 60 percent. This pattern held true even in counties where Lincoln lost. In 1856, Menard County gave Buchanan 52.4 percent of its votes, Fillmore 41 percent, and Fremont 6.6 percent, while in 1860, Douglas won a plurality with 49.9 percent compared to Lincoln's 46.4 percent.[56]

Some of these changes, of course, resulted from the addition of new voters to the electorate, and as the work of Jon Grinspan and other historians has demonstrated, the Republicans' message of change and the pageantry of Wide Awake parades won over many "virgin voters." Nevertheless the counties analyzed in the preceding examples presented only a small increase in total voters, suggesting a concerted turn toward Lincoln by Fillmore voters rather than a youthful surge for the Rail Splitter.[57]

Lincoln and his Illinois Republican allies had swayed these voters through their appeals to the Constitution as a sacred document and by their commitment to reinstating the policies of the Founding generation. For voters disgusted by the Buchanan administration's corruption, disturbed by the extremism of slaveholding Southern Democrats, and shocked by the disastrous course of popular sovereignty in Kansas, the Republican argument made perfect sense. In casting their ballots for Lincoln, they hoped to send a message to arrogant slaveholders and corrupt Democratic officeholders that they would not permit the desecration of the Constitution or the degradation of the Union.

"Illinois Redeemed!"

Throughout the Prairie State, the Republican press reveled in the ecstasy of a national triumph and the elevation of their own favorite son to the chief magistracy. Their vision of the Union as a nation for the advancement of free white men everywhere had been vindicated. "There is yet hope for freedom, for honesty, for purity," boasted the *Chicago Press and Tribune,* for the results proved that "maxims of Jefferson, of Franklin, of Adams, of Madison, of Clay and of Jackson, survive." Beneath a crowing rooster, the *Woodstock Sentinel* gloated, "Douglas played out at home. For devout Republicans have buried him in popular sovereignty." In Springfield, the *Illinois State Journal* proclaimed "THE UNION SAFE!" with "MR. LINCOLN'S ELECTION CERTAIN!!" The *Pantagraph* of Bloomington also saw smooth sailing ahead as the nation entered "on a path of glory, and a career of moral power unequaled in the world's history" even as "liberty and moral right are struggling into existence in Europe, here they will be working and wielding their power." Fully confident that the slaveholding South, despite its bluster, would eventually accept the election as fair and constitutional, Republicans dismissed any thought of secession or war.[58]

Yet, in distant South Carolina the election result threatened to dissolve the Union. That political bond of fraternity, treasured by Illinoisans of all political stripes and praised as the noblest experiment on the face of the earth, now teetered on the brink of destruction. The *Charleston Mercury* announced, "The tea has been thrown overboard—the revolution of 1860 has been initiated," as the state's citizens expressed "their determination to resist LINCOLN's election at all hazards." Voicing the determination of the Southern planter class, the *Charleston Courier* concurred and pronounced "the failure of the great American experiment of Federal self government." In the weeks and months that followed, Illinoisans would frantically fight with one another in the hope of reversing this calamity, even as events in Charleston harbor poised to draw them together, for once at least, under the same banner.[59]

CHAPTER 7

THE UNION IN PERIL

The canon that had boomed in jubilation on election night in Springfield now rested in uneasy silence, covered in a blanket of snow as the cold north wind swept across the prairie. The unwelcome events of the early winter reminded the capital's residents that their oversized noisemaker had been cast for a far grimmer purpose. In the aftermath of the 1860 presidential contest, the jubilation of Illinois Republicans had initially drowned out the crisis that threatened to rend the Union. While Douglas Democrats had taken the threat of Southern disunion more seriously, the rapid unilateral secession of South Carolina in December startled both parties. For the remainder of the so-called secession winter, as six other Deep South states voted to sever their ties to the federal government, Illinoisans of all political parties and factions fiercely debated how best to save the Union. As historian Adam I. P. Smith has stated, the question was not whether the "dismemberment of the nation" should be met with resistance but rather "what form that should take and how it would be justified."[1]

Indeed, even as some radical elements on the political margins embraced national dissolution as the least of several evils, the essential conservatism of mainstream Republicans and Democrats throughout the Prairie State—their underlying devotion to preserving the Constitution and institutions established by the Founders—led them to debate the means of national preservation rather than the ends. The uncertainty of the secession crisis, permeated with rumor and misinformation, placed great strain on both major political parties as Lincoln and Douglas struggled to maintain tenuous coalitions. The president-elect and most other Illinois Republican leaders believed that by standing firm on the Chicago platform they could both maintain their party's diverse coalition and squelch Southern intransigence. Douglas and his allies, better informed on the extent of disunionist power throughout the slaveholding states, worked to craft a compromise that would satisfy conditional unionists in the South and avert a clash of arms without acknowledging the legitimacy of secession. Amid rising tensions, each party accused the other of covertly aiding Southern extremists and undermining the Union. Ultimately, however, a common devotion to maintaining law and order as established by the Constitution drove the followers of both Lincoln and Douglas into a united front to protect the Union after secessionists fired on the Stars and Stripes. This alliance did not signal an end to partisan divisions in Illinois or anywhere else in the North, but it did reveal the common core of unconditional unionism that bridged the party divide.[2]

The Question of Secession

After listening to the seemingly empty threats of Southern Fire-Eaters for more than a decade, most Illinois Republicans initially dismissed the agitation in the Cotton South in the election's aftermath as mere bluster. Having promised voters that Lincoln's election would restore order and good government, the state Republican press blithely brushed off the threat posed by secessionists and instead emphasized the nation's bright future under Republican governance. With an overzealous confidence that revealed the ignorance of editors Charles H. Ray and Joseph Medill, the *Chicago Tribune* announced the day after the election that "there will be no secession—not even of a single state." Instead, they predicted only a "few impotent howels" from slaveholding extremists "and the disunion farce will be permanently withdrawn from Southern boards." According to the *Illinois State Journal,* far from creating a crisis, Lincoln's election marked an end to national turmoil. "The people," they argued, "are tired of wrangling and agitations in which the Democracy have so needlessly embroiled the nation, and they have elected Mr. Lincoln for the express purpose of ending them." The *Pantagraph* of Bloomington concurred, promising its readers "the Union will enjoy a quiet it has not known for years." A constituent writing to Lyman Trumbull "had no fears from the bluster of South Carolina and Georgia" and contended that misguided Southern fears "could be easily (and perhaps should be) allayed" through a public letter reiterating Republican policy. As such, in Republican eyes, the crisis appeared within the norm of political bluster, and many turned their attention to the matter of securing patronage positions within the Lincoln administration.[3]

Illinois Douglas Democrats, who had warned of the danger of disunion throughout the campaign, now positioned themselves uneasily as opponents of both the incoming administration and secession. Mimicking the antisecessionist stance Douglas had taken up his campaign tour of the South, the *Illinois State Register* noted that while Lincoln's election marked "national calamity" that would "destroy the comity that ought to exist between the states," it insisted that" under no circumstances, can disunion be the remedy or the redress for the unfortunate choice." Editor Charles H. Lanphier further declared that any act of secession "being an act not within the constitutional power of any state, will become rebellion and treason" and that those who might attempt it "should be seized and punished just as any other rebel or traitor would be seized or punished." The *Rock Island Argus* concurred, expressing disgust at the Republicans' "party policy" but insisting "Douglas men cannot give practical effect to their notions of popular sovereignty any other way than by heartily sustaining Mr. Lincoln in enforcing the laws of the land and the decisions of the courts." Douglas subsequently sustained these editorials in his first public address since the election, delivered to the citizens of New Orleans on November 13. The Little Giant denounced the "aggressive policy which [Lincoln] and his party are understood to represent" but insisted that "as a good citizen and law-abiding man" he could never accept secession and called on Southerners to help preserve "the Union under the Constitution as our fathers made it" by trusting in the minority rights safeguarded by that document. In the immediate aftermath of the election, Douglas and his allies, unlike the Republicans, took secessionist sentiment seriously but still hoped that a combination of concessions by Lincoln and pro-Union feelings among ordinary Southern citizens could defuse the crisis before any state acted. Lincoln would become president in accordance with the law, and the South needed to recognize his constitutional authority, but since Lincoln's party advocated measures unconstitutional in the eyes of most Democrats, the president-elect would also need to renounce Republican orthodoxy to fulfill his oath of office.[4]

As they had during the campaign, Douglas Democrats blamed the emerging calamity on the "extremism" of both the Republicans and the Democracy's pro-Southern wing. President Buchanan drew special ire for his role in destroying the national party organization and in emboldening the worst Southern Fire-Eaters. From Scott County in west-central Illinois, one Douglas supporter denounced the outgoing president as "a selfish old man, who has an unsatisfied first for malice and national disorder" and had sown the political seeds "now germinating into rebellion—revolution—and civil war." The *Salem Advocate* blamed William Yancey, John C. Breckinridge, and the selfish "leaders of the Cotton States" who stood poised to dismember "this glorious country" from a heedless "desire to rule." Always suspicious of the Republicans' claims to unionism, Douglas Democrats interpreted the Republican dismissal of Southern threats as covert support for disunion. The *Illinois State Register* predicted "that the republican leaders will wink at the secession of the southern states" to achieve a permanent electoral majority in the North. The *Quincy Herald* also identified the Republicans as the abettors of disunion, arguing that Lincoln did not give "a tinker's damn whether the Union is preserved or broken up" and condemned the president-elect for lacking "the courage to go to the south and tell the people there that the Union must be preserved!" For Douglas Democrats, Lincoln's public silence amid Southern upheaval signaled either an indifference to the fate of the Union or a fatal indecision, either of which deserved sharp condemnation.[5]

While Douglas and the Illinois Democracy emerged as the principal advocates of compromise and conciliation in the months that followed, their marked hostility to James Buchanan's appeasement efforts drew a clear boundary on how far they would go to achieve national reconciliation. As alluded to earlier, Douglas Democrats in Illinois blamed Buchanan as much as the Republicans for bringing the Union to the brink of dissolution. "Oh my soul what a disgrace has Jas Buchanan brought upon himself and his country," wrote one constituent from Union County to Douglas. "Infamy & shame must forever cover his name."[6]

This feeling only grew following Buchanan's annual message to Congress in early December, in which he denounced the "intrinsic unsoundness" of popular sovereignty, urged Congress to adopt a territorial slave code, and washed his hands of any responsibility for secession by announcing, "The Executive has no authority to decide what shall be the relations between the Federal Government and South Carolina." Douglas's supporters in Illinois recoiled at such a policy, inadvertently echoing contemporary Republican claims that such a concession would undermine popular self-government. As the *Illinois State Register* explained, the demand for a federally enforced slave code in the territories unfairly asked "three million four hundred thousand voters of the country to abandon their views, and acquiesce in those of six hundred thousand," as it required all who had "voted for Douglas, Bell and Lincoln, in the late election to come down to the dogma upon which Mr. Buchanan and his associates disrupted the democratic party." Another supporter urged Douglas to stand firm, writing that in his part of the state, "no Douglas or Lincoln man can approve of an act by Congress that gives any prefference to slavery in the territory." Having long ignored the will of most Northern Democrats as well as moderate Southern ex-Whigs, Buchanan had put himself in an untenable position when his Southern extremist allies abandoned the Union. "It is after all to his own blundering, if no worse, that Mr. Buchanan is indebted for the unfortunate necessity which compels him to close his administration with so lugubrious a jeremiad," wrote the *Ottawa Free Trader*. "These disasters are solely attributable to his own folly, this crowning catastrophe of a Union dissolved and the fairest political fabric on the face of the earth in ruins, must damn the administration of James Buchanan to immortal infamy."[7]

A minority of Illinois Democrats, principally from the marginalized Danite faction with strong ties to the South, refused to assign equal blame to the crisis and placed sole responsibility on the Republicans. Deep in southern Illinois's Little Egypt, Allen Bainbridge, a Tennessean by birth, wrote to Douglas that he and his neighbors proposed: "If the South or any portion are determined to secede . . . let them go peaceably" and warned that if the federal government sought to "compel any state to remain in the Union . . . they would go South, & defend the South." Yet, as historian Matthew E. Stanley has noted, the overwhelming majority of Democrats in southern Illinois expressed "some gradation of conservative Unionism," and while Little Egypt remained "geographically, culturally, and politically the southernmost part of any free state," prosecession sentiment remained "atypical."[8]

Trepidation, indecision, and self-contradiction proved far more common reactions among mainstream Douglas Democrats in Illinois as the Deep South hurtled toward secession. While Douglas Democrats had taken a firm posture against secession during the campaign, they now needed to balance that rigid stance with liberal concessions to preserve peace. Samuel Snowden Hayes, a confused Douglas ally, initially supported efforts to organize a "Union Meeting" of anti-Republican forces in Chicago to promote compromise but then hesitated to act further, as he thought "nothing should be done here which will look like opposition to the position that you [Douglas] may be about to take." With disunion at their doorstep, Douglas Democrats needed to develop a coherent policy that would promote both unconditional unionism and peaceful compromise.[9]

These efforts revealed an underlying tension in Democratic conceptions of the Union. As proponents of an affective theory of the Union, many Douglas Democrats believed the Union could only endure as long as mutual affinity bound the states together. But unlike their Southern counterparts, who maintained the rights of individual states to withdraw from the compact, Douglas Democrats insisted that the Union could only be dissolved with the consent of all the states. Thus, no legal or political mechanism could dissolve the Union, which was established in perpetuity, but violent antagonism between the states might create a revolution that would make any reconstruction under republican institutions impossible. Therefore, Douglas and his fellow Illinois Democrats would denounce secession as treason and support the president's right to defend federal property in any seceded states, but they would also not support a war of conquest to reconstruct the Union. A constituent urged Douglas against using force, arguing that any offensive action would "most assuredly divide & destroy [the Union]." Negotiations could bring the recalcitrant states back into the fold (especially if only a handful seceded), while an attack by the federal government on American citizens might permanently harden the hearts of Southerners against the Union and doom the country to perpetual anarchy.[10]

These commitments to both the Union and peace, while not mutually exclusive, created serious dilemmas for Douglas and his allies. They could achieve their two goals only if Congress or a convention of the states adopted a grand compromise akin to that of 1850 or if the South backed down. If these efforts failed and the South stood firm, they would face the unthinkable possibility of confronting either permanent disunion or some form of civil war. As such, throughout the secession winter pro-compromise Northern voices, such as the former Constitutional Unionist vice presidential candidate Edward Everett, exhibited behavior best characterized as erratic. Usually noted for his stoicism, the New England sage instead experienced "wild swings" between hope and despair as the prospects of civil war waxed and waned. Douglas Democrats in Illinois underwent similar emotional turbulence as events in the South and in the halls of Congress unfolded. In December, the dissolution of pro-Breckinridge organizations in the Upper South provided a major boon to the advocates of compromise, even as letters from Douglas supporters in the Deep South gave him little hope for unionist victories there. Back in Illinois, most Democrats looked either to Congress or a national convention to resolve the crisis without bloodshed.[11]

Yet even amid denunciations of Republican warmongering by Democratic organs, clues began to appear that Douglas Democrats might not oppose a war for Union if the federal government was assailed directly by Southern secessionists. Douglas Democrats and Upper South unionists decried "coercion" of the seceded states, but this word, *coercion,* so commonly used throughout the secession crisis, did not rule out defensive action. As Adam I. P. Smith has aptly summarized, for Douglas Democrats, "coercion . . . a full-scale armed invasion of the slave states was one thing, but 'manly' resistance to secession was, implicitly, something different," especially as it became clear that Southerners might themselves reject compromise. In such a case, it might become necessary to use force to enforce the laws and preserve the Union under the Constitution, as Andrew Jackson had promised to do during the Nullification Crisis of 1832–33. For Douglas's ally newspaper editor James W. Sheahan, that principle remained paramount even as he doubted that the occupants of the White House would rise to the occasion. Longstanding partisan animosity, rather than opposition to military force, shaped Sheahan's position on secession. In frustration, he wrote to Douglas, if "secession and disunion could be averted by force then I would be for that course, but under Buchanan or Lincoln it is not possible." A contemporaneous letter to John A. McClernand from a misinformed Illinois Democrat offers another revealing perspective. Alerted, incorrectly, to the news that South Carolina secessionists had seized Fort Moultrie in Charleston Harbor and expelled the federal garrison, Charles B. Phillips demanded immediate action so "justice [might] deal a damnation on treason to our glorious constitution and country wherever it is found." Phillips's instinct to rally to the flag when assailed foreshadowed the mass reaction among Douglas Democrats to genuine secessionist aggression.[12]

As the secession crisis intensified, Douglas Democrats in Illinois did their best to position themselves as the voice of reason within the sectional melee. Disgusted by the perceived intransigence of their Republican adversaries, they nevertheless refused to countenance a permanent dissolution of the Union or an attack on the flag of the United States. Convinced the people would support their effort to preserve both peace and Union, they began to explore potential compromises that could satisfy the South without alienating Northern moderates. Republicans, meanwhile, needed to tread lightly to maintain both party unity and their claim to conservatism.

The Hardline Stance

For some time, Illinois Republicans remained confident they could suppress any threat posed by secessionist intransigence and maintained a firm stance against any compromise with the South. Historians have often contrasted this hardline stance with the "conservative" position taken by conciliationists. But this ideological label obscures more than it reveals, as many hardline

Republicans, especially those in Illinois, believed that they maintained an authentic conservative position in opposition to the constitutional innovations proposed by the proponents of compromise. As the *Chicago Tribune* put it, "That instrument [the Constitution] admits of no tinkering; it is, as applicable to the country at large, the wisest of all human labor, and as such the North is determined to maintain it." To be sure, some hardliners in northern Illinois, especially in the First and Third Congressional Districts, opposed compromise out of sympathy with radical abolitionism and a sense of religious duty. But for many others throughout the state, the question of concession raised fundamental questions about the nature of the republic. Having fairly won a presidential contest on the promise of redeeming the Union from corruption and restoring the vision of the Founders, Lincoln, and his moderate allies could not, in good conscience, retreat from their position. In their minds, compromising on the status of slavery in the territories, far from a conservative measure, would advance the radical agenda of Southern Fire-Eaters to spread slavery still further beyond the limits intended for it in the Constitution. Just as importantly, they believed that when reminded of the Republicans' intentions to merely limit slavery's extension—not abolish it in the states where it existed—a resurgence of Southern unionism would readily extinguish the flames ignited by the Fire-Eaters.[13]

In short, hardline Illinois Republicans believed that reasonable white men in both sections would eventually accept the legitimacy of Lincoln's presidency if met with resolve. Reviewing the Chicago Platform's recognition of slavery in the states where it existed, and Republican support for the Fugitive Slave Law, Bloomington's Republican organ dismissed the "cutting up and cavorting" of Deep South secessionists. "Lincoln is conservative and national, and those disunioinists know it," insisted the editor of the *Pantagraph*. "They could not put forth a more flimsy pretext for secession." Confident that its Democratic neighbors in Illinois would not countenance disunion, the *Waukegan Gazette* dismissed and denounced secessionist bluster by asserting, "All parties at the North will act together against all treasonable projects.... Republicans and Douglas men, Wide Awakes and Invincibles stand united."[14]

Since he believed his previous speeches on the subject made his conservative intentions perfectly clear, Lincoln felt little need to issue a statement outlining his intentions on slavery. Still, he attended a Republican rally at Springfield on November 20 and permitted Lyman Trumbull to speak implicitly on his behalf, offering him some notes to sprinkle into his prepared remarks. Trumbull's speech clearly outlined the conservative intentions of the

Republicans to "bring the government back to the policies of the fathers" and praised Lincoln as a man "whom in the Constitution in all its parts, has not a more faithful supporter, nor the Union an abler defender." Dismissing any direct threat to the South, he reiterated the Republican position that the federal government has "no more right to meddle with slavery in a state, than it has to interfere with serfdom in Russia." Addressing the same audience a few minutes later, governor-elect Richard Yates outlined the stakes for ordinary white men as the new administration faced down the disunionists, and he demanded, "Let us know once and forever whether a majority or minority shall rule. Let us know whether the millions of freemen of this nation are to get on their knees to Slavery at every Presidential election." While Yates conveniently neglected to mention that Lincoln had secured only 39 percent of the national popular vote. Given the opposition of Douglas and Bell voters to federal protection for slavery in the territories—a core demand of the Southern Fire-eaters—his point still carried weight, but as events in Washington would prove, appeals to majority rule could cut both ways.[15]

Indeed, once proponents of conciliation presented compromise plans in Congress in early December, it became clear that Bell, Douglas, and even many Lincoln voters outside of Illinois supported concessions. Douglas, eager to preserve popular sovereignty, initially offered a constitutional amendment that would have applied that policy in future territories once they reached fifty thousand inhabitants. But given the South's rejection of popular sovereignty at Charleston in 1860, one might doubt whether Douglas could have mustered much support beyond his base. The Constitutional Unionist senator John J. Crittenden of Kentucky offered a more promising proposal when he detailed a series of constitutional amendments that would have permanently reinstituted the Missouri Compromise line of 36 degrees 30 minutes, offered federal protection for slavery south of that line, and applied to all future territorial acquisitions. The Crittenden Compromise also prohibited abolition in the District of Columbia without the permission of Virginia and Maryland, banned congressional interference in the interstate slave trade, and provided federal compensation for the owners of enslaved fugitives. Crittenden believed plan gave the South the protection for slavery where it was most vulnerable while maintaining for the North the territory designated for freedom back in 1820–21. Given that the Republican Party emerged from outrage over the repeal of the Missouri Compromise, such a promise might carry some weight.[16]

Yet the winter of 1860–61 was not 1854, and the events of the last seven years had hardened most Republicans' position on the extension of slavery. A minority of Republicans, led by soon-to-be secretary of state William H.

Seward, believed their party could afford to grant some concessions because the progress of slavery would stall in the desert climate of the American Southwest. For Lincoln and most Republicans, however, the Crittenden Compromise was unacceptable because it recognized slavery in all territories south of the line "hereafter acquired" by the United States, which opened the door to the extension of slavery into the Caribbean and Central America. While Seward's ally Thurlow Weed lobbied Lincoln in Springfield to accept some form of territorial compromise, the president-elect firmly rejected such a proposal, forcing Seward to vote with his fellow Republicans against Crittenden's plan in the Senate. In the eyes of Republican hardliners, Southerners had acted in bad faith before—one need only look at the initial repeal of the Missouri Compromise and the farce of popular sovereignty in Kansas—and would certainly do so again if given a chance.[17]

Thus, even as Elihu B. Washburne alerted Lincoln to the disunionists' earnestness, writing how "the secession feeling has assumed proportions of which I had but a faint conception" before arriving in Washington, Lincoln pressed the congressman to hold firm "as with a chain of steel." He urged Washburne to "prevent, as far as possible, any of our friends from demoralizing themselves, and our cause, by entertaining propositions for compromise of any sort, on '*slavery extension*.'" The president-elect insisted, "There is no possible compromise upon it, but which puts us under again, and leaves all our work to do over again." For upon the adoption of any such line, "filibustering and extending slavery" would recommence "immediately" and create yet another sectional crisis. In the mind of Lincoln and his fellow hardline Republicans, concessions on the extension of slavery would not save the Union but further distort it and empower Southern radicals to play fast and loose with the Constitution. The editors of the *Chicago Tribune* aptly captured this stance: "The country desires peace . . . but peace on an enduring basis of equality and justice. It wants to offer no new temptations to the lawlessness of Slavery. It desires no tampering with the Constitution which has wrought so glorious a work in this American Republic. Our territory, as it is, the Constitution and the laws as they are written, and the Union as the fathers made it—these are the points upon which no compromise can be made."[18] While such insistence on holding to the party line revealed a partisan imperative, as Lincoln feared that the fracturing of the Republican Party would doom his presidency, it also reflected the underlying commitment of self-identified conservatives in the party to stand fast against Southern bullying.[19]

Yet it is a mistake to interpret this determination to stand fast to the Chicago Platform and its vision of the Union as the Republican hardliners inviting the most destructive war in American history. Lincoln and his fellow Illinois Republicans, largely disconnected from the events in the South, maintained a distorted and hopelessly optimistic perspective of the situation. Although party leaders had ties to the northern tier of slaveholding states, especially to Kentucky, the birthplace of Yates, John M. Palmer, Orville H. Browning, and Lincoln himself, they lacked exposure to the perspectives of Deep South secessionists and misunderstood the conditional nature of unionism for most in the Upper South. By assuming that unconditional unionism was as widespread throughout the entire South as it was in Kentucky, hardliners mistakenly believed that a unionist resurgence would inevitably sweep through the Cotton States.

Even Trumbull, who, from his position in Washington, observed the fiery demonstrations of secessionists firsthand, was reinforced in his hardline stance by correspondence from unconditional unionists in the Border South. In mid-December, Kentuckian Elisha Smith, a self-identified "Old Whig," wrote Trumbull that he did not "blame the North . . . but the South" for the nation's troubles as a result of "the great breach of faith" perpetrated by Southerners in repealing the Missouri Compromise and urged the senator to stand opposed to the advocates of "nullification or secession." Predisposed to believe that most ordinary white Southerners maintained a stronger allegiance to the Union than to slavery, Illinois Republicans deluded themselves into believing that any conflict would pit slaveholding autocrats, and perhaps a few of their dupes, against the great mass of Union-loving people North and South.[20]

The formal secession of South Carolina on December 20 did little to alter hardline Republican opinion throughout Illinois. A *Belleville Advocate* correspondent confidently predicted that the "country will ride triumphantly through the impending storm," as "that Revolutionary Element, mostly concentrated in South Carolina," will "be thwarted and restrained by the Conservative Elements of the country." From Springfield, the *Illinois State Journal* disparaged South Carolina as a "pestilent little plantation," an aberration in the Union that "had more tories in it in Revolutionary days than all the other states combined" and whose descendants now reprised that treasonous role. Dismissing the significance of the state's secession, the *Journal* asserted that "Union exists to-day exactly the same as it existed when South Carolina, the other day passed the ordinance of secession, and South Carolina's vote to the contrary has no more dissolved the Union than it was dissolved in 1780 by the British conquest of that state." Out of a combination of ignorance and erroneous optimism, many Illinois Republicans seemed convinced that South Carolina would stand alone, just as it had in the Nullification Crisis of

1832–33, prompting the *Waukegan Gazette* to smugly reflect on how the state had been left "standing out in the cold" and how South Carolinians would "be glad enough one of these days to get back to the old hearth stone to warm their fingers, which must soon begin to feel the bitter frost of isolation."[21]

In short, the hardline stance among Illinois Republicans, far from embracing a new radical program, reflected a fundamental misunderstanding of the political reality in the South. Believing most Southerners shared their underlying commitment to the Union, they supposed only a few extremists would embrace disunion and war to protect slavery in the territories. Illinois Republicans remained too distant from events in both Washington and the Deep South to realize that most white Southerners viewed their party as an imminent threat to slavery in their states and would support drastic measures to avoid living under a Republican president. While some Republicans may well have continued to hold their uncompromising position if given more accurate assessments, the erroneous assumptions of the party's leaders at this stage shaped policy for months to come.

Holding Together a Fractured Republic

While the state's Douglas Democrat also expressed disdain toward South Carolina's secession, they correctly recognized the event all but guaranteed the secession of the Cotton States and possibly others. Writing from Washington ten days earlier, McClernand informed Lanphier that while the "secession of S.C., Fld., Ala. & Miss. is certain," he believed "if we can retain the border states, the Union will endure, and slowly but certainly the seceding states will come back." Douglas and his supporters hoped, along with the Republican minority committed to conciliation, that the adoption of a compromise would halt the domino effect and leave the seceded states too weak to survive as an independent confederacy and produce a reconstruction of the Union. In such a sense, the plan did not differ dramatically from the Republican expectation that a lonely South Carolina would limp meekly back into the fold. Thus, while conciliationist Northerners more accurately sensed the conditional nature of Upper South unionism, they shared the hardliners' naivete that Deep South secessionists would voluntarily return, humbled and dejected, to the Union. Given the vast popular support for secession, once it had occurred throughout the Deep South, one might reasonably question that such a reunion could have occurred even had the conciliationists cobbled together a compromise. Of course, such knowledge remained inaccessible for Illinoisans living through the secession winter, and as such, each party expressed perfect confidence in the flawed logic underlying their stances while denouncing their opponents as the covert operatives of disunion.[22]

Indeed, while eager to present themselves as moderate peacemakers, Illinois's Douglas Democrats recognized their vulnerability to Republican charges of winking at treason and sought to counter it. "We must not be put in the fix of antagonism to the Union in any shape," Lanphier wrote to McClernand, recognizing that all but the most ardent partisans would repudiate the Democracy if it appeared to sympathize with the Fire-Eaters. McClernand concurred and revealed the depth of his commitment to maintaining the Union, even if force became the only alternative. "The Northwest cannot afford to submit to disunion except as an unavoidable necessity." He insisted that Illinois "ought to hasten to arm herself. Common prudence requires it." Responding to a rumor that Breckinridge Democrat Benjamin Butler of Massachusetts had condoned South Carolina's secession, the *Rock Island Argus* soundly denounced Butler as a "contemptible reptile" who had consumed "southern dirt by the bushel" and had done his best to "break up the democratic party and 'precipitate the cotton states into a revolution.'" The *Quincy Herald* went even further, appealing to the material interests of all Illinoisans in its opposition to a division of the country, promising its southern neighbors that "the people of Illinois will fight for the free navigation of the Mississippi River, to the last ditch, to the last day, and till very late in the evening."[23]

In Washington, where the Senate's designated Committee of Thirteen voted down Crittenden's Compromise proposal at the end of December, Douglas blended bitterness toward the Republicans with a determination to preserve the Union at all hazards. Writing to Lanphier, he explained that he believed that for "partizan reasons" many Republican leaders actually hoped to dissolve the Union and achieve "permanent Republican ascendency in the Northern states." In the face of what he interpreted as Republican double-dealing, Douglas urged Illinois Democrats to stay true to the Union for the sake of patriotism and self-preservation. "We can never acknowledge the right of a state to secede and cut us off from the Ocean and the world, without our consent" he wrote with determination. The unliteral secession of states in the lower Mississippi valley threatened to undermine the prospects of free white men in Illinois and throughout the Northwest. Even if egged on by the machinations of two-faced Republicans, slaveholder separatists would undercut the American experiment in social, political, and economic liberty for white men by creating artificial borders and imposing limits on commerce. For Douglas and other Democrats, these were the exact limitations that the

Framers of the Constitution had worked to overcome in the national charter, and the failure of their offspring to maintain it would prove catastrophic for both their material interests and the future of republican government.[24]

Thus, even while they fiercely deplored antislavery agitation, criticized perceived Republican intransigence, and castigated coercion, Illinois Douglas Democrats hedged as they considered a conflict in defense of the Union. Following a full-throated denunciation of the Republicans and Lincoln, the *Mount Carmel Democrat* concluded that despite all of that, "we must not permit feelings in opposing his Administration, to put out of our [s]ight those distinctive principles of the Democracy—the maintenance of the Union at all hazards, and the enforcement of the laws in every quarter of the Union." This conservative disposition to enforce the law and maintain order became a Republican staple over the course of the secession crisis, but it also received attention from Democrats. As such, while the *Illinois State Register* maintained that "for peace, democrats should be—are—willing to concede much," it also emphasized that "salvation from anarchy" required that Southerners recognize "*our* rights are infringed by their secession and destruction of [the] Union—rights which we are bound to maintain."[25]

As the winter dragged on, Illinois Republicans stressed that the maintenance of such rights and the government might require force but that such force would not constitute "coercion." Noting that the state Democracy had embraced Henry Clay as the Great Compromiser, the former Whig editors of the *Illinois State Journal* pointed out how the Sage of Ashland had also advocated the defensive use of force, quoting him as reflecting that "government . . . would lose all respect, and fall into disgrace and contempt, if it did not possess potentiality, and would not, in extreme cases, practically exercise the right of employing force." In a similar vein, the *Quincy Whig and Republican* emphasized that if a clash did come, "it will not be a contest to 'coerce' patriotism, but 'to preserve, protect and defend the Constitution of the United States.'" The editor insisted that the Lincoln administration would not require Southern states to send representatives to Congress, appoint federal postal officers, or otherwise take an active part in the government of the nation, and instead promised that only "'the Union, the Constitution, and the enforcement of the laws' will be maintained at any and every hazard." So long as the secessionists did not seek to dislodge federal military personnel or interfere with the collection of tariff duties, the federal government would take no action against them. Anticipating Lincoln's inaugural address, the paper argued that the secessionists alone had the power to start a war.[26]

A degree of common ground emerged between the partisans in Illinois in support of the regular operations of the federal government. In January, as rumors swirled through the nation that secessionist forces would prevent Lincoln from being inaugurated in Washington, the *Belvidere Standard* resolutely declared, "Republicans will cower before no mobs. If half a million of men are wanted to secure the proper inauguration of Honest Old Abe, let the word go out, and they will be forthcoming." Remarkably, the *Salem Advocate,* one of the most stridently anti-coercion Democratic organs, abandoned any sympathy toward the secessionists on this issue. Reporting that Chief Justice Roger B. Taney had promised to inaugurate Lincoln, even "*if he was obliged to go to Springfield to do so,*" the editor applauded the pledge, suggesting that the "secession gentlemen . . . will find before they are much older, that the spirit of patriotism is not dead in this country, and enough of it survives to quench all treasonable schemes." While scholars have previously observed a moment of bipartisan cooperation in the wake of South Carolina's attack on the federal supply vessel *Star of the West,* the incident did not spark a significant reaction in Illinois, as a swirl of other rumors regarding Southern military action dampened the magnitude of the assault. It seems that the shared instinct to ratify the result of the election and ensure a transfer of power reflected a deeper commitment common to both Republicans and Douglas Democrats in Illinois to protect and preserve the Constitution.[27]

This shared ground did not, however, paper over the very real difference that existed both between and within the parties. The rapid secession of Mississippi (January 9), Florida (January 10), Alabama (January 11), Georgia (January 19), Louisiana (January 26), and Texas (February 1), together with the adoption of a provisional constitution for the Confederate States of America (February 8), raised the stakes for conciliationists and hardliners alike. In Illinois, the state legislature bubbled with tension as Democratic resolutions demanded a "peaceful resolution" to the crisis through the adoption of "additional explanatory amendments to the Constitution" while Republican governor John Wood advocated reorganizing and arming the state militia so that "should exigencies arise," Illinois regiments might reflect the state's "past glory." Meanwhile, Illinois Democrats squabbled among themselves as delegates to the annual state convention in Springfield sought to strike a balance between their fervent desire for compromise and their dedication to perpetual Union. The *Illinois State Register* embodied these internal tensions as, within a single page, it both denounced Governor Wood's militia plan as the "popinjay trappings of military despotism" and praised Congressman McClernand's declaration that "submission" to a division of the Union "would be a disgrace" and his intention to support "coercion to . . . uphold the laws and the constitution." Following a contentious day of discussion, the convention adopted a set of conciliatory resolutions, but the delegates balanced their opposition to coercion with a warning to both the federal government and the seceding states to "stay the arm of military power, and on no pretext whatever to bring on the nation the horrors of civil war." This pivot to the middle, standing between the two extremes, reprised an old move in state politics and gave the state's Douglas Democrats leeway to reconsider their opposition to coercion should the secessionist South strike first.[28]

Illinois Republicans, meanwhile, dealt with their own internal tensions as pressure from the pro-conciliation wing of the national party provoked a notable defection. William Kellogg, Illinois's representative on the House Committee of Thirty-Three (the equivalent of the Senate Committee of Thirteen) and the fourth district's Republican congressman, shifted into the conciliation camp in early February, prompting applause from Douglas Democrats and a fierce backlash among his Republican constituents. Although Lincoln had ordered Kellogg to entertain "no proposition for a compromise in regard to the extension of slavery," explaining that "the tug has to come & better now than later," Kellogg had grown increasingly sympathetic to the desperation of Southern unionists and their pleas for concessions on the issue of slavery in the territories. In a remarkable speech delivered to the House on February 8, Kellogg endorsed a version of the Crittenden Compromise, claiming that the measure would do much to cool sectional tensions while reserving a vast stretch of the West for free white labor. To combat Republican insistence that such a policy would only promote slavery's expansion into South America, Kellogg proposed that all future territorial acquisitions should require a congressional supermajority. Not entirely alone in his views, Kellogg's embrace of compromise reflected the views of Leonard Swett and some other downstate Illinoisans with Whig antecedents who feared their party might throw away all they had gained through obstinacy over the New Mexico territory. With the party already internally strained by cabinet appointments and patronage decisions, denunciations and defenses of Kellogg by Republican organs further exacerbated tensions among Illinois Republicans.[29]

Indeed, the *Chicago Tribune* responded venomously, accusing Kellogg of "laying broad and deep the foundation of a slave empire, embracing the *whole* territory, present and prospective, of the Unite States." As this denunciation indicates, the division within the Republican ranks centered less on the question of slavery in the presently held territory of New Mexico since the climate seemed especially unsuited to plantation agriculture. In fact, Lincoln would eventually consent to a plan that would have allowed New Mexico to enter the Union as a slave state, and even John Wentworth's *Chicago Democrat,* whose hardline position at times seemed to welcome the prospect of civil war, admitted that slavery in New Mexico posed no real threat. Much more important to the hardliners was the promise of slavery for new territories acquired south of 36 degrees 30 minutes. Even with congressional checks on the annexation of new territory, many Republicans believed Southern slaveholders and their Northern allies would inevitably demand further slave territory and again threaten disunion. But a minority within the party echoed the *Chicago Journal,* which defended Kellogg and insisted that "if republicans can, by honorable means, secure peace to the country and permanency to the Union, it is their duty to do it." In Kellogg's district, a Republican convention in Peoria adopted resolutions protesting his support for compromise with the South and reiterating their support for the Chicago Platform, but in an illustration of uncertainty within party ranks, the gathering narrowly voted down a resolution calling for Kellogg's resignation, by a vote of 88 to 79.[30]

Predictably, Illinois Democrats reacted warmly to Kellogg's embrace of compromise and disorder in the Republican ranks. The *Ottawa Free Trader* gloated over the "frightful demoralization in the Republican Party" created by Kellogg's address. In Washington, McClernand gladly welcomed Kellogg and anyone else "willing to join conservative men of all parties to save the country." Publicly taking up McClernand's appeal to antipartisan partisanship, the *Rock Island Argus* applauded Kellogg for not caring "a copper for all the party platforms" and for his determination to "save the union" and "restore peace to the country." Douglas took heart in the convening of a peace conference in Washington, chaired by former president John Tyler, which attracted delegates from twenty-one states, including Illinois. Douglas took the time to visit Illinois's delegate, Palmer, a Republican, in the hope of convincing him to embrace some sort of compromise. This effort ultimately proved futile, as the convention repeated the debates that had already occurred in Congress. In the end, a well-timed absence allowed the conference to narrowly approve a variation of the Crittenden Compromise, but since the body lacked any constitutional authority, it merely returned the measure to the senators and congressman who had already rejected it.[31]

In the midst of these deliberations, Lincoln emerged from his seclusion in Springfield to begin a circuitous thirteen-day journey to Washington by rail, which would carry him through Illinois, Indiana, Ohio, Pennsylvania, New York, New Jersey, and Maryland. Although he had kept mum in public,

Lincoln had made his own hardline views clear to party leaders in both Illinois and around the country as he worked throughout the preceding three months to assemble a cabinet and lay the ground for his administration. His purpose remained fixed on the eve of his trip when he privately concurred with Browning that "no concession by the free States short of surrender . . . would satisfy the South" and that "far less evil & bloodshed would result from an effort to maintain the Union and the Constitution, than from disruption and the formation of two confederacies." As he set out on February 11, Lincoln hoped to convince the Northern public of the soundness of that position. But in his first major address, before an immense crowd in Indianapolis, Lincoln fumbled, clumsily offending his audience with a coarse joke that compared the Southern conception of Union to a "free-love arrangement" rather than a "regular marriage" and alarming listeners by casually speculating on the prospect of "marching an army into South Carolina." In the days that followed, Lincoln avoided innuendo, but he blundered further by dismissing the national crisis as "artificial" and maintaining the jocular air of a stump speaker rather than the solemnity that many expected from a statesman in a time of national peril. Nevertheless, Lincoln's tour did bolster party hardliners, particularly following an address to the New Jersey General Assembly in which Lincoln stated, "It may be necessary to put the foot down firmly." While Lincoln's political enemies, and some historians, have criticized the president-elect's statement as aggressive, most Republicans, determined to limit slavery's influence and defend the rights of free white men, saw Lincoln's determination as a principled commitment to restoring the Founders' vision for the territories.[32]

Predictably, the press in Illinois reacted to Lincoln's journey along partisan lines. The *Illinois State Journal* lauded the public's enthusiastic reaction to Lincoln, reflecting, "When we see the masses laying aside party prejudices, and forgetting partisan bitterness, and uniting to pay homage to [the presidency] . . . we feel that we need not despair of the Republic." Of course, not all Americans had put aside partisan prejudices, and the credible threat of an assassination attempt led Lincoln to forgo a public appearance in Baltimore and arrive at Washington unannounced and ahead of schedule. This embarrassing finale bolstered the president's critics and seemed to further confirm the view of the *Illinois State Register,* which reprinted an unfriendly editorial describing how Lincoln had approached "the capital of the country more in the character of a harlequin, dealing with the great issues which agitate and agonize the minds of thoughtful men, as if they were only absurdities of a pantomime which would all be put to right by a touch of his magic wand."

All too eager to paint Lincoln as a buffoon, the Democratic press ruthlessly capitalized on Lincoln's gaffes to undermine both his moral authority and political prestige.[33]

Yet, for all their gleeful partisanship, as Lincoln's inauguration neared, Illinois Democrats walked a fine line. Congressman McClernand remained especially worried that the Republicans might yet frame their party as disloyal. The effort to reform the militia placed "the Illinois democracy in a delicate position," and McClernand again reminded Lanphier, "If we become entangled with diusnionism we will be lost as a party." Writing publicly to a friendly editor in Peoria, McClernand reminded his fellow Democrats, "Whilst we maintain our independence of black republicanism, we must be equally clear of fire-eating disunionism" and discouraged the use of the word *coercion* as "in its present application" it had become "a term coined by disunionists for the purpose of misleading the public mind." Douglas, likewise, despite his deep frustration with the hardline Republicans, knew the danger of appearing disloyal and greeted Lincoln courteously upon his arrival in Washington, calling on him twice prior to his inauguration. Such maneuvering reflected a combination of genuine patriotism and political pragmatism. McClernand, Douglas, and other Illinois Democratic leaders recognized that while they could and would continue to oppose Lincoln politically, neither their consciousnesses nor their constituents would support attempts to undermine him in his new role as chief executor of the laws. However mistaken or misguided Lincoln might be until he openly violated his oath of office and assumed powers beyond those prescribed in Article II of the Constitution, he remained the legitimate choice of the people, and the Democrats would need to support his efforts to enforce the laws or risk ostracism across the North.[34]

Rejecting the Anarchy of Disunion

Lincoln's first weeks in Washington fully aroused him to the peril facing his incoming administration. Although he remained firm on the question of slavery in the territories and largely dismissed the work of the Washington Peace Convention, Lincoln assisted Republican conciliationist Thomas Corwin in his effort to pass a constitutional amendment recognizing slavery's legitimacy in the states where it existed and earnestly worked to cultivate good relations with Virginia's conditional unionists. Returning to his inaugural address, originally drafted in January, Lincoln accepted revisions from two advisors with decidedly conservative dispositions, the conciliationist Seward and his Illinois hardliner Browning. Old Whigs with strong commitments to the Union, the pair adapted language to position Lincoln as a defender of law and order, redefining secessionist treason as "revolutionary" and softening the demand for the South to "submit" to merely "acquiesce" to the constitutional order. Although as determined as Lincoln to defend the Union through force of arms, if necessary, Browning astutely recognized that Lincoln's pledge to "retake" forts and other public property from secessionists would make the federal government the aggressor in any conflict. Instead, by pledging merely "to hold, occupy, and possess the property, and places belonging to the government," the president positioned himself in a defensive role. Any conflict would begin with an unprovoked assault by armed insurgents on government property rather than federal troops assaulting the citizens of Southern states.[35]

With these modifications, Lincoln's inaugural address struck a remarkable balance that pleased Republican hardliners and many Northern Democratic conciliationists. Adopting a sober tone absent from the speeches given on his Northern tour, Lincoln reiterated that he had no intention to interfere with slavery in the slaveholding states, denounced violent abolitionists, promised to faithfully execute the Fugitive Slave Law in accordance with the Constitution, and approved the new constitutional amendment to recognize slavery's legitimacy in the states. In his defense of the Union, Lincoln rejected the state compact theory and traced the origin of the Union to the First Continental Congress. He explained that unilateral secession by individual states violated the spirit of the Union, which placed ultimate authority in the hands of the American people. He further pledged there would "be no bloodshed or violence; and there shall be none, unless it be forced upon the national authority" and that in the spirit of the affective theory of Union, he would do all in his power to bring about "the restoration of fraternal sympathie and affections" between the sections. Finally, Lincoln made a conservative appeal to law and order as well as to majority rule, two principles with bipartisan support across the North, labeling secession "the essence of anarchy" and pointing out that by "rejecting the majority principle, anarchy, or despotism in some form, is all that is left." Adopting a pacific posture, Lincoln promised peace and order under the Constitution to Southerners willing to accept it "the government will not assail you. You can have no conflict, without being yourselves the aggressors."[36]

Illinois Republicans eagerly accepted the president's calm, but firm promises as a vindication of their commitment to the intentions of the Founding Fathers and the Union they created. The *Belvidere Standard* praised the message's "admirable" temper and the "firm and unswerving purpose" in Lincoln's words, and the *Waukegan Gazette* likewise endorsed the address's "wisdom, patriotism, and sound sense." Picking up on the public's frustration with partisanship in such a moment of crisis, the *Chicago Tribune* argued that the address "comes from the heart and brain of a sincere man" and "[was not] tied up in red tape and sealed with the stamp of a party caucus." The *Quincy Whig and Republican* furthered this sentiment, exclaiming that the inaugural "revived the hopes of patriotism every where."[37]

To the surprise of many, throughout the speech Douglas made his approval of the address known to all around him, muttering affirmations like "Good," "That's so," and "Good again." Two days later, on the Senate floor, Douglas defended Lincoln's address, claiming the new president had "sunk the partisan in the patriot" and was "entitled to the thanks of all conservative men to that extent." While the speech drew harsh criticism from the press in the Upper South (the *Richmond Enquirer* labeled Lincoln's address the "deliberate language of the fanatic with the purpose of pursing the promptings of fanaticism"), Illinois's Democratic organs responded favorably. The *Illinois State Register* declared that he had "succeeded in expressing a deal of patriotism" albeit within "a mountain of ambiguity." The *Joliet Signal* thought the inaugural left "grounds of hope" for "mild, moderate, and conservative measures." The *Rock Island Argus* endorsed the speech as "a conservative document, favoring compromise and peace," and the *Ottawa Free Trader* applauded "the spirit of the utmost forbearance" expressed in the address and endorsed his decision to avoid war "unless it is forced upon him, as by an attack on Fort Sumpter, for instance." Although the *Free Trader* was clearly eager to avoid conflict, its subtle endorsement of Lincoln's defensive policy had profound implications in the coming months.[38]

Although Lincoln's moderate tone proved attractive to both Illinois Republicans and Democrats, it left genuine radicals deeply disgruntled. Committed abolitionists found little to cheer about in Lincoln's promise to respect slavery's legal status throughout the South and rigorously enforce the Fugitive Slave Law. Frederick Douglass castigated the inaugural address as "a double tongued document," a speech "wholly discreditable to the head and heart of Mr. Lincoln," and damned the "inhuman coldness" of Lincoln's defense of slavery in the Southern states. From the pages of the *Liberator,* William Lloyd Garrison likewise denounced Lincoln as an "accomplice in man-stealing" and argued that the speech revealed how Lincoln was "anxious to perpetuate the thraldom of the millions already in bondage." For both editors, the prospect of disunion and freedom throughout a truncated United States was more appealing than remaining tied to Southern slaveholders. This indifference to the Union's fate placed radical abolitionists like Douglass and Garrison well outside of the Northern political mainstream and relegated their voices to the margins of public discourse.[39]

Much to Lincoln's chagrin, within a day of his inaugural address, news from Fort Sumter undercut his proposal to passively defend the remaining government property in the seceding states. An incomplete sea fort intended to defend Charleston harbor from attack by a foreign fleet, Sumter now sat surrounded by the hostile guns of South Carolina secessionists. Although the post's commander, Maj. Robert Anderson, had maintained an uneasy peace since late December, by March, his small garrison of federal troops had consumed most of their stores. Within hours of taking his oath of office, Lincoln learned that Anderson's men would exhaust their supply of hardbread within twenty-eight days. The army's senior officer, Maj. Gen. Winfield Scott, estimated that he would need a force of twenty-five thousand men to retain Sumter if it came under attack, but the entire army had only sixteen thousand soldiers in the ranks—most of them scattered in garrisons throughout the far West. Lincoln's entire cabinet, with the single exception of Postmaster General Montgomery Blair, concurred that evacuating Fort Sumter had become a matter of military necessity and urged the new president to withdraw the soldiers. Yet Lincoln recognized that such an evacuation would ruin him politically, alienating him from his hardline followers while simultaneously emboldening the secessionists and encouraging European powers to look favorably on Southern claims to independence. As the time for a final decision drew ever closer, Lincoln agonized with his cabinet over the options available to them as speculation swirled around Washington City and a host of office seekers invaded the executive mansion.[40]

The five weeks after Lincoln's inauguration proved equally anxious for the wider public as rumors of a withdrawal from Sumter or an impending withdrawal proliferated through the press. Fed the latest intelligence clandestinely by Secretary of State Seward, who still hoped to avoid a clash of arms in Charleston, on March 7 Douglas detailed Major Anderson's dire circumstances on the floor of the Senate and predicted a peaceful withdrawal of the garrison on the grounds of military necessity. Both Douglas and Seward clung to the vain hope that by delaying any violent confrontation, unionist sentiment would reemerge throughout the South and prompt a voluntary reconstruction. In Illinois, the Democratic press urged Douglas's policy of inaction and voluntary reunion, arguing that "the adoption of the peace policy by the administration will in a month break the backbone of southern secession. The only hope of the Jeff Davis government is in a collision with the Northern States ... [that] will at once bring to their side the border states, with Virginia at the head." Hardline Republicans, in contrast, voiced their displeasure, with one Illinois paper stating: "If Fort Sumter cannot be reinforced without a great sacrifice of life, we hope it will be blown into the air by firing the magazine, sooner than submit that it should become the property of a little nest of traitors." If indeed it proved necessary, the Republicans insisted Lincoln redouble the federal presence at the last remaining federal installation in the seceding states, Fort Pickens, off the coast of Pensacola, Florida. Notably, Illinois Democrats did not object to such a measure, as they expressed their support for a policy which would "place [forts] that could be reinforced and defended without necessarily producing a collision, in a perfect state of defense."[41]

Indeed, although Illinois partisans disagreed on whether the evacuation of Sumter would promote reunion, they concurred that the Lincoln administration needed to strengthen the resolve of unionists throughout the South by some combination of firmness and magnanimity. Douglas Democrats believed a prolonged lull would bring the mass of the Southerners back to their allegiance to the Constitution, while Republicans feared Southerners would see a delay as weakness and interpret forbearance as a lack of resolve. According to the *Chicago Tribune,* "If anything can foster a Union sentiment at the South ... it is an unmistakable demonstration on the part of the Government both of the intention and the ability to maintain the Union and protect those who are loyal to it." Thus, even as they diverged on the means to achieve it, mainstream Illinois Democrats and Republicans shared a goal to promote unionism and empower loyal white Southerners to redeem their states.[42]

In the White House, Lincoln received yet another grim report from South Carolina. Following his inauguration, the president had sent an ally from Illinois, state representative Stephen A. Hurlbut, back to his native Charleston to investigate the situation on the ground. To Lincoln's dismay, Hurlbut stated flatly that "the sentiment of National Patriotism always feeble in Carolina, has been extinguished." No unionist resurgence would occur in the Palmetto State. While Lincoln could yet hold out hope for a pro-Union reaction elsewhere in the South, South Carolina would remain obstinate, and evacuating the fort would only embolden the secessionists. Although some evidence exists that Lincoln still considered a withdrawal to conciliate conditional unionists in Virginia, in the end, he decided that his constitutional oath required him to resupply Sumner. Working closely with former naval officer Gustavus Fox, Lincoln organized a relief expedition to Charleston and notified South Carolina governor Francis Pickens of his intention to support the garrison with food, though not munitions or reinforcements.[43]

In the eyes of the South Carolina forces assembled around Fort Sumter, Lincoln's decision justified going to war. Secessionists viewed Sumter's garrison as a hostile foreign force occupying the sovereign soil of South Carolina and the Confederate States of America and made ready to expel the "enemy" by force. Under orders from Jefferson Davis and the Confederate government, the secessionists, commanded by Brig. Gen. Pierre Gustave Toutant Beauregard, ordered Major Anderson to surrender the fort or face an attack. Following Anderson's refusal, Confederate guns opened fire early on the morning of April 12. While the beleaguered Union troops did their best to return fire in a show of defiance, the engagement was thoroughly lopsided. On the afternoon of April 13, Anderson agreed to surrender Fort Sumter, under the condition that he and his men be allowed to return North with all the honors of war. Enthusiastic Southerners rejoiced at what they believed represented the permanent ejection of US forces from the Confederate States. But in fact, the Charleston secessionists had pushed the great mass of Northerners to the point of no return and had inaugurated four bloody years of civil war. On April 15, Lincoln called on seventy-five thousand state volunteers to preserve the Union and suppress the rebellion.[44]

While historians have accurately captured the period between the firing on Fort Sumter and the war's first major battle at First Bull Run as a moment of *rage militaire* in both sections, in their earnestness to explain the secession of the Upper South and detail the process of mobilization, few have explained why Northerners of both major political parties joined the fray with such earnestness.[45] Some scholars, eager to discern emancipation as a Northern war aim from the outset of the conflict, ignore the preponderance of the available evidence to claim that Northern soldiers enlisted to destroy slavery.[46] Similarly, studies of Northern nationalism have often overlooked the perspectives of moderates in the Midwest in favor of the most radical Eastern voices to emphasize Northern disdain for the South the frame the war as a clash of civilizations.[47]

In contrast, the best recent works on this period have taken the time to discern how politically polarized Northerners agreed to wage war in defense of the Union. Gary Gallagher's *The Union War* aptly captures the motivating power of unionism that propelled young Northern men into the ranks and sustained them there for four years. As Adam I. P. Smith has observed, in the aftermath of the assault on Fort Sumter, Northern military action "was no longer a military response to secession per se, but a military response to an assault on the flag: a subtle, but vital distinction." The imperative to defend the Union and the promise of republican government embodied in the Constitution provided a common platform upon which nearly all white Northerners could stand. Most recently, Elizabeth R. Varon has discussed how Republicans and Northern Democrats alike waged war to redeem their Southern countrymen from the clutches of a slaveholding oligarchy and restore them to their rightful place within a Union of equal rights for all white men.[48]

Rallying to the Flag of the Union

In Illinois, as elsewhere in the North, Republicans and Douglas Democrats overcame deep partisan animosities to wage war in defense of the Union. While a few rumblings of dissatisfaction emerged from the Democratic press, such dissent was quickly overwhelmed by popular support for the war. As Russell McClintock reminds us, "as antagonistic and entrenched as partisan battles were, the sides did share that mutual aim of preserving the Constitution and the Union." While Republicans had long denounced Douglas Democrats as Southern flunkies, in the aftermath of Fort Sumter, they warmly welcomed Douglasites into the Union military and began to reconstruct their own political organizations to include loyal Democrats. In turn, as much as they resented Republicans and denounced their radicalism as a cause of the conflict, Illinois Democrats shouldered arms in astonishing numbers. Indeed, as historians Matthew Stanley and Christopher Phillips have both observed, by the end of 1861, Illinois had exceeded its quota for volunteers by 71.5 percent, and devoutly Democratic Little Egypt enlisted a higher proportion of its young men than any other region in the Union.[49]

The decisive Republican response to the outbreak of hostilities came as no surprise, but the degree to which party members emphasized the limited and lawful nature of the conflict yields important insights. The *Illinois State Journal* carefully justified the necessity of a military response, explaining that facing "an armed and aggressive usurpation within its own territory," the national government needed to "assert and maintain its title to that which the people have invested it with, or else it must surrender entirely, and cease to be a government." Similarly, the *Ottawa Republican* emphasized that "there is no issue but the Union and the enforcement of the laws," and the *Chicago Tribune* claimed that "all issues of slavery in the Territories, or slavery anywhere else, are subordinated, lost in the mighty strife now inaugurated. Have we a government? Have we a country?... These questions have swallowed all other controversies." Even as they deprecated the slaveholders who initiated the war, Illinois Republicans made clear that they waged war not against slavery but instead to enforce the law, preserve republican self-government, and thereby protect "the freedom and happiness of thirty millions of white men." With such a cause, they hoped that Illinois would "be united as one man, Republicans, Democrats and Americans alike forgetting all other considerations for the higher and holier cause of their country."[50]

Although they did not entirely forget their partisan identity, and continued to snipe at Republicans, Illinois Democrats quickly embraced the war for Union. Even as they criticized "[Secretary of the Treasury] Chase and the war wing of the cabinet" for subjecting the nation to "the horrors of fraternal strife," the editors of the *Rock Island Argus* nevertheless argued that it "is made apparent no patriot can hesitate to do his duty—he must sustain the administration in every proper effort to defend and sustain the stars and stripes." Likewise, the *Illinois State Register* lamented the conflict as "the consequence of sectional agitations by northern and southern extremists" but insisted that "the patriot can only sympathize with his government and with the flag ... with which are blended all our hopes of future greatness, happiness and prosperity, of civil and religious liberty and the cause of democratic republican government." The *Galena Courier* concurred, despite its previous opposition to armed conflict "now, that war has commenced—that the first gun has been fired by the Secessionists—[Democrats] cannot desire the old flag of the Union disgraced by defeat" and called on citizens to take up arms. The *Freeport Bulletin* agreed, declaring that it would "never permit the reptile flag of disunion to wave in triumph over one foot of the soil or territory of the United States."[51]

From Washington, Stephen A. Douglas made it clear to both his followers and the nation that for all their past differences, he would stand firmly behind Lincoln. In a statement to the press, Douglas insisted that while he remained "unalterably opposed to the administration on all its political issues," he would nonetheless "sustain the President in the exercise of his constitutional functions to preserve the Union, and maintain the government, and defend the Federal Capital" and endorsed a "firm policy and prompt action" by President Lincoln. Writing to a St. Louis editor sympathetic to the Confederates, Douglas resolutely declared, "I am with my country and for my country, under all circumstances, and in every contingency." In a meeting with Lincoln shortly before his call for volunteers, Douglas recommended that he ask for two hundred thousand men rather than seventy-five thousand

and recommended that he immediately strengthen key positions in Virginia, such as Fortress Monroe and Harpers Ferry, in anticipation of a secessionist push to seize the positions.[52]

Leading the charge for the defense of the Union back in Illinois, McClernand had, in fact, endorsed a war policy in a note to Lincoln drafted two days before the Confederate bombardment of Fort Sumter, reflecting that civil war had become "unavoidable unless the United States surrender what would compromise their honor and safety" and therefore advocated the loyal states "at once ... take up arms in their defence against the rebellion of the Confederate States." Although "not desiring either civil or military position," McClernand declared his willingness to "lend my assistance to give practical effect" to these suggestions and "if need be my life." Delivered to Lincoln in the aftermath of Sumter, the message must have given the president great hope that he could rally his longtime opponents to the national standard.[53]

Indeed, while a few Democratic organs—particularly those that had earlier supported the Buchanan administration—initially responded sullenly to the call for arms, public pressure from all sides soon necessitated a change in tune. On April 16, the *Joliet Signal* hesitated to come out in favor of the war and stated that "on the eve of a calamity more terrible than any that has yet befallen a nation ... it behooves us to act with caution," but a week later it backtracked and announced that "Democrats never were disunionists or traitors" and therefore hoped "the Democratic members of our Legislature will join their Republican opponents in voting supplies to assist the Government in its present hour of need and danger. Likewise, on April 14 the *Peoria Democratic Union* bitterly noted that news of war "must fill every patriotic heart with intense sorrow" and lambasted the Republicans for their eagerness to take up arms, but four days later, it denounced a New York official rumored to be aiding the South and explained, "The treachery of such an act is only less than that of [Benedict] Arnold because its outflowing consequences are likely to effect less injury to the government than those contemplated by the first named traitor."[54]

Writing to his son away at college, Lincoln's old campaign manager and future Supreme Court justice David Davis described how "the whole country is in a blaze of excitement" and reflected that such "a united North may strike terror to the southern people & thus end the war sooner." Although the unity of the North did not leave the Rebels quaking in their boots, as the subsequent secession of Virginia, Arkansas, North Carolina, and Tennessee illustrated, it did allow the Lincoln administration to employ military force to preserve the integrity of the Union. The longstanding partisan divisions, visible throughout the secession crisis, remained after the attack on Fort Sumter.

After all, Douglas Democrats had earnestly sought to avoid a violent conflict and now took up arms only to restore the Union to the status quo of October 1860. Republicans, while not yet committed to remaking the South in their own image, sought to maintain and extend the political power they had won with Lincoln's elevation to the presidency.[55]

Still, a common political center remained for Illinoisans and the North as a whole. The fierce devotion to the Union, the Constitution, and the rule of law, common to Douglas Democrats, Republicans, and those few old Whigs and Know-Nothings who still found themselves in between, allowed bitter political opponents to enlist in the same regiments, serve under the same officers, and fight for the same flag. While the course of the war would bring new challenges, most profoundly the process of emancipation initiated by the enslaved men and women of the South even before most volunteers had mastered the manual of arms, this common core remained intact and proved sufficient to carry fierce partisans through four bloody years of war.

EPILOGUE

Addressing a joint session of the Illinois General Assembly on April 25, 1861, Stephen A. Douglas made clear his stance on the recently inaugurated conflict. Quivering with anger, the Little Giant denounced the Southern "secessionists and disunionists" for this "war of aggression and of extermination" waged "against the government established by our fathers." The Southern rebellion contained "all the elements of the French Revolution," and if allowed to succeed, its radicalism would drown the nation in blood. He called on all loyal citizens—"men of all parties"—to take up arms in defense of "the best government the sun of heaven ever shed its rays upon." For if they did not, he declared, "not only is our constitutional government to be stricken down; not only is our flag to be blotted out; but the very foundations of social order are to be undermined and destroyed." Should they abandon "the government established by Washington, Madison, Hamilton, and their compeers," Douglas warned that the United States would degenerate into anarchy and follow the course of Mexico, a nation where political rivals "seized upon the presidential chair by the use of the bayonet." In short, unless these politicians set aside their differences and committed to a war for the Union, they would lose everything. They owed it to themselves, their children, and "the friends of constitutional liberty and self government around the world" to defend the government they had "inherited as a priceless legacy from our patriotic fathers."[1]

For once, Springfield's two rival political organs had something they could both praise. The *Illinois State Journal* exalted Douglas's address as "a triumphant call to arms in defense of country, Government and Constitutional Liberty," while the *Illinois State Register* echoed the senator's call "to maintain the governmental authority for the preservation of the Union, of law and order, and to resist the anarchy which secessionists would spread abroad in the land." By framing the Southern rebellion as an unjustified revolution and insisting that Northern arms merely sought to preserve the Constitution of their fathers, Douglas appealed to the conservative impulses that motivated most Illinoisans. The conservatism of Douglas's bipartisan address stood in stark contrast to a speech the radical abolitionist Wendell Phillips made to a Boston audience, in which the activist appealed to the positive example of revolutions in France and Mexico as antislavery forces, noting with pleasure that emancipation arrived as "the child of convulsion." From the pages of his newspaper, Frederick Douglass echoed this radical sentiment and presented the conflict as an opportunity for Northerners "to make the cause of their country the cause of freedom." But as Douglas had made clear, for white Illinoisians, the war was a cataclysm and not an opportunity. The insurrection of the slaveholding states posed a dire threat to white freedom, and the potential for Black liberation did not factor into their reasoning. Only much later would some come to embrace emancipation as an essential, if haphazard, tool in putting down the rebellion.[2]

Prior to the speech, the Little Giant had met cordially with the state's Republican leaders and had reached an agreement with Orville H. Browning that ensured Democratic support for all the military funding bills facing the legislature. Deeply impressed by Douglas's course, Browning noted in his diary that the senator went "much farther in his conversations than he did in his speech and declare[d] without conditions that the Government must be sustained and rebellion put down." Such bipartisanship became even more necessary as politicians transformed into military officers. On the day Douglas delivered his address in Springfield, Republican politico Richard J. Oglesby became the colonel of the Eighth Illinois Volunteer Infantry. Shortly thereafter, Congressman John A. McClernand, Douglas's longtime ally, secured a commission as a brigadier general. While politics would continue to spark conflicts within the ranks throughout the war, for these first few weeks, at least, partisans became brother officers. Douglas's hardline stance, reiterated in a speech in Chicago on May 5, also helped to prompt hesitant Democrats from southern Illinois, such as Congressman John A. Logan, to embrace the war for Union. Logan, too, soon commanded Union troops in the field. Within the boisterous atmosphere of recruiting, McClernand and Logan gave speeches encouraging enlistments, including one on June 18 for a regiment under the command of a former regular army officer from Galena named Ulysses S. Grant.[3]

But by then, however, Illinois Democrats knew they would need to find a new leader. Douglas's health began to fail shortly after he delivered his speech in Springfield, and by May 10, "a severe attack of rheumatism" had weakened him to the point where he could no longer hold a pen. Mentally exhausted from years of political turmoil and physically wrecked by heavy drinking, Douglas became increasingly ill. His liver began to fail, and he was confined to a bed at a Chicago hotel for the remainder of the month. On the morning of June 3, the Little Giant's five physicians concluded he would not recover. Asked if he had a final message for his two young sons, Douglas asked that their mother tell them "to obey the laws and support the Constitution of the United States." Four hours later, Douglas died, at the age of forty-eight.[4]

Douglas's sudden death shocked and saddened Illinoisans from across the political spectrum. Within hours of the Little Giant's demise, a bipartisan committee assembled in Springfield to request he be buried in the state. Members included longtime allies such as John A. McClernand and Charles Lanphier, more recent friends like Benjamin S. Edwards, and a cadre of political adversaries including Lyman Trumbull, Edward L. Baker, and Gustave Koerner. Illinois Republicans deeply appreciated Douglas's commitment to maintaining the Union. Even the irascible John Wentworth encouraged his readers in the *Chicago Democrat* "to forget all that was wrong in [Douglas's] eventful career and remember only that which was right." In Washington, President Lincoln had the White House draped in mourning and wondered who could emerge to fill the void left by Douglas. While Lincoln had never admired the Little Giant, Douglas had proved immensely helpful in the war's opening weeks in rallying men to the Union's cause.[5]

By standing shoulder to shoulder with the president, Douglas ensured the Union army would enjoy overwhelming public support in its first campaign. Through his support for a vigorous military response to Confederate aggression, he successfully channeled his party's unconditional unionism of into the war effort and quashed the hopes of Southern secessionists who believed they could break up the Union without bloodshed. It is impossible to know how the politics of the Civil War would have evolved had Douglas lived, but following his death, and especially after the first year of the war, the Northern Democrats splintered. Many continued to loyally back the war effort, and some even accepted emancipation as a military necessity. Others, led by the Ohioan Clement L. Vallandingham, gave up hope for a military triumph, demanded peace at any price, and flirted with treason. A third group, distressed by the Republican policy of emancipation but unwilling to abandon the Union, stood uncomfortably between the two camps—politically rudderless.[6]

Back in 1854, Douglas had introduced the Kansas-Nebraska Act to speed the construction of a railroad to the Pacific and bolster the economic power of the West within the American Union. At that time, slavery had appeared an incidental issue, a mere bump on the road to continental domination. The policy of popular sovereignty, dependent as it was on the popular will, could overcome any opposition. The hubris of that belief may never have appeared as apparent to Douglas as to subsequent generations, but in his final weeks, he recognized its failure. The slavery question had shattered the Union. If not quickly reconstructed, the onetime United States would likely fragment into several rival confederacies. Douglas called on "every citizen in the great basin between the Rocky Mountains and the Alleghanies, in the valleys of the Ohio, Mississippi and Missouri" to rally to the Union's call, lest their neighbors "isolate us from the markets of the world and make us dependent provinces." To the end, he blamed everyone but himself, stating his "irreconcilable and undying opposition both to the Republicans and the Secessionists," who together had brought the nation to the brink of self-destruction.[7]

By disavowing the Missouri Compromise, Douglas turned his back on a critical precedent and upended the political order that had maintained sectional peace—if not sectional harmony—for decades. Even as those within the political mainstream clung to the mantle of conservativism—and worked fervently to preserve and restore that which had maintained that peace, the volatility of the slavery question, when combined with a host of ethnocultural tensions that accompanied economic growth and changing demographics, blurred the lines between parties and factions. In the years that followed, the opponents of the Kansas-Nebraska Act built up a viable political organization and began to win electoral majorities. But the ability of Douglas and his wing of the Democratic Party to claim the high ground of the conservative center, especially after the Lecompton crisis, continued to pose challenges for the new Republican Party. Ultimately, the political genius of Abraham Lincoln and the extremism manifested by Southern Democrats provided an opening for the Republicans to win power in 1860. The subsequent crisis compelled Lincoln and his inveterate Northern rivals to set aside their many ideological differences to preserve their most important points of common ground: majority rule, constitutional democracy, and the Union.

They would succeed in that task and, in the process, extirpate slavery from American soil. Yet before they did so, some seven hundred thousand Americans would go prematurely to their graves.

NOTES

Introduction

1. *Chicago Journal,* reprinted in the *Illinois State Journal* (Springfield), Sept. 1, 1856.

2. Among the most notable recent works on abolitionists and antislavery radicals are Kate Masur, *Until Justice Be Done: America's First Civil Rights Movement from the Revolution to Reconstruction* (New York: W. W. Norton, 2021); Kellie Carter Jackson, *Force and Freedom: Black Abolitionists and the Politics of Violence* (Philadelphia: Univ. of Pennsylvania Press, 2019; David W. Blight, *Frederick Douglass: Prophet of Freedom* (New York: Simon & Schuster, 2018); Richard J. M. Blackett, *The Captive's Quest for Freedom: Fugitive Slaves, the 1850 Fugitive Slave Law, and the Politics of Slavery* (New York: Cambridge Univ. Press, 2018); Corey M. Brooks, *Liberty Power: Antislavery Third Parties and the Transformation of American Politics* (Chicago: Univ. of Chicago Press, 2016).

3. Adam I. P. Smith, *The Stormy Present: Conservatism and the Problem of Slavery in Northern Politics, 1846–1865* (Chapel Hill: Univ. of North Carolina Press, 2017), 3. For other recent works emphasizing the role of self-identified conservatives and political moderates, see Andrew F. Lang, *A Contest of Civilizations: Exposing the Crisis of American Exceptionalism in the Civil War Era* (Chapel Hill: Univ. of North Carolina Press, 2021); Michael F. Holt, *The Election of 1860: "A Campaign Fraught with Consequences"* (Lawrence: Univ. Press of Kansas, 2017); Matthew Mason, *Apostle of Union: A Political Biography of Edward Everett* (Chapel Hill: Univ. of North Carolina Press, 2016); Daniel W. Crofts, *Lincoln and the Politics of Slavery: The Other Thirteenth Amendment and the Struggle to Save the Union* (Chapel Hill: Univ. of North Carolina Press, 2016). Slightly older works of note include Robert McCluer Calhoon, *Political Moderation in America's First Two Centuries* (New York: Cambridge Univ. Press, 2009); Patrick Allit, *The Conservatives: Ideas and Personalities throughout American History* (New Haven: Yale Univ. Press, 2009); Edward L. Ayers, *In the Presence of Mine Enemies: The Civil War in the Heart of America, 1859–1863* (New York: W. W. Norton, 2003); Peter B. Knupfer, *The Union as It Is: Constitutional Unionism and Sectional Compromise, 1787–1861* (Chapel Hill: Univ. of North Carolina Press, 1991).

4. Gary Gallagher, *The Union War* (Cambridge, MA: Harvard Univ. Press, 2011), 3.

5. *Ottawa Free Trader,* July 28, 1855.

6. For examples of this pledge across the political spectrum in Illinois, see *Capital Enterprise* (Springfield), Aug. 26, 1854; *Illinois State Register* (Springfield), Oct. 5, 1854; *Rock Island Argus,* Feb. 28, 1856; *Chicago Press and Tribune,* Aug. 4, 1858; *Jonesboro Gazette,* July 28, 1860.

7. Michael Holt, *The Political Crisis of the 1850s* (New York: John Wiley & Sons, 1978), 5. Other scholars who have emphasized the role significance of republicanism include David M. Potter, *The Impending Crisis, 1848–1861,* comp. and ed. Don E. Fehrenbacher (New York: Harper & Row, 1976); William E. Gienapp, *The Origins of the Republican Party, 1852–1856* (New York: Oxford Univ. Press, 1987); Emily Pears, *Cords of Affection: Constructing Constitutional Union in Early American History* (Lawrence: Univ. Press of Kansas, 2021).

8. Lang, *Contest of Civilizations,* 12.

9. Lang, *Contest of Civilizations,* 15.

10. Smith, *Stormy Present,* 7.

11. *Islander and Argus* (Rock Island), July 25, 1859.

12. For example, Joshua A. Lynn has argued that antebellum Democrats created the intellectual framework for the New Right that emerged in the United States after the Second World War. See Lynn, *Defending the White Man's Republic: Jacksonian Democracy, Race, and the Transformation of American Conservatism* (Charlottesville: Univ. of Virginia Press, 2019) 178–80. In another recent study, Michael F. Conlin excludes nearly all Republicans from the ranks of antebellum conservatives and argues that conservatives primarily sought to perpetuate hierarchies. See Conlin, "Dangerous *Isms* and Fanatical *Ists:* Antebellum Conservatives in the South and North Confront the Modernist Conspiracy," *Journal of the Civil War Era* 4 (June 2014): 205–33.

13. James Oakes, *The Crooked Path to Abolition: Abraham Lincoln and the Antislavery Constitution* (New York: W. W. Norton, 2021), xiv. See also James Oakes, *The Scorpion's Sting: Antislavery and the Coming of the Civil War* (New York: W. W. Norton, 2014); James Oakes, *Freedom National: The Destruction of Slavery in the United States, 1861–1865* (New York: W. W. Norton, 2013). Other recent works that emphasize the radicalism of the Republican Party in the 1850s include Graham A. Peck, *Making an Antislavery Nation: Lincoln, Douglas, and the Battle over Freedom* (Urbana: Univ. of Illinois Press, 2017), and Matthew Karp, "The People's Revolution of 1856: Antislavery Populism, National Politics, and the Emergence of the Republican Party," *Journal of the Civil War Era* 9 (Dec. 2019): 524–45.

14. *Chicago Journal,* reprinted in the *Illinois State Journal* (Springfield), Sept. 1, 1856.

15. Robert E. Ankli, "Agricultural Growth in Antebellum Illinois," *Journal of the Illinois State Historical Society* 63 (Winter 1970): 387–98; John J. Binder, "The Transportation Revolution and Antebellum Sectional Disagreement," *Social Science History* 35 (Spring 2011): 23–37.

16. William Cronon, *Nature's Metropolis: Chicago and the Great West* (New York: W. W. Norton, 1991), 27, 92; *1860 Census,* State of Illinois—Population of Cities and Towns, 90.

17. Frank Cicero Jr., *Creating the Land of Lincoln: The History and Constitutions of Illinois, 1778–1870* (Champaign: Univ. of Illinois Press, 2015), 136–62. While this book

confines itself to Illinois, it has benefited from a host of recent scholarship highlighting the significance of the Lower Midwest in this period. See Matthew Stanley, *The Loyal West: Civil War and Reunion in Middle America* (Urbana: University of Illinois Press, 2017); Christopher Phillips, *The Rivers Ran Backward: The Civil War and the Remaking of the American Middle Border* (New York: Oxford Univ. Press, 2016); Kristin L. Hoganson, *The Heartland: An American History* (New York: Penguin, 2019); John K. Lauck, *The Lost Region: Towards a Revival of Midwestern History* (Iowa City: Univ. of Iowa Press, 2013). See also John Craig Hammond, "Midcontinent Borderlands: Illinois and the Early American Republic, 1774–1854," *Journal of the Illinois State Historical Society* 111 (Spring–Summer 2017): 31–54.

18. The classification *Border North* is borrowed from William W. Freehling, *Becoming Lincoln* (Charlottesville: Univ. of Virginia Press, 2018), 167–68. Adapting a geographic distinction long applied to the Southern border states, Freehling includes New Jersey, Pennsylvania, Ohio, Indiana, Illinois, and Iowa within the Border North. For the results of the 1856 election, see "Elections: 1856," *The American Presidency Project*, by John Woolley and Gerhard Peters, Univ. of California, Santa Barbara, https://www.presidency.ucsb.edu/statistics/elections/1856.

19. Jack Furniss, "Devolved Democracy: Federalism and the Party Politics of the Late Antebellum North," *Journal of the Civil War Era* 9 (Dec. 2019): 546–68; Gienapp, *Origins of the Republican Party*, 6; Holt, *Political Crisis of the 1850s*, 14. See also Roy Franklin Nichols, *The Disruption of American Democracy* (New York: Macmillan, 1948), viii.

20. Among many worthy titles are Don E. Fehrenbacher, *Prelude to Greatness: Lincoln in the 1850s* (Palo Alto, CA: Stanford Univ. Press, 1962); David Herbert Donald, *Lincoln* (New York: Simon & Schuster, 1996); Richard Carwardine, *Lincoln: A Life of Purpose and Power* (New York: Alfred A. Knopf, 2006), 32–44; William C. Harris, *Lincoln's Rise to the Presidency* (Lawrence: Univ. Press of Kansas, 2007); Michael Burlingame, *Abraham Lincoln: A Life*, 2 vols. (Baltimore: Johns Hopkins Univ. Press, 2008); Allen C. Guelzo, *Lincoln and Douglas: The Debates That Defined America* (New York: Simon & Schuster, 2008); Eric Foner, *The Fiery Trial: Abraham Lincoln and American Slavery* (New York: W. W. Norton, 2010); Freehling, *Becoming Lincoln*.

21. Michael E. Woods, *Arguing until Doomsday: Stephen Douglas, Jefferson Davis, and the Struggle for American Democracy* (Chapel Hill: Univ. of North Carolina Press, 2020), 5. The authoritative work on Douglas's political career remains Robert W. Johannsen's *Stephen A. Douglas*, 2nd ed. (Urbana: Univ. of Illinois Press, 1997). Other recent works that emphasize Douglas's significance include James L. Huston, *Stephen A. Douglas and the Dilemmas of Democratic Equality* (Lanham, MD: Rowan & Littlefield, 2007) and Martin H. Quitt, *Stephen A. Douglas and Antebellum Democracy* (New York: Cambridge Univ. Press, 2012).

22. Such a vision for a free-labor world has long been associated with the antebellum Republican Party. See Eric Foner, *Free Soil, Free Labor, Free Men: The Ideology of the Republican Party before the Civil War*, 2nd ed. (New York, Oxford Univ. Press, 1995). This book joins Adam I. P. Smith and others in arguing that Northerners of all parties subscribed to its basic tenets. See Smith, *Stormy Present*, 17.

23. Stephen A. Douglas repeatedly expressed his relief that Illinois was not burdened by slavery. In his first joint debate with Lincoln in 1858, he announced, "There is no man in the State who would be more strenuous in his opposition to the introduction

of slavery than I would." See First Joint Debate, Aug. 21, 1858, *The Lincoln-Douglas Debates*, ed. Robert W. Johannsen (New York: Oxford Univ. Press, 1965), 47.

24. The complete exclusion of Black activists in Illinois contrasts in important ways with the experiences of those in Northern states that enfranchised Black men. In Massachusetts, for example, African Americans developed a working partnership with the state's Know-Nothing Party that led to the desegregation of the state's schools in April 1855. See Stephen Kantrowitz, *More Than Freedom: Fighting for Black Citizenship in a White Republic: 1829–1889* (New York: Penguin, 2012), 164–68.

25. For the Republican–Democratic coalition in Indiana, see Gregory Peek, "'The True and Ever Living Principle of States Rights and Popular Sovereignty': Douglas Democrats and Indiana Republicans Allied, 1857–1859," *Indiana Magazine of History* 111 (Dec. 2015): 381–421.

26. For accounts of the partisan press and its significance in this period, see David B. Sachsman and Gregory A. Borchard, eds., *The Antebellum Press: Setting the Stage for Civil War* (New York: Routledge, 2019). See also Thomas C. Leonard, *News for All: America's Coming-of-Age with the Press* (New York: Oxford Univ. Press, 1995), 47–52.

1. Prologue

1. Webster quoted in Stephen E. Maizlish, *A Strife of Tongues: The Compromise of 1850 and the Ideological Foundations of the American Civil War* (Charlottesville: Univ. of Virginia Press, 2018), 220; *New-York Tribune*, Sept. 10, 1850. See also *New York Herald*, Sept. 10, 1850.

2. For more on antiparty feelings in antebellum political culture, see Ronald P. Formisano, "The 'Party Period' Revisited," *Journal of American History* 86 (June 1999): 93–120.

3. For analysis of the results of the 1848 election, see James L. Huston, "The Illinois Political Realignment of 1844–1860: Revisiting the Analysis," *Journal of the Civil War Era* 1 (Dec. 2011): 511–14; *Illinois State Register* (Springfield), Sept. 13, 1850; *Illinois Journal* (Springfield), Sept. 14, 1850 (Springfield); *Alton Telegraph and Democratic Review*, Sept. 20, 1850.

4. Johannsen, *Stephen A. Douglas*, 298. References to the Compromise of 1850 as a "final settlement" appeared frequently throughout the period, most notably in President Millard Fillmore's annual message of 1850 and the Whig Platform of 1852; see the *Republic* (Washington, DC), Dec. 3, 1850, and the *New York Times*, June 25, 1852.

5. Potter, *Impending Crisis, 1848–1861*, 121–38; Holt, *Political Crisis of the 1850s*, 87–94; Woods, *Arguing until Doomsday*, 94–110. For a state-by-state analysis of Whig disorganization in the wake of the Compromise of 1850, see Michael F. Holt, *The Rise and Fall of the American Whig Party: Jacksonian Politics and the Onset of the Civil War* (New York: Oxford Univ. Press, 1999), 554–97.

6. For a discussion of the cultural clashes between Upland Southerners and Northerners in the antebellum Midwest, see Nicole Etcheson, *The Emerging Midwest: Upland Southerners and the Political Culture of the Old Northwest, 1787–1861* (Bloomington: Indiana Univ. Press, 1996), 1–9. Historians fiercely contest the causes, consequences, and dynamics of this "market revolution." For an interpretation that

emphasizes the coercive nature of these changes for Northern white farmers and workers, see Charles Sellers, *The Market Revolution: Jacksonian America, 1815-1846* (New York: Oxford Univ. Press, 1991). Daniel Walker Howe offers a critique of Sellers's arguments and argues that many of these "ordinary Americans" embraced the new world of integrated markets in *What Hath God Wrought: The Transformation of America, 1815-1848* (New York: Oxford Univ. Press, 2007). John Lauritz Larson offers a synthesis of both arguments and highlights the ambiguities of this period in *The Market Revolution in America: Liberty, Ambition, and the Eclipse of the Common Good* (New York: Cambridge Univ. Press, 2010). Clerk of the House of Representatives, *Abstract of the Returns of the Fifth Census* (Washington, DC: Duff Green, 1832), 39; Joseph C. Kennedy, *Population of the United States in 1860* (Washington, DC: GPO, 1864), iv.

7. For discussions on the economic and political implications of mid-century theological debates, see Sellers, *Market Revolution*, 393–95; Carwardine, *Lincoln*, 32–44; Daniel Walker Howe, *The Political Culture of the American Whigs* (Chicago: University of Chicago Press, 1979) 166–67; Howe, *What Hath God Wrought*, 166–82. See also Stephen L. Hansen, *The Making of the Third Party System: Voters and Parties in Illinois, 1850–1876* (Ann Arbor: UMI Research Press, 1980), 60–67; W. F. Short, "Early Religious Leaders and Methods in Illinois," *Transactions of the Illinois State Historical Society for the Year 1902* (Springfield: Illinois State Historical Library, 1902), 56–62; Barton E. Price, "Religion, Reform, and Patriotism in Southern Illinois: A Case Study, 1852–1900," *Journal of the Illinois State Historical Society* 107 (Summer 2014): 175–88.

8. For statistics on the Midwest's foreign-born and Catholic populations, see Luke Ritter, *Inventing America's First Immigration Crisis: Political Nativism in the Antebellum West* (New York: Fordham Univ. Press, 2021), 15–19. For helpful discussions of German immigrants and politics in this period, see Christina Bearden-White, "Illinois Germans and the Coming of the Civil War: Reshaping Ethnic Identity," *Journal of the Illinois State Historical Society* 109 (Fall 2016): 231–51; Alison Clark Efford, *German Immigrants, Race, and Citizenship in the Civil War Era* (New York: German Historical Institute and Cambridge Univ. Press, 2013); Bruce Levine, *The Spirit of 1848: German Immigrants, Labor Conflict, and the Coming of the Civil War,* (Urbana: Univ. of Illinois Press, 1992). For an insightful discussion of the role of Irish immigrants in Chicago's political culture, see Patricia Kelleher, "Class and Catholic Irish Masculinity in Antebellum America: Young Men on the Make in Chicago," *Journal of American Ethnic History* 28 (Summer 2009): 7–42.

9. Lovejoy quoted in Ritter, *Inventing America's First Immigration Crisis*, 37.

10. For recent studies on the Black Hawk War and its legacy, see John W. Hall, *Uncommon Defense: Indian Allies in the Black Hawk War* (Cambridge, MA: Harvard Univ. Press, 2009) and Nicholas A. Brown and Sarah E. Kanouse, *Re-Collecting Black Hawk: Landscape, Memory, and Power in the American Midwest* (Pittsburgh: Univ. of Pittsburgh Press, 2015). For Lincoln's service in the conflict, see Burlingame, *Abraham Lincoln*, 1:67–71. See also Roger L. Nichols, *Black Hawk and the Warriors Path* (Arlington Heights, IL: Harlan Davidson, 1992).

11. M. Scott Heerman, *The Alchemy of Slavery: Human Bondage in the Illinois Country, 1730–1865* (Philadelphia: Univ. of Pennsylvania Press, 2018), 25–27, 36–37, 50–53.

12. *1840 Census*, Compendium of Population: Illinois, 86; Jerome B. Meites, "The 1847 Illinois Constitutional Convention and Persons of Color," *Journal of the Illinois*

State Historical Society 108 (Fall–Winter 2015), 271–75; Leslie A. Schwalm, *Emancipation's Diaspora: Race and Reconstruction in the Upper Midwest* (Chapel Hill: Univ. of North Carolina Press, 2009), 16–22; James Simeone, *Democracy and Slavery in Frontier Illinois: The Bottomland Republic* (DeKalb: Northern Illinois Univ. Press, 2000), 148–53, 155–57, 178–85, 215–18; Alan Taylor, *American Republics: A Continental History of the United States, 1783–1850* (New York W. W. Norton, 2021), 178–80. See also John Craig Hammond, *Slavery, Expansion, and Freedom in the Early American West* (Charlottesville: Univ. of Virginia Press, 2007).

13. Heerman, *Alchemy of Slavery*, 139–50.

14. For more on the colonization movement in Illinois, see Kurt E. Leichtle and Bruce G. Carveth, *Crusade against Slavery: Edward Coles, Pioneer of Freedom* (Carbondale: Southern Illinois Univ. Press, 2011), 126–28; Merton Lynn Dillon, "The Antislavery Movement in Illinois: 1824–1835," *Journal of the Illinois State Historical Society* 47 (Summer 1954): 149–66. Ficklin quoted in Charles R. McKirdy, *Lincoln Apostate: The Matson Slave Case* (Jackson: Univ. Press of Mississippi, 2011), 110.

15. *Frederick Douglass' Paper* (Rochester, NY), Mar. 18, 1853; *National Era* (Washington, DC), Mar. 17, 1853.

16. Meities, "1847 Illinois Constitutional Convention and Persons of Color," 275–86; Stanley, *Loyal West*, 20–26; Eugene H. Berwanger, *The Frontier against Slavery: Western Anti-Negro Prejudice and the Slavery Extension Controversy* (Urbana: Univ. of Illinois Press, 1967), 38–41.

17. In 1850, Illinois had only 5,436 Black residents out of a total population of more than 850,000. This figure grew slightly over the succeeding decade to 7,628 but shrank as a proportion of the total population as the Prairie State grew to encompass 1.7 million residents by 1860. *1850 Census*, Comparative Table of Population, ix; *1860 Census*, State of Illinois—Population by Color and Condition, 86–90.

18. Masur, *Until Justice Be Done*, 225–67; Christopher Robert Reed, "The Early African American Settlement of Chicago, 1833–1870," *Journal of the Illinois State Historical Society* 108 (Fall–Winter 2015): 230–33; Jennifer R. Harbour, *Organizing Freedom: Black Emancipation Activism in the Civil War Midwest* (Carbondale: Southern Illinois Univ. Press, 2020), 10–25, 54–57. See also Blackett, *Captive's Quest for Freedom*, 137–79; William F. Moore and Janet Ann Moore, *Collaborators for Emancipation: Abraham Lincoln and Owen Lovejoy* (Urbana: Univ. of Illinois Press, 2014).

19. Letter in *Frederick Douglass' Paper* (Rochester, NY), May 13, 1853; William J. Simmons, *Men of Mark: Eminent, Progressive, and Rising* (Cleveland: George M. Rewell & Co., 1887), 679–84; Brent M. S. Campney, *Hostile Heartland: Racism, Repression, and Resistance in the Midwest* (Urbana: Univ. of Illinois Press, 2019), 34–46; Brent M. S. Campney, "'The Peculiar Climate of This Region': The 1854 Cairo Lynching and the Historiography of Racist Violence against Blacks in Illinois," *Journal of the Illinois State Historical Society* 107 (Summer 2014): 143–70.

20. Hiram M. Drache, "The Impact of John Deere's Plow," *Illinois History Teacher* 8, no. 1 (2001): 2–13; Cronon, *Nature's Metropolis*, 313–18; *1850 Census*, Statistics of Illinois—Agriculture, 728–35; *1860 Census*, State of Illinois—Agriculture, 30–37. See also Paul Wallace Gates, "Large-Scale Farming in Illinois, 1850 to 1870," *Agricultural History* 6, no. 1 (1932): 14–25; David E. Schob, "Sodbusting on the Upper Midwestern Frontier, 1820–1860," *Agricultural History* 47, no. 1 (1973): 47–56.

21. For the breakdown of traditional party positions on railroads, see Holt, *Political Crisis of the 1850s*, 112–13. Huston, *Stephen A. Douglas and the Dilemmas of Democratic Equality*, 39–41; Cronon, *Nature's Metropolis*, 72.

22. Simon Cordery, *The Iron Road in the Prairie State: The Story of Illinois Railroading* (Bloomington: Univ. of Indiana Press, 2016), 9–21.

23. Johannsen, *Stephen A. Douglas*, 315; Cordery, *Iron Road*, 21–31; *Western Whig* (Bloomington), Aug. 6, 1851. For sectionalism and the railroad, see William Earl Weeks, *Building the Continental Empire: American Expansion from the Revolution to the Civil War* (Chicago: Ivan R. Dee, 1996), 84–85; William G. Thomas, *The Iron Way: Railroads, the Civil War, and the Making of Modern America* (New Haven: Yale Univ. Press, 2011), 37–44. See also Binder, "Transportation Revolution and Antebellum Sectional Disagreement," 19–57. While Binder convincingly argues that internal improvements strengthened economic ties between the Midwest and Northeast, at the expense of the South, he misleadingly claims that by 1860 midwesterners had become ambivalent to commercial access to the Mississippi River.

24. *Bloomington Intelligencer*, June 2, 1852. On the convergence of Illinois Whigs and Democrats in the early 1850s, see Graham Peck, "Was There a Second Party System? Illinois as a Case Study in Antebellum Politics," in *Practicing Democracy: Popular Politics in the United States from the Constitution to the Civil War*, ed. Daniel Peart and Adam I. P. Smith (Charlottesville: Univ. of Virginia Press, 2015), 159.

25. Yonatan Eyal, *The Young America Movement and the Transformation of the Democratic Party* (New York: Cambridge Univ. Press, 2007), 147; *Western Whig* (Bloomington), Aug. 6, 1851. Foner's *Free Labor, Free Soil, Free Men* argues that this commitment to social advancement through free labor and enterprise formed the ideological crux of the emerging Republican Party in the 1850s. In his limited treatment of the Democrats, Foner acknowledges that Douglas's branch of the party largely agreed with Republican critiques of slavery and the South in principle, even as they dampened the intensity of this criticism to maintain national unity. Further investigation into the origins of this Northern consensus reveals that the section's endorsement of free labor preceded the breakup of the Second Party System. Although a powerful force throughout the 1850s, free labor provided neither a coherent ideology nor a clear set of policy initiatives. In many respects, the policy debates between Republicans, Northern Know-Nothings, and Douglas Democrats in the 1850s centered on the best means of advancing free-labor society within the political structures of the American Union. For recent argument that this sectional consensus emerged earlier, in the debates surrounding the Compromise of 1850, see Maizlish, *Strife of Tongues*, 6–9.

26. *New York Herald*, June 4, 1852; Eyal, *Young America Movement*, 52–64; Mark Power Smith, *Young America: The Transformation of Nationalism Before the Civil War* (Charlottesville: Univ. of Virginia Press, 2022), 148–49; Quitt, *Stephen A. Douglas and Antebellum Democracy*, 99–103.

27. *Rock Island Republican*, Oct. 18, 1851; Stephen A. Douglas to Charles H. Lanphier, Dec. 30, 1851, in *The Letters of Stephen A. Douglas*, ed. Robert. W. Johannsen (Urbana: Univ. of Illinois Press, 1961), 235; Jeremy Atack, Matthew Jaremski, and Peter L. Rousseau, "American Banking and the Transportation Revolution before the Civil War," *Journal of Economic History* 74 (Dec. 2014): 943–86. For overviews of banking in antebellum Illinois, see George William Dowrie, "The Development of Banking in

Illinois, 1817–1863" (PhD diss., Univ. of Illinois, 1913), and Francis Murray Hutson, *Financing an Empire: History of Banking in Illinois*, vol. 1, ed. Andrew Russel (Chicago: S. J. Clarke Publishing Company, 1926).

28. *Ottawa Free Trader*, July 23, 1853; *Rock Island Republican*, Oct. 5, 1853; *Quincy Whig*, Nov. 4, 1853. Some historians contend that cultural outlook contributed to this continued animosity, for an exploration of the expectations of Whigs and Democrats for the individual, state, and society, see Joseph W. Pearson, *The Whigs' America: Middle-Class Political Thought in the Age of Jackson and Clay* (Lexington: Univ. Press of Kentucky, 2020).

29. Holt, *Rise and Fall of the American Whig Party*, 754–66; Johannsen, *Stephen A. Douglas*, 386–400; Stephen A. Douglas to Charles H. Lanphier, Nov. 11, 1853, in *Letters of Stephen A. Douglas*, 267–68.

2. A Hell of a Storm

1. *Mount Carmel Register*, May 31, 1854.

2. Debate regarding Douglas's motivations for proposing the Kansas-Nebraska Act dates back to the introduction of the bill, when Salmon P. Chase and his fellow political abolitionists accused Douglas of working on behalf of the Slave Power in their "Appeal of the Independent Democrats." Following Union victory in the Civil War, the Republican Party's antebellum emphasis on the Slave Power conspiracy remained the predominant narrative throughout the North. Professional historians first challenged this consensus in the early twentieth century, with the publication of P. Orman Ray's *The Repeal of the Missouri Compromise: Its Origin and Authorship* (Cleveland: Arthur H. Clark, 1909), which emphasized Douglas's intense desire for a central railroad route. Scholars returned the Slave Power thesis to a position of prominence during civil rights era, see Larry Gara, "Slavery and the Slave Power: A Key Distinction," *Civil War History* 15 (Mar. 1969): 5–18. For modern analyses that privilege the role of Southern slaveholders in shaping the Kansas-Nebraska Act, see Leonard L. Richards, *The Slave Power: The Free North and Southern Domination, 1780–1860* (Baton Rouge: Louisiana State Univ. Press, 2000), 162–89; Michael Landis, *Northern Men with Southern Loyalties: The Democratic Party and the Sectional Crisis* (Ithaca, NY: Cornell Univ. Press, 2014), 106–19; Alice Elizabeth Malavasic, *The F Street Mess: How Southern Senators Rewrote the Kansas-Nebraska Act* (Chapel Hill: Univ. of North Carolina Press, 2017). For an explanation that suggests that Douglas sought to resolve the slavery question in favor of proslavery forces, see Peck, *Making an Antislavery Nation*, 113–21.

3. For an interpretation that argues that Douglas was inspired by a constitutional commitment to popular sovereignty, see Quitt, *Stephen A. Douglas and Antebellum Democracy*, 121–23. For scholars who emphasize Douglas's desire to revitalize Democratic fortunes and position himself as the party's leader, see Holt, *Political Crisis of the 1850s*, 139–49, and Gienapp, *Origins of the Republican Party*, 69–78. Versions of this argument within their regional context appear in Michael A. Morrison, *Slavery and the American West: The Eclipse of Manifest Destiny and the Coming of the Civil War* (Chapel Hill: Univ. of North Carolina Press, 1997), 141–43, and Phillips, *Rivers Ran Backward*, 90–91.

4. For contemporary explanations that emphasize Douglas's ideological commitment to Western development, see Potter, *Impending Crisis,* 147–61; Robert W. Johannsen, *The Frontier, the Union, and Stephen A.* Douglas (Urbana: Univ. of Illinois Press, 1989), 77–102; Huston, *Stephen A. Douglas and the Dilemmas of Democratic Equality,* 100–101. For the role of generation and the Young America movement in Douglas's decision, see Eyal, *Young America Movement,* 221–22; Mark Power Smith, *Young America,* 139–42. Michael E. Woods has recently weaved together several of these analytical threads and outlined a synthesis in *Arguing until Doomsday,*129–30.

5. Stephen A. Douglas to Asa Whitney, Oct. 15, 1845, *Letters of Stephen A. Douglas,* 127–33. A proposed central route to the Pacific placed Chicago in competition with St. Louis as eastern terminus. For details on this rivalry, see Cronon, *Nature's Metropolis,* 299–305. At times, Douglas also advocated for a second northern route that would have run from Lake Superior to Puget Sound. See Potter, *Impending Crisis,* 152. See also Cong. Globe, 32nd Cong., 2nd Sess., 1111–17 (1853).

6. Johannsen, *Stephen A. Douglas,* 390–400; Cong. Globe, 32nd Cong., 1st Sess., 1760 (1852).

7. Cong. Globe, 32nd Cong., 2nd Sess., 544, 556–65 (1853); Potter, *Impending Crisis,* 151–52.

8. Stephen A. Douglas to J. H. Crane, M. D. Johnson, and L. J. Eastin, Dec. 17, 1853, *Letters of Stephen A. Douglas,* 270.

9. Malavasic, *F-Street Mess,* 75–95; Potter, *Impending Crisis,* 155–57; Sean Wilentz, *The Rise of American Democracy: Jefferson to Lincoln* (New York: W. W. Norton, 2007), 672. For a discussion of the F Street Mess within the broader context of congressional social dynamics, see Rachel Shelden, *Washington Brotherhood: Politics, Social Life, and the Coming of the Civil War* (Chapel Hill: Univ. of North Carolina Press, 2013), 96–119.

10. Douglas to the editor of the *State Capitol Reporter* (Concord, NH), Feb. 16, 1854, *Letters of Stephen A. Douglas,* 289; Even Douglas's harshest critics do not think he believed that slavery would spread into Nebraska or Kansas. See Peck, *Making an Antislavery Nation,* 117. For thoughtful analyses of Douglas's strategy in January 1854, see Johannsen, *Stephen A. Douglas,* 405–17; Potter, *Impending Crisis,*156–61; Holt, *Political Crisis of the 1850s,* 144–45; Yonatan Eyal, "With His Eyes Open: Stephen A. Douglas and the Kansas-Nebraska Disaster of 1854," *Journal of the Illinois State Historical Society* 91 (Winter 1998): 175–217.

11. For the reaction of Southern Whigs, see Holt, *Rise and Fall of the American Whig Party,* 813–25; Salmon P. Chase et al., *Appeal of the Independent Democrats in Congress to the People of the United States: Shall Slavery Be Permitted in Nebraska* (Washington, DC: Towers' Printers, 1854), 7; Gienapp, *Origins of the Republican Party,* 72–75; Smith, *Stormy Present,* 76–77.

12. *Illinois State Journal* (Springfield), Jan. 16, 21, 1854. For the traditional Whig commitment to colonization, see Howe, *Political Culture of the American Whigs,* 133–36.

13. *Alton Telegraph,* Jan. 21, 1854; Jeff L. Dugger to Richard Yates, Jan. 22, 1854, box 1, folder 5, Yates Family Papers, ALPL; *Quincy Whig,* Jan. 31, 1854.

14. For more on Lincoln's view of Clay, see Kevin J. Portteus, "'My Beau Ideal of a Statesman': Abraham Lincoln's Eulogy of Henry Clay," *Journal of the Abraham Lincoln Association* 41 (Summer 2020): 1–24.

15. Zachary J. Lechner, "Black Abolitionist Response to the Kansas Crisis, 1854–1856," *Kansas History: A Journal of the Central Plains* 31 (Spring 2008): 14–31; *Frederick Douglass' Paper* (Rochester, NY), Jan. 13, Feb. 17, Mar. 3, 1854.

16. *Illinois State Register* (Springfield), Jan. 31, 1854; *Ottawa Free Trader*, Feb. 11, 1854.

17. Stephen A. Douglas to Edward Coles, Feb. 18, 1854, *Letters of Stephen A. Douglas*, 297. Edward Coles had grown up in Albemarle County, Virginia, as a neighbor and correspondent of Thomas Jefferson and had served as James Madison's personal secretary during his presidency. A determined opponent of slavery, Coles freed the slaves he had inherited from his father and moved to Illinois with them in 1819. During his term as governor, from 1822 to 1826, he vigorously opposed a constitutional convention to make Illinois a slave state. Coles's original objection to Douglas over the Nebraska Bill was published in the Washington, DC, *National Intelligencer* on February 18, 1854. For a recent biography of Coles, see Leichtle and Carveth, *Crusade against Slavery*.

18. *Quincy Herald*, Mar. 15, 16, 1854; *Salem Advocate*, Mar. 9, 1854.

19. Cong. Globe, 33rd Cong., 1st Sess., Appendix, 443, 447 (1854); *Salem Advocate*, Mar. 30, 1854.

20. Stephen A. Douglas to Charles H. Lanphier, Feb. 13, 1854, box 1, folder 5, Charles Henry Lanphier Papers, ALPL.

21. David Davis to John A. Rockwell, July 15, 1854, box 2, folder 4, David Davis Family Papers, ALPL.

22. Carwardine, *Lincoln*, 60.

23. John F. Henry to David Davis, July 15, 1854, box 2, folder 4, Davis Family Papers.

24. Ritter, *Inventing America's First Immigration Crisis*, 38–59. Prohibition measures received the title "Maine Law," following Maine's adoption of them in 1851. The passage of the law marked a major shift in the temperance movement, which had previously relied on voluntary pledges of abstinence, using tactics of moral suasion similar to that of abolitionists like William Lloyd Garrison. For background, see Jack S. Blocker Jr., *American Temperance Movements: Cycles of Reform* (Boston: Twayne, 1989), 54–60. Although native-born evangelical Protestants dominated the temperance and Sabbatarian movements, they were joined throughout the Midwest by small groups of pietistic Protestant immigrants, especially English and Welsh Methodists, Scottish and Irish Presbyterians, Scandinavian Lutherans, and members of the Dutch Reformed Church. This dynamic sometimes complicated the politics connecting nativism, moral reform, and anti-Catholicism. For a thoughtful discussion of these pietistic immigrants and their political affinities with native-born evangelicals, see Paul Kleppner, *The Cross of Culture: A Social Analysis of Midwestern Politics, 1850–1900*, 2nd ed. (New York: Free Press, 1970), 84–89. For background on the role of evangelical Protestants in Northern political life, see Daniel Walker Howe, "The Evangelical Movement and Political Culture in the North during the Second Party System," *Journal of American History* 77 (March 1991): 1216–39; Richard J. Carwardine, *Evangelicals and Politics in Antebellum America*, 2nd ed. (Knoxville: Univ. of Tennessee Press, 1997), 199–218. See also Bridget Ford, *Bonds of Union: Religion, Race, and Politics in a Civil War Borderland* (Chapel Hill: Univ. of North Carolina Press, 2016).

25. Thomas M. Keefe, "Chicago's Flirtation with Political Nativism, 1854–1856," *American Catholic Historical Society* 82 (Sept. 1971): 131–32; Hansen, *Making of the*

Third Party System, 54. For a discussion of Koerner and other anti-Nebraska Germans, see Levine, *Spirit of 1848*, 202–7.

26. Historians have offered a variety of interpretations for the collapse of the Second Party System and subsequent realignment in Illinois. The traditional position places the question of slavery's extension at the heart of the realignment. See Fehrenbacher, *Prelude to Greatness*. The so-called ethnocultural and geographical interpretations, notably advanced by Paul Kleppner and Stephen L. Hansen, respectively, and supported to varying extents by the works Michael F. Holt, William E. Gienapp, and Joel H. Silbey, emphasize religious, linguistic, and cultural divisions between pietists, liturgists, Yankees, immigrants, and Southerners as leading factors. See Paul Kleppner, *The Third Electoral System, 1853–1892: Parties, Voters, and Political Cultures* (Chapel Hill: Univ. of North Carolina Press, 1979); Hansen, *Making of the Third Party System*; Holt, *Political Crisis of the 1850s*; Gienapp, *Origins of the Republican Party*; Joel H. Silbey, *The Partisan Imperative: The Dynamics of American Politics before the Civil War* (New York: Oxford Univ. Press, 1985); Mark Voss-Hubbard, *Beyond Party: Cultures of Antipartisanship in Northern Politics before the Civil War* (Baltimore: Johns Hopkins Univ. Press, 2002). Recent literature has largely returned to the traditional "fundamentalist" interpretation but acknowledges the role of ethnocultural issues and geography. See Bruce Levine, "Conservatism, Nativism, and Slavery: Thomas R. Whitney and the Origins of the Know-Nothing Party," *Journal of American History* 88 (Sept. 2001): 455–88; Foner, *Fiery Trial*, 72–73; Bruce Levine, "'The Vital Element of the Republican Party': Antislavery, Nativism, and Abraham Lincoln" *Journal of the Civil War Era* 1 (Dec. 2011): 481–505; Huston, "Illinois Political Realignment of 1844–1860," 506–35; Peck, *Making an Antislavery Nation*, 105–7

27. *Alton Courier,* Nov. 7, 1853; *Mount Carmel Register,* July 19, Dec. 27, 1854. The numbering of the Ten Commandments remains disputed among Christians. Most Protestants consider "Remember the sabbath day, to keep it holy" as the Fourth Commandment. Roman Catholics and Lutherans consider this the Third Commandment.

28. *Mount Carmel Register,* Mar. 15, 1854; *Chicago Tribune,* June 7, 1854.

29. *Capital Enterprise* (Springfield), Sept. 2, 1854; Richard Hofstadter, *The Paranoid Style in American Politics, and Other Essays* (New York: Alfred A. Knopf, 1965), 19–23. For background on early American anti-Catholicism, see Ritter, *America's First Immigration Crisis*, 86–87. See also Ira M. Leonard and Robert D. Parment, *American Nativism, 1830–1860* (New York: Van Nostrand Reinhold, 1971).

30. For background on antipartisan partisanship, see Adam I. P. Smith, *No Party Now: Politics in the Civil War North* (New York: Oxford Univ. Press, 2006), 9–24. For details on the antipartisan impulse in the Whig Party and its collapse, see Howe, *Political Culture of the American Whigs,* 278–80, and Holt, *Rise and Fall of the American Whig Party,* 845–50. *Capital Enterprise,* Aug. 26, Sept. 2, 1854; Tyler Anbinder, *Nativism and Slavery: The Northern Know Nothings and the Politics of the 1850s* (New York: Oxford Univ. Press, 1992), 125. See also William E. Gienapp, "Nativism and the Creation of a Republican Majority in the North before the Civil War," *Journal of American History* 72 (Dec. 1985): 530.

31. Hansen, *Making of the Third Party System,* 49; Abraham Lincoln to Richard Yates, Aug. 18, 1854, in *The Collected Works of Abraham Lincoln,* ed. Roy Basler, 9 vols.

(New Brunswick, NJ: Rutgers Univ. Press, 1953), 2:226; Benjamin Brown Hamilton to Richard Yates, Apr. 17, 1854, box 1, folder 5, Yates Family Papers; Matthew Pinsker, "Not Always Such a Whig: Abraham Lincoln's Partisan Realignment in the 1850s," *Journal of the Abraham Lincoln Association* 29 (Summer 2008): 33–34; Abraham Lincoln to Richard Yates, Oct. 30, 1854, and Abraham Lincoln to Richard Yates, Oct. 31, 1854, both in in *Collected Works of Abraham Lincoln*, 2:284–85; Thomas L. Harris to Charles H. Lanphier, Oct. 23, 1854, box 1, folder 5, Lanphier Papers; Daniel C. Brown to Richard Yates, Nov. 18, 1854, box 1, folder 5, Yates Family Papers.

32. The anti-Nebraska moment secured at least 47 percent votes in each congressional district except for Little Egypt's Ninth District, where the Democrat Samuel S. Marshall secured 64 percent of the vote. For details, see Peck, *Making an Antislavery Nation*, 130. Hansen, *Making of the Third Party System*, 44–45; Gienapp, *Origins of the Republican Party*, 123–24; Victor B. Howard, "Illinois Republican Party: Part I: A Party Organizer for the Republicans in 1854," *Journal of the Illinois State Historical Society* 64 (Summer 1971): 151; Moore and Moore, *Collaborators for Emancipation*, 13–18. For an overview of the Liberty Party and the Fugitive Slave Act, see Brooks, *Liberty Power*, 70–71, 162–63.

33. Gienapp, *Origins of the Republican Party*, 87–160; Holt, *Political Crisis of the 1850s*, 146–58; Smith, *Stormy Present*, 74–75.

34. Foner, *Free Soil, Free Labor, Free Men*, 94–95; Richard H. Sewell, *Ballots for Freedom: Antislavery Politics in the United States, 1837–1860*, 2nd ed. (New York: W. W. Norton, 1980), 262–63; James McPherson, *Battle Cry of Freedom: The Civil War Era* (New York: Oxford Univ. Press, 1988), 126–29. See also Brooks, *Liberty Power*.

35. Speech at Bloomington, Illinois, Sept. 12, 1854, and Speech at Peoria, Illinois, Oct. 16, 1854, both in *Collected Works of Abraham Lincoln*, 2:230–34, 247–83.

36. *Illinois State Journal* (Springfield), Oct. 17, 1854. Lincoln had contributed pseudonymous pieces to the *Journal* throughout his political career. The paper's editor, Simeon Francis, shared Lincoln's commitment to internal improvements and a protective tariff and campaigned furiously for the Whigs in Sangamon and throughout the state. Over the years, Lincoln and Francis had become close friends, and Lincoln's biographers have credited the editor with the reconciling Lincoln with Mary Todd after he broke off their first engagement. Throughout the 1854 campaign, Francis took a conservative antiextension and anti-Nebraska position, staunchly denying any connection with abolitionists and repudiating the label as "an odious epithet." Francis would sell the paper to William Bailhache and Edward Baker in 1855. *Illinois State Journal* (Springfield), Oct. 19, 1854. For details of the Lincoln and Francis's relationship, see Burlingame, *Abraham Lincoln*, 1:95, 123–35, 194.

37. The three most notable biographies of Trumbull are Horace White, *The Life of Lyman Trumbull* (Cambridge, MA: Riverside, 1913), Mark M. Krug, *Lyman Trumbull: Conservative Radical* (New York: A. S. Barnes & Company, 1965), and Ralph J. Roske, *His Own Counsel: The Life and Times of Lyman Trumbull* (Reno: Univ. of Nevada Press, 1979). Of these, Krug most directly engages with the question of Trumbull's political philosophy. Although his label "conservative radical" recognizes the profound implications of Trumbull's self-identified conservatism, the term *radical* imposes a label Trumbull never embraced and alludes to debates during Congressional Reconstruc-

tion. In keeping with Trumbull's antebellum understanding of the term, my own analysis will refer to Trumbull as a conservative, and his policies as advancing a philosophy of conservatism. Krug, *Conservative Radical*, 20–25; Roske, *His Own Counsel*, 2–10. Trumbull's extended family included the Connecticut governor Jonathan Trumbull and the noted artist John Trumbull. For Trumbull's views on the Alton riot, see the November 12, 1837, letter reprinted in White, *Life of Lyman Trumbull*, 8–11. For his work to end slavery in Illinois, see Heerman, *Alchemy of Slavery*, 139–50.

38. Krug, *Conservative Radical*, 91–93; *Alton Courier*, Oct. 12, 1854; *Alton Telegraph*, Oct. 12, 1854; Peck, *Making an Antislavery Nation*, 131, 202; James Shields to Charles H. Lanphier, Oct. 25, 1854, box 1, folder 5, Lanphier Papers.

39. Lyman Trumbull to John M. Palmer, Nov. 23, 1854, "A Collection of Letters from Lyman Trumbull to John M. Palmer, 1854–1858," ed. George T. Palmer, *Journal of the Illinois State Historical Society* 16 (Apr.–July 1923): 20–24. Lyman Trumbull to John Trumbull, Dec. 4, 1854, box 1, folder 3, Lyman Trumbull Family Papers, ALPL.

40. Abraham Lincoln to Thomas J. Henderson, Nov. 27, 1854, Abraham Lincoln to Elihu N. Powell, Nov. 27, 1854, and Abraham Lincoln to Elihu B. Washburne, Dec. 19, 1854, all in *Collected Works of Abraham Lincoln*, 2:288, 289, 295; Freehling, *Becoming Lincoln*, 174–75.

41. James Shields to Charles H. Lanphier, Nov. 23, 1854, and Stephen A. Douglas to Charles H. Lanphier, Dec. 18, 1854, both in box 1, folder 5, Lanphier Papers; Stephen A. Douglas to James W. Sheehan, Feb. 6, 1855, *Letters of Stephen A. Douglas*, 333.

42. James W. Sheehan to Charles H. Lanphier, Jan. 17, 1855, box 1, folder 5, Lanphier Papers; Robert D. Bridges, "Antebellum Struggles for Citizenship," *Journal of the Illinois State Historical Society* 108 (Fall–Winter 2015): 307; *Journal of the House of Representatives of the Nineteenth General Assembly of the State of Illinois* (Springfield: Lanphier & Walker, 1855), 50, 68, 266–67. Hackney's party affiliation is described in R. Waite Joslyn and Frank W. Joslyn, *History of Kane County, Ill.* (Chicago: Pioneer Publishing, 1908), 447–48. An account of Diggins as a conductor on the Underground Railroad appears in the *Belvidere Standard*, Mar. 19, 1897. McCune Smith quoted in Dana Elizabeth Weiner, *Race and Rights: Fighting Slavery and Prejudice in the Old Northwest, 1830–1870* (Ithaca, NY: Cornell Univ. Press, 2013), 210.

43. *Journal of the House of Representatives of the Nineteenth General Assembly of the State of Illinois*, 348–61; Joseph C. Howell to Richard Yates, Feb. 11, 1855, box 1, folder 6, Yates Family Papers. See Fehrenbacher, *Prelude to Greatness*, 39; Roske, *His Own Counsel*, 25–27; Freehling, *Becoming Lincoln*, 177–79.

44. F. I. Herriott, "Senator Stephen A. Douglas and the Germans in 1854," in *Transactions of the Illinois State Historical Society 1912* (Springfield: Illinois State Historical Library, 1914), 150–55.

45. *Chicago Tribune*, Mar. 7, 14, 1855;' Keefe, "Chicago's Flirtation with Political Nativism," 139–42.

46. *Chicago Tribune*, Mar. 14, 1855; Bearden-White, "Illinois Germans and the Coming of the Civil War," 236; Sam Mitrani, *The Rise of the Chicago Police Department: Class and Conflict, 1850–1894* (Urbana: Univ. of Illinois Press, 2013), 13–16.

47. *Chicago Tribune*, Apr. 24, 1855; *Alton Courier*, Apr. 26, 1855; *Moline Workman*, Apr. 25, 1855; *Republican* (Rock Island), Apr. 23, 1855.

48. For an overview of the 1855 Free School Law, see Paul E. Belting, "The Development of the Free Public High School in Illinois to 1860," *Journal of the Illinois State Historical Society* 11 (Jan. 1919): 500–512. For Protestant establishment within public education, see Steven K. Green, *The Second Disestablishment: Church and State in Nineteenth-Century America* (New York: Oxford Univ. Press, 2010), 251–53. For sectarian antagonism in the Chicago public schools, see James W. Sanders, *The Education of an Urban Minority: Catholics in Chicago, 1833–1965* (New York: Oxford Univ. Press, 1977), 20–24. For details on voters in the 1855 prohibition referendum, see Gienapp, *Origins of the Republican Party*, 520; Hansen, *Making of the Third Party System*, 62–66; *Cairo City Times*, Apr. 18, 1855.

49. *Moline Workman*, July 13, 1855. For the growth of the Know Somethings, or "Jonathans," see Charles H. Ray to Elihu B. Washburne, Apr. 21, 1855, image 220, E. B. Washburne Papers, Library of Congress, Washington, DC, available at https://www.loc.gov/resource/mss44651.002/?sp=220&st=image.

50. For a list of these factions, see Hansen, *Making of the Third Party System*, 74. Stephen A. Douglas to Howell Cobb, Oct. 6, 1855, *Letters of Stephen A. Douglas*, 342.

3. The Common Cause

1. Lyman Trumbull to John M. Palmer, Jan. 22, 1856, "Collection of Letters," 27.

2. For details on the national Know-Nothing organization's disagreements over slavery in the summer of 1855, see Anbinder, *Nativism and Slavery*, 167–72; Lyman Trumbull to Owen Lovejoy, Aug. 20, 1855, and Silas Ramsey to Lyman Trumbull, Dec. 28, 1855, and J. M. Palmer to Lyman Trumbull, Dec. 22, 1855, both in box 1, folder 4, Lyman Trumbull Family Papers, ALPL; Samuel Pike to Charles H. Lanphier, Nov. 20, 1855, box 1, folder 5, Charles Henry Lanphier Papers, ALPL.

3. Stephen A. Douglas to James W. Sheahan, Jan. 11, 1856, *Letters of Stephen A. Douglas*, 347–48; Franklin Pierce, "Third Annual Message to Congress," Dec. 31, 1855, *Presidential Speeches*, Miller Center, University of Virginia, https://millercenter.org/the-presidency/presidential-speeches/december-31-1855-third-annual-message.

4. Throughout the antebellum period, Congress generally assembled on the first Monday in December, in keeping with Article 1, Section 4, of the Constitution. A Congress's first session often stretched into the summer, while its second (lame-duck) session ended with the expiration of its term on March 4. While the Senate held a brief special session immediately following the inauguration of a president in March to confirm executive appointments, new members of the House typically took their seats in December, more than a year after being elected.

5. For details on Kansas in this period, including vote totals, see Potter, *Impending Crisis, 1848–1861*, 199–208. For Douglas's illness and the reactions of Pierce and Douglas to events in Kansas, see Johannsen, *Stephen A. Douglas*, 484–93.

6. See Cong. Globe, 34th Cong., 1st Sess., 562–84 (1856). See also *Alton Courier*, Mar. 13, 1856. Shelden, *Washington Brotherhood*, 150; Lyman Trumbull to John Trumbull and Erastus Trumbull, Jan. 22, 1856, box 1, folder 5, Trumbull Family Papers.

7. For details surrounding the pair's confrontation, see White, *Life of Lyman Trumbull*, 58–62; Krug, *Lyman Trumbull*, 123–25; Johannsen, *Stephen A. Douglas*, 495–96. For the text of Trumbull's speech, see Cong. Globe, 34th Cong., 1st Sess., 200–206, appendix (1856). For national coverage, see *New-York Tribune*, Mar. 19, 1856, *Pittsburgh Gazette*, Mar. 24, 1856; *National Era* (Washington, DC), Mar. 27, 1856.

8. Introduced by Senator William H. Seward of New York in 1850, this "higher law" doctrine claimed that despite the protections for slavery inscribed in the Constitution, divinely instituted natural law forbade slavery and this higher law ought to govern slavery's extension into the territories. Stephen A. Hurlbut to Lyman Trumbull, May 2, 1856, microfilm, reel 2, Lyman Trumbull Correspondence, Library of Congress. For another such response, see Charles H. Ray to Lyman Trumbull, Mar. 18, 1856, and Lyman Trumbull to John Trumbull, Mar. 2, 1856, both in box 1, folder 6, Trumbull Family Papers.

9. *Illinois State Journal* (Springfield), Feb. 27, 1856; Speech at Decatur, Illinois: February 22, 1856, in *Collected Works of Abraham Lincoln*, 2:333; Freehling, *Becoming Lincoln*, 182–83. Elihu B. Washburne to Thomas Gregg, Mar. 4, 1856, Elihu B. Washburne Papers, Illinois History and Lincoln Collections, University of Illinois Urbana-Champaign; George T. Brown to Lyman Trumbull, Mar. 6, 1856, box 1, folder 6, Trumbull Family Papers.

10. *Illinois State Journal* (Springfield), Feb. 27, 1856; Foner, *Fiery Trial*, 77.

11. Lyman Trumbull to Joseph Gillespie, Feb. 25, 1856, Small Collection 558, box 27, Joseph Gillespie Papers, ALPL; Roske, *His Own Counsel*, 36; *Alton Courier*, Apr. 3, 1856; Lewis Brown to Lyman Trumbull, May 1, 1856, N. B. Risigner to Lyman Trumbull, May 2, 1856, S. M. Skinner to Lyman Trumbull, May 3, 1856, and James Bain to Lyman Trumbull, May 3, 1856, all in microfilm, reel 2, Lyman Trumbull Correspondence. For the determination of anti-Nebraska Democrats in Illinois to break free of Douglas through a new coalition, see Foner, *Free Soil, Free Labor Free Men*, 161–62; Jean H. Baker, *Affairs of Party: The Political Culture of Northern Democrats in the Mid-Nineteenth Century*, 2nd ed. (New York: Fordham Univ. Press, 1998), 145. These efforts by Trumbull and others to attract longtime Democratic voters in Little Egypt by appealing to a set of common values complicates the narrative offered by historian Eric Michael Burke, who argues that Republican leaders sought to remake southern Illinois in the North's image. See Burke, "Egyptian Darkness: Antebellum Reconstruction, 'Republicanization,' and Southern Illinois in the Republican Imagination, 1854–61," *Civil War History* 67 (Sept. 2021): 167–99.

12. Robin L. Einhorn, *Property Rules: Political Economy in Chicago, 1833–1872* (Chicago: Univ. of Chicago Press, 1991), 165–67; Norman B. Judd to Lyman Trumbull, Mar. 23, 1856, box 1, folder 6, Trumbull Family Papers.

13. Ebenezer Peck to Lyman Trumbull, Feb. 24, 1856, box 1, folder 5, Trumbull Family Papers; William Bissell to Joseph Gillespie, Jan. 21, 1856, Small Collection 558, box 27, Gillespie Papers; William Bissell to Lyman Trumbull, May 5, 1856, microfilm, reel 2, Trumbull Correspondence.

14. *Ottawa Free Trader*, May 10, 1856; George T. Brown to Lyman Trumbull, May 12, 1856, microfilm, reel 2, Trumbull Correspondence; *Alton Courier*, May 15, 1856; *National Era* (Washington, DC), July 24, 1856; *Ottawa Free Trader*, Aug. 16, 1856.

15. Orville H. Browning to Lyman Trumbull, May 19, 1856, microfilm, reel 2, Trumbull Correspondence; Roger Williams, *A Short Review of the Illinois Know Nothing Platform* (Petersburg, IL: H. L. Clay, 1855); Anbinder, *Nativism and Slavery*, 209–10.

16. William H. Bailhache to John Bailhache, Feb. 22, 1856, William H. Bailhache to John Bailhache, Feb. 26, 1856, and William H. Bailhache to John Bailhache, Mar. 7, 1856, all in box 1, folder 8, Bailhache-Brayman Families Papers, ALPL. For an insightful discussion of the animosity many Western antiextensionists felt toward abolitionists and Blacks, see James D. Bilotta, *Race and the Rise of the Republican Party, 1848–1865* (New York: Peter Lang, 1992), 163–66.

17. *Cairo City Times*, Sept. 5, 1855; *Peoria News*, Feb. 27, 1856; Thomas L. Harris to Charles H. Lanphier, Mar. 7, 1856, Thomas L. Harris to Charles H. Lanphier, Mar. 18, 1856, and *To Sangamon Whigs* (Springfield, IL: Richard & Smith's Job Office Print, 1856), all in box 1, folder 6, Lanphier Papers.

18. Among others, Michael F. Holt asserts that these two events allowed the slavery question to displace immigration as the primary issue among Whiggish conservatives throughout the Border North in 1856. See Holt, *Political Crisis*, 192–95, and Michael F. Holt, *Political Parties and American Political Development from the Age of Jackson to the Age of Lincoln* (Baton Rouge: Louisiana State Univ. Press, 1992), 278–80.

19. Nicole Etcheson, *Bleeding Kansas: Contested Liberty in the Civil War Era* (Lawrence: Univ. Press of Kansas, 2004), 75–95.

20. Potter, *Impending Crisis*, 203–4.

21. Kristen Tegtmeier Oertel, *Bleeding Borders: Race, Gender, and Violence in Pre–Civil War Kansas* (Baton Rouge: Louisiana State Univ. Press, 2009), 85–87; Adam Wesley Dean, *An Agrarian Republic: Farming, Antislavery Politics, and Nature Parks in the Civil War Era* (Chapel Hill: Univ. of North Carolina Press, 2015), 50–58.

22. *New-York Tribune*, May 26, 1856; *Alton Courier*, May 29, 1856; *Freeport Journal*, May 27, 1856. For an analysis of newspaper coverage of events in Kansas, see Craig Miner, *Seeding Civil War: Kansas in the National News, 1854–1858* (Lawrence: Univ. Press of Kansas, 2008).

23. Joanne B. Freeman, *The Field of Blood: Violence in Congress and the Road to Civil War* (New York: Farrar, Straus & Giroux, 2018), 217–34; Manisha Sinha, "The Caning of Charles Sumner: Slavery, Race, and Ideology in the Age of the Civil War," *Journal of the Early Republic* 23 (Summer 2003): 233–62.

24. William E. Gienapp, "The Crime against Sumner: The Caning of Charles Sumner and the Rise of the Republican Party," *Civil War History* 25 (Sept. 1979): 218–45; Brooks D. Simpson "'Hit Him Again': The Canning of Charles Sumner," in *Congress and the Crisis of the 1850s*, ed. Paul Finkelman and Donald R. Kennon (Athens: Ohio Univ. Press, 2012), 213–18; Michael E. Woods, *Emotional and Sectional Conflict in the Antebellum United States* (New York: Cambridge Univ. Press, 2014), 150; *New-York Tribune*, May 24, 1856.

25. *Chicago Democrat*, May 22, 1856; *Pantagraph* (Bloomington), May 28, 1856; *Illinois State Journal* (Springfield), May 24, 1856; *Freeport Journal*, May 29, 1856; *Ottawa Free Trader*, May 31, 1856. See also *Salem Advocate*, May 29, 1856; *Mount Carmel Register*, May 29, 1856.

26. E. W. Hazard to Lyman Trumbull, May 23, 1856, Abraham Jonas to Lyman Trumbull, May 26, 1856, Ebenezer Peck to Lyman Trumbull, May 26, 1856, Joseph Gillespie to Lyman Trumbull, May 29, 1856, and Benjamin Franklin Lemen to Lyman Trumbull, June 1, 1856, all in microfilm, reel 2, Trumbull Correspondence; "The Massacre of Glencoe," in *The Poetical Works of Sir Walter Scott*, 10 vols. (Edinburgh: Archibald Constable & Co., 1821), 7:477–80,1. 40; all in microfilm, reel 2, Trumbull Correspondence.

27. *Illinois State Journal*, June 2, 1856; *Moline Workman*, June 11, 1856.

28. Quote concerning Douglas in E. W. Hazard to Lyman Trumbull, May 23, 1856, microfilm, reel 2, Trumbull Correspondence. Denunciation of Pierce quoted in *Alton Courier*, June 12, 1856.

29. Charles H. Sumner, *The Crime against Kansas—The Apologies for the Crime—The True Remedy* (Boston: John P. Jewett & Co., 1856); *Alton Courier*, June 12, 1856.

30. Woods, *Emotional and Sectional Conflict*, 166.

31. Sewell, *Ballots for Freedom*, 279–81; Foner, *Free Soil, Free Labor, Free Men*, 198–200; Peck, *Making an Antislavery Nation*, 166–68; Gienapp, *Origins of the Republican Party*, 299–303; Gienapp, "Crime against Sumner," 229–32; Smith, *Stormy Present*, 84–88; Freehling, *Becoming Lincoln*, 184–85.

32. For the idea of the lowest common denominator on the slavery question, see Foner, *Fiery Trial*, 87–88. For the argument that the ultimate goal of the antebellum Republican Party was to establish a "cordon of freedom," see Oakes, *Scorpion's Sting*, 13–14; *Illinois State Journal* (Springfield), May 29, 1856. For an alternate interpretation of the 1856 contest that stresses radical antislavery militancy and populism as decisive factors, see Karp, "People's Revolution of 1856," 524–45.

33. "Landmark Major's Hall Razed for Parking," *Pantagraph* (Bloomington), Feb. 6, 2011; *1850 Census*, Statistics of Illinois—Population by Subdivision of Counties, 712; *1860 Census*, State of Illinois—Population of Cities and Towns, 97; J. H. Burnham, *History of Bloomington and Normal in McLean County, Illinois* (Bloomington, IL: J. H. Burnham, 1879), 61–96; *Illinois State Journal* (Springfield), May 10, 1856.

34. A detailed account of the entire convention and its legacy can be found in Ezra M. Prince, ed., "Meeting of May 29, 1900 Commemorative of the Convention of May 29, 1856 that Organized the Republican Party in the State of Illinois," *The Transactions of the McLean County Historical Society* 3 (1900): 3–184; contemporary coverage as printed in the *Alton Courier*, June 5, 1856. See also J. O. Cunningham, "The Bloomington Convention of 1856 and Those Who Participated in It," *Transactions of the Illinois State Historical Society* 10 (1906): 101–10.

35. *Alton Courier*, June 5, 1856.

36. Prince, *Transactions of the McLean County Historical Society*, 82–83.

37. Quoted in Freehling, *Becoming Lincoln*, 187.

38. *Alton Courier*, June 5, 1856. For a compelling and concise explanation of how and why some Northern Jacksonians embraced such arguments, see Jonathan H. Earle, *Jacksonian Antislavery and the Politics of Free Soil* (Chapel Hill: Univ. of North Carolina Press, 2004), 196–98.

39. For the Free-Soilers and racial rhetoric, see Eric Foner, "Politics and Prejudice: The Free Soil Party and the Negro, 1849–1852," *Journal of Negro History* 50 (Oct. 1965):

239–56. Wickliffe Kitchell to Lyman Trumbull, May 25, 1856, microfilm, reel 2, Trumbull Correspondence.

40. *Peru Chronicle*, June 5, 1856. Hoffman would subsequently be found ineligible for office because of the state's residency and naturalization requirements. He was replaced on the ticket by John Wood, an ex-Whig of German descent who was popular among German immigrants in west-central Illinois. For details, see May 28, 29, 1856, *The Diary of Orville Hickman Browning*, ed. Theodore Calvin Pease (Springfield: Illinois State Historical Society, 1925), 237–39; *Quincy Whig*, Sept. 29, 1856; J. H. A Lacher, "Francis A. Hoffman of Illinois and Hans Buschbauer of Wisconsin," *Wisconsin Magazine of History* 13 (June 1930): 337–38; Reg Ankrom, "Wood's German heritage helped him rise to governor," *Herald-Whig* (Quincy), July 12, 2015.

41. Prince, *Transactions of the McLean County Historical Society*, 110–12. For details on the organizational weakness of the Know-Nothing / American Party's weakness in Illinois prior to the Bloomington Convention, see James C. Sloo to Lyman Trumbull, May 16, 1856, and Orville H. Browning to Lyman Trumbull, May 19, 1856, both in microfilm, reel 2, Trumbull Correspondence; For the anti-Nebraska/Republican nominations, see *Alton Courier*, June 5, 1856.

42. Jonathan B. Turner, "On the Bloomington Convention," box 1, folder 7, Yates Family Papers, ALPL.

43. *Illinois State Journal* (Springfield), May 31, 1856; Foner, *Fiery Trial*, 79–80; Freehling, *Becoming Lincoln*, 186; Gienapp, *Origins of the Republican Party*, 295; Moore and Moore, *Collaborators for Emancipation*, 40–41.

44. Quoted in *Peru Chronicle*, June 5, 1856.

45. As previously stated, the label *Republican* remained controversial for some party activists throughout the 1856 contest. I refer to the party organized at Bloomington as the *Illinois Republican Party* and all of its adherents as *Republicans* to emphasize party unity in the aftermath of the convention. This choice adheres to the contentions of recent scholars, including Graham Peck and William Freehling. See Peck, *Making an Antislavery Nation*, 137, and Freehling, *Becoming Lincoln*, 191.

46. For examples of these attacks on popular sovereignty, see the *Illinois State Journal* (Springfield), June 5, 1856; *Freeport Journal*, June 9, 1856; *Quincy Whig*, June 9, 1956; *Pantagraph* (Bloomington), June 11, 1856; *Alton Courier*, June 12, 1856.

47. James Knox to Richard Yates, June 9, 1856, box 1, folder 7, Yates Family Papers; Holt, *Political Crisis of the 1850s*, 186–87; Johannsen, *Stephen A. Douglas*, 506–20; Woods, *Arguing until Doomsday*, 146–47. Historian Joshua A. Lynn has also suggested that Buchanan's status as a bachelor appealed to a conservative desire among disconcerted Democrats for restrained and dispassionate manhood in their standard bearer. See Lynn, "A Manly Doughface: James Buchanan and the Sectional Politics of Gender," *Journal of the Civil War Era* 8 (Dec. 2018): 591–620.

48. *Illinois State Journal* (Springfield), June 6, 1856; *Freeport Journal*, June 11, 1856.

49. "1856 Democratic Party Platform," June 2, 1856, *The American Presidency Project*, University of California, Santa Barbara, https://www.presidency.ucsb.edu/documents/1856-democratic-party-platform.

50. Although northern Illinois had been predominately settled by Northern Democrats, the antislavery proclivities of these voters had alienated them from the national

party as early as 1848. For a detailed discussion of voting patterns in this region over time, see Huston, "Illinois Political Realignment of 1844–1860," 525–28. See also Hansen, *Making of the Third Party System*, 51–57.

51. Johannsen, *Stephen A. Douglas*, 534–37; Huston, *Stephen A. Douglas and the Dilemmas of Democratic Equality*, 119–22. *Ottawa Free Trader*, June 7, 1856.

52. Peck, *Making an Antislavery Nation*, 137–38; Smith, *Stormy Present*, 87.

53. *Ottawa Free Trader*, Oct. 18, 1856.

54. Benjamin S. Edwards to Lyman Trumbull, July 24, 1856, microfilm, reel 2, Trumbull Correspondence.

55. *Salem Advocate*, July 24, 1856. For the Democratic reaction to Republicans' perceived Puritanism, see Joel H. Silbey, "The Surge of Republican Power: Partisan Antipathy, American Social Conflict, and the Coming of the Civil War," in *Essays on American Antebellum Politics, 1840–1860*, ed. Stephen E. Maizlish and John J. Kushma (College Station: Texas A & M Univ. Press, 1982), 216–24.

56. *Rock Island Argus*, Sept. 20, 1856; *Ottawa Free Trader*, Aug. 8, 1856.

57. Merrit Ransom to Lyman Trumbull, July 28, 1856, microfilm, reel 2, Trumbull Correspondence; *Freeport Journal*, July 16, 1856.

58. James Knox to Richard Yates, Mar. 17, 1856, box 1, folder 7, Yates Family Papers; G. D. A. Parks to Lyman Trumbull, June 13, 1856, microfilm, reel 2, Trumbull Correspondence.

59. Ebenezer Peck to Lyman Trumbull, June 10, 1856, and Abraham Jonas to Lyman Trumbull, June 11, 1856, both in microfilm, reel 2, Trumbull Correspondence; Roske, *His Own Counsel*, 36–37.

60. Henry Julian Abraham, *Justices, Presidents, and Senators: A History of the US. Supreme Court from Washington to Clinton*, 3rd ed. (Lanham, MD: Rowman & Littlefield, 1999), 72–73. Gienapp, *Origins of the Republican Party*, 311–16.

61. To Lyman Trumbull: June 7, 1856, in *Collected Works of Abraham Lincoln*, 2:342–43.

62. "Republican Party Platform of 1856"; Gienapp, *Origins of the Republican Party*, 340–41; Wilentz, *Rise of American Democracy*, 695–97. Chase quoted in Sewell, *Ballots for Freedom*, 285.

63. Foner, *Free Soil, Free Labor, Free Men*, 248–50; Gienapp, *Origins of the Republican Party*, 316–29; Holt, *Political Crisis of the 1850s*, 175–81. Gender historian Michael D. Pierson offers an excellent account of Jessie Frémont's political significance during the 1856 campaign in his work *Free Hearts and Free Homes: Gender and American Antislavery Politics* (Chapel Hill: Univ. of North Carolina Press, 2003), 144–50. See also Lauren N. Haumesser, *The Democratic Collapse: How Gender Politics Broke a Party and a Nation, 1856–1861* (Chapel Hill: Univ. of North Carolina Press, 2022), 14–19.

64. Foner, *Fiery Trial*, 80–81; Freehling, *Becoming Lincoln*, 189–90; Roske, *His Own Counsel*, 37.

65. *Salem Advocate*, Sept. 25, 1856; Bissell did come under fire from Democrats throughout the campaign for having nearly fought a duel with Jefferson Davis in 1850. Although sectional animosity helped to spark the incident, the dispute centered around the performance of each man's unit at the Battle of Buena Vista. While Bissell's acceptance of Davis's challenge would have him ineligible to hold state office under an antidueling provision in the Illinois Constitution, the fact that Bissell, at the

time a Democrat, had retained the support of his party and that several other prominent Illinois Democrats were involved in the affair helped the Republicans to sidestep the issue. See *Illinois State Chronicle* (Decatur), Aug. 14, 1856.

66. The Democratic press raised the issue of Bissell's Catholicism on occasion to drive a wedge between the Republicans and Know-Nothings. See *Chicago Times*, Sept. 11, 1856; *Dewitt Courier* (Clinton), Oct. 22, 1856. On at least one occasion, the Republicans responded by falsely claiming that Bissell remained a Protestant. See *Chicago Tribune*, Sept. 17, 1856.

67. *Chicago Tribune*, Sept. 9, 1856; *Alton Courier*, Aug. 7, 1856; *Belvidere Standard*, Aug. 12, 1856. The Republican claim of being the only truly national party paralleled the antipartisan ideology of the early republic period. For an extended discussion of antipartisanship in late antebellum politics, see Smith, *No Party Now*, 10–30. See also Voss-Hubbard, *Beyond Partisanship*, 178–216.

68. William H. Herndon to Lyman Trumbull, July 12, 1856, microfilm, reel 2, Trumbull Correspondence; Form Letter to Fillmore Men, Sept. 8, 1856, in *Collected Works of Abraham Lincoln*, 2:374. See also Foner, *Fiery Trial*, 81–82.

69. William H. Bailhache to John Bailhache, June 21, 1856, William H. Bailhache to John Bailhache, Aug. 1, 1856, William H. Bailhache to John Bailhache, Aug. 2, 1856, William H. Bailhache to John Bailhache, Oct. 30, 1856, and John Bailhache to William H. Bailhache, Nov. 3, 1856, all in box 1, folder 8, Bailhache-Brayman Families Papers; William B. Archer to Lyman Trumbull, Aug. 11, 1856, microfilm, reel 2, Trumbull Correspondence.

70. *Illinois State Register* (Springfield), Sept. 20, 1856; *Rock Island Argus*, Aug. 1, 1856; *Moline Workman*, Aug. 20, 1856.

71. *Conservative* (Springfield), Aug. 14, 28, Sept. 4, Oct. 30, 1856; Howe, *Political Culture of the American Whigs*, 52–53.

72. *Chicago Tribune*, Sept. 17, 1856; *Illinois State Journal* (Springfield), Sept. 26, 1856; For the influence of Democratic campaign traditions on Trumbull and other ex-Democrats, see Foner, *Free Soil, Free Labor, Free Men*, 165–68.

73. *Illinois State Journal* (Springfield), Sept. 1, 1856.

74. *Illinois State Journal* (Springfield), Sept. 17, Oct. 10, 1856; *Quincy Whig*, July 26, 1856.

75. Oakes, *Crooked Path to Abolition*, xiii–vv; Sean Wilentz, *No Property in Man: Slavery and Antislavery at the Nation's Founding* (Cambridge, MA: Harvard Univ. Press, 2018). For the prevailing view of the Constitution among historians, see David Waldstreicher, *Slavery's Constitution: From Revolution to Ratification* (New York: Hill & Wang, 2010).

76. Dickey would eventually abandon the Republicans altogether, supporting Stephen A. Douglas's campaigns in 1858 and 1860. Abraham Lincoln to Henry C. Whitney, July 9, 1856, in *Collected Works of Abraham Lincoln*, 2:347; Abraham Lincoln to David Davis, July 7, 1856 in *Collected Works of Abraham Lincoln: First Supplement, 1832–1865*, ed. Roy P. Basler (Westport, CT: Greenwood, 1973), 27; David Davis to T. Lyle Dickey, July 18, 1856, ser. 1, box 6, David Davis Papers, Chicago History Museum; *Ottawa Republican*, July 19, Aug. 16, 1856; Vermilion Republicans to David Davis, Oct. 31, 1856, box 2, folder 5, David Davis Family Papers, ALPL. See also Freehling, *Becoming Lincoln*, 190–91; Moore and Moore, *Collaborators for Emancipation*, 43–50.

77. *Proceedings of the State Convention of Colored Citizens of the State of Illinois* (Chicago: Hays & Thompson, 1856), 17–19; Victoria L. Harrison, "We Are Here Assembled; Illinois Colored Conventions, 1853–1873," *Journal of the Illinois State Historical Society* 108 (Fall–Winter 2015): 332–33; Robert L. Harris Jr., "H. Ford Douglas: Afro-American Antislavery Emigrationist," *Journal of Negro History* 62 (July 1977): 217–34; Alvan Stewart, *A Legal Argument before the Supreme Court of the State of New Jersey for the Deliverance of 4,000 Persons from Bondage* (New York: Finch & Weed, 1845); Sewell, *Ballots for Freedom*, 49–51.

78. For examples, see *Rock Island Argus*, June 16, 1856; *Ottawa Free Trader*, July 12, 1856; *Salem Advocate*, July 31, Aug. 14, 1856.

79. *Illinois State Chronicle* (Decatur), Aug. 28, 1856; *Freemonter* (Dixon), Aug. 29, 1856; *Belvidere Standard*, July 1, 1856; *Chicago Tribune*, Sept. 9, 13, 1856. For an informative discussion of the uses of racist rhetoric by early Republicans, see Bilotta, *Race and the Rise of the Republican Party*, 231–49. Historian James L. Huston has argued that the clash over popular sovereignty in the 1850s forced Republicans to recognize the human rights of enslaved people; yet as these examples show, many in the party chose to ignore or demean Black rights in clashes with Douglas Democrats. See James L. Huston, "Putting African Americans in the Center of National Political Discourse: The Strange Fate of Popular Sovereignty," in *Politics and Culture in the Civil War Era: Essays in Honor of Robert W. Johannsen*, ed. Daniel McDonough and Kenneth W. Noe (Selinsgrove, PA: Susquehanna Univ. Press, 2006), 96–128.

80. Gienapp, *Rise of the Republican Party*, 413; Potter, *Impending Crisis*, 265.

81. Foner, *Free Soil, Free Labor, Free Men*, 163–65; Freehling, *Becoming Lincoln*, 193; Gienapp, *Rise of the Republican Party*, 417; Hansen, *Making of the Third Party System*, 81–87; Holt, *Political Crisis of the 1850s*, 198–99. For the role of Germans in the 1856 election in Illinois, see Zachary Stuart Garrison, *German Americans on the Middle Border: From Antislavery to Reconciliation, 1830–1877* (Carbondale: Southern Illinois Univ. Press, 2020), 61–64.

82. Walter Dean Burnham, *Presidential Ballots, 1836–1892* (Baltimore: Johns Hopkins Univ. Press, 1955), 368–91; Huston, "Illinois Political Realignment of 1844–1860," 526–29.

83. See Potter, *Impending Crisis*, 261–62; McPherson, *Battle Cry of Freedom*, 157

84. Sidney Blumenthal, *All the Powers of the Earth: The Political Life of Abraham Lincoln, 1856–1860* (New York: Simon & Schuster, 2019), 261.

85. Stephen A. Douglas to John A. McClernand, Dec. 23, 1856, *Letters of Stephen A. Douglas*, 371; Johannsen, *Stephen A. Douglas*, 533–39; Woods, *Arguing until Doomsday*, 146–48.

4. No Man's Land

1. The weather in Springfield in late January 1857 is recorded in Jan. 22, 24, 25, 26, 1857, *Diary of Orville Hickman Browning*, 273. Thomas L. Harris to Charles H. Lanphier, Jan. 20, 1857, box 1, folder 6, Charles Henry Lanphier Papers, ALPL.

2. Kenneth M. Stampp, *America in 1857: A Nation on the Brink* (New York: Oxford Univ. Press, 1990).

3. Stampp, *America in 1857;* Burnham, *Presidential Ballots,* 368.

4. Affidavit signed by William H. Bissell certifying the freedom of John Shelby, a free man of color of Springfield, Illinois, Feb. 19, 1861, Louisiana Digital Library, https://louisianadigitallibrary.org. *National Era* (Washington, DC), Dec. 18, 1856; *Chicago Times* reprinted in the *Rock Island Argus,* Feb. 21, 1857. The *Ottawa Free Trader* expressed a similar sentiment in an earlier editorial, on January 3, 1857. David Davis to John F. Henry, Feb. 7, 1857, series 1, box 6, David Davis Papers, Chicago History Museum.

5. Thomas L. Harris to Charles H. Lanphier, Jan. 3, 1857, box 1, folder 6, Lanphier Papers; Stephen A. Douglas to Samuel Treat, Feb. 5, 1857, *Letters of Stephen A. Douglas,* 372. For details on Buchanan's cabinet appointments and its fallout within the Democratic Party, see Stampp, *America in 1857,* 56–63; Johannsen, *Stephen A. Douglas,* 550–55; Woods, *Arguing until Doomsday,* 148–49.

6. Johannsen, *Stephen A. Douglas,* 539–40; *Rock Island Republican,* May 26, 1855; *Ottawa Free Trader,* Nov. 15, 1856. See also Johannsen, *Frontier, the Union, and Stephen A. Douglas,* 77–98.

7. Cong. Globe, 34th Cong., 3rd Sess., 850–51 (1857).

8. Cong. Globe, 34th Cong., 3rd Sess., 852–53 (1857).

9. The radical antislavery *National Era* (Washington, DC) was one of the few national organs to give the debate between Thompson and Douglas extensive coverage and editorial commentary. See *National Era,* Mar. 12, 1857. For details on abrasive speeches intended for to please constituents, commonly known as *buncombe,* see Shelden, *Washington Brotherhood,* 36–38. Although the *Rock Island Argus* reprinted Douglas's speech, the *Ottawa Free Trader*'s more muted coverage offers a representative sample by both Democratic and Republican papers throughout Illinois. See *Rock Island Argus,* Mar. 27, 1857; *Ottawa Free Trader,* Feb. 28, 1857. For attention to the issue of foreign voters, see *Alton Courier,* Mar. 5, 1857.

10. Historian Graham A. Peck has resolutely denied that Stephen A. Douglas was antislavery in any meaningful sense. This position, which Michael Todd Landis and Joshua A. Lynn have endorsed in other recent works, serves a corrective to the overly sympathetic interpretation of Douglas's views advanced by his primary biographer, Robert W. Johannsen. Douglas's own view of slavery remains largely obscure, though it appears he did not criticize the institution beyond occasionally stating his own preference to live in a free labor society. In this sense, Douglas might have shared what historian Adam I. P. Smith has called the "antislavery consensus," in which Northerners of all parties "shared a commitment to defend a free labor society in which white men could govern themselves, build communities, and make their way in the world." Yet, even more importantly, as recently illustrated by Michael E. Woods, Douglas was not proslavery in the eyes of Southerners, who demanded dedication "to slavery's perpetual stability, grounded in masters' right to impose the burden of slavery on any community they chose." Douglas's refusal to surrender the rights of local white majorities to the prerogatives of slaveholders ultimately mattered more to Southerners than their mutual loathing of abolitionists and their common dedication to white supremacy. See Smith, *Stormy Present,* 17; Graham A. Peck, "Was Stephen A. Douglas Antislavery?" *Journal of the Abraham Lincoln Association* 26 (Summer 2005): 1–21; Landis, *Northern Men with Southern Loyalties,* 1–9; Lynn, *Defending the White Man's Republic,* 17; Woods, *Arguing until Doomsday,* 155.

11. James Buchanan, draft of inaugural address, Mar. 4, 1857, American Manuscripts, NYHS Digital Collections, New-York Historical Society Museum & Library, https://digitalcollections.nyhistory.org/islandora/object/nyhs%3A3599#page/1/mode/2up; *Rock Island Argus*, Mar. 11, 1857; *Randolph County Democrat*, Mar. 19, 1857; *Chicago Tribune*, Mar. 5, 1857; *Pantagraph* (Bloomington), Mar. 12, 1857.

12. For discussion of Dred Scott, see Don E. Fehrenbacher, *The Dred Scott Case: Its Significance in American Law and Politics* (New York: Oxford Univ. Press, 1978); Paul Finkelman, *An Imperfect Union: Slavery, Federalism, and Comity* (Chapel Hill: Univ. of North Carolina Press, 1981), 274–84; Paul Finkelman, *Supreme Injustice: Slavery in the Nation's Highest Court* (Cambridge, MA: Harvard Univ. Press, 2018), 204–17. Most scholars agree that Taney sought to establish the legitimacy an extreme Southern interpretation of the Constitution's protections for slavery in his ruling in the Dred Scott decision. Mark A. Graber has offered a notable dissent from this view, arguing that Taney's ruling actually reflected a bisectional consensus. See Mark A. Graber, *Dred Scott and the Problem of Constitutional Evil* (New York: Cambridge Univ. Press, 2006).

13. Roger B. Taney, *The Dred Scott Decision: Opinion of Chief Justice Taney*, with an introduction by Dr. J. H. Van Evrie (New York: Van Evrie, Horton, & Co., 1860), 19; *Chicago Tribune*, Apr. 15, 1857; *National Era* (Washington, DC), Apr. 30, 1857.

14. *Belvidere Standard*, Mar. 24, 1857; *Chicago Tribune*, Mar. 19, 1857; *Chicago Democrat*, Mar. 21, 1857; *Pantagraph* (Bloomington), Mar. 11, 1857. For a discussion of the Republican Party's use of states' rights rhetoric, see Michael E. Woods, "'Tell Us Something about State Rights': Northern Republicans, States' Rights, and the Coming of the Civil War," *Journal of the Civil War Era* 7 (June 2017): 242–68.

15. Edward S. Corin, "The Dred Scott Decision, in Light of Contemporary Legal Doctrine," *American Historical Review* 17 (Oct. 1911): 52–69.

16. *Alton Courier*, Mar. 26, 1857; *Illinois State Journal* (Springfield), Apr. 8, 1857; *Waukegan Gazette*, Mar. 28, 1857; *Chicago Democrat*, Mar. 21, 1857.

17. *Illinois State Register* (Springfield), Mar. 18, 1857; *Ottawa Free Trader*, Apr. 18, 1857.

18. *Mount Carmel Register*, Apr. 1, 1857; *Times and Delta* (Cairo), Apr. 8, 1857.

19. *Mount Carmel Register*, Apr. 1, 1857.

20. *Randolph County Democrat* (Chester), Mar. 26, 1857.

21. Speech printed in the *Ottawa Free Trader*, June 27, 1857.

22. Speech printed in the *Ottawa Free Trader*, June 27, 1857.

23. Speech at Springfield, Illinois, June 26, 1857, in *Collected Works of Abraham Lincoln*, 2:398–410.

24. Speech at Springfield, June 26, 1857, 398–410. By claiming that securing freedom in Kansas would prevent interracial sex, Lincoln echoed the professions of actual settlers in Kansas. For a concise analysis of this discourse, see Oertel, *Bleeding Borders*, 111–14.

25. Trumbull's speech was printed in the *Chicago Tribune*, July 3, 1857.

26. *Illinois State Chronicle* (Decatur), Aug. 13, 1857.

27. Stampp, *America in 1857*, 196–203; Lincoln's Speech at Springfield, IL, June 26, 1857, 399.

28. For a discussion of Lincoln's opposition to popular sovereignty and the distinction between his critique and those of other Republican leaders, see Nicole Etcheson,

"'A Living, Creeping Lie': Abraham Lincoln on Popular Sovereignty," *Journal of the Abraham Lincoln Association* 29 (Summer 2008): 1–25; *Chicago Tribune*, July 3, 1857.

29. *Ottawa Free Trader,* May 30, 1857; *Rock Island Argus,* June 9, July 11, 1857; Potter, *Impending Crisis,* 297–304; Stampp, *America in 1857,* 168.

30. *Chicago Tribune,* July 16, 1857; C. D. Hay to Lyman Trumbull, July 10, 1857, microfilm, roll 3, Lyman Trumbull Correspondence, Library of Congress.

31. *Illinois State Journal* (Springfield), July 7, 1857; *Chicago Tribune,* July 9, 1857.

32. Although a native of Pennsylvania, Walker had moved to Natchez, Mississippi, in the 1820s and served as senator from that state from 1835 to 1845, before his appointment to President Polk's cabinet as secretary of the Treasury. Resolutions printed in *Charleston Mercury,* July 8, 1857; *Central Transcript* (Clinton), July 23, 1857; Stampp, *America in 1857,* 169; Potter, *Impending Crisis,* 303–4.

33. *Ottawa Free Trader,* May 30, 1857; Stephen A. Douglas to Robert J. Walker, July 21, 1857, *Letters of Stephen A. Douglas,* 386.

34. Free-state men in had established a shadow government at Topeka in the wake of fraudulent territorial elections and the most partisan advocates of free soil refused to consider any state constitution except that drafted by that government in the fall of 1855. *Ottawa Free Trader,* July 18, 1857; *Rock Island Argus,* July 24, July 30, 1857; *Quincy Whig,* July 23, 1857.

35. William H. Bissell to Joseph Gillespie, July 11, 1857, folder 1, Joseph Gillespie Papers, ALPL; *Illinois State Journal* (Springfield), July 13, 1857; *Chicago Tribune,* June 27, 1857.

36. Article from the *Congregational Herald* reprinted in *National Era* (Washington, DC), July 9, 1857; *Ottawa Free Trader,* July 18, 1857. For more on the role of racism in the Illinois Republican Party, see Berwanger, *Frontier against Slavery,* 132–35; Bilotta, *Race and the Rise of the Republican Party,* 233–37; Stanley, *Loyal West,* 33–36. For a dissenting interpretation, see John M. Rozett, "Racism and Republican Emergence in Illinois, 1848–1860: A Re-Evaluation of Republican Negrophobia," *Civil War History* 22 (June 1976):101–15.

37. Ford Douglas quoted in Harris, "H. Ford Douglas," 223; Richard Junger, "'God Helped Those Who Helped Themselves': John and Mary Jones and the Culture of African American Self-Sufficiency in Mid-Nineteenth Century Chicago," *Journal of Illinois History* 11 (Summer 2008): 111–32; *Illinois State Journal* (Springfield), Feb. 25, 1857; *Journal of the House of Representatives of the Twentieth General Assembly of the State of Illinois* (Springfield: Lanphier & Walker, 1857), 629, 889–91.

38. Some historians identify the failure of the Ohio Life Insurance & Trust Company on August 24 as the beginning of the panic: see Stampp, *America in 1857,* 213–36. Others emphasize the sudden drop in railroad stocks at the end of September: see Charles W. Calomiris and Larry Schweikart, "The Panic of 1857: Origins, Transmission, and Containment," *Journal of Economic History* 51 (Dec. 1991): 807–34. See also James L. Huston, *The Panic of 1857 and the Coming of the Civil War* (Baton Rouge: Louisiana State Univ. Press, 1987), 14–24. For the effect on financial institutions and railroads in Illinois, see Hutson, *Financing an Empire,* 150–53; Charles Leroy Brown, "Abraham Lincoln and the Illinois Central Railroad," *Journal of the Illinois State Historical Society* 36 (June 1943): 121–63; Johannsen, *Stephen A. Douglas,* 587; Thomas, *Iron Way,*

44–55. *Pantagraph* (Bloomington), Sept. 1, 1857; *Quincy Whig*, Oct. 7, 1857; *Ottawa Free Trader*, Oct. 10, 1857.

39. *Quincy Whig*, Oct. 5, 14, 1857; *Rock Islander and Argus*, Oct. 6, 1857.

40. *Illinois State Journal* (Springfield), Oct. 10, 1857; *Rock Islander and Argus*, Oct. 14, 1857.

41. Pearl T. Ponce, *To Govern the Devil in Hell: The Political Crisis in Territorial Kansas* (DeKalb: Northern Illinois Univ. Press, 2014), 162–70; Potter, *Impending Crisis*, 307–20; Stampp, *American in 1857*, 264–81; *Alton Courier*, Nov. 19, 1857.

42. *Rock Islander and Argus*, Oct. 16, 1857; *Ottawa Free Trader*, Nov. 7, 21, 1857; Stephen A. Douglas to John A. McClernand, Nov. 23, 1857, box 1, folder 12, John A. McClernand Papers, ALPL. In a list published on December 28, 1857, the *Illinois State Register* of Springfield identified only two pro-Lecompton Democratic newspapers in Illinois. Although this count misrepresented a few papers that had yet to take a stand, it reflected the anti-Lecompton consensus among the state's Democrats.

43. Smith, *Stormy Present*, 121; *Rock Islander and Argus*, Dec. 8, 1857; *Illinois State Register* (Springfield), Dec. 17, 1857.

44. W. N. Coles to Stephen A. Douglas, Nov. 28, 1857, box 9, folder 10, James W. Sheahan to Stephen A. Douglas, Dec. 9, 1857, box 10, folder 5, and George C. Lanphere to Stephen A. Douglas, Dec. 24, 1857, box 11, folder 16, all in Stephen A. Douglas Papers, Hanna Holborn Gray Special Collections Research Center, University of Chicago Library.

45. Stephen A. Douglas to Charles H. Lanphier, Dec. 6, 1857, and Thomas L. Harris Douglas to Charles H. Lanphier, Dec. 3, 1857, both in box 1, folder 6, Lanphier Papers; *Quincy Herald*, Jan. 4, 1858; *Rushville Times*, reprinted in the *Quincy Herald*, Jan. 4, 1858.

46. Smith, *Stormy Present*, 116; *New York Herald*, Jan. 6, 1858; *Illinois State Register* (Springfield), Jan. 12, 1858.

47. *Rockford Register*, Dec. 19, 1857.

48. *New-York Tribune*, Dec. 17, 25, 1857; *Missouri Democrat* reprinted in *Central Transcript* (Clinton), Dec. 11, 1857; *Chicago Tribune*, Dec. 29, 1857.

49. Norman B. Judd to Lyman Trumbull, Nov. 21, 1857, Charles H. Ray to Lyman Trumbull, Nov. 24, 1857, and Charles L. Wilson to Lyman Trumbull, Nov. 26, 1857, all microfilm, reel 3, Trumbull Correspondence; *Chicago Democrat*, Dec. 26, 1857.

50. Lyman Trumbull to Abraham Lincoln, Dec. 5, 1857, and Lyman Trumbull to Abraham Lincoln, Dec. 25, 1857, both in box 1, folder 8, Lyman Trumbull Family Papers, ALPL. Most scholars mark December 3, 1857, as the moment when Douglas made a final break with Buchanan, following a testy meeting between the two men at the White House. Yet this break only became clear to the public on December 9, when Douglas denounced Lecompton on the Senate floor. See Damon Wells, *Stephen Douglas: The Last Years, 1857–1861* (Austin: Univ. of Texas Press, 1971), 34–35.

51. Indiana Republican Henry S. Lane quoted in Peek, "The True and Ever Living Principle of States Rights and Popular Sovereignty," 414.

52. Abraham Lincoln to Lyman Trumbull, Dec. 28, 1857," in *Collected Works of Abraham Lincoln*, 2:430.

53. Lyman Trumbull to Abraham Lincoln, Jan. 3, 1858, ser. 1, General Correspondence, 1833–1916, Abraham Lincoln Papers at the Library of Congress, http://hdl.loc.

gov/loc.mss/mss000001.mss30189a.0073100. For contrasting interpretations of the role of state and local party activists in this period, see Glenn C. Altschuler and Stuart M. Blumin, *Rude Republic: Americans and Their Politics in the Nineteenth Century* (Princeton, NJ: Princeton Univ. Press, 2000), 41, and Mark E. Neely Jr., *The Boundaries of American Political Culture in the Civil War Era* (Chapel Hill: Univ. of North Carolina Press, 2005), 8.

54. Potter, *Impending Crisis*, 318; Stephen A. Douglas to Charles H. Lanphier, Jan. 6, 1858, box 1, folder 7, Lanphier Papers.

5. The Great Debates

1. Exchange quoted in Johannsen, *Stephen A. Douglas*, 586.

2. *Illinois State Register* (Springfield), Jan. 6, 1858. For the importance of party loyalty, see Baker, *Affairs of Party*, 317–27. See also Silbey, *Partisan Imperative*, 33–49. For a discussion of the free-soil potential of popular sovereignty and the potential for political for realignment in the wake of Lecompton, see Smith, *Stormy Present*, 121–27. For a concise overview of the intraparty divisions in Illinois at the beginning of 1858, see Allen C. Guelzo, "Houses Divided: Lincoln, Douglas, and the Political Landscape of 1858," *Journal of American History* 94 (Sept. 2007): 391–417.

3. *Quincy Herald*, Jan. 18, 1858; *Randolph County Democrat* (Chester), Jan. 21, 1858.

4. *Peoria Democratic Union*, Feb. 5, 8, 12, 13, 1858; *Times and Delta* (Cairo), Feb. 24, 1858. The term *Danite* initially referred to an alleged secret order of Mormons who acted as spies to suppress non-Mormon activities. Douglas Democrats subsequently applied the epithet to Buchanan supporters in Illinois.

5. *Illinois State Register* (Springfield), Feb. 8, 1858; Thomas L. Harris Douglas to Charles H. Lanphier, Jan. 21, 1858, box 1, folder 7, Charles Henry Lanphier Papers, ALPL; Thomas L. Harris to John A. McClernand, Feb. 16, 1858, box 1, folder 12, John A. McClernand Papers, ALPL.

6. *Ottawa Free Trader*, Feb. 13, 1858; *Quincy Herald*, Feb. 15, 1858; *Islander and Argus* (Rock Island), Feb. 6, 1858.

7. *Waukegan Gazette*, Feb. 13, 1858; *Illinois State Journal* (Springfield), Feb. 24, 1858; *Central Transcript* (Clinton), Feb. 26, 1858; *Alton Courier*, Feb. 18, 1858.

8. *Illinois State Register* (Springfield), Feb. 8, 1858.

9. Ozias M. Hatch to Lyman Trumbull, Jan. 25, 1858, Jeff L. Dugger to Lyman Trumbull, Jan 28, 1858, and Ozias M. Hatch to Lyman Trumbull, Feb. 6, 1858, all in microfilm, reel 3, Lyman Trumbull Correspondence, microfilm, Library of Congress.

10. Abraham Jonas to Lyman Trumbull, Feb. 13, 1858, Norman B. Judd to Lyman Trumbull, Mar. 7, 1858, and Mark T. Skinner to Lyman Trumbull, Mar. 8, 1858, all in, microfilm, reel 3, Trumbull Correspondence.

11. Johannsen, *Stephen A. Douglas*, 601–5; Don E. Fehrenbacher, "The Post Office in Illinois Politics of the 1850's," *Journal of the Illinois State Historical Society* 46 (Spring 1953): 60–70; Stephen A. Douglas to Samuel Treat, Feb. 28, 1858, *Letters of Stephen A. Douglas*, 418–19; Samuel Treat to Stephen A. Douglas, Mar. 5, 1858, box 16, folder 13, Stephen A. Douglas Papers, Hanna Holborn Gray Special Collections Research Center, University of Chicago Library.

12. Alexander Starne to Charles H. Lanphier, Mar. 3, 1858, and Calvin Goudy to Charles H. Lanphier, Mar. 22, 1858, both in box 1, folder 7, Lanphier Papers; *Carbondale Transcript,* Apr. 15, 1858. This antipathy for proslavery ideology and commitment to free labor echoes the Republican critique of the South best articulated in Eric Foner's *Free Soil, Free Labor, Free Men.* For a discussion of how Northern Democrats harnessed public antipathy toward slavery for their partisan advantage, see Woods, *Emotional and Sectional Conflict in the Antebellum United States,* 174–77.

13. Abraham Lincoln to Owen Lovejoy, Mar. 8, 1858, *Collected Works of Abraham Lincoln,* 2:435; William C. Goudy to Stephen A. Douglas, Mar. 21, 1858, box 17, folder 3, Douglas Papers, UCL; Abraham Lincoln to Richard Yates, Mar. 9, 1858, *Collected Works of Abraham Lincoln, First Supplement,* 28–29. Burnham, *Presidential Ballots,* 368–91. One might reasonably wonder whether voter turnover through migration, a common phenomenon throughout the West, might decrease the significance of these percentages. Historian Kenneth J. Winkle, however, notes that persistent (multielection) voters in central Illinois held disproportionate power within the electorate, see Winkle, "The Voters of Lincoln's Springfield: Migration and Political Participation in an Antebellum City," *Journal of Social History* 25 (Spring 1992): 595–611. For details on Lovejoy's effort to secure his renomination, see Jane Ann Moore and William F. Moore, *Owen Lovejoy and the Coalition for Equality* (Urbana: Univ. of Illinois Press, 2019), 121.

14. Charles H. Ray to Lyman Trumbull, Mar. 9, 1858, Norman B. Judd to Lyman Trumbull, Mar. 19, 1858, and Jesse K. Dubois to Lyman Trumbull, Mar. 22, 1858, all in Trumbull Correspondence, microfilm, reel 4; Charles H. Ray to Abraham Lincoln, Apr. 14, 1858, ser. 1, General Correspondence, 1833–1916, Abraham Lincoln Papers at the Library of Congress, https://www.loc.gov/resource/ma1.0074600/?sp=2&r=-0.604,-0.086,2.207,1.011,0.

15. Abraham Lincoln to Ozias M. Hatch, Mar. 24, 1858, *Collected Works of Abraham Lincoln, First Supplement,* 29–30; Abraham Lincoln to Thomas A. Marshall, Apr. 23, 1858, and Abraham Lincoln to Elihu B. Washburne, Apr. 26, 1858, both in *Collected Works of Abraham Lincoln,* 2:443.

16. Potter, *Impending Crisis,* 320–26.

17. Johannsen, *Stephen A. Douglas,* 622–31; *Times and Delta* (Cairo), Apr. 28, 1858.

18. *Freeport Bulletin,* Apr. 22, 1858.

19. Cong. Globe, 35th Cong., 1st Sess., 1963–65 (1858).

20. *Illinois State Journal* (Springfield), May 3, 1858. Although downplayed in many recent works that argue the early Republican Party was essential radical in nature, the older scholarship of Eugene Berwanger and V. Jacque Voegeli offers conclusive evidence of pervasive racism throughout the Midwest. This issue has more recently been explored from the African American perspective in studies by Brent S. Campney and Jennifer R. Harbour. See Berwanger, *Frontier against Slavery;* V. Jacque Voegeli, *Free but Not Equal: The Midwest and the Negro during the Civil War* (Chicago: Univ. of Chicago Press, 1968); Campney, *Hostile Heartland;* Harbour, *Organizing Freedom.*

21. Cong. Globe, 35th Cong., 1st Sess., 1964–65.

22. *Ottawa Free Trader,* May 15, 1858; *Islander and Argus* (Rock Island), May 18, 1858, *Illinois State Journal* (Springfield), May 13, 1858; *Illinois State Register* (Springfield), May 15, 1858; Lyman Trumbull to John M. Palmer, May 20, 1858, box 1, folder 1, John McAuley Palmer Papers, ALPL; *Illinois State Register* (Springfield), May 21, 1858.

23. *Pantagraph* (Bloomington), May 20, 1858. For conservative reactions to rioting at mid-century, see Smith, *Stormy Present*, 31–42. See also David Grimsted, *American Mobbing, 1828–1861: Toward Civil War* (New York: Oxford Univ. Press, 1998).

24. Lyman Trumbull to John M. Palmer, May 20, 1858, box 1, folder 1, Palmer Papers; *Illinois State Journal* (Springfield), May 14, 17, 1858.

25. James W. Sheahan to Stephen A. Douglas, May 30, 1858, box 20, folder 7, Douglas Papers. *Illinois State Register* (Springfield), May 19, 1858; Smith, *Stormy Present*, 133.

26. For a discussion of Douglas's evolving relationship with Know-Nothing voters, see Steven Hansen and Paul Nygard, "Stephen A. Douglas, the Know-Nothings, and the Democratic Party in Illinois, 1854–1858," *Illinois Historical Journal* 87, no. 2 (1994): 109–30.

27. David Davis to Ward Hill Lamon, May 25, 1858, box 8, folder A-25, David Davis Family Papers, ALPL; Owen Lovejoy to Lucy Lovejoy, June 7, 1858, box 1, folder 8, Owen Lovejoy Papers, William L. Clements Library, University of Michigan; Ward Hill Lamon to Abraham Lincoln, June 9, 1858, ser. 1, General Correspondence. 1833–1916, Abraham Lincoln Papers at the Library of Congress, https://www.loc.gov/item/ma10085900/; Abraham Lincoln to Ward Hill Lamon, June 11, 1858, *Collected Works of Abraham Lincoln*, 2:458–59.

28. "A House Divided": Speech at Springfield, June 16, 1858, *Collected Works of Abraham Lincoln*, 2:461; *Illinois State Journal* (Springfield), June 17, 1858.

29. June 16, 1858, *Diary of Orville Hickman Browning*, 327. For evidence that Browning sought to preempt Douglas and tack to the center, see B. Gratz Brown to Orville Hickman Browning, June 10, 1858, box 1, folder 1, Orville Hickman Browning Papers, ALPL. *Illinois State Journal* (Springfield), June 17, 1858; *Chicago Tribune*, June 19, 1858; *Illinois State Register* (Springfield), June 18, 1858; *National Anti-Slavery Standard* (New York), June 26, 1858.

30. "A House Divided": Speech at Springfield, June 16, 1858, *Collected Works of Abraham Lincoln*, 2:461–69; Freehling, *Becoming Lincoln*, 206–7. See also David Zarefsky, *Lincoln, Douglas, and Slavery: In the Crucible of Public Debate* (Chicago: Univ. of Chicago Press, 1990), 44–45.

31. Clay's letter calling for slavery's "ultimate extinction," dated February 14, 1840, was later reprinted in Illinois in the *Alton Telegraph and Democratic Review*, Mar. 23, 1849. For radical calls for slavery's extinction, see the *Liberator* (Boston), May 2, 1856. For an overview of the North's gradual emancipation efforts, see Arthur Zilversmit, *The First Emancipation: The Abolition of Slavery in the North* (Chicago: Univ. of Chicago Press, 1967).

32. John L. Scripps to Abraham Lincoln, June 22, 1858, ser. 1, General Correspondence. 1833–1916, Abraham Lincoln Papers at the Library of Congress, https://www.loc.gov/resource/ma1.0090600/?st=gallery; Abraham Lincoln to John L. Scripps, June 23, 1858, *Collected Works of Abraham Lincoln*, 2:471. Historians and biographers have struggled to make sense of the "House Divided" speech and have offered competing interpretations for the address's significance. My interpretation of it as the unintentional political blunder of a still conservative statesman largely matches that of Allen C. Guelzo in his book *Lincoln and Douglas:* 57–64. Conversely, Douglas biographer Robert W. Johannsen believes Lincoln revealed his underlying sympathy for radical abolitionism in the speech. In his examination of the "House Divided" address,

Daniel Walker Howe encounters the Whig commitment to moral homogeneity and parallels to earlier anti-Catholic conspiracies in Lincoln's charges against Douglas. While William W. Freehling has built on interpretations offered by David Herbert Donald and Allen C. Guelzo by highlighting Lincoln's effort to frame Douglas as a party to a proslavery conspiracy, Eric Foner, James Oakes, and Graham A. Peck view the conspiracy charges as secondary to Lincoln's underlying commitment to antislavery nationalism. Michael G. Burlingame, reviving Don E. Fehernbacher's classic interpretation of the speech, gives equal weight to the incompatibility of slavery and freedom and the threat of a slaveholder conspiracy. Howe, *Political Culture of the American Whigs*, 286; Freehling, *Becoming Lincoln*, 206–10; Donald, *Lincoln*, 206–9; Guelzo, *Lincoln and Douglas*, 57–61; Foner, *Fiery Trial*, 98–103; James Oakes, *The Radical and the Republican: Frederick Douglass, Abraham Lincoln, and the Triumph of Antislavery Politics* (New York: W. W. Norton, 2007), 55–58; Oakes, *Crooked Path to Abolition*, 113;. Peck, *Making an Antislavery Nation*, 171–73; Burlingame, *Abraham Lincoln*, 1:457–65; Fehrenbacher, *Prelude to Greatness*, 70–95.

33. *Illinois State Register* (Springfield), June 26, 1858. For the antiparty sentiments of Whigs, see Howe, *Political Culture of the American Whigs*, 51–55. Michael E. Woods points to the profound limitations of Douglas's appeal in the South after Lecompton in *Arguing until Doomsday*, 168–75.

34. Lyman Trumbull to John M. Palmer, June 19, 1858, box 1, folder 1, Palmer Papers; P. L. Randle to Stephen A. Douglas, July 4, 1858, box 21, folder 1, Douglas Papers.

35. Guelzo, *Lincoln and Douglas*, 75–76; Johannsen, *Stephen A. Douglas*, 640–41.

36. Address printed in the *Illinois State Register* (Springfield), July 13, 1858; Johannsen, *Stephen A. Douglas*, 641–43; Guelzo, *Lincoln and Douglas*, 69–70; Rodney O. Davis, "Dr. Charles Lieb: Lincoln's Mole?" *Journal of the Abraham Lincoln Association* 24 (Summer 2003): 20–35; Charles Lieb to Lyman Trumbull, July 20, 1858, microfilm, reel 4, Trumbull Correspondence.

37. *Mount Carmel Register*, July 16, 23, 1858; *Islander and Argus* (Rock Island), July 15, 1858.

38. Address printed in *Illinois State Journal* (Springfield), July 14, 1858.

39. Address printed in *Illinois State Journal* (Springfield), July 14, 1858.

40. Address printed in *Illinois State Journal* (Springfield), July 14, 1858; undated, "Fragments: Notes for Speeches," *Collected Works of Abraham Lincoln*, 3:399.

41. *Illinois State Journal* (Springfield), July 16, 1858; *Olney Times*, Aug. 6, 1858; *Waukegan Gazette*, July 31, 1858.

42. Krug, *Lyman Trumbull*, 140–41; Lyman Trumbull to John Trumbull June 20, 1858, box 1, folder 8, Lyman Trumbull Family Papers, ALPL; Norman B. Judd to Lyman Trumbull, July 16, 1858, Jesse K. Dubois to Lyman Trumbull, July 17, 1858, and Charles Henry Ray, July 17, 1858, all in microfilm, reel 4, Trumbull Correspondence.

43. *Chicago Press and Tribune*, Aug. 9, 1858.

44. *Chicago Press and Tribune*, Aug. 9, 1858.

45. *Waukegan Gazette*, Aug. 14, 1858; *Illinois State Journal* (Springfield), Aug. 14, 1858; *Louisville Journal*, Aug. 14, 1858; *Chicago Press and Tribune*, Aug. 17, 1858.

46. Henry C. Whitney to Abraham Lincoln, July 31, 1858, ser. 1, General Correspondence. 1833–1916, Abraham Lincoln Papers at the Library of Congress, https://www.loc.gov/item/ma10110800/; David Davis to Abraham Lincoln, Aug. 2, 1858, ser. 2, box

7, David Davis Papers, Chicago History Museum. For background on T. Lyle Dickey, see Guelzo, *Lincoln and Douglas*, 109. *Chicago Times*, Aug. 9, 1858, reprinted in *Ottawa Free Trader*, Aug. 14, 1858.

47. *Chicago Press and Tribune*, Aug. 11, 23, 1858; *Illinois State Journal* (Springfield), Aug. 30, 1858; *Central Transcript* (Clinton), Sept. 17, 1858.

48. *Frederick Douglass' Paper* (Rochester, NY), Sept. 17, 1858.

49. *Jonesboro Gazette*, July 10, 1858; *Times and Delta* (Cairo), Aug. 11, Sept. 29, 1858; *Chicago Democrat*, Aug. 28, 1858

50. *Peoria Democratic Union*, Oct. 5, 1821, Oct. 21, 1858.

51. R. B. Carpenter to James Buchanan, June 23, 1858, Small Collections 254, box 10, R. B. Carpenter Letter, ALPL; Phillip A. Hoyal to Sidney Breese, Aug. 23, 1858, and Isaac L. Cook to Sidney Breese, Aug. 27, 1858, both in Small Collections 165, box 7, Sidney Breese Papers, ALPL; *Illinois State Register* (Springfield), Sept. 8, Oct. 18, 1858; James L. McCook to Thomas L. Harris, Sept. 15, 1858, and Thomas L. Harris to Charles H. Lanphier, Sept. 21, 1858, both in box 1, folder 7, Lanphier Papers.

52. Many of the excellent works documenting the Lincoln–Douglas debates can be found throughout the notes of this chapter. The works of Allen C. Guelzo and David Zarefsky provide the best recent political and rhetorical analyses of the debates. See also John Burt, *Lincoln's Tragic Pragmatism: Lincoln, Douglas, and Moral Conflict* (Cambridge, MA: Harvard Univ. Press, 2013).

53. "A Statement Showing the Political Complexion of the Germans in Different Parts of Illinois," Aug. 1858, and Report from Louis Didier to Stephen A. Douglas on the German Press and German Politics in the State of Illinois, Aug. 1858, both in box 21, folder 10, Douglas Papers. German Republicans framed Douglas as a hypocrite and troublemaker: see *Illinois Staats Zeitung* (Chicago), Sept. 16, 1858.

54. First Joint Debate, Aug. 21, 1858, *Lincoln-Douglas Debates*, 43–45; Douglas revealed his ignorance of Lincoln's 1854 positions in a letter to Charles H. Lanphier of the *Illinois State Register* shortly before the first joint debate. See Stephen A. Douglas to Charles H. Lanphier, Aug. 15, 1858, *Letters of Stephen A. Douglas*, 426–27.

55. Fourth Joint Debate, Charleston, Sept. 18, 1858, *Lincoln-Douglas Debates*, 162.

56. Seventh Joint Debate, Alton, Oct. 15, 1858, *Lincoln-Douglas Debates*, 316.

57. Peck, *Making an Antislavery Nation*, 172. The supporter in question was Republican congressional candidate Jehu Baker. See *Alton Courier*, Oct. 4, 1858.

58. Sixth Joint Debate, Quincy, Oct. 13, 1858, *Lincoln-Douglas Debates*, 268.

59. Seventh Joint Debate, Alton, Oct. 15, 1858, *Lincoln-Douglas Debates*, 289–90.

60. Johannsen, *Stephen A. Douglas*, 652–53; Guelzo, *Lincoln and Douglas*, 273–77.

61. *Pantagraph* (Bloomington), Oct. 30, 1858; *Illinois State Journal* (Springfield), Oct. 15, 1858; *Chicago Press and Tribune*, Oct. 13, Oct. 30, 1858; *Alton Courier*, Oct. 28, 1858; Abraham Lincoln to Norman B. Judd, Oct. 20, 1858, *Collected Works of Abraham Lincoln*, 3:329–30.

62. Returns found in *The Tribune Almanac for the Years 1838 to 1868*, inclusive, 30 vols. (New York: New York Tribune, 1868), 21:60–61; percentages in Guelzo, "Houses Divided," 415.

63. Hansen, *Making of the Third Party System*, 114–15; Gienapp, "Nativism and the Creation of a Republican Majority in the North before the Civil War," 553. Guelzo has

pointed to the fact that several key races for legislative seats were decided by razor-thin margins while others proved decisive Democratic victories. Collins has offered evidence that local issues, such as railroad monopolies, may have played a significant role in a handful of swing districts. Guelzo, "Houses Divided," 414–16; Bruce Collins, "The Lincoln-Douglas Contest of 1858 and Illinois' Electorate," *Journal of American Studies* 20 (Dec. 1986): 391–420. Nonetheless, the regional analysis presented by James L. Huston, which challenges elements of both Hansen's and Gienapp's analyses, supports Gienapp's conclusion that most former Fillmore voters in central and southern Illinois migrated into the Republican camp. See Huston, "Illinois Political Realignment of 1844–1860," 510–11.

64. *Tribune Almanac*, 60–61. Steven L. Hansen and Paul Nygard have argued that Douglas decisively won the support of former Fillmore voters by noting that in the twenty-two counties where Fillmore had won 30 percent or more of the vote, all but two went Democratic in 1858. Yet, many of these same counties had returned a Democratic majority in 1856. For example, in 1856, Menard County posted a return of 854 votes for Buchanan, 668 for Fillmore, and 109 for Frémont, while in 1858, the county delivered 871 votes for Fondey, 766 for Miller, and 13 for Dougherty. See Hansen and Nygard, "Stephen A. Douglas, the Know-Nothings, and the Democratic Party in Illinois, 1854–1858," 129–30.

65. *Central Transcript* (Clinton), Nov. 12, 1860. Quotation from the *Chicago Journal* reprinted in the *Illinois State Journal* (Springfield), Dec. 29, 1858.

6. Race to the White House

1. "House Journal Entry on the Election of Stephen Douglas to the Senate (1859)," *100 Most Valuable Documents at the Illinois State Archives: The Online Exhibit*, Office of the Illinois Secretary of State, https://www.ilsos.gov/departments/archives/online_exhibits/100_documents/1859-journal-douglas-senate.html; *Chicago Times*, Jan. 13, 1859; Johannsen, *Stephen A. Douglas*, 685–87; Woods, *Arguing until Doomsday*, 181.

2. For accounts of Lincoln's thinking in this period, see Doris Kearns Goodwin, *Team of Rivals: The Political Genius of Abraham Lincoln* (New York: Simon & Schuster, 2009), 211–12; Burlingame, *Abraham Lincoln*, 1:588–89; Carwardine, *Lincoln*, 92–94; Foner, *Fiery Trial*, 132–36; Freehling, *Becoming Lincoln*, 224–26.

3. Charles H. Ray to O. M. Hatch, Dec. 1858, box 1, folder 3, Ozias Mather Hatch Papers, ALPL; Johannsen, *Stephen A. Douglas*, 682–83; Woods, *Arguing until Doomsday*, 180.

4. Cong. Globe, 35th Cong., 2nd Sess., 1256, 1259 (1859); Johannsen, *Stephen A. Douglas*, 694–97; Woods, *Arguing until Doomsday*, 2–3, 183.

5. *Illinois State Register*, Mar. 2, 1859; *Quincy Herald*, Mar. 7, 1859; *Chicago Press and Tribune*, Mar. 1, 1859.

6. *Chicago Times*, Jan. 13, 1859.

7. Foner, *Free Soil, Free Labor, Free Men*, 250–53; Levine, *Spirit of 1848*, 241. See also Dale Baum, "Know-Nothingism and Republican Majority in Massachusetts: The Political Realignment of the 1850s," *Journal of American History* 64 (Mar. 1979): 959–86.

8. Gary Ecelbarger, *The Great Comeback: How Abraham Lincoln Beat the Odds to Win the 1860 Republican Nomination* (New York: Thomas Dunne Books, 2008), 39–41; *Islander and Argus* (Rock Island), Mar. 17, 1859; Gustave Koerner to Abraham Lincoln, Apr. 4, 1859, ser. 1, General Correspondence. 1833–1916, Abraham Lincoln Papers at the Library of Congress, https://www.loc.gov/resource/mal.0168700/?sp=1&r=-0.042,0.499,1.176,0.568,0; Abraham Lincoln to Gustave Koerner, Apr. 11, 1859, *Collected Works of Abraham Lincoln*, 3:376.

9. Don E. Fehrenbacher, "The Judd–Wentworth Feud," *Journal of the Illinois State Historical Society* 45 (Autumn 1952): 197–211; Abraham Lincoln to Lyman Trumbull, Feb. 3, 1859, *Collected Works of Abraham Lincoln*, 3:355–56; *Chicago Press and Tribune*, Apr. 19, 1859.

10. Ecelbarger, *Great Comeback*, 35–38; *Central Transcript* (Clinton), July 1, 1859; Abraham Lincoln to the Editor of the *Central Transcript*, July 3, 1859, *Collected Works of Abraham Lincoln*, 3:389–90. For Yates's interest in the governor's race, see Richard Yates to Joseph T. Eccles, Dec. 7, 1859, box 21, Small Collections 440, Box 21, Joseph T. Eccles Papers, ALPL.

11. Simmons, *Men of Mark*, 681–82; Junger, "'God and Man Helped Those Who Helped Themselves,'" 130; Henry O. Wagoner to Wendell Phillips, Nov. 6, 1859, *Kansas Memory*, Kansas Historical Society, https://www.kshs.org/index.php?url=km/items/view/5342; Jackson, *Force and Freedom*, 129.

12. Potter, *Impending Crisis*, 356–84; Elizabeth Varon, *Disunion! The Coming of the American Civil War, 179–859* (Chapel Hill: Univ. of North Carolina Press, 2008), 326–35. Ayers, *In the Presence of Mine Enemies*, 34–60. For the range of Northern reactions to Brown's Raid, see Paul Finkelman, ed., *His Soul Goes Marching On: Responses to John Brown and the Harpers Ferry Raid* (Charlottesville: Univ. of Virginia Press, 1995). See also Joshua D. Rothman, "'But How and in What Balance Weigh John Brown': Northern Reactions to John Brown's Raid" (MA thesis, Univ. of Virginia, 1995).

13. David Davis to George Davis, Oct. 20, 1859, box 8, folder 3, David Davis Family Papers, ALPL; *Pantagraph* (Bloomington), Dec. 10, 1859; *Chicago Press and Tribune*, Dec. 9, 1859; *Chicago Times*, Oct. 19, 1859; *Ottawa Free Trader*, Oct. 22, 1859. See also *Chicago Times*, Dec. 6, 1859; *Illinois State Register* (Springfield), Dec. 6, 1859. Many Republican papers that expressed sympathy with Brown did so with some caveats. They often labeled Brown insane, ascribing his mental illness to his grief at losing a son to proslavery bushwhackers in Kansas. The *Chicago Press and Tribune* balanced its publication of a "Requiem for John Brown" with a denunciation of "the midnight horrors and atrocities" Brown sought, including the "brutal ravishing of delicate women by untamed beasts" and "the braining of children against the door-posts of their fathers' dwellings." Other papers pointed to Southern hypocrisy in prosecuting Brown for treason while offering clemency to proslavery filibusters and international slave traders. See *Chicago Press and Tribune*, Dec. 3, 1859; *Illinois State Journal* (Springfield), Nov. 9, 1859; *Waukegan Gazette*, Dec. 10, 1859; *Central Transcript* (Clinton), Dec. 15, 1859.

14. For Danite interference in the state party apparatus, see Stephen A. Douglas to Charles H. Lanphier, Oct. 1, 1859, box 1, folder 8, Charles Henry Lanphier Papers, ALPL; Stephen A. Douglas to John A. McClernand, Oct. 1, 1859, box 1, folder 12, John A. McClernand Papers, ALPL; *Illinois State Register* (Springfield), Oct. 27, 1859; *Illinois State Journal* (Springfield), Oct. 29, Nov. 16, 1859.

15. Fehrenbacher, "Judd-Wentworth Feud," 201–9; *Chicago Democrat*, Nov. 5, Dec. 3, 1859; *Illinois State Journal* (Springfield), Oct. 28, 1859. For Wentworth's radicalism as political sabotage, see Don E. Fehrenbacher, *Chicago Giant: A Biography of "Long John" Wentworth* (Madison: American History Research Center, 1957), 178–81 and Sally Heinzel, "'To Protect the Rights of the White Race': Illinois Republican Racial Politics in the 1860 Campaign and the Twenty-Second General Assembly," *Journal of the Illinois State Historical Society* 108 (Fall–Winter 2015): 384–86.

16. Hinton Rowan Helper, *The Impending Crisis of the South: How to Meet It* (New York: A. B Burdick, 1859), v; Potter, *Impending Crisis*, 386–88; Johannsen, *Stephen A. Douglas*, 717–18. For the reaction of the Southern Opposition to Brown's Raid and the Republicans, see William A. Link, *Roots of Secession: Slavery and Politics in Antebellum Virginia* (Chapel Hill: Univ. of North Carolina Press, 2005), 188–89.

17. While Buchanan's annual message was dated December 19, the written address was delivered and read to the Senate on December 27. Potter, *Impending Crisis*, 388–92; Johannsen, *Stephen A. Douglas*, 719–21; Cong. Globe, 36th Cong., 1st Sess., 256 (1859); Cong. Globe, 36th Cong., 1st Sess., Appendix, 1–7, 64–66 (1859); Victor Hicken, "John A. McClernand and the House Speakership Struggle of 1859," *Journal of the Illinois State Historical Society* 53 (Summer 1960): 163–78; John A. McClernand to Charles H. Lanphier, Dec. 27, 1859, box 1, folder 8, Lanphier Papers; Charles H. Lanphier to John A. McClernand, Dec. 27, 1859, box 1, folder 12, John A. McClernand Papers, ALPL; *New York Times*, Feb. 2, 1860.

18. Henry J. Atkins to Lyman Trumbull, Dec. 27, 1859, Lyman Trumbull Correspondence, microfilm, reel 5, Library of Congress; Woods, *Arguing until Doomsday*, 192–95; A. H. Mozier to Stephen A. Douglas, Apr. 14, 1860, box 32, folder 17, Stephen A. Douglas Papers, Hanna Holborn Gray Special Collections Research Center, University of Chicago Library; *Chicago Press and Tribune*, Jan. 5, 1860.

19. Maruice G. Baxter, *Orville H. Browning: Lincoln's Friend and Critic* (Bloomington: Indiana Univ. Press, 1957), 95–98; Robert S. Eckley, *Lincoln's Forgotten Friend, Leonard Swett* (Carbondale: Southern Illinois Univ. Press, 2012), 64–68; Fehrenbacher, *Prelude to Greatness*, 151–53.

20. Scholars have carefully detailed Lincoln's pursuit of the Republican nomination for president in 1859 and 1860. See Burlingame, *Abraham Lincoln*, 579–94; Carwardine, *Lincoln*, 92–111; Donald, *Lincoln*, 235–46; Ecelbarger, *Great Comeback*, 121–30; Foner, *Fiery Trial*, 132–40; Goodwin, *Team of Rivals*, 211–39; Harris, *Lincoln's Rise to the Presidency*, 176–99. My interpretation of Lincoln's revisions largely concurs with that of William W. Freehling; see Freehling, *Becoming Lincoln*, 223–23. See also Smith, *Stormy Present*, 163–64. Historian Graham Peck, in contrast, has called Lincoln's conservative edits "a masterpiece of misdirection," and James Oakes has insisted that Lincoln's renewed emphasis antislavery constitutionalism "appealed to the more radical base of the party." See Peck, *Making an Antislavery Nation*, 176; Oakes, *Crooked Path to Abolition*, 94.

21. Speech at Columbus, Ohio, Sept. 16, 1859, and Address before the Wisconsin State Agricultural Society, Milwaukee, Wisconsin, Sept. 30, 1859, both in *Collected Works of Abraham Lincoln*, 3:404, 479.

22. Address before the Wisconsin State Agricultural Society; Speech at Indianapolis, Indiana, Sept. 19, 1859, in *Collected Works of Abraham Lincoln*, 3:470.

23. Freehling, *Becoming Lincoln*, 232–34. See also Harold Holzer, *Lincoln at Cooper Union: The Speech That Made Abraham Lincoln President* (New York: Simon & Schuster, 2004).

24. For competing twenty-first-century evaluations of the relationship of the Constitution and slavery, see Waldstreicher, *Slavery's Constitution* and Wilentz, *No Property in Man*. Address at Cooper Institute, New York City, Feb. 27, 1860, *Collected Works of Abraham Lincoln*, 3:522–50.

25. Address at Cooper Institute.

26. *New-York Tribune*, Feb. 28, Mar. 10, 1860; *Hartford (CT) Courant*, Feb. 29, Mar. 6, 1860; *Vermont Phoenix* (Brattleboro), Mar. 3, 1860; *Boston Transcript*, Mar. 6, 1860; *Poughkeepsie (NY) Eagle*, Mar. 3, 1860.

27. *Chicago Herald*, Jan. 21, 1860; *Ottawa Free Trader*, Mar. 31, 1860; *Rock Island Argus*, Apr. 9, 1860; *Chicago Times*, Jan. 29, 1860; *Olney Press*, Mar. 9, 1860.

28. John A. McClernand to Charles A. Lanphier, Mar. 30, 1860, and John A. McClernand to Charles A. Lanphier, Apr. 4, 1860, both in box 1, folder 9, Lanphier Papers.

29. Murray McConnel to Stephen A. Douglas, Apr. 22, 1860, box 32, folder 22, Douglas Papers.

30. *Charleston Mercury*, Apr. 21, 1860. For accounts of the Charleston Convention, see Douglas R. Egerton, *Year of the Meteors: Stephen Douglas, Abraham Lincoln, and the Election that Brought on the Civil War* (New York: Bloomsbury, 2010), 51–83; William W. Freehling, *The Road to Disunion*: vol. 2, *Secessionists Triumphant* (New York: Oxford Univ. Press, 2007), 288–308; Holt, *Election of 1860*, 50–67; Nichols, *Disruption of American Democracy*, 288–322. See also Barbara L. Bellows, "Of Time and the City: Charleston in 1860," *South Carolina Historical Magazine* 112 (July–Oct. 2011): 157–72.

31. Moses Bates to Stephen A. Douglas, Apr. 24, 1860, and C. P. Culver to Stephen A. Douglas, Apr. 24, 1860, both in box 32, folder 23, Douglas Papers; Carl Becker, "The Unit Rule in National Nominating Conventions," *American Historical Review* 5 (Oct. 1899): 64–82. See also Huston, *Stephen A. Douglas and the Dilemmas of Democratic Equality*, 165–69.

32. John G. Parkhurst, *Official Proceedings of the Democratic National Convention, Held in 1860, at Charleston and Baltimore, Proceedings at Charleston, April 23–May 3* (Cleveland: Nevins' Print, 1860). Pugh quoted in in Holt, *Election of 1860*, 60.

33. *Ottawa Free Trader*, May 5, 1860; *Salem Advocate*, May 10, 1860; *Quincy Herald*, May 9, 1860; *Illinois State Register* (Springfield), May 14, 1860.

34. *Chicago Tribune*, May 8, 1860; *Belvidere Standard*, May 8, 1860.

35. Holt, *Election of 1860*, 79–84; *Illinois State Journal* (Springfield), May 12, 1860. For a perspective more sympathetic to the strategy of Bell and Everett, see A. James Fuller, "The Last True Whig: John Bell and the Politics of Compromise in 1860," in *The Election of 1860 Reconsidered*, ed. A. James Fuller (Kent, OH: Kent State Univ. Press, 2013), 103–39. See also Mason, *Apostle of Union*, 249–55.

36. *Illinois State Journal* (Springfield), May 10, 11, 1860. For further details on the gubernatorial contest, see Alexander Sympson to O. M. Hatch, Feb. 29, 1960; box 1, folder 7, Hatch Papers: James Berdan to Richard Yates, Feb. 13, 1860, box 1, folder 11, Yates Family Papers, ALPL. For an excellent account of the Decatur Convention and its significance, see James T. Hickey, "Oglesby's Fence Rail Dealings and the 1860

Decatur Convention," *Journal of the Illinois State Historical Society* 54 (Spring 1961): 5–24. See also Michael S. Green, "The Political Organizer: Abraham Lincoln's 1860 Campaign," in Fuller, *Election of 1860 Reconsidered*, 7–27.

37. *Chicago Press and Tribune*, May 9, 11, 1860; Mark A. Plummer, *Lincoln's Rail-Splitter: Governor Richard J. Oglesby* (Urbana: Univ. of Illinois Press, 2001) 41–43; Burlingame, *Abraham Lincoln*, 1:589–99; Freehling, *Becoming Lincoln*, 245.

38. Seward's address is printed in the Cong. Globe, 36th Cong., 1st Sess., 910–14 (1860).

39. Jesse K. DuBois to Abraham Lincoln, May 13, 1860, and Nathan M. Napp to Abraham Lincoln, May 14, 1860, both in Abraham Lincoln Papers at the Library of Congress, https://www.loc.gov/resource/ma1.026470o/?sp=1&r=-0.098,0.204,1.327,0.641,0, https://www.loc.gov/item/ma10267200/;*Chicago Democrat*, May 19, 1860; Ecelbarger, *Great Comeback*, 197–200; Burlingame, *Abraham Lincoln*, 608–11.

40. *Chicago Press and Tribune*, May 19, 1860; Harris, *Lincoln's Rise to the Presidency*, 209–11.

41. Republican National Platform reprinted in *Illinois State Journal* (Springfield), May 19, 1860.

42. Charles Balance to Lyman Trumbull, May 7, 1860, microfilm, reel 6, Trumbull Correspondence.

43. J. W. Maxwell to Stephen A. Douglas, May 31, 1860, box 34, folder 18, and S. A. Washington to Stephen A. Douglas, box 334, folder 29, both in Douglas Papers; *Illinois State Register* (Springfield), June 12, 16, 1860.

44. Stephen A. Douglas to William A. Richardson, June 20, 1860, *Letters of Stephen A. Douglas*, 492; John A. McClernand to Stephen A. Douglas, June 21, 1860, box 35, folder 9, Douglas Papers; Holt, *The Election of 1860*, 119–27; Egerton, *Year of the Meteors*, 162–70.

45. F. W. S. Brawley to Stephen A. Douglas, June 24, 1860, box 35, folder 10, Douglas Papers.

46. Stephen A. Douglas to Charles H. Lanphier, July 5, 1860, *Letters of Stephen A. Douglas*, 497–98; *Illinois State Register* (Springfield), June 27, 1860; *Ottawa Free Trader*, July 14, 1860, The Rock Island resolutions were reprinted in the *Rock Island Argus*, July 2, 1860.

47. *Chicago Press and Tribune*, June 27, 1860; *Illinois State Journal* (Springfield), July 19, 1860; Oglesby's speech reprinted in the *Pantagraph* (Bloomington), Aug. 4, 1860; *Chicago Press and Tribune*, Aug. 10, 13, Sept. 11, 1860. For more on the role of Illinois women in the campaign of 1860, see Erika Rozinek, "Trembling for the Nation: Illinois Women and the Election of 1860," *Constructing the Past* 2, no.1 (2001): 6–24. For the role of corruption in shaping public opinion and electoral politics, see Mark W. Summers, *The Plundering Generation: Corruption and the Crisis of the Union, 1849–1861* (New York: Oxford Univ. Press, 1987).

48. David Davis et al. to Orville H. Browning, May 21, 1860, box 1, folder 1, Orville Hickman Browning Papers, ALPL. For details on Bates's endorsement, see Burlingame, *Abraham Lincoln*, 1:643. Thurlow Weed to Leonard Swett, June 7, 1860, ser. 1, box 8, David Davis Papers, Chicago History Museum. These endorsements did not mark a full reconciliation between the rival candidates, as both Bates and Seward viewed Lincoln

as a second-rate candidate. Rather, their acquiescence signaled a commitment to party regularity, and their loyalty prompted their followers to take an active role in the 1860 campaign. David Davis to Abraham Lincoln, June 7, 1860, ser. 1, box 8, Davis Papers; Cyrus Edwards to Joseph Gillespie, July 4, 1860, Small Collections 558, box 27, Joseph Gillespie Papers, ALPL. Details of the Southern tour discussed in David Davis to Richard J. Oglesby, July 13, 1860, box 1, folder 10, Oglesby Family Papers, ALPL.

49. *Liberator* (Boston, MA), June 22, July 13, 1860; *Anti-Slavery Bugle* (Lisbon, OH), Oct. 6, 1860. It is important to note that Black abolitionist leaders outside of Illinois did not share Ford Douglas's sense of alienation and continued to work the Republicans. In New York, for example, Black leaders worked with radical state party leaders to place universal adult male suffrage on the ballot in 1860. Unfortunately, the referendum received only tacit support from more moderate leaders and rank-and-file Republicans, and the proposal was solidly rejected by voters at the November election, with only 36.4 percent in favor. Those same voters simultaneously awarded Lincoln the Empire State's electoral votes—53.7 percent. See Phyllis F. Field, *The Politics of Race in New York: The Struggle for Black Suffrage in the Civil War Era* (Ithaca: Cornell Univ. Press, 1982), 114–32. See also Leslie M. Alexander, *African or American? Black Identity and Political Activism in New York City, 1784–1861* (Urbana: Univ. of Illinois Press, 2008), 136–38.

50. Blackett, *Captive's Quest for Freedom*, 172–77; John Hossack, *Speech of John Hossack Convicted of Violation of the Fugitive Slave Law: Before Judge Drummond, of the U.S. District Court of Chicago* (Chicago: James Barnet, 1860), available at the Newberry Library, CARLI Digital Collections, https://collections.carli.illinois.edu/digital/collection/nby_chicago/id/5404. *Belvidere Standard,* Oct. 16, 23, 1860; *Illinois State Register* (Springfield), Oct. 10, 1860; *Illinois State Journal* (Springfield), Oct. 11, 1860; *Chicago Tribune,* Oct. 13, 1860; *Ottawa Free Trader,* Oct. 13, 1860.

51. Johannsen, *Stephen A. Douglas*, 776–96; *Woods Arguing until Doomsday*, 206–7; *Cairo City Gazette*, July 5, 1860. For Douglas's cooperation with Bell supporters, see Blaton Duncan to Stephen A. Douglas, Aug. 14, 1860, box 36, folder 5, Douglas Papers. See the attempt to remove a pro-Douglas mail agent in N. A. Goodrich et al. to John A. McClernand, Oct. 3, 1860, box 1, folder 14, McClernand Papers.

52. *Quincy Herald,* Sept. 17, 1860; *Rock Island Argus,* Sept. 21, 1860; D. Roberts to Stephen A. Douglas, Oct. 17, 1860, box 36, folder 11, Douglas Papers.

53. *Ottawa Free Trader,* Sept. 1, Oct. 6, 1860; *Illinois State Register* (Springfield), Oct. 25, 1860.

54. Johannsen, *Stephen A. Douglas*, 797–803; James L. Huston, "The 1860 Southern Sojourns of Stephen A. Douglas and the Irrepressible Separation," in Fuller, *Election of 1860 Reconsidered*, 46–51.

55. Holt, *Election of 1860*, 192–99.

56. Burnham, *Presidential Ballots*, 368–91.

57. Jon Grinspan, *The Virgin Vote: How Young Americans Made Democracy Social, Politics Personal, and Voting Popular in the Nineteenth Century* (Chapel Hill: Univ. of North Carolina Press, 2016), 1–3.

58. *Quincy Whig and Republican,* Nov. 10, 1860; *Chicago Press and Tribune,* Nov. 7, 1860; *Woodstock Sentinel,* Nov. 7, 1860; *Illinois State Journal* (Springfield), Nov. 7, 1860; *Pantagraph* (Bloomington), Nov. 7, 1860.

59. *Charleston Mercury,* Nov. 8, 1860; *Charleston Courier,* Nov. 8, 1860.

7. The Union in Peril

1. Smith, *Stormy Present*, 279.

2. My argument that Illinois Republicans and Democrats shared an unconditional commitment to the Union echoes the preeminent study of Northern politics during the secession crisis is Russell McClintock's *Lincoln and the Decision for War: The Northern Response to Secession* (Chapel Hill: Univ. of North Carolina Press, 2008). McClintock's study details the "bitter polarization" of the secession winter but emphasizes how the firing on Fort Sumter "laid bare the common Northern nationalism usually hidden by the fierce battles more typical of the political arena" (255–57). Although a first-class work of history in many respects, *Lincoln and the Decision for War* muddles ideological distinctions—intermixing terms like *radical* and *conservative* with more accurate ones like *hardliner* and *conciliationist*—and mischaracterizes the factions within the Illinois Republican Party, something this study seeks to correct. McClintock builds on a foundation Kenneth Stampp laid in *And the War Came: The North and the Secession Crisis, 1860–1861* (Baton Rouge: Louisiana State Univ. Press, 1950), which, while still helpful in many ways, shows its age after seven decades. William J. Cooper's *We Have the War upon Us: The Onset of the Civil War, November 1860–April 1861* (New York: Alfred A. Knopf, 2012) is another worthy study, but its characterization of Republicans as sectional radicals largely overlooks how most Republicans saw themselves. Nevertheless, Cooper's emphasis on the critical role of political leaders echoes the best of the so-called neo-revisionist tradition exemplified in David M. Potter's *Impending Crisis* and Michael F. Holt's *The Political Crisis of the 1850s*. Shearer Davis Bowman's *At the Precipice: Americans North and South during the Secession Crisis* (Chapel Hill: Univ. of North Carolina Press, 2010) provides excellent analysis of issues race and gender during the Secession Winter while Daniel W. Crofts's *Lincoln and the Politics of Slavery* accurately captures confusion and continency of the crisis in its examination of the Corwin Amendment.

3. *Chicago Tribune*, Nov. 7, 1860; *Illinois State Journal* (Springfield), Nov. 8, 1860; *Pantagraph* (Bloomington), Nov. 19, 1860. John Olney to Lyman Trumbull, Lyman Trumbull Correspondence, microfilm, reel 7, Library of Congress. For internecine battles over patronage and cabinet appointments within the Illinois Republican party, see McClintock, *Lincoln and the Decision for War*, 41–46.

4. *Illinois State Register* (Springfield), Nov. 7, 1860; *Rock Island Argus*, Nov. 9, 1860; "To Ninety-Six New Orleans Citizens," *Letters of Stephen A. Douglas*, 499–503.

5. John Abbot to Stephen A. Douglas, Nov. 14, 1860, box 36, folder 12, Stephen A. Douglas Papers, Hanna Holborn Gray Special Collections Research Center, University of Chicago Library; *Salem Advocate*, Nov. 22, 1860; *Illinois State Register* (Springfield), Nov. 24, 1860; *Quincy Herald*, Nov. 17, 1860.

6. J. J. Harvey to Stephen A. Douglas, Dec. 4, 1860, box 36, folder 15, Douglas Papers.

7. Buchanan's address printed in the *New York Herald*, Dec. 5, 1860; *Illinois State Register* (Springfield), Dec. 10, 1860; A. B. Darind to Stephen A. Douglas, Dec. 20, 1860, box 36, folder 23, Douglas Papers; *Ottawa Free Trader*, Dec. 8, 1860.

8. Allen Bainbridge to Stephen A. Douglas, Dec. 13, 1860, box 36, folder 19, Douglas Papers; Stanley, *Loyal West*, 45–45. See also Phillips, *Rivers Ran Backward*, 108–9.

9. Samuel Snowden Hayes to Stephen A. Douglas, Dec. 14, 1860, box 36, folder 19, Douglas Papers.

10. For details on the affective theory of Union as envisioned by both Northerners and Southerners, see Woods, *Emotional and Sectional Conflict*, 25–31. For Democratic fears that civil war would result in permanent disunion, see Joel H. Silbey, *A Respectable Minority: The Democratic Party in the Civil War Era* (New York: W. W. Norton, 1977), 37–38. Walter B. Scotes to Stephen A. Douglas, Dec. 17, 1860, box 36, folder 21, Douglas Papers.

11. For descriptions of Everett during the secession winters, see Mason, *Apostle of Union*, 264–66. For the disintegration of the pro-Breckinridge Democracy in the Upper South along pro-Union and pro-Secession lines, see Daniel Crofts, *Reluctant Confederates: Upper South Unionists in the Secession Crisis* (Chapel Hill: Univ. of North Carolina Press, 1989), 133–34. For examples of Deep South letters to Douglas, see Thomas J. Wiggin to Stephen A. Douglas, Nov. 25, 1860, box 36, folder 13, and J. A. Stewart to Stephen A. Douglas, Dec. 26, 1860, box 37, folder 1, both in Douglas Papers.

12. See, for example, *Rock Island Argus*, Dec. 12, 1860; *Quincy Herald*, Dec. 12, 1860; Smith, *Stormy Present*, 174; James W. Sheahan to Stephen A. Douglas, Dec. 17, 1860, box 36, folder 21, Douglas Papers; C. B. Phillips to John A. McClernand, Dec. 17, 1860, box 1, folder 14, John A. McClernand Papers, ALPL.

13. *Chicago Tribune*, Dec. 29, 1860. Cooper is especially critical of Republicans for their apparent moral intransigence; see *We Have the War upon Us*, 60–62. For a more balanced perspective that engages Illinois directly, see Crofts, *Lincoln and the Politics of Slavery*, 167–71. Although somewhat dated after eight decades, David M. Potter's *Lincoln and His Party in the Secession Crisis* (New Haven: Yale Univ. Press, 1942) still offers sharp insights into the skepticism of Republicans at the outset of the secession crisis and their surprise at the South's intransigence.

14. *Pantagraph* (Bloomington), Nov. 15, 1860; *Waukegan Gazette*, Nov. 17, 1860.

15. Passage Written for Lyman Trumbull's Speech at Springfield, Illinois, Nov. 20, 1860, in *Collected Works of Abraham Lincoln*, 4:141–43; Trumbull's and Yates' speeches, Nov. 20 printed in the *Illinois State Journal* (Springfield), Nov. 21, 22, 1860.

16. Johannsen, *Stephen A. Douglas*, 814–18; Woods, *Arguing until Doomsday*, 218–19; Crofts, *Reluctant Confederates*, 196–97; Isaiah A. Woodward, "Lincoln and the Crittenden Compromise," *Negro History Bulletin* 22 (Apr. 1959): 153–55. See also Quitt, *Stephen A. Douglas and Antebellum Democracy*, 170–72.

17. Daniel W. Crofts, "Secession Winter: William Henry Seward and the Decision for War," *New York History* 65 (July 1984): 229–56; McClintock, *Lincoln and the Decision for War*, 70–79. For Southern plans to seize the Caribbean and Central America as a slave empire, see Robert E. May, *The Southern Dream of a Caribbean Empire: 1854–1861* (Baton Rouge: Louisiana State Univ. Press, 1973); Matthew Karp, *This Vast Southern Empire: Slaveholders at the Helm of American Foreign Policy* (Cambridge, MA: Harvard Univ. Press, 2016).

18. *Chicago Tribune*, Dec. 24, 1860.

19. Elihu B. Washburne to Abraham Lincoln, Dec. 9, 1860, ser. 1, General Correspondence, 1833–1916, Abraham Lincoln Papers at the Library of Congress, https://www.loc.gov/resource/mal.0491700/?sp=1&r=-0.506,0.209,2.012,0.969,0; Abraham

Lincoln to Elihu B. Washburne, Dec. 13, 1860, *Collected Works of Abraham Lincoln,* 4:151; Burlingame, *Abraham Lincoln,* 1:708–10; Carwardine, *Lincoln,* 140–45; Freehling, Becoming Lincoln, 264–66. See also Charles Desmond Hard, "Why Lincoln Said 'No': Congressional Attitudes on Slavery Expansion, 1860–1861," *Social Science Quarterly* 49 (Dec. 1968): 732–41.

20. Elisha Smith to Lyman Trumbull, Dec. 12, 1860, Trumbull Correspondence, microfilm, reel 7; McClintock, *Lincoln and the Decision for War,* 94–95. For another example of a misleading Kentucky correspondent, see Samuel Haycraaft to Abraham Lincoln, Nov. 9, 1860, ser. 1, General Correspondence, 1833–1916, Abraham Lincoln Papers at the Library of Congress, https://www.loc.gov/resource/mal.0439100/?sp=1&r=-0.228,0.012,1.607,0.774,0.

21. *Belleville Advocate,* Dec. 21, 1860; *Illinois State Journal* (Springfield), Dec. 25, 27, 1860; *Waukegan Gazette,* Dec. 29, 1860.

22. John A. McClernand to Charles H. Lanphier, Dec. 10, 1860, box 1, folder 9, Charles Henry Lanphier Papers, ALPL; Freehling, *Road to Disunion,* 2:496–98. See also Stephen A. West, "Minute Men, Yeomen, and the Mobilization for Secession in the South Carolina Upcountry," *Journal of Southern History* 71 (Feb. 2005): 75–104.

23. Charles H. Lanphier to John A. McClernand, Dec. 19, 1860, box 1, folder 14, McClernand Papers; *Rock Island Argus,* Dec. 21, 1860; *Quincy Herald,* Dec. 21, 1860.

24. The Senate's Committee of Thirteen had been assigned by the main body to devise a compromise proposal and consisted of three Northern Democrats (including Douglas), five Republicans, Crittenden, and four Southern Democrats. Stephen A. Douglas to Charles H. Lanphier, Dec. 25, 1860, box 1, folder 9, Charles Henry Lanphier Papers, ALPL; Johannsen, *Stephen A. Douglas,* 818–19.

25. *Mount Carmel Democrat,* Jan. 4, 1861; *Illinois State Register* (Springfield), Jan. 15, 1861.

26. *Illinois State Journal* (Springfield), Dec. 12, 1860; *Quincy Whig and Republican,* Jan. 7, 1860.

27. *Belvidere Standard,* Jan. 8, 1861; *Salem Advocate,* Jan. 17, 1861; McClintock, *Lincoln and the Decision for War,* 129–36.

28. *Journal of the Senate of the Twenty-Second General Assembly of the State of Illinois* (Springfield: Bailhache & Baker, 1861), 16–18, 26–28, 67–68; *Illinois State Register* (Springfield), Jan. 16, 17, 1861.

29. Abraham Lincoln to William Kellogg, Dec. 11, 1860, *Collected Works of Abraham Lincoln,* 4:150; Cong. Globe, 36th Cong., 2nd Sess., 690–91, 1259 (1861); *Speech of Hon. Wm. Kellogg of Illinois in Favor of the Union Delivered in the House of Representatives, Feb. 8, 1861* (Washington, DC: Lemuel Towers, 1861); McClintock, *Lincoln and the Decision for War,* 160–63; Eckley, *Lincoln's Forgotten Friend,* 87–92.

30. *Chicago Tribune,* Feb. 9, 1861; *Chicago Democrat,* Feb. 9, 1861; quotation from the *Chicago Journal* reprinted in the *Illinois State Register* (Springfield), Feb. 9, 1861; Freehling, *Becoming Lincoln,* 264–65; *Pantagraph* (Bloomington), Feb. 23, 1861, *Rock Island Argus,* Feb. 25, 1861.

31. *Ottawa Free Trader,* Feb. 9, 1861; John A. McClernand to Charles H. Lanphier, Feb. 8, 1861, box 1, folder 10, Lanphier Papers; *Rock Island Argus,* Feb. 13, 1861; Johannsen, *Stephen A. Douglas,* 834–36. For more on the Washington Peace Conference,

see Cooper, *We Have the War upon Us*, 173–83; McClintock, *Lincoln and the Decision for War*, 183–85. See also Mark Tooley, *The Peace That Almost Was: The Forgotten Story of the 1861 Washington Peace Conference and the Final Attempt to Avert the Civil War* (Nashville: Thomas Nelson, 2015).

32. Feb. 9, 1861, *Diary of Orville Hickman Browning*, 453; Speech from the Balcony at the Bates House in Indianapolis, Indiana, Feb. 11, 1861, and address to the New Jersey General Assembly at Trenton, Feb. 21, 1861, both in *Collected Works of Abraham Lincoln*, 4:194–96, 236–37. Ted Widmer's *Lincoln on the Verge: Thirteen Days to Washington* (New York: Simon & Schuster, 2020) offers a helpful day-by-day account of the journey to Washington. Harold Holzer also provides an insightful narrative overview of the larger interregnum period in *Lincoln President-Elect: Abraham Lincoln and the Great Secession Winter, 1860–1861* (New York: Simon & Schuster, 2008). See also Burlingame, *Abraham Lincoln*, 2:4–51; Freehling, *Becoming Lincoln*, 273–79.

33. *Illinois State Journal* (Springfield), Feb. 15, 1861; *Illinois State Register* (Springfield), Feb. 22, 1861.

34. John A. McClernand to Charles H. Lanphier, Feb. 14, 1861, box 1, folder 10 Lanphier Papers; *Illinois State Register* (Springfield), Feb. 18, 1861; Johannsen, *Stephen A. Douglas*, 841–42.

35. First Inaugural Address—First and Revised Editions, Mar. 4, 1861, and First Inaugural Address—Final Text, both in *Collected Works of Abraham Lincoln*, 4:249–62, 262–71; Crofts, *Lincoln and the Politics of Slavery*, 231–37.

36. First Inaugural Address—Final Text, 262–71.

37. *Belvidere Standard*, Mar. 12, 1861; *Waukegan Gazette*, Mar. 9, 1861; *Chicago Tribune*, Mar. 5, 1861; *Quincy Whig and Republican*, Mar. 9, 1861.

38. Johannsen, *Stephen A. Douglas*, 844; Cong. Globe, 37th Cong., Special Session of the Senate, 1437–38 (1861). *Illinois State Register* (Springfield), Mar. 6, 1861; *Joliet Signal*, Mar. 12, 1861; *Rock Island Argus*, Mar. 6, 1861; *Ottawa Free Trader*, Mar. 9, 1861.

39. *Douglass' Monthly* (Rochester, NY), Apr. 1861; *Liberator* (Boston), Mar. 8, 1861.

40. McClintock, *Lincoln and the Decision for War*, 202–5; Cooper, *We Have the War upon Us*, 229–30.

41. McClintock, *Lincoln and the Decision for War*, 211–12; Cong. Globe, 37th Cong., Senate—Special Sess., 1142; *Ottawa Free Trader*, Mar. 16, 1861; *Belvidere Standard*, Mar. 19, 1861.

42. *Chicago Tribune*, Mar. 21, 1861.

43. Stephen A. Hurlbut to Abraham Lincoln, Mar. 27, 1861, ser. 1. General Correspondence, 1833–1916, Abraham Lincoln Papers at the Library of Congress, https://www.loc.gov/resource/ma1.0838800/?sp=5&r=-0.975,0.074,2.95,1.436,0; McClintock, *Lincoln and the Decision for War*, 241–44; Burlingame, *Abraham Lincoln*, 105, 123–25; Bowman, *At the Precipice*, 279–82.

44. McPherson, *Battle Cry of Freedom*, 273–75.

45. For example, in his magisterial *Battle Cry of Freedom*, James M. McPherson devotes only two paragraphs to the Northern reaction to Fort Sumter, while he examines the Upper South for an entire chapter (274–75). Similarly, while Ed Ayers offers a bit more attention to the North than does McPherson in his award-winning book *In the Presence of Mine Enemies*, his focus remains primarily on the South and on the logistics of Union (150–87).

46. See Oakes, *Freedom National*, 78–83 and Chandra Manning, *What This Cruel War Was Over: Soldiers, Slavery and the Civil War* (New York: Alfred A. Knopf, 2007), 44–45.

47. See Susan-Mary Grant, *North over South: Northern Nationalism and American Identity in the Antebellum* Era (Lawrence: Univ. Press of Kansas, 2002) and Melinda Lawson, *Patriot Fires: Forging a New American Nationalism in the Civil War North* (Lawrence: Univ. Press of Kansas, 2002).

48. Gallagher, *Union War*; Smith, *Stormy Present*, 179; Elizabeth R. Varon, *Armies of Deliverance: A New History of the Civil War* (New York: Oxford Univ. Press, 2019), 2–15.

49. McClintock, *Lincoln and the Decision for War*, 280; Stanley, *Loyal West*, 47–53; Phillips, *Rivers Ran Backward*, 126.

50. *Illinois State Journal* (Springfield), Apr. 13, 15, 1861; *Ottawa Republican*, Apr. 13, 1861; *Chicago Tribune*, Apr. 15, 1861. See also *Naperville Sentinel*, Apr. 18, 1861; *Tazewell Republican* (Perkin, IL), Apr. 19, 1861; *Chicago Democrat*, Apr. 20, 1861.

51. *Rock Island Argus*, Apr. 15, 1861; *Illinois State Register* (Springfield), Apr. 15, 1861; *Galena Courier*, n.d., reprinted in the *Quincy Herald*, Apr. 17, 1861.

52. Statement, Apr. 14, 1861, and Stephen A. Douglas to James L. Faucett, Apr. 17, 1861, both in *Letters of Stephen A. Douglas*, 509, 510; Johannsen, *Stephen A. Douglas*, 559–60. Historian Matthew Norman has cogently argued that this moment revealed that for all their political differences, "Lincoln and Douglas believed the Constitution established a system of government that essentially obviated the necessity for revolution" and thus put aside their differences to sustain the Union in the face of an unjustifiable rebellion. See Matthew Norman, "Abraham Lincoln, Stephen A. Douglas, the Model Republic, and the Right of Revolution, 1848–1861," in *Politics and Culture in the Civil War Era: Essays in Honor of Robert W. Johannsen,* ed. Daniel McDonough and Kenneth W. Noe (Selinsgrove, PA: Susquehanna Univ. Press, 2006), 154–77.

53. John A. McClernand to Abraham Lincoln, Apr. 10, 1861, box 2, folder 2, McClernand Papers.

54. *Joliet Signal*, Apr. 16, 23, 1861; *Peoria Democratic Union*, Apr. 14, 18, 1861.

55. David Davis to George P. Davis, Apr. 22, 1861, Box 8, Folder 5, David Davis Family Papers, ALPL.

Epilogue

1. Stephen A. Douglas, *Speech of Senator Douglas before the Legislature of Illinois, April 25, 1861, in Compliance with a Joint Resolution of the two Houses* (N.p.: n.p., 1861), 1–3, 5, 8.

2. *Illinois State Journal* (Springfield), Apr. 26, 1861; *Illinois State Register* (Springfield), Apr. 26, 1861; *New York Times*, Apr. 28, 1861; *Douglass' Monthly* (Rochester, NY), May 1861.

3. Apr. 25, 26, 1861, *Diary of Orville Hickman Browning*, 465–66; Plummer, *Lincoln's Rail-Splitter*, 63; Richard J. Oglesby to Benjamin M. Prentiss, May 18, 1861, ser. 1, box 2, folder 1, Oglesby Family Papers, ALPL. Richard Yates to John A. McClernand, May 18, 1861, box 2, folder 2, John A. McClernand Papers, ALPL; Richard L. Kiper, *Major General John Alexander McClernand: Politician in Uniform* (Kent, OH: Kent State Univ. Press, 1999), 19–25; Victor Hicken, *Illinois in the Civil War*, 2nd ed. (Urbana: Univ.

of Illinois Press, 1991), 5; James P. Jones, *"Black Jack": John A. Logan and Southern Illinois in the Civil War Era* (Tallahassee: Florida State Univ. Studies, 1967), 77–90; McClintock, *Lincoln and the Decision for War*, 267–69; Stanley, *Loyal West*, 48–49; Etcheson, *Emerging Midwest*, 137–39; Philips, *Rivers Ran Backward*, 128–29; Smith, *No Party Now*, 37; Ron Chernow, *Grant* (New York: Penguin, 2017), 138. See also Robert I. Girardi, "Illinois' First Response to the Civil War," *Journal of the Illinois State Historical Society* 105 (Summer–Fall 2012): 167–72.

4. Stephen A. Douglas to Virgil Hickox, May 10, 1861, *Letters of Stephen A. Douglas*, 511; Johannsen, *Stephen A. Douglas*, 865–74.

5. *Illinois State Register* (Springfield), June 4, 1861; *Chicago Democrat*, June 8, 1861; Carwardine, *Lincoln*, 166.

6. For studies of Northern Democrats and party conflict during the Civil War, see Silbey, *Respectable Minority*; Mark E. Neely Jr., *The Union Divided: Party Conflict in the Civil War North* (Cambridge, MA: Harvard Univ. Press, 2002); Mark E. Neely Jr., *Lincoln and the Democrats: The Politics of Opposition in the Civil War* (New York: Cambridge Univ. Press, 2017); J. Matthew Gallman, *The Cacophony of Politics: Northern Democrats and the American Civil War* (Charlottesville: Univ. of Virginia Press, 2021). For party conflict in Illinois in the leadup to the 1862 midterms, see Bruce Tap, "Race, Rhetoric, and Emancipation: The Election of 1862 in Illinois," *Civil War History* 39 (June 1993):101–25; Bruce S. Allardice, "'Illinois Is Rotten with Traitors': The Republican Defeat in the 1862 State Election," *Journal of the Illinois State Historical Society*, 104, nos. 1–2 (2011): 97–114.

7. Woods, *Arguing until Doomsday*, 222–23; Douglas, *Speech of Senator Douglas before the Legislature of Illinois*, 4.

BIBLIOGRAPHY

Manuscript and Archival Sources

Abraham Lincoln Presidential Library (ALPL)
    Bailhache-Brayman Families Papers
    Sidney Breese Papers
    Orville Hickman Browning Papers
    R. B. Carpenter Letter
    David Davis Family Papers
    Joseph T. Eccles Papers
    Joseph Gillespie Papers
    Ozias Mather Hatch Papers
    Charles Henry Lanphier Papers
    John McAuley Palmer Papers
    John A. McClernand Papers
    Oglesby Family Papers
    Lyman Trumbull Family Papers
    Yates Family Papers
Chicago History Museum
    David Davis Papers
Library of Congress
    Lyman Trumbull Correspondence
University of Chicago, Hanna Holborn Gray Special Collections Research Center
    Stephen A. Douglas Papers
University of Illinois Urbana–Champaign, Illinois History and Lincoln Collections
    Elihu B. Washburne Papers
University of Michigan, William Clements L. Library
    Owen Lovejoy Papers

Digitally Accessible Primary Sources

Abraham Lincoln Papers at the Library of Congress, https://www.loc.gov/collections/abraham-lincoln-papers/

Elihu B. Washburne Papers at the Library of Congress, https://www.loc.gov/collections/e-b-washburne-papers/

Kansas Memory. Kansas Historical Society, https://www.kshs.org/portal_kansas_memory

Louisiana Digital Library, https://louisianadigitallibrary.org

Newberry Library, CARLI Digital Collections, https://collections.carli.illinois.edu/digital/collection/nby_chicago/id/5404

New-York Historical Society Digital Collections, New-York Historical Society Museum & Library, https://digitalcollections.nyhistory.org/islandora/object/islandora%3Aroot

100 Most Valuable Documents at the Illinois State Archives: The Online Exhibit, Office of the Illinois Secretary of State, https://www.ilsos.gov/departments/archives/online_exhibits/100_documents/main-menu.html

Presidential Speeches, Miller Center, University of Virginia, https://millercenter.org/the-presidency/presidential-speeches

Woolley, John, and Gerhard Peters. *The American Presidency Project*, University of California Santa Barbara, https://www.presidency.ucsb.edu

Edited Collections of Primary Sources

Browning, Orville Hickman. *The Diary of Orville Hickman Browning*, edited by Theodore Calvin Pease. Springfield: *Illinois State Historical* Society, 1925.

Douglas, Stephen. *The Letters of Stephen A. Douglas*, edited by Robert. W. Johannsen. Urbana: Univ. of Illinois Press, 1961.

Johannsen, Robert W, ed. *The Lincoln–Douglas Debates*. New York: Oxford Univ. Press, 1965.

Lincoln, Abraham. *The Collected Works of Abraham Lincoln*. 9 vols, edited by Roy P. Basler. New Brunswick, NJ: Rutgers Univ. Press, 1953.

———. *Collected Works of Abraham Lincoln: First Supplement, 1832–1865*, edited by Roy P. Basler. Westport, CT: Greenwood Press, 1973.

Trumbull, Lyman. "A Collection of Letters from Lyman Trumbull to John M. Palmer, 1854–1858," edited by George T. Palmer. *Journal of the Illinois State Historical Society* 16 (Apr.–July 1923): 20–41.

Published Primary Sources

Chase, Salmon P., Charles Sumner, Joshua Giddings, Edward Wade, Gerrit Smith, and Alexander De Witt. *Appeal of the Independent Democrats in Congress to the People of the United States: Shall Slavery Be Permitted in Nebraska?* Washington, DC: Towers' Printers, 1854.

Clerk of the House of Representatives, *Abstract of the Returns of the Fifth Census*. Washington, DC: Duff Green, 1832.

Congressional Globe

Douglas, Stephen A. *Speech of Senator Douglas before the Legislature of Illinois, April 25, 1861, in Compliance with a Joint Resolution of the two Houses*. N.p.: n.p., 1861.
Helper, Hinton R. *The Impending Crisis of the South: How to Meet It*. New York: A. B. Burdick, 1859.
Journal of the House of Representatives of the Nineteenth General Assembly of the State of Illinois. Springfield: Lanphier & Walker, 1855.
Journal of the House of Representatives of the Twentieth General Assembly of the State of Illinois. Springfield: Lanphier & Walker, 1857.
Journal of the Senate of the Twenty-Second General Assembly of the State of Illinois. Springfield: Bailhache & Baker, 1861.
Kellogg, William. *Speech of Hon. Wm. Kellogg of Illinois in Favor of the Union Delivered in the House of Representatives, Feb. 8, 1861*. Washington, DC: Lemuel Towers, 1861.
Kennedy, Joseph C. *Population of the United States in 1860*. Washington, DC: GPO, 1864.
Parkhurst, John G. *Official Proceedings of the Democratic National Convention, Held in 1860, at Charleston and Baltimore, Proceedings at Charleston, April 23–May 3*. Cleveland: Nevins' Print, 1860.
Proceedings of the State Convention of Colored Citizens of the State of Illinois. Chicago: Hays & Thompson, 1856.
Scott, Walter. "The Massacre of Glencoe." In *The Poetical Works of Sir Walter Scott*. Edinburgh: Archibald Constable & Co., 1821.
Stewart, Alvan. *A Legal Argument before the Supreme Court of the State of New Jersey for the Deliverance of 4,000 Persons from Bondage*. New York: Finch & Weed, 1845.
Sumner, Charles. *The Crime against Kansas—The Apologies for the Crime—The True Remedy*. Boston: John P. Jewett & Co., 1856.
Taney, Roger B. *The Dred Scott Decision: Opinion of Chief Justice Taney with an Introduction by Dr. J. H. Van Evrie*. New York: Van Evrie, Horton, & Co., 1860.
The Tribune Almanac for the Years 1838 to 1868, inclusive. 30 vols. New York: New-York Tribune, 1868.
United States Census, 1840.
United States Census, 1850.
United States Census, 1860.
Williams, Roger. *A Short Review of the Illinois Know Nothing Platform*. Petersburg, IL: H. L. Clay, 1855.

Newspapers

Connecticut
    Hartford Courant
Illinois
    Alton Courier
    Alton Telegraph / Alton Telegraph and Democratic Review
    Belleville Advocate
    Belvidere Standard
    Bloomington Intelligencer
    Cairo City Gazette

Cairo City Times
Capital Enterprise (Springfield)
Carbondale Transcript
Central Transcript (Clinton)
Chicago Democrat
Chicago Herald
Chicago Journal
Chicago Times
Chicago Tribune / Chicago Press and Tribune
Congregational Herald (Chicago)
Conservative (Springfield)
Dewitt Courier (Clinton)
Freemonter (Dixon)
Freeport Bulletin
Freeport Journal
Galena Courier
Illinois State Chronicle (Decatur)
Illinois Journal / Illinois State Journal (Springfield)
Illinois State Register (Springfield)
Illinois Staats Zeitung (Chicago)
Joliet Signal
Jonesboro Gazette
Moline Workman
Mount Carmel Register / Democrat
Naperville Sentinel
Olney Press
Olney Times
Ottawa Free Trader
Ottawa Republican
Pantagraph (Bloomington)
Peoria Democratic Union
Peoria News
Peru Chronicle
Rock Island Republican / Republican/ Rock Island Argus / Islander and Argus (Rock Island)
Quincy Herald
Quincy Whig / Quincy Whig and Republican
Randolph County Democrat (Chester)
Rockford Register
Rushville Times
Salem Advocate
Tazewell Republican (Perkin)
Times and Delta (Cairo)
Waukegan Gazette
Western Whig (Bloomington)
Woodstock Sentinel

Kentucky
  Louisville Journal
Massachusetts
  Boston Transcript
  Liberator (Boston)
Missouri
  Missouri Democrat (St. Louis)
New York
  Douglass' Monthly (Rochester)
  Frederick Douglass' Paper (Rochester)
  National Anti-Slavery Standard (New York)
  New York Herald
  New York Times
  New-York Tribune
  Poughkeepsie Eagle
Ohio
  Anti-Slavery Bugle (Lisbon)
Pennsylvania
  Pittsburgh Gazette
South Carolina
  Charleston Courier
  Charleston Mercury
Vermont
  Vermont Phoenix (Brattleboro)
Washington, DC
  National Era
  National Intelligencer
  Republic

Unpublished Dissertations and Theses

Dowrie, George William. "The Development of Banking in Illinois, 1817–1863." PhD diss. Univ. of Illinois, 1913.

Rothman, Joshua D. "'But How and in What Balance Weigh John Brown': Northern Reactions to John Brown's Raid," MA thesis, Univ. of Virginia, 1995.

Books, Articles, and Chapters

Abraham, Henry Julian. *Justices, Presidents, and Senators: A History of the U.S. Supreme Court from Washington to Clinton*, 3rd ed. Lanham, MD: Rowman & Littlefield, 1999.

Alexander, Leslie M. *African or American? Black Identity and Political Activism in New York City, 1784–1861*. Urbana: Univ. of Illinois Press, 2008.

Allardice, Bruce S. "'Illinois Is Rotten with Traitors': The Republican Defeat in the 1862 State Election." *Journal of the Illinois State Historical Society* 104, nos. 1–2 (2011): 97–114.

Allit, Patrick. *The Conservatives: Ideas and Personalities Throughout American History*. New Haven: Yale Univ. Press, 2009.

Altschuler, Glenn C., and Stuart M. Blumin, *Rude Republic: Americans and Their Politics in the Nineteenth Century*. Princeton, NJ: Princeton Univ. Press, 2000.

Anbinder, Tyler. *Nativism and Slavery: The Northern Know Nothings and the Politics of the 1850s*. New York: Oxford Univ. Press, 1992.

Ankli, Robert E. "Agricultural Growth in Antebellum Illinois." *Journal of the Illinois State Historical Society* 63 (Winter 1970): 387–98.

Atack, Jeremy, Matthew Jaremski, and Peter L. Rousseau. "American Banking and the Transportation Revolution before the Civil War." *Journal of Economic History* 74 (Dec. 2014): 943–86.

Ayers, Edward. *In the Presence of Mine Enemies: The Civil War in the Heart of America, 1859–1863*. New York: W. W. Norton, 2003.

Baker, Jean H. *Affairs of Party: The Political Culture of Northern Democrats in the Mid-Nineteenth Century*, 2nd ed. New York: Fordham Univ. Press, 1998.

Baxter, Maurice G. *Orville H. Browning: Lincoln's Friend and Critic*. Bloomington: Indiana Univ. Press, 1957.

Baum, Dale. "Know-Nothingism and Republican Majority in Massachusetts: The Political Realignment of the 1850s." *Journal of American History* 64 (Mar. 1979): 959–86.

Bearden-White, Christina. "Illinois Germans and the Coming of the Civil War: Reshaping Ethnic Identity." *Journal of the Illinois State Historical Society* 109 (Fall 2016): 231–51.

Becker, Carl. "The Unit Rule in National Nominating Conventions." *American Historical Review* 5 (Oct. 1899): 64–82.

Bellows, Barbara L. "Of Time and the City: Charleston in 1860." *South Carolina Historical Magazine* 112, (July–Oct. 2011): 157–72.

Belting, Paul E. "The Development of the Free Public High School in Illinois to 1860." *Journal of the Illinois State Historical Society* 11 (Jan. 1919): 500–512.

Berwanger, Eugene H. *The Frontier against Slavery: Western Anti-Negro Prejudice and the Slavery Extension Controversy*. Urbana: Univ. of Illinois Press, 1967.

Bilotta, James D. *Race and the Rise of the Republican Party, 1848–1865*. New York: Peter Lang, 1992.

Binder, John J. "The Transportation Revolution and Antebellum Sectional Disagreement." *Social Science History* 35 (Spring 2011): 23–37.

Blackett, Richard J. M. *The Captive's Quest for Freedom: Fugitive Slaves, the 1850 Fugitive Slave Law, and the Politics of Slavery*. New York: Cambridge Univ. Press, 2018.

Blight, David. *Frederick Douglass: Prophet of Freedom*. New York: Simon & Schuster, 2018.

Blocker, Jack S. Jr. *American Temperance Movements: Cycles of Reform*. Boston: Twayne, 1989.

Blumenthal, Sidney. *All the Powers of the Earth: The Political Life of Abraham Lincoln, 1856–1860*. New York: Simon & Schuster, 2019.

Bowman, Shearer Davis. *At the Precipice: Americans North and South during the Secession Crisis*. Chapel Hill: Univ. of North Carolina Press, 2010.

Bridges, Robert D. "Antebellum Struggles for Citizenship." *Journal of the Illinois State Historical Society* 108 (Fall–Winter 2015): 296–321.

Brooks, Corey M. *Liberty Power: Antislavery Third Parties and the Transformation of American Politics*. Chicago: Univ. of Chicago Press, 2016.

Brown, Charles Leroy. "Abraham Lincoln and the Illinois Central Railroad." *Journal of the Illinois State Historical Society* 36 (June 1943): 121–63.
Brown, Nicholas A., and Sarah E. Kanouse. *Re-Collecting Black Hawk: Landscape, Memory, and Power in the American Midwest.* Pittsburgh: Univ. of Pittsburgh Press, 2015.
Burke, Eric Michael. "Egyptian Darkness: Antebellum Reconstruction, 'Republicanization,' and Southern Illinois in the Republican Imagination, 1854–61." *Civil War History* 67 (Sept. 2021): 167–99.
Burlingame, Michael. *Abraham Lincoln: A Life.* 2 vols. Baltimore: Johns Hopkins Univ. Press, 2008.
Burnham, J. H. *History of Bloomington and Normal in McLean County, Illinois.* Bloomington, IL: J. H. Burnham, 1879.
Burnham, Walter Dean. *Presidential Ballots, 1836–1892.* Baltimore: Johns Hopkins Univ. Press, 1955.
Burt, John. *Lincoln's Tragic Pragmatism: Lincoln, Douglas, and Moral Conflict.* Cambridge, MA: Harvard Univ. Press, 2013.
Calhoon, Robert McCluer. *Political Moderation in America's First Two Centuries.* New York: Cambridge Univ. Press, 2009.
Calomiris, Charles W., and Larry Schweikart. "The Panic of 1857: Origins, Transmission, and Containment." *Journal of Economic History* 51 (Dec. 1991): 807–34.
Campney, Brent M. S. *Hostile Heartland: Racism, Repression, and Resistance in the Midwest.* Urbana: Univ. of Illinois Press, 2019.
———. "'The Peculiar Climate of This Region': The 1854 Cairo Lynching and the Historiography of Racist Violence against Blacks in Illinois." *Journal of the Illinois State Historical Society* 107 (Summer 2014): 143–70.
Carwardine, Richard J. *Evangelicals and Politics in Antebellum America,* 2nd ed. Knoxville: Univ. of Tennessee Press, 1997.
———. *Lincoln: A Life of Purpose and Power.* New York: Alfred A. Knopf, 2006.
Chernow, Ron. *Grant.* New York: Penguin, 2017.
Cicero, Frank Jr. *Creating the Land of Lincoln: The History and Constitutions of Illinois, 1778–1870.* Champaign: Univ. of Illinois Press, 2015.
Collins, Bruce. "The Lincoln-Douglas Contest of 1858 and Illinois' Electorate." *Journal of American Studies* 20 (Dec. 1986): 391–420.
Conlin, Michael F. "Dangerous *Isms* and Fanatical *Ists:* Antebellum Conservatives in the South and North Confront the Modernist Conspiracy." *Journal of the Civil War Era* 4 (June 2014): 205–33.
Cooper, William J. *We Have the War upon Us: The Onset of the Civil War, November 1860–April 1861.* New York: Alfred A. Knopf, 2012.
Cordery, Simon. *The Iron Road in the Prairie State: The Story of Illinois Railroading.* Bloomington: Univ. of Indiana Press, 2016.
Corin, Edward S. "The Dred Scott Decision, in Light of Contemporary Legal Doctrine." *American Historical Review* 17 (Oct. 1911): 52–69.
Crofts, Daniel W. *Lincoln and the Politics of Slavery: The Other Thirteenth Amendment and the Struggle to Save the Union.* Chapel Hill: Univ. of North Carolina Press, 2016.
———. *Reluctant Confederates: Upper South Unionists in the Secession Crisis.* Chapel Hill: Univ. of North Carolina Press, 1989.

———. "Secession Winter: William Henry Seward and the Decision for War." *New York History* 65 (July 1984): 229–56.

Cronon, William. *Nature's Metropolis: Chicago and the Great West.* New York: W. W. Norton, 1991.

Cunningham, J. O. "The Bloomington Convention of 1856 and Those Who Participated in It." *Transactions of the Illinois State Historical Society* 10 (1906): 101–10.

Davis, Rodney O. "Dr. Charles Lieb: Lincoln's Mole?" *Journal of the Abraham Lincoln Association* 24 (Summer 2003): 20–35.

Dean, Adam Wesley Dean. *An Agrarian Republic: Farming, Antislavery Politics, and Nature Parks in the Civil War Era.* Chapel Hill: Univ. of North Carolina Press, 2015.

Dillon, Merton Lynn. "The Antislavery Movement in Illinois: 1824–1835." *Journal of the Illinois State Historical Society* 47, No. 2 (Summer 1954): 149–66.

Donald, David Herbert. *Lincoln.* New York: Simon & Schuster, 1996.

Drache, Hiram M. "The Impact of John Deere's Plow." *Illinois History Teacher* 8, no. 1 (2001): 2–13.

Earle, Johnathan H. *Jacksonian Antislavery and the Politics of Free Soil.* Chapel Hill: Univ. of North Carolina Press, 2004.

Ecelbarger, Gary. *The Great Comeback: How Abraham Lincoln Beat the Odds to Win the 1860 Republican Nomination.* New York: Thomas Dunne Books, 2008.

Eckley, Robert S. *Lincoln's Forgotten Friend, Leonard Swett.* Carbondale: Southern Illinois Univ. Press, 2012.

Egerton, Douglas R. *Year of the Meteors: Stephen Douglas, Abraham Lincoln, and the Election that Brought on the Civil War.* New York: Bloomsbury, 2010.

Efford, Alison Clark. *German Immigrants, Race, and Citizenship in the Civil War Era.* New York: German Historical Institute and Cambridge Univ. Press, 2013.

Einhorn, Robin L. *Property Rules: Political Economy in Chicago, 1833–1872.* Chicago: Univ. of Chicago Press, 1991.

Etcheson, Nicole. *Bleeding Kansas: Contested Liberty in the Civil War Era.* Lawrence: Univ. Press of Kansas, 2004.

———. *The Emerging Midwest: Upland Southerners and the Political Culture of the Old Northwest, 1787–1861.* Bloomington: Indiana Univ. Press, 1996.

———. "'A Living, Creeping Lie': Abraham Lincoln on Popular Sovereignty." *Journal of the Abraham Lincoln Association* 29 (Summer 2008): 1–25.

Eyal, Yonatan. *The Young America Movement and the Transformation of the Democratic Party.* New York: Cambridge Univ. Press, 2007.

———. "With His Eyes Open: Stephen A. Douglas and the Kansas-Nebraska Disaster of 1854." *Journal of the Illinois State Historical Society* 91 (Winter 1998): 175–217.

Fehrenbacher, Don E. *Chicago Giant: A Biography of "Long John" Wentworth.* Madison: American History Research Center, 1957.

———. *The Dred Scott Case: Its Significance in American Law and Politics.* New York: Oxford Univ. Press, 1978.

———. "The Judd–Wentworth Feud." *Journal of the Illinois State Historical Society* 45 (Autumn 1952): 197–211.

———. "The Post Office in Illinois Politics of the 1850's." *Journal of the Illinois State Historical Society* 46 (Spring 1953): 60–70.

———. *Prelude to Greatness: Lincoln in the 1850s*. Palo Alto, CA: Stanford Univ. Press, 1962.
Field, Phyllis F. *The Politics of Race in New York: The Struggle for Black Suffrage in the Civil War Era*. Ithaca, NY: Cornell Univ. Press, 1982.
Finkelman, Paul. *An Imperfect Union: Slavery, Federalism, and Comity*. Chapel Hill: Univ. of North Carolina Press, 1981.
———. *Supreme Injustice: Slavery in the Nation's Highest Court*. Cambridge, MA: Harvard Univ. Press, 2018.
———, ed. *His Soul Goes Marching On: Responses to John Brown and the Harpers Ferry Raid*. Charlottesville: Univ. of Virginia Press, 1995.
Foner, Eric. *The Fiery Trial: Abraham Lincoln and American Slavery*. New York: W. W. Norton, 2010.
———. *Free Soil, Free Labor, Free Men: The Ideology of the Republican Party before the Civil War*. 2nd ed. New York, Oxford Univ. Press, 1995.
———. "Politics and Prejudice: The Free Soil Party and the Negro, 1849–1852." *Journal of Negro History* 50 (Oct. 1965): 239–56.
Ford, Bridget. *Bonds of Union: Religion, Race, and Politics in a Civil War Borderland*. Chapel Hill: Univ. of North Carolina Press, 2016.
Formisano, Ronald P. "The 'Party Period' Revisited." *Journal of American History* 86 (June 1999): 93–120.
Freehling, William W. *Becoming Lincoln*. Charlottesville: Univ. of Virginia Press, 2018.
———. *The Road to Disunion*. Vol. 2, *Secessionists Triumphant*. New York: Oxford Univ. Press, 2007.
Freeman, Joanne B. *The Field of Blood: Violence in Congress and the Road to Civil War*. New York: Farrar, Straus & Giroux, 2018.
Fuller A. James, ed. *The Election of 1860 Reconsidered*. Kent, OH: Kent State Univ. Press, 2013.
Furniss, Jack. "Devolved Democracy: Federalism and the Party Politics of the Late Antebellum North." *Journal of the Civil War Era* 9 (Dec. 2019): 546–68.
Gallagher, Gary. *The Union War*. Cambridge, MA: Harvard Univ. Press, 2011.
Gallman, J. Matthew. *The Cacophony of Politics: Northern Democrats and the American Civil War*. Charlottesville: Univ. of Virginia Press, 2021.
Gara, Larry. "Slavery and the Slave Power: A Key Distinction." *Civil War History* 15 (Mar. 1969): 5–18.
Garrison, Zachary Stuart. *German Americans on the Middle Border: From Antislavery to Reconciliation, 1830–1877*. Carbondale: Southern Illinois Univ. Press, 2020.
Gates, Paul Wallace, "Large-Scale Farming in Illinois, 1850 to 1870." *Agricultural History* 6, no. 1 (1932): 14–25.
Graber, Mark A. *Dred Scott and the Problem of Constitutional Evil*. New York: Cambridge Univ. Press, 2006.
Gienapp, William E. "The Crime against Sumner: The Caning of Charles Sumner and the Rise of the Republican Party." *Civil War History* 25 (Sept. 1979): 218–45.
———. "Nativism and the Creation of a Republican Majority in the North before the Civil War." *Journal of American History* 72 (Dec. 1985): 529–59.
———. *The Origins of the Republican Party, 1852–1856*. New York: Oxford Univ. Press, 1987.
Girardi, Robert I. "Illinois' First Response to the Civil War." *Journal of the Illinois State Historical Society* 105 (Summer–Fall 2012): 167–72.

Goodwin, Doris Kearns. *Team of Rivals: The Political Genius of Abraham Lincoln.* New York: Simon & Schuster, 2009.
Grant, Susan-Mary. *North over South: Northern Nationalism and American Identity in the Antebellum Era.* Lawrence: Univ. Press of Kansas, 2002.
Green, Steven K. *The Second Disestablishment: Church and State in Nineteenth-Century America.* New York: Oxford Univ. Press, 2010.
Greenberg, Amy S. *Manifest Manhood and the Antebellum American Empire.* New York: Cambridge Univ. Press, 2005.
Grimsted, David. *American Mobbing, 1828–1861: Toward Civil War.* New York: Oxford Univ. Press, 1998.
Grinspan, Jon. *The Virgin Vote: How Young Americans Made Democracy Social, Politics Personal, and Voting Popular in the Nineteenth Century.* Chapel Hill: Univ. of North Carolina Press, 2016.
Guelzo, Allen C. "Houses Divided: Lincoln, Douglas, and the Political Landscape of 1858." *Journal of American History* 94 (Sept. 2007): 391–417.
———. *Lincoln and Douglas: The Debates That Defined America.* New York: Simon & Schuster, 2008.
Hall, John W. *Uncommon Defense: Indian Allies in the Black Hawk War.* Cambridge, MA: Harvard Univ. Press, 2009.
Hammond, John Craig. "Midcontinent Borderlands: Illinois and the Early American Republic, 1774–1854." *Journal of the Illinois State Historical Society* 111 (Spring–Summer 2017): 31–54.
———. *Slavery, Expansion, and Freedom in the Early American West.* Charlottesville: Univ. of Virginia Press, 2007.
Hansen, Stephen L. *The Making of the Third Party System: Voters and Parties in Illinois, 1850–1876.* Ann Arbor: UMI Research Press, 1980.
Hansen, Stephen L., and Paul Nygard. "Stephen A. Douglas, the Know-Nothings, and the Democratic Party in Illinois, 1854–1858." *Illinois Historical Journal* 87, no. 2 (1994): 109–30.
Harbour, Jennifer. *Organizing Freedom: Black Emancipation Activism in the Civil War Midwest.* Carbondale: Southern Illinois Univ. Press, 2020.
Hard, Charles Desmond. "Why Lincoln Said 'No': Congressional Attitudes on Slavery Expansion, 1860–1861." *Social Science Quarterly* 49 (Dec. 1968): 732–41.
Harris, Robert L., Jr. "H. Ford Douglas: Afro-American Antislavery Emigrationist." *Journal of Negro History* 62 (July 1977): 217–34.
Harris, William C. *Lincoln's Rise to the Presidency.* Lawrence: Univ. Press of Kansas, 2007.
Harrison, Victoria L. "We Are Here Assembled; Illinois Colored Conventions, 1853–1873." *Journal of the Illinois State Historical Society* 108 (Fall–Winter 2015): 322–46.
Haumesser, Lauren N. *The Democratic Collapse: How Gender Politics Broke a Party and a Nation, 1856–1861.* Chapel Hill: Univ. of North Carolina Press, 2022.
Heerman, M. Scott, *The Alchemy of Slavery: Human Bondage in the Illinois Country, 1730–1865.* Philadelphia: Univ. of Pennsylvania Press, 2018.
Heinzel, Sally. "'To Protect the Rights of the White Race': Illinois Republican Racial Politics in the 1860 Campaign and the Twenty-Second General Assembly." *Journal of the Illinois State Historical Society* 108 (Fall–Winter 2015): 374–406.

Herriott, F. I. "Senator Stephen A. Douglas and the Germans in 1854." In *Transactions of the Illinois State Historical Society 1912*. Springfield: Illinois State Historical Library, 1914.
Hicken, Victor. *Illinois in the Civil War*, 2nd ed. Urbana: Univ. of Illinois Press, 1991.
———. "John A. McClernand and the House Speakership Struggle of 1859." *Journal of the Illinois State Historical Society* 53 (Summer 1960): 163–78.
Hickey, James T. "Oglesby's Fence Rail Dealings and the 1860 Decatur Convention." *Journal of the Illinois State Historical Society* 54 (Spring 1961): 5–24.
Hofstadter, Richard. *The Paranoid Style in American Politics, and Other Essays*. New York: Alfred A. Knopf, 1965.
Hoganson, Kristen L. *The Heartland: An American History*. New York: Penguin, 2019.
Holt, Michael F. *The Election of 1860: "A Campaign Fraught with Consequences."* Lawrence: Univ. Press of Kansas, 2017.
———. *The Political Crisis of the 1850s*. New York: John Wiley & Sons, 1978.
———. *Political Parties and American Political Development from the Age of Jackson to the Age of Lincoln*. Baton Rouge: Louisiana State Univ. Press, 1992.
———. *The Rise and Fall of the American Whig Party: Jacksonian Politics and the Onset of the Civil War*. New York: Oxford Univ. Press, 1999.
Holzer, Harold. *Lincoln at Cooper Union: The Speech That Made Abraham Lincoln President*. New York: Simon & Schuster, 2004.
———. *Lincoln President-Elect: Abraham Lincoln and the Great Secession Winter, 1860–1861*. New York: Simon & Schuster, 2008.
Howard, Victor B. "The Illinois Republican Party: Part I: A Party Organizer for the Republicans in 1854." *Journal of the Illinois State Historical Society* 64 (Summer 1971): 125–60.
Howe, Daniel Walker. "The Evangelical Movement and Political Culture in the North during the Second Party System." *Journal of American History* 77 (Mar. 1991): 1216–39.
———. *The Political Culture of the American Whigs*. Chicago: Univ. of Chicago Press, 1979.
———. *What Hath God Wrought: The Transformation of America, 1815–1848*. New York: Oxford Univ. Press, 2007.
Huston, James L. "The Illinois Political Realignment of 1844–1860: Revisiting the Analysis." *Journal of the Civil War Era* 1 (Dec. 2011): 506–35.
———. *The Panic of 1857 and the Coming of the Civil War*. Baton Rouge: Louisiana State Univ. Press, 1987.
———. *Stephen A. Douglas and the Dilemmas of Democratic Equality*. Lanham, MD: Rowan & Littlefield, 2007.
Hutson, Francis Murray. *Financing an Empire: History of Banking in Illinois*. Vol. 1, edited by Andrew Russel. Chicago: S. J. Clarke Publishing Company, 1926.
Jackson, Kellie Carter. *Force and Freedom: Black Abolitionists and the Politics of Violence*. Philadelphia: Univ. of Pennsylvania Press, 2019.
Johannsen, Robert W. *The Frontier, the Union, and Stephen A. Douglas*. Urbana: Univ. of Illinois Press, 1989.
———. *Stephen A. Douglas*. 2nd ed. Urbana: Univ. of Illinois Press, 1997.
Jones, James P. *"Black Jack": John A. Logan and Southern Illinois in the Civil War Era*. Tallahassee: Florida State Univ. Studies, 1967.

Joslyn, R. Waite and Frank W. Joslyn. *History of Kane County, Ill.* Chicago: Pioneer Publishing, 1908.

Junger, Richard. "'God Helped Those Who Helped Themselves': John and Mary Jones and the Culture of African American Self-Sufficiency in Mid-Nineteenth Century Chicago." *Journal of Illinois History* 11 (Summer 2008): 111–32.

Kantrowitz, Stephen. *More Than Freedom: Fighting for Black Citizenship in a White Republic: 1829–1889.* New York: Penguin, 2012.

Karp, Matthew. "The People's Revolution of 1856: Antislavery Populism, National Politics, and the Emergence of the Republican Party." *Journal of the Civil War Era* 9 (Dec. 2019): 524–45.

———. *This Vast Southern Empire: Slaveholders at the Helm of American Foreign Policy.* Cambridge, MA: Harvard Univ. Press, 2016.

Keefe, Thomas M. "Chicago's Flirtation with Political Nativism, 1854–1856." *American Catholic Historical Society* 82 (Sept. 1971): 131–58.

Kelleher, Patricia. "Class and Catholic Irish Masculinity in Antebellum America: Young Men on the Make in Chicago." *Journal of American Ethnic History* 28 (Summer 2009): 7–42.

Kiper, Richard L. *Major General John Alexander McClernand: Politician in Uniform.* Kent, OH: Kent State Univ. Press, 1999.

Kleppner, Paul. *The Cross of Culture: A Social Analysis of Midwestern Politics, 1850–1900,* 2nd ed. New York: Free Press, 1970.

———. *The Third Electoral System, 1853–1892: Parties, Voters, and Political Cultures.* Chapel Hill: Univ. of North Carolina Press, 1979.

Knupfer, Peter B. *The Union as It Is: Constitutional Unionism and Sectional Compromise, 1787–1861.* Chapel Hill: Univ. of North Carolina Press, 1991.

Krug, Mark M. *Lyman Trumbull: Conservative Radical.* New York: A. S. Barnes & Company, 1965.

Lacher, J. H. A. "Francis A. Hoffman of Illinois and Hans Buschbauer of Wisconsin." *Wisconsin Magazine of History* 13 (June 1930): 337–38.

Landis, Michael. *Northern Men with Southern Loyalties: The Democratic Party and the Sectional Crisis.* Ithaca, NY: Cornell Univ. Press, 2014.

Lang, Andrew F. *A Contest of Civilizations: Exposing the Crisis of American Exceptionalism in the Civil War Era.* Chapel Hill: Univ. of North Carolina Press, 2021.

Larson, John Lauritz. *The Market Revolution in America: Liberty, Ambition, and the Eclipse of the Common Good.* New York: Cambridge Univ. Press, 2010.

Lauck, John K. *The Lost Region: Towards a Revival of Midwestern History.* Iowa City: Univ. of Iowa Press, 2013.

Lawson, Melinda. *Patriot Fires: Forging a New American Nationalism in the Civil War North.* Lawrence: Univ. Press of Kansas, 2002.

Lechner, Zachary J. "Black Abolitionist Response to the Kansas Crisis, 1854–1856." *Kansas History: A Journal of the Central Plains* 31 (Spring 2008): 14–31.

Leichtle, Kurt E., and Bruce G. Carveth. *Crusade against Slavery: Edward Coles, Pioneer of Freedom.* Carbondale: Southern Illinois Univ. Press, 2011.

Leonard, Ira M., and Robert D. Parment. *American Nativism, 1830–1860.* New York: Van Nostrand Reinhold, 1971.

Leonard, Thomas C. *News for All: America's Coming-of-Age with the Press.* New York: Oxford Univ. Press, 1995.

Levine, Bruce. "Conservatism, Nativism, and Slavery: Thomas R. Whitney and the Origins of the Know-Nothing Party." *Journal of American History* 88 (Sept. 2001): 455–88.

———. *The Spirit of 1848: German Immigrants, Labor Conflict, and the Coming of the Civil War.* Urbana: Univ. of Illinois Press, 1992.

———. "'The Vital Element of the Republican Party': Antislavery, Nativism, and Abraham Lincoln." *Journal of the Civil War Era* 1 (Dec. 2011): 481–505.

Link, William A. *Roots of Secession: Slavery and Politics in Antebellum Virginia.* Chapel Hill: Univ. of North Carolina Press, 2005.

Lynn, Joshua A. *Defending the White Man's Republic: Jacksonian Democracy, Race, and the Transformation of American Conservatism.* Charlottesville: Univ. of Virginia Press, 2019.

———. "A Manly Doughface: James Buchanan and the Sectional Politics of Gender." *Journal of the Civil War Era* 8 (Dec. 2018): 591–620.

Maizlish, Stephen E. *A Strife of Tongues: The Compromise of 1850 and the Ideological Foundations of the American Civil War.* Charlottesville: Univ. of Virginia Press, 2018.

Malavasic, Alice Elizabeth. *The F Street Mess: How Southern Senators Rewrote the Kansas-Nebraska Act.* Chapel Hill: Univ. of North Carolina Press, 2017.

Manning, Chandra *What This Cruel War Was Over: Soldiers, Slavery and the Civil War.* New York: Alfred A. Knopf, 2007.

Mason, Matthew. *Apostle of Union: A Political Biography of Edward Everett.* Chapel Hill: Univ. of North Carolina Press, 2016.

Masur, Kate. *Until Justice Be Done: America's First Civil Rights Movement, From Revolution to Reconstruction.* New York: W. W. Norton, 2021.

May, Robert E. *The Southern Dream of a Caribbean Empire: 1854–1861.* Baton Rouge: Louisiana State Univ. Press, 1973.

McClintock, Russell. *Lincoln and the Decision for War: The Northern Response to Secession.* Chapel Hill: Univ. of North Carolina Press, 2008.

McDonough, Daniel, and Kenneth W. Noe, eds. *Essays in Honor of Robert W. Johannsen.* Selinsgrove, PA: Susquehanna Univ. Press, 2006.

McKirdy, Charles R. *Lincoln Apostate: The Matson Slave Case.* Jackson: Univ. Press of Mississippi, 2011.

McPherson, James. *Battle Cry of Freedom: The Civil War Era.* New York: Oxford Univ. Press, 1988.

Meites, Jerome B. "The 1847 Illinois Constitutional Convention and Persons of Color." *Journal of the Illinois State Historical Society* 108 (Fall–Winter 2015): 266–95.

Miner, Craig. *Seeding Civil War: Kansas in the National News, 1854–1858.* Lawrence: Univ. Press of Kansas, 2008.

Mitrani, Sam. *The Rise of the Chicago Police Department: Class and Conflict, 1850–1894.* Urbana: Univ. of Illinois Press, 2013.

Moore, Jane Ann, and William F. Moore. *Owen Lovejoy and the Coalition for Equality.* Urbana: Univ. of Illinois Press, 2019.

Moore, William F., and Jane Ann Moore. *Collaborators for Emancipation: Abraham Lincoln and Owen Lovejoy.* Urbana: Univ. of Illinois Press, 2014.

Morrison, Michael A. *Slavery and the American West: The Eclipse of Manifest Destiny and the Coming of the Civil War*. Chapel Hill: Univ. of North Carolina Press, 1997.
Neely, Mark E. Jr. *The Boundaries of American Political Culture in the Civil War Era*. Chapel Hill: Univ. of North Carolina Press, 2005.
———. *Lincoln and the Democrats: The Politics of Opposition in the Civil War*. New York: Cambridge Univ. Press, 2017.
———. *The Union Divided: Party Conflict in the Civil War North*. Cambridge, MA: Harvard Univ. Press, 2002.
Nichols, Roger L. *Black Hawk and the Warriors Path*. Arlington Heights, IL: Harlan Davidson, 1992.
Nichols, Roy Franklin. *The Disruption of American Democracy*. New York: Macmillan, 1948.
Oakes, James. *The Crooked Path to Abolition: Abraham Lincoln and the Antislavery Constitution*. New York: W. W. Norton, 2021.
———. *Freedom National: The Destruction of Slavery in the United States, 1861–1865*. New York: W. W. Norton, 2013.
———. *The Radical and the Republican: Frederick Douglass, Abraham Lincoln, and the Triumph of Antislavery Politics*. New York: W. W. Norton, 2007.
———. *The Scorpion's Sting: Antislavery and the Coming of the Civil War*. New York: W. W. Norton, 2014.
Oertel, Kristen Tegtmeier. *Bleeding Borders: Race, Gender, and Violence in Pre–Civil War Kansas*. Baton Rouge: Louisiana State Univ. Press, 2009.
Pears, Emily. *Cords of Affection: Constructing Constitutional Union in Early American History*. Lawrence: Univ. Press of Kansas, 2021.
Pearson, Joseph W. *The Whigs' America: Middle-Class Political Thought in the Age of Jackson and Clay*. Lexington: Univ. Press of Kentucky, 2020.
Peck, Graham A. *Making an Antislavery Nation: Lincoln, Douglas, and the Battle over Freedom*. Urbana: Univ. of Illinois Press, 2017.
———. "Was Stephen A. Douglas Antislavery?" *Journal of the Abraham Lincoln Association* 26 (Summer 2005): 1–21.
———."Was There a Second Party System? Illinois as a Case Study in Antebellum Politics." In *Practicing Democracy: Popular Politics in the United States from the Constitution to the Civil War*, edited by Daniel Peart and Adam I. P. Smith, 145–72. Charlottesville: Univ. of Virginia Press, 2015.
Peek, Gregory. "'The True and Ever Living Principle of States Rights and Popular Sovereignty': Douglas Democrats and Indiana Republicans Allied, 1857–1859." *Indiana Magazine of History* 111 (Dec. 2015): 381–421.
Phillips, Christopher. *The Rivers Ran Backward: The Civil War and the Remaking of the American Middle Border*. New York: Oxford Univ. Press, 2016.
Pierson, Michael D. *Free Hearts and Free Homes: Gender and American Antislavery Politics*. Chapel Hill: Univ. of North Carolina Press, 2003.
Pinsker, Matthew. "Not Always Such a Whig: Abraham Lincoln's Partisan Realignment in the 1850s." *Journal of the Abraham Lincoln Association* 29 (Summer 2008): 26–46.
Plummer, Mark A. *Lincoln's Rail-Splitter: Governor Richard J. Oglesby*. Urbana: Univ. of Illinois Press, 2001.
Ponce, Pearl T. *To Govern the Devil in Hell: The Political Crisis in Territorial Kansas*. DeKalb: Northern Illinois Univ. Press, 2014.

Portteus, Kevin J. "'My Beau Ideal of a Statesman': Abraham Lincoln's Eulogy of Henry Clay." *Journal of the Abraham Lincoln Association* 41 (Summer 2020): 1–24.
Potter, David M. *The Impending Crisis: America before the Civil War, 1848–1861.* Completed and edited by Don E. Fehrenbacher. New York: Harper & Row, 1976.
———. *Lincoln and His Party in the Secession Crisis.* New Haven: Yale Univ. Press, 1942.
Price, Barton E. "Religion, Reform, and Patriotism in Southern Illinois: A Case Study, 1852–1900." *Journal of the Illinois State Historical Society* 107 (Summer 2014): 175–88.
Prince, Ezra M, ed.. *The Transactions of the McLean County Historical Society* 3 (1900): 3–184.
Quitt, Martin H. *Stephen A. Douglas and Antebellum Democracy.* New York: Cambridge Univ. Press, 2012.
Ray, P. Orman. *The Repeal of the Missouri Compromise: Its Origin and Authorship.* Cleveland: Arthur H. Clark, 1909.
Reed, Christopher Robert. "The Early African American Settlement of Chicago, 1833–1870." *Journal of the Illinois State Historical Society* 108 (Fall–Winter 2015): 211–65.
Richards, Leonard L. *The Slave Power: The Free North and Southern Domination, 1780–1860.* Baton Rouge: Louisiana State Univ. Press, 2000.
Ritter, Luke. *Inventing America's First Immigration Crisis: Political Nativism in the Antebellum West.* New York: Fordham Univ. Press, 2021.
Roske, Ralph J. *His Own Counsel: The Life and Times of Lyman Trumbull.* Reno: Univ. of Nevada Press, 1979.
Rozett, John M. "Racism and Republican Emergence in Illinois, 1848–1860: A Re-Evaluation of Republican Negrophobia." *Civil War History* 22 (June 1976): 101–15.
Rozinek, Erika. "Trembling for the Nation: Illinois Women and the Election of 1860." *Constructing the Past* 2, no. 1 (2001): 6–24.
Sachsman, David B., and Gregory A. Borchard, eds. *The Antebellum Press: Setting the Stage for Civil War.* New York: Routledge, 2019.
Sanders, James W. *The Education of an Urban Minority: Catholics in Chicago, 1833–1965.* New York: Oxford Univ. Press, 1977.
Schob, David E. "Sodbusting on the Upper Midwestern Frontier, 1820–1860." *Agricultural History* 47, no. 1 (1973): 47–56.
Schwalm, Leslie A. *Emancipation's Diaspora: Race and Reconstruction in the Upper Midwest.* Chapel Hill: Univ. of North Carolina Press, 2009.
Sellers, Charles. *The Market Revolution: Jacksonian America, 1815–1846.* New York: Oxford Univ. Press, 1991.
Sewell, Richard H. *Ballots for Freedom: Antislavery Politics in the United States, 1837–1860,* 2nd ed. New York: W. W. Norton, 1980.
Shelden, Rachel. *Washington Brotherhood: Politics, Social Life, and the Coming of the Civil War.* Chapel Hill: Univ. of North Carolina Press, 2013.
Short, W. F. "Early Religious Leaders and Methods in Illinois." *Transactions of the Illinois State Historical Society for the Year 1902.* 56–62. Springfield: Illinois State Historical Library, 1902.
Silbey, Joel H. *The Partisan Imperative: The Dynamics of American Politics before the Civil War.* New York: Oxford Univ. Press, 1985.
———. *A Respectable Minority: The Democratic Party in the Civil War Era.* New York: W. W. Norton, 1977.

———. "The Surge of Republican Power: Partisan Antipathy, American Social Conflict, and the Coming of the Civil War." In *Essays on American Antebellum Politics, 1840–1860*, edited by Stephen E. Maizlish and John J. Kushma, 199–229. College Station: Texas A & M Univ. Press, 1982.

Simeone, James. *Democracy and Slavery in Frontier Illinois: The Bottomland Republic*. DeKalb: Northern Illinois Univ. Press, 2000.

Simmons, William J. *Men of Mark: Eminent, Progressive, and Rising*. Cleveland: George M. Rewell & Co., 1887.

Sinha, Manisha. "The Caning of Charles Sumner: Slavery, Race, and Ideology in the Age of the Civil War." *Journal of the Early Republic* 23 (Summer 2003): 233–62.

Simpson, Brooks D. "'Hit Him Again: 'The Canning of Charles Sumner." In *Congress and the Crisis of the 1850s*, edited by Paul Finkelman and Donald R. Kennon, 202–20. Athens: Ohio Univ. Press, 2012.

Smith, Adam I. P. *No Party Now: Politics in the Civil War North*. New York: Oxford Univ. Press, 2006.

———. *The Stormy Present: Conservatism and the Problem of Slavery in Northern Politics, 1846–1865*. Chapel Hill: Univ. of North Carolina Press, 2017.

Smith, Mark Power. *Young America: The Transformation of Nationalism before the Civil War*. Charlottesville: Univ. of Virginia Press, 2022.

Stampp, Kenneth M. Stampp, *America in 1857: A Nation on the Brink*. New York: Oxford Univ. Press, 1990.

———. *And the War Came: The North and the Secession Crisis, 1860–1861*. Baton Rouge: Louisiana State Press, 1950.

Stanley, Matthew. *The Loyal West: Civil War and Reunion in Middle America*. Urbana: Univ. of Illinois Press, 2017.

Summers, Mark W. *The Plundering Generation: Corruption and the Crisis of the Union, 1849–1861*. New York: Oxford Univ. Press, 1987.

Tap, Bruce. "Race, Rhetoric, and Emancipation: The Election of 1862 in Illinois." *Civil War History* 39 (June 1993):101–25.

Taylor, Alan. *American Republics: A Continental History of the United States, 1783–1850*. New York W. W. Norton, 2021.

Thomas, William G. *The Iron Way: Railroads, the Civil War, and the Making of Modern America*. New Haven: Yale Univ. Press, 2011.

Tooley, Mark. *The Peace That Almost Was: The Forgotten Story of the 1861 Washington Peace Conference and the Final Attempt to Avert the Civil War*. Nashville: Thomas Nelson, 2015.

Varon, Elizabeth R. *Armies of Deliverance: A New History of the Civil War*. New York: Oxford Univ. Press, 2019.

———. *Disunion! The Coming of the American Civil War, 179–859*. Chapel Hill: Univ. of North Carolina Press, 2008.

Voss-Hubbard, Mark. *Beyond Party: Cultures of Antipartisanship in Northern Politics before the Civil War*. Baltimore: Johns Hopkins Univ. Press, 2002.

Waldstreicher, David. *Slavery's Constitution: From Revolution to Ratification*. New York: Hill & Wang, 2010.

Weeks, William Earl. *Building the Continental Empire: American Expansion from the Revolution to the Civil War*. Chicago: Ivan R. Dee, 1996.

Weiner, Dana Elizabeth. *Race and Rights: Fighting Slavery and Prejudice in the Old Northwest, 1830–1870*. Ithaca, NY: Cornell Univ. Press, 2013.

Wells, Damon. *Stephen Douglas: The Last Years, 1857–1861*. Austin: Univ. of Texas Press, 1971), 34–35.

West, Stephen A. "Minute Men, Yeomen, and the Mobilization for Secession in the South Carolina Upcountry." *Journal of Southern History* 71 (Feb. 2005): 75–104.

White, Horace. *The Life of Lyman Trumbull*. Cambridge, MA.: Riverside, 1913.

Widmer, Ted. *Lincoln on the Verge: Thirteen Days to Washington*. New York: Simon & Schuster, 2020.

Wilentz, Sean. *No Property in Man: Slavery and Antislavery at the Nation's Founding*. Cambridge, MA: Harvard Univ. Press, 2018.

——. *The Rise of American Democracy: Jefferson to Lincoln*. New York: W. W. Norton, 2007.

Winkle, Kenneth J. "The Voters of Lincoln's Springfield: Migration and Political Participation in an Antebellum City." *Journal of Social History* 25 (Spring 1992): 595–611.

Woods, Michael E. *Arguing until Doomsday: Stephen Douglas, Jefferson Davis, and the Struggle for American Democracy*. Chapel Hill: Univ. of North Carolina Press, 2020.

——. *Emotional and Sectional Conflict in the Antebellum United States*. New York: Cambridge Univ. Press, 2014.

——. "'Tell Us Something about State Rights': Northern Republicans, States' Rights, and the Coming of the Civil War." *Journal of the Civil War Era* 7 (June 2017): 242–68.

Woodward, Isaiah A. "Lincoln and the Crittenden Compromise." *Negro History Bulletin* 22 (Apr. 1959): 153–55.

Voegeli, Jacque. *Free but Not Equal: The Midwest and the Negro during the Civil War*. Chicago: Univ. of Chicago Press, 1968.

Zarefsky, David. *Lincoln, Douglas, and Slavery: In the xCrucible of Public Debate*. Chicago: Univ. of Chicago Press, 1990.

Zilversmit, Arthur. *The First Emancipation: The Abolition of Slavery in the North*. Chicago: Univ. of Chicago Press, 1967.

INDEX

abolitionists/abolitionism, 2, 125; Black, 16–17, 28, 73–74, 79, 95–96, 149–50; Dred Scott decision and, 85–86; in Illinois, 15–17, 31, 35, 38, 85–86, 95, 136, 138, 149–54, 159, 168, 173; Lincoln and, 125–26, 131, 134, 139–40, 154–58, 169, 170, 182–206; marginalization of, 40, 51, 126–27; party politics and, 116, 123; popular sovereignty and, 47, 49, 50, 54–55, 57–58, 61, 69, 72, 75, 111; radical, 28, 57, 73–74, 78–79, 82, 84, 102, 124, 126, 137, 150, 170, 182, 196, 204
Adams, John Quincy, 66, 161
African Americans, 143; abolitionists, 16–17, 28, 73–74, 79, 95–96, 149–50; civil and political rights of, 6, 62, 86, 94–95, 106, 120, 121, 129, 137–38, 171; deportation of, 15, 73, 88, 112; exclusion, 15–16, 120, 121; French-speaking, 14–15; in Illinois, 6, 14–15, 22, 40, 52, 78–79, 89–90, 121–22, 129; natural rights of, 6, 16, 82, 94–95
Agricultural Society of Wisconsin, 155
Alabama, 159–60, 189
Allison, John, 68
Alton Courier, 38, 52, 56, 69–70, 112; nativism, 33, 43; Nebraska Bill, 30, 50, 55; popular sovereignty, 84, 98
Alton Democrat, 77
Alton Telegraph and Democratic Review, 10, 27, 38, 70
American Party, 32, 33, 34, 61, 84. *See also* Know-Nothing Party
American Revolution, 3, 53, 74, 80

American System, 30
Anderson, Robert, 196, 198
Anti-Nebraska Ticket, 62
Anti-Slavery Bugle, 16
Appeal of the Independent Democrats, 27
Archer, William B., 61, 70
Arkansas, 28, 201
Arnold, Benedict, 58, 201
Atchison, David R., 25–26, 58
Atkins, Henry J., 153

Bacon Academy, 37
Bailhache, John, 70
Bailhache, William H., 53, 70–72, 78
Bainbridge, Allen, 179
Baker, Edward L., 53, 72, 78, 205
Baker, Jean H., 51
Balance, 166
Banks, Nathaniel P., 48, 50, 67
Barksdale, William, 56
Bates, Edward L., 154, 155, 157, 162–64, 169
Battle of Bad Axe, 13
Beauregard, Pierre Gustave Toutant, 198
Becoming Lincoln (Freehling), 125
Beecher, Henry Ward, 156
Bell, John, 94, 162, 169, 171, 173, 178, 183
Belleville Advocate, 185
Belvidere Standard, 70, 74, 83, 171, 189, 194–95
Benton, Thomas Hart, 26, 50, 68
Bissell, William, 40, 61, 67, 69, 70, 78, 94; 1856 election, 51–54, 75, 102, 134
Black Codes/Laws, 14–15, 40, 95, 96

Black Hawk, 13
Black Hawk War, 30
Blair, Francis P., 67, 112
Blair, Montgomery, 196
Boone, Levi, 42–43
Bowers, Theodore S., 32
Breckinridge, John C., 63, 141, 144, 168, 171–73, 178, 180, 187; 1856 election, 172; 1860 election, 41, 143–76
Breese, Sidney, 137
Bright, Jesse D., 63, 79, 104
British Empire, 14. *See also* Great Britain
Brooks, Preston, 56–58, 62, 112
Brown, Albert G., 153
Brown, George T., 30, 32, 60, 84, 112; *Alton Courier*, 30, 33, 38, 43, 50, 52, 55, 56, 69–70, 84, 98, 112
Brown, John, 96, 149–54; Harpers Ferry raid, 150–52, 154
Brown, Josiah, 121
Brown, Lewis, 51
Browning, Orville H., 13, 52–53, 60–61, 124, 154, 164, 169, 185, 192, 194, 204
Buchanan, James, 4, 6, 47, 78–79, 103, 144, 147, 158, 169, 201; 1856 election, 66, 74–76, 86, 142, 172; Dred Scott decision, 81–93; Lecompton constitution, 106, 110, 114, 118, 124, 128–29, 137; popular sovereignty, 47, 59, 62–70; slavery, 48, 77, 96–102, 108–9, 111–13, 115, 132–33, 153, 173, 177–79
Butler, Andrew P., 25, 56
Butler, Benjamin, 187

Cairo City Gazette, 77, 171
Cairo City Times, 44
Calhoun, John C., 72, 92, 98, 170
California, 9, 24, 172
Cameron, Simon, 154
Capital Enterprise, 34
Cass, Lewis, 157
Central Transcript, 92, 112, 135, 149
Chaffee, Calvin C., 86
Charleston Courier, 174
Charleston Mercury, 69, 159
Chase, Salmon P., 27, 36, 67, 68, 154, 200
Chicago & Alton Railroad, 18
Chicago City Council, 16
Chicago Democrat, 56, 83, 148, 151, 164, 191, 205
Chicago Herald, 158
Chicago Journal, 1, 3, 103, 143, 191
Chicago Press and Tribune, 134, 135, 147–50, 163, 168, 174. See also *Chicago Tribune*
Chicago & Rock Island Railroad, 96

Chicago Times, 77, 79, 99–100, 114, 116, 122; 1854 elections, 41; 1855 election, 40, 105; 1856 elections, 47, 86, 102; 1860 elections, 144, 147, 158
Chicago Tribune, 33, 43, 56, 72, 82–83, 91–92, 95, 103, 116, 182, 184, 190, 195, 197, 199; 1848 elections, 32; 1854 elections, 41; 1855 elections, 41; 1856 elections, 74; 1858 elections, 124; 1860 elections, 171, 176. See also *Chicago Press and Tribune*
Cincinnati Platform of 1856, 93, 107
Civil War, 1–2, 6, 16, 125, 198–206
Clay, Henry, 9–10, 27–30, 60, 64, 88, 126, 131, 139–40, 163, 171, 173, 188; and Daniel Webster, 37, 53, 94, 157
Cobb, Howell, 158
Codding, Ichabod, 35
Coles, Edward, 29
Collins, Bruce, 142
colonization movement, 15, 27, 88, 112
Colored Conventions, 96
Coltrin, I. N., 149
Committee on Territories, 49
Compromise of 1820, 71
Compromise of 1850, 9–11, 18–19, 23–24, 26–29, 36, 53, 64, 71
Confederates States of America, 1, 189, 198, 201, 205
Congressional Herald, 95
Conservative, 71
Constitutional Unionists, 158, 161–62, 168, 180, 183
Cook, Isaac L., 114, 119, 137
Cooper Institute, 145, 156–58, 162, 164
Corwin, Thomas, 193
Crittenden, John J., 94, 116, 127–28, 141, 143, 162, 183
Crittenden Compromise, 3, 184, 187, 190–91
Cromwell, Nance, 15
Cuba, 59, 117, 146
Cushing, Caleb, 160

Daily Republican, 43
Danforth, John B., 43
Davis, David, 30, 31, 44, 79, 116, 123, 149–50, 154, 163, 169, 201
Davis, Jefferson, 11, 146–47, 153, 197–98
Dayton, William, 68
Decatur Resolutions, 50, 53
Declaration of Independence, 86–87, 131, 138, 154
Deere, John, 17
Democratic Club of Rock Island, 168

Democratic Party/Democrats: anti-Catholicism, 32–34, 69; anti-Lecompton, 102–3, 111–13, 116–17, 122, 130, 147, 152–53; anti-Nebraska, 30–32, 35, 38, 40–41, 44, 46–47, 49–52, 54–57, 104–5, 118; Baltimore convention, 161–62, 166–68; banking platform, 20; Buchanan, 6, 108, 110, 114–15, 118, 129, 147, 158, 160; commercial, 17–18, 20; conservatives in, 3, 102–6; Convention for the Eighth Congressional District, 38; Danites, 110, 115, 118–19, 129–30, 136–37, 141–44, 151, 158, 179; Douglas, 3, 6, 32, 50, 81, 93, 101, 105, 108–14, 114–44, 153–54, 158–62, 168, 175, 177, 178–81, 187–90, 197, 199, 202; Fire-Eater, 11, 34, 92, 159, 161, 168, 176–77, 182–83, 187; fundraising, 128; Illinois, 5, 10–11, 20–22, 28, 32, 38, 46, 53, 64, 79, 84–86, 91, 98, 100–102, 104, 107, 109–11, 113–14, 119, 121, 137, 151, 158, 161, 171, 175, 177, 179, 181, 189, 195–97, 199–200; Indiana, 6; interracial sex and, 88, 95; Irish, 13, 75, 135, 147; Jacksonian, 20–21, 23, 32, 34, 37–38, 44, 51, 69, 79, 83, 99, 124; Jeffersonian, 63, 65; National, 141; National Convention of 1856, 47, 53–66; National Convention of 1860 (Charleston), 145, 151, 154, 158–62, 168, 183; national expansion, 30; nativism, 32, 36, 63, 69, 81, 147; New York, 128; Northern, 10–11, 26, 30, 34, 63, 65, 76, 82, 91–92, 101, 109, 130, 153, 157–59, 161, 170, 172, 179, 181, 194, 199; popular sovereignty and, 26, 29–30, 51, 64, 65, 101, 110, 137, 153, 157, 161, 177; pro-Nebraska, 41, 51–52, 61; Protestant, 33, 65, 147; slavery and, 27, 29–30, 32, 36, 38, 61, 64, 65, 69, 71–72, 81–93, 96, 106, 122, 152–53, 160–61, 182, 199; Southern, 11, 23, 49, 62, 63, 69, 87, 93–94, 109, 122, 127–28, 144, 153, 159, 160, 171, 176–77, 180, 182–83, 206; Springfield Convention, 52; temperance, 32–33, 36, 40, 51; Union and, 159, 179–80, 187–88, 194, 200–206; unit rule, 160; Yankee, 32; Young America movement, 19

Democratic Union, 110–11
Deutcher Demokrat, 138
Dewitt Courier, 43
Dickey, T. Lyle, 73, 134, 141, 143
Didier, Louis, 138
Diggins, Wesley, 40
District of Columbia, 9
Dixon, Archibald, 26
Dougherty, John, 142
Douglas, H. Ford, 73–74, 95, 170
Douglas, Stephen, 4–5, 11, 37–39, 41, 43, 45, 57, 58, 69, 78, 84, 88, 98, 123, 145–46, 152, 156; 1856 election, 47–49, 51, 54, 62–63, 76; 1860 election, 41, 143, 144–74, 183; Democrats, 3, 6, 32, 50, 81, 93, 101, 105, 108–14, 114–44, 153–54, 158–62, 168, 175, 177, 178–81, 187–90, 197, 199, 202; abolitionists and, 28; birth, 10; conservatism/moderation, 120, 122–23; death, 5, 205; health issues, 204–5; "Little Giant" nickname, origin of, 10; popular sovereignty and, 19, 29–30, 39, 46–47, 62, 64, 77, 87, 89–90, 93, 100–119, 128–29, 133–34, 138, 140, 146, 153, 183, 206; railroad expansion and, 18, 21–24, 26, 30, 97, 205; Senate campaign, 1858, 124–44; slavery and, 29, 46–47, 74, 79–81, 86, 100–119, 125–32, 134, 139–40, 146, 154, 179, 205; support of Lincoln, 200–206; Tremont House speech, 128–29; Union and, 127–28, 177, 200–206; westward expansion and, 80
Douglass, Frederick, 16, 17, 73, 96, 136, 150, 195–96, 204
Dred Scott v. Sandford, 77, 82–93, 106, 124–25, 130, 133, 138, 140, 172
Dubois, Jesse K., 116, 164

Edwards, Benjamin S., 35, 65, 134, 205
Edwards, Cyrus, 41, 169
Eighth Illinois Volunteer Infantry, 204
elections: 1848, 32, 157; 1852, 21, 26, 34; 1854, 35–41, 48, 159; 1855, 40–42, 105, 132; 1856, 1, 4, 46, 47–54, 74–76, 86, 102, 134, 142, 145, 172; 1858, 118–19, 123–43, 148; 1860, 41, 143–76, 183
Electoral College, 159, 161, 171–73
Emerson, John, 82
Emigrant Aid Company, 48, 55
English, William H., 118
English Bill, 118
Everett, Edward, 162, 169, 180

federalism, 4, 63
Fessenden, William P., 120–21
Ficklin, Orlando B., 15
Fillmore, Millard, 66–67, 69, 70–72, 78, 84, 112, 116–17, 127, 134–35, 169, 173; 1856 election, 4, 53–54, 75–76, 102, 134, 142–43
First Continental Congress, 194
Fitzpatrick, Benjamin, 167
Florida, 189, 197
Fondey, William B., 142
Forney, John W., 128
Fort Moultrie, 181
Fort Pickens, 197
Fortress Monroe, 201

Fort Sumter, 3, 5, 196–99, 201–2
Foulke, Phillip B., 38
Fourth Commandment/Sabbath, 33
Fox, Gustavus, 198
Francis, Simeon, 27
Frederick Douglass' Paper, 28
Free banking system, 20
Freehling, William W., 125
Freeport Bulletin, 119–200
Freeport Doctrine, 130, 140, 144–46, 159, 172
Freeport Journal, 56–57
Free School law, 43
Free-Soil Party, 10, 11, 18, 23, 27–28, 32, 36, 40, 48, 58, 61, 102, 120, 134; popular sovereignty and, 80–82
Free State Hotel, 55
free white labor, 23, 38, 47, 54, 58, 60–61, 64, 74, 78, 80–81, 85, 129–30, 141, 187, 190; morality of, 72, 115, 139, 152–56
Frémont, Jesse Benton, 68
Frémont, John C., 4, 66–73, 75–76, 78, 112, 142–43
French, Augustus C., 20
French Empire, 14
French Revolution, 203–4
Front Street Theater, 167
F-Street Mess, 25, 26
Fugitive Slave Law/Act, 6, 9, 11, 16–17, 35–36, 50, 58, 67, 138, 171, 182, 194–95
Furniss, Jack, 4
fusion movement, 35–42, 63, 116–17; anti-Nebraska, 52; barriers to, 47–54; nativism, 40

Galena & Chicago Union Railroad, 18
Galena Courier, 200
Gallagher, Gary, 198
Garrison, William Lloyd, 72, 85, 126, 170, 195–96
Georgia, 37, 68, 172, 176, 189
Giddings, Joshua P., 27
Gienapp, William E., 4, 142
Gillespie, Joseph, 13, 38, 57, 94, 114
Gray, Jim, 171
Great Britain, 24, 155. *See also* British Empire
Greeley, Horace, 49, 55–56, 102–3, 105, 118, 156–57, 164
Grinspan, Jon, 173
Guelzo, Allen C., 142

Hackney, Bejamin, 40
Hall, Willard P., 25
Hamilton, Alexander, 203
Hammond, James Henry, 115, 156
Hanks, John, 163
Hansen, Stephen L., 142

Harpers Ferry, 150–52, 154, 201
Harris, Thomas L., 35, 53–54, 77, 79, 100, 111–12, 118, 122, 151
Hatch, Ozias M., 113, 117
Hayes, Samuel Snowden, 179
Hazard, E. W., 57
Helper, Hinton R., 152
Henry, John F., 31
Henry, Patrick, 49
Herndon, William, 70, 149
Hoffman, Francis A., 61, 163
Hofstadter, Richard, 34
Holt, Michael F., 2, 4, 162
Hossack, John, 170–71
Houston, Sam, 162
Howard, Volney, 25
Howe, Daniel Walker, 71
Hunter, Robert M. T., 25
Hurlbut, Stephen A., 49–50, 197
Huston, James L., 17

Illinois: abolitionists in, 28, 64; African Americans in, 6, 14–17, 22, 28, 40, 52, 74, 78–79, 89–90, 95–96, 121–22, 129; Catholics, 13, 22, 31–32, 42–43, 135; Chicago, 4, 11, 14, 16, 18, 24, 28, 35, 42–43, 51, 80; debt, 18; Democrats, 5, 11, 15, 20–22, 28, 32, 38, 46, 53, 64, 79, 84–86, 91, 98, 100–102, 104, 107, 109–11, 113–14, 119, 121, 137, 151, 158, 161, 171, 175, 177, 179, 181, 189, 195–97, 199–200; demographics, 4, 12; Eighth Congressional District, 40; First Congressional District, 117, 182; Germans in, 31–33, 42–43, 51, 54, 135, 138; immigrants and immigration, 4, 12, 13, 22, 43–44; Native Americans in, 13–14; nativism, 13, 31–34, 44; police force, 42; population, 4, 12; prohibition/temperance movement, 6, 31, 33, 41–44; Protestants, 12–13, 23, 31–34, 42–43, 135; public schools, 31–32, 40–41, 43; Republicans, 5, 6, 35–36, 47, 63–64, 69, 74–78, 83–84, 87–88, 92–94, 106–10, 112–13, 115–16, 118, 120–22, 131–32, 134, 147–51, 154, 161, 170, 175–76, 185, 188, 190, 194, 197, 200; Second Congressional District, 35; Seventh Congressional District, 117; Sixth Congressional District, 151; slavery, 5–6, 14, 29, 41, 64, 119, 126, 129, 139; State Assembly, 10; Supreme Court, 10, 15, 37; Third Congressional District, 73, 134, 182; Whigs, 11, 15, 19, 31
Illinois Central Railroad, 4, 18, 24, 96
Illinois Constitution, 23, 49; of 1818, article VI, 14; of 1847, 15; of 1848, 20

Illinois General Assembly, 203
Illinois Journal, 10, 27. See also *Illinois State Journal*
Illinois & Michigan Canal, 4, 18
Illinois Republican Central Committee, 148
Illinois Staats-Anzeiger, 148
Illinois State Chronicle, 89–90
Illinois State Journal, 37, 59, 62, 70, 72, 78, 84, 92, 94, 97, 112, 185, 188, 192, 199, 203; 1856 elections, 53, 134; 1858 elections, 118–19, 122, 124, 131, 134–35, 148; 1860 elections, 41, 162, 169, 171, 174, 176. See also *Illinois Journal*
Illinois State Register, 10, 20, 28, 57, 77, 94–95, 99–101, 106, 111–13, 121–22, 124, 127, 131, 137, 147, 151, 161, 166–68, 171, 188–89, 192, 195, 200, 203–4; 1856 elections, 54, 172; 1858 elections, 118–19, 123–43, 148; 1860 elections, 41, 172, 183
Impending Crisis of the South, The (Helper), 152–53
Indiana, 6, 16, 36, 118, 172
Iowa, 36
Islander and Argus, 3, 112, 129, 148

Jackson, Andrew, 10, 17, 19–20, 23, 32, 34, 37–38, 44, 51, 69, 79, 83, 99, 108, 124, 181
Jackson, Kellie Carter, 150
Jefferson, Thomas, 29, 36–37, 63, 65, 72, 85, 88, 92, 99, 133, 155, 157
Johnson, Herschel V., 167
Joliet Signal, 195, 201
Jonas, Abraham, 57
Jones, John, 15–16, 96, 149
Jones, Mary, 96, 149
Joseph Jarrot, a colored man v. Julia Jarrot, 15, 38
Judd, Norman B., 51, 68, 103, 114, 148–49, 152, 154, 162–63, 169

Kansas, 90, 124; admission to the Union, 71, 78, 91, 93–94, 99–100, 104, 110–12, 118; Constitution, 93–96; Lecompton constitution, 54–55, 77, 91, 93, 98, 101–3, 105–19, 125–27, 130, 133–34, 138, 140, 143, 184, 206; free-soilers, 46, 48, 55, 58, 73, 93, 106, 111, 113, 120; slavery, 46–76, 78, 79, 91–93, 98–99, 101, 104, 106–7, 109, 111–12, 119, 140, 150, 174, 184; Topeka convention, 54–55, 63, 73, 76, 83, 149–54
Kansas Constitutional Convention, 91
Kansas-Nebraska Act, 5, 28, 31–32, 35–36, 42, 44, 49, 53, 58, 68–69, 90, 108, 113, 122, 125, 127, 145, 148, 162, 205; popular sovereignty and, 22–24, 29, 46, 51, 63, 72, 84, 100, 110, 130, 206
Keitt, Lawrence M., 112
Kellogg, William, 190–91
Kentucky, 31, 80, 126
Kentucky Resolution, 63
King James Bible, 32
Kitchell, Wickliffe, 61
Know-Nothing Party, 4, 32–34, 36, 39–45, 47, 53–54, 57, 67, 69–71, 78, 109, 113, 117, 127, 134–36, 138, 140–43, 147, 148, 153, 158, 163, 202; 1856 national convention, 53; Northern, 48, 114; Southern, 48, 80, 118. See also American Party
Knox, James, 63, 66
Koerner, Gustave, 32, 38, 41, 52, 75, 148, 205

Lager Beer Riot, 41, 42–43
Lamon, Ward Hill, 123
Lane, Joseph, 168, 171
Lang, Andrew F., 2
Lanphere, George C., 100
Lanphier, Charles H., 20, 39, 40, 54, 77, 111, 153, 168, 177, 186–87, 193, 205
Latter Day Saints' Reformation of 1856–57, 90
Lecompton Convention, 93, 98–99, 111
Lee, Robert E., 150
Lemen, Franklin, 57
Liberator, 170, 195
Liberia, 88
Liberty Association, 16
Liberty Party, 35
Lincoln, Abraham, 5–6, 13, 15–16, 18, 35, 39–40, 104, 105–6, 109, 112, 115–17, 123–24, 152; 1860 election, 144–74, 183; Alton speech, 139–40; birth, 30, 185; conservative appeal, 168–74; Cooper Institute speech, 145, 156–58, 162, 164; Decatur Convention, 163–66; election to House of Representatives, 31; hardline stance, 181–86; House Divided speech, 124–28, 131–32, 139, 164; inaugural address, 193–99; Lost Speech, 60; popular sovereignty and, 87–89, 130; as president of the United States, 175–206; Republican nomination in 1860, 41, 145; Republican Party and, 41, 50–51, 53, 54, 67–68, 70; Senate campaign, 1858, 124–44, 148–49, 154–55; slavery, 125–26, 131, 134, 139–40, 154–58, 169, 170, 182–206; speaking tours, 154–58; Union and, 194–206; Whig Party and, 30, 32, 36–37, 44
Linder, Usher F., 134
Logan, John A., 204
Louisiana, 189

Louisiana Purchase, 80
Louisville Journal, 134
Lovejoy, Elijah, 13, 38
Lovejoy, Owen, 13, 15–16, 35, 40, 47, 50, 61, 73, 75, 102, 115–16, 123, 134, 149, 162

Madison, James, 85, 99, 134, 203
Maine Law, 31, 43
Major's Hall, 59
manifest destiny, 18, 85, 146
Maryland Institute Hall, 168
Mason, James M., 25
Matheny, Jim, 70, 116
Matson, James, 15
Matteson, Joel, 40–41, 124, 149
Maxwell, J. W., 166
McClernand, John A., 111, 151–53, 159–60, 181, 186–87, 189–91, 193, 201, 204–5
McClintock, Russell, 199
McConnel, Murray, 159
McCormick, Cyrus, 4
McLean, John, 66–68, 71, 154, 162
Medill, Joseph, 176
Mexican-American War, 31, 61, 68
Mexican Cession of 1848, 9
Mexico, political violence in, 203–4
Michigan, 36
Miller, James, 35, 61, 142
Minnesota, 79, 80, 82, 86, 172
Mississippi, 153–54, 189
Missouri, 24, 28; admission to the Union, 26; slavery in, 26, 48, 54–55, 58, 125
Missouri Compromise, 26–29, 32, 36–37, 40–41, 50–51, 53, 57–59, 134, 140, 183–85, 206; repeal of, 3, 22–23, 26, 30, 69, 71–72, 82–83, 117
Missouri Democrat, 102
Moline Workman, 43–44
Monroe, James, 66
Mormons, 90
Morris, Isaac, 153
Mount Carmel Register, 32–33, 85, 129, 188

National Era, 16
National Liberty Party, 72
Native American Party, 33. *See also* Know-Nothing Party
Nebraska: Native peoples in, 24–25; slavery in, 26, 37, 79; territorial government, 24
Nebraska Bill, 26, 27, 29–33, 37–38, 40, 44, 63, 76
New Jersey General Assembly, 192
New Mexico, 9, 26, 190–91
New York Herald, 101
New-York Tribune, 49, 55, 102, 105, 156–57

North Carolina, 201
Northwest Ordinance, 14, 28–29, 36, 40, 155, 157, 172
Nullification Crisis of 1832–33, 181, 185–86

Oakes, James, 3, 72–73
Oglesby, Richard J., 163, 204
Ohio, 36
Olney Times, 131, 158–59
Oregon, 16, 24, 79, 80, 120–21, 172
Osman, William, 65
Ostend Manifesto, 59
Ottawa Free Trader, 28–29, 57, 64–65, 80, 84–86, 93, 95, 99, 112, 158, 161, 168, 172, 179, 191, 195
Ottawa Republican, 199

Pacific railroad, 21, 24
Paine, Seth, 136
Paine, Thomas, 37
Palmer, John M., 38–39, 46, 54, 68, 121, 127, 148, 151–52, 185, 191
Panic of 1837, 18, 97
Panic of 1857, 77–78, 96–102, 106
Pantagraph, 56–57, 82–83, 97, 121, 174, 176, 182
Parks, G. D. A., 66
Peck, Ebenezer, 51, 57
Peck, Graham, 139–40
Pennington, William, 153
Pennsylvania, 172
People's Party, 36, 62
Peoria Democratic Union, 110, 201
Peoria Union, 77
Peru Chronicle, 61
Philadelphia Convention, 62, 66–69
Phillips, Charles B., 181, 199
Phillips, Wendell, 96, 204
Pickens, Francis, 198
Pierce, Franklin, 21, 30, 47, 55, 58, 60, 62–63, 78; Annual Message to Congress, 48
Plymouth Church, 156
popular sovereignty, 3, 6, 40, 47–48, 55, 76–78, 87, 89, 98–99, 109, 118, 128–29, 137–38, 140, 146–47, 172, 174, 178, 183; Democratic Party and, 26, 29–30, 51, 64, 65, 101, 110, 137, 153, 157, 161, 177; free-soil potential of, 80–82; Kansas-Nebraska Act and, 22–24, 29, 46, 51, 63, 72, 84, 100, 110, 130, 206; Republican Party and, 62, 100, 112–13, 130, 134
Potter, David M., 55
Poughkeepsie Eagle, 157–58
Price, William, 114
principle of nonintervention, 26
Pugh, George E., 160

Quincy Herald, 29, 77, 100, 110, 112, 147, 171, 178, 187
Quincy Whig, 27, 94, 97
Quincy Whig and Republican, 188, 195

Radical Abolition Party, 52, 73, 79, 171
railroads, 17–8, 20, 22, 23–26, 30, 96
Randolph County Democrat, 81–82, 86, 110
Ray, Charles H., 103, 116, 146, 176
Repeal Association, 16
Republican Party/Republicans, 103, 104, 113, 119, 138, 143; anti-Catholicism, 135, 148; Black, 110, 145, 171; Bloomington Convention, 46, 51–52, 54, 56, 59, 62, 67, 73, 124; Chicago Convention, 162–63; Chicago Platform, 182, 184, 191; conservativism, 123, 156–57, 168–74, 181–82; Decatur Convention, 163–66; German, 70, 75, 148; hardline stance, 181–86; Illinois, 5, 6, 35–36, 47, 63, 64, 69, 74–78, 83–84, 87, 88, 92–94, 106–10, 112–13, 115–16, 118, 120–22, 131–32, 134, 147–51, 154, 161, 170, 175–76, 185, 188, 190, 194, 197, 200; Indiana, 164; interracial sex and, 88, 95; Massachusetts, 147–48; National Central Committee, 39, 154; National Convention, 1860, 152; National Platform, 165–66; nativism, 135; New York, 156; Northern, 126; policy of federal exclusion, 146; popular sovereignty, 62, 100, 112–13, 130, 134; Protestants, 148; racial egalitarianism, 121–22; slavery and, 44–46, 53, 65, 67, 70, 73, 79, 82–93, 130, 131, 136, 145, 151–54, 159, 161–62, 164, 169, 183–206; Springfield convention, 35–36, 61, 123–28, 132; State Central Committee, 148; Union and, 159, 178, 200–206; unity, 162–66, 181; white supremacy, 130–31, 133, 135, 156
Revolutions of 1848, 13
Reynolds, John M., 136
Richardson, William A., 24, 63, 69, 76, 79, 167
Richmond Inquirer, 69, 195
Rockford Register, 102
Rock Island Argus, 65–66, 81, 91, 94, 97, 99, 158, 171–72, 177, 187, 191, 195, 200
Rock Island Republican, 20, 33
Roman Catholic Church, 33–34
Rushville Times, 101

Sack of Lawrence, 150
Salem Advocate, 29, 65, 178, 189
Scott, Dred, 82–93
Scott, Walter, 57
Scott, Winfield, 21, 34, 196

Scripps, John L., 126
Second Great Awakening, 12
Second Party System, 36, 51, 83, 104, 138
Seward, William H., 30, 36, 67, 116, 120–21, 151, 154–56, 163–64, 183–84, 193, 196; Irrepressible Conflict speech, 164
Sewell, Richard H., 58
Shannon, Wilson, 55
Sheahan, James W., 40, 47, 100, 114, 116, 122, 181
Shelden, Rachel A., 49
Sherman, John, 152
Shields, James, 38– 41, 124
Singleton, James, 134
Skinner, Mark T., 114
slave catchers, 16
slavery, 14, 35, 44–45, 53, 57–58, 71–72, 136; Atlantic slave trade, 146; chattel, 1; emancipation, 126, 172, 204–5; extension of, 6, 9, 17, 21–22, 23, 25–26, 32, 36, 38–39, 41, 46–76, 78–83, 88, 92, 98, 104–5, 109, 116–19, 125–26, 129, 132, 139–40, 145–46, 154–58, 161–62, 164, 172, 182–85, 190, 194; gradual elimination of, 15, 85, 126, 130, 131, 154–55, 169; Lincoln and, 125–26, 131, 134, 139–40, 154–58, 169, 170, 182–206; morality of, 72, 115, 139, 155–56; politics and, 2, 27; principle of congressional exclusion of, 28; protection of, 5–6, 26–27, 78, 98–99, 111–13, 146–47, 153, 160, 183; Southern Slave Power, 56, 58–60, 62, 64, 68, 113, 115, 123, 128, 132–33, 140, 143, 145–46, 155, 158, 173, 179, 185, 196, 199; technology replacing, 17; territorial slave code, 146–47, 154, 161, 178
Smith, Adam I. P., 2–3, 64, 99, 175, 198–99
Smith, Elisha, 185
Smith, Gerrit, 52, 72–73, 171
Smith, James McCune, 40
South Carolina, 174, 175, 178, 181, 185–87, 189, 196–98
Southern Opposition, 147, 152–53
Southern Rights, 158–59
Spencer, Joseph, 17
Stampp, Kenneth M., 77
Stanley, Matthew E., 179, 199
Star of the West, 189
state compact theory, 194
Stephens, Alexander H., 11
Stewart, Alvan, 74
St. Louis Railroad, 26
Stuart, John T., 13, 134
Sumner, Charles, 46, 54, 56–58, 112; "Crime Against Kansas" speech, 58
Swett, Leonard, 73, 149, 154, 163–64, 169, 190

Taney, Roger B., 82, 78, 82–84, 87, 106, 172, 189
Taylor, Zachary, 31, 70
Tennessee, 201
territorial expansion, 18
Texas, 9, 189
Thirtieth Congress, 18
Thirty-Fifth Congress, 79
Thirty-Fourth Congress, 46, 48, 80
Thirty-Second Congress, 24
Thirty-Six Congress, 147
Thirty-Third Congress, 25
Three-Fifths Compromise, 50
Thompson, John B., 80, 81
Times and Delta, 85, 111, 136–37
Toombs, Robert, 11
Topeka Constitution, 120
Treaty of Paris of 1783, 155
Tremont House, 128–29, 164
Trumbull, Benjamin, 37
Trumbull, Lyman, 7, 15, 44, 57, 60–61, 66–68, 71–72, 103–6, 113, 116, 182, 185, 205; 1856 elections, 46, 47–54; 1860 elections, 41, 148, 176, 183; on popular sovereignty, 90–91, 134; on slavery, 37–39, 53, 65, 88, 89, 120–24, 127, 132–33
Turner, Jonathan B., 61–62
Tyler, John, 67, 191

Underground Railroad, 16, 40
Union, 47, 123, 173; preservation of, 2–3, 46, 62–66, 69, 78, 114, 145–46, 158–59, 168, 172, 174, 199–202; secession from, 6, 60, 69, 153–54, 159, 172, 174–206
Union War, The (Gallagher), 198
United States Constitution, 2, 37, 46, 50, 53, 56, 120, 134, 146, 164, 172–74, 176, 181–82, 194, 197, 199, 204; Article II, 193; Bill of Rights, 82; Fifth Amendment, 67; Seventeenth Amendment, 123; slavery and, 64, 72–74, 92, 99, 111, 156–58, 184, 188
United States House of Representatives, 31, 70; Committee of Thirty-Three, 190
United States Senate, 10–11, 123–24, 144, 156; 1858 election, 124–43, 148; Committee of Thirteen, 187, 190
United States Supreme Court, 83–86, 89, 106, 132–33
Utah, 9, 26, 90

Vallandingham, Clement L., 205
Van Buren, Martin, 23
Vanderbilt, Cornelius, 128
Varon, Elizabeth R., 199
Virginia, 4, 12, 14, 24, 62, 63, 73, 85, 99; delegates, 150, 164, 166, 172, 173; secession, 183, 193, 197, 200, 201
Virginia Resolutions, 63, 99

Wabash Railroad, 18
Wade, Benjamin, 67
Wagoner, Henry O., 17, 52, 73–74, 79, 149–50
Walker, Robert J., 91–93, 98, 111
War of 1812, 13, 63
Washburne, Elihu B., 39, 50, 117, 164, 184
Washington, 79
Washington, George, 72, 92, 157, 203
Washington Peace Convention, 193
Watkins, William J., 28
Waukegan Gazette, 84, 112, 131, 133, 182, 186, 195
Webster, Daniel, 9–11, 27, 37, 49, 53, 64, 94, 157
Weed, Thurlow, 164, 169, 184
Wentworth, John E. "Long John," 29, 62, 83, 191, 205; 1858 elections, 119, 136, 148; 1860 elections, 149, 151–52, 154, 162, 164, 171
Western Citizen, 15
Western Whig, 19
Whigs, 5, 10, 23, 32–34, 36, 38, 40–41, 44, 47, 51–53, 57, 58, 60, 62, 64–65, 69–71, 73, 75, 78, 114, 117, 122, 124, 131, 134–35, 138, 140–42, 147, 154, 158, 159, 162–63, 169, 188, 190, 194, 202; anti-Nebraska, 35, 39, 52, 54, 118; fracturing, 30, 52–53, 108; Illinois, 11, 15, 19, 21, 28, 31, 67, 171; Northern, 11, 30, 49; slavery and, 32, 94, 133, 170; Southern, 11, 27, 30, 128
Whitney, Asa, 24
Wide Awakes, 169
Wigwam, 164
Wilentz, Sean, 72
Wilmot Proviso, 9, 11
Wilson, Charles L., 103
Wisconsin, 36, 155
Wood, John, 189
Woods, Michael E., 5, 56, 58, 137

Yancey, William L., 11, 159, 160, 178
Yates, Richard, 18–19, 27–29, 35, 52, 66, 70, 116, 185; 1860 elections, 149, 154, 163–64, 183
Young, Brigham, 90